THE BEECHWOOD
AIRSHIP INTERVIEWS

DAN RICHARDS

D1613089

The Friday Project
An imprint of HarperCollins*Publishers*
1 London Bridge Street
London SE1 9GF

www.harpercollins.co.uk

First published by The Friday Project in 2015

1

A catalogue record for this book is
available from the British Library

ISBN 978-0-00-810521-1

Printed and bound in Spain by Rodesa

For Jo

Many are prepared to suffer for their art.
Few are prepared to learn to draw.

– Simon Munnery

CONTENTS

LIMINAL SPACE

In the summer of 2006 I moved to Norwich from my family home in Bristol to begin a Creative Writing MA at the Art School.

It was a year since I'd graduated from an English Literature and Philosophy BA at the University of East Anglia. I had spent the intervening months working in a bookshop staffed entirely by graduates sheltering from an indifferent world, presided over by a weirdly ageless Brylcreemed man who, when he wasn't smoking on the roof – arcing his dog-ends languidly into the yard of the adjacent church – would lock himself in his attic office or materialise at your elbow to relate how his father nursed the captive Rudolf Hess.

The shop had a very limited selection of Art books and an even meaner smattering of Photography and Transport.* There was no demand, we were told, and it was this message that we passed on to any customer who enquired, taking great pleasure in directing them up to the 'better stocked, less expensive shop' at the top of the road ('where we would much prefer to work').

---

* Our Mind, Body & Spirit section, it should be noted, was unaccountably massive.

I had no idea what I was doing at the shop but day after day I'd be there, going through the motions of retail. I'd reached an impasse. It was relatively easy work and brought in a small wage, which I'd eke out during the week so I could catch a train to the South Coast to see my girlfriend at weekends. Sometimes I'd get to Brighton and she'd be happy to see me. Sometimes not. Sometimes she'd say, 'I'm not sure how I feel about you being here . . . turning up like this . . .' and I'd freeze there on the doorstep; tired and punctured, foolish – as if I'd spoilt the most simple of tasks: just turn up and don't be shit. Life in Barcelona-on-Sea unravelled as a mess of well-meant gestures and hissed upset. I was sure we *had it in us* to be happy but we weren't; we really weren't.

This went on for months.

I'd think about us all the week while stickering 3 for 2s or directing people up the road, but in my head she smiled more and shouted less.

In retrospect I'd been sleepwalking through many things. She left fairly suddenly. She had indeed been unhappy for a long time. I received a postcard quoting Virginia Woolf's suicide note as an unequivocal gesture of severance.

That was it.

I moved up to Norwich earlier than planned and drank a lot of gin on my own in a conservatory.

Then I got a cat.

Then I got a night job washing dishes in a pub.

I'd return home in the small hours covered in sink dross, drink more gin and complain to the cat about love.

It became clear that I needed direction, to begin something new, or I'd go mad, fill my sink-drossed smock with bricks and throw myself into a pond.

I threw myself into the art school instead.

•   •   •   •   •

2

In the weeks before term started, I began working in the Student Union bar – a large timber-beamed hall above the canteen – a building which put me in mind of St Pancras Station, all mustard brickwork, corkscrew chimneys and gothic arches; an eccentric building which seemed to embody the idea of an art school.

Accessed up a spiral staircase in a turret tucked away, the bar had a welcoming, secret feel and it was always great to see freshers double-take on first discovery, as I had – caught out by the size of the space, drawn in by the warmth towards the silhouetted people clustered around long tables and stood at the bar while candle shadows flickered the roof joists high above.

Like a massive womb . . . with Jägermeister.

Hulking cast-iron radiators hugged the walls and creaked, their heat rippling the curtains. The hall was always warm, even on the dark mornings as I swept and served coffee to the few brave souls awake – or yet to go to sleep.

On quiet evenings, the staff would play Scrabble or perch at the bar and talk, and it was on one of these slow nights that Rob, the manager, and I hit upon the idea of an airship.

We were staring into space, I remember; talking about the bar.

At this point the bar was one of the few places in the school where students could exhibit their work, and the walls, ledges and large windowsills were crammed with sculptures and paintings. A huge canvas by Bill Drummond hung on one side of the hall which said GET YOUR HAIR CUT, one of a series of works the artist had lent to Rob to display in the bar. I think Rob and I were talking about this as we stared up into the eaves, discussing GET YOUR HAIR CUT, the student art on show, the roof – our conversation spinning off at intervals but always arcing back to large student work and the roof space.

That morning I had been exploring Norwich and discovered the brass plaques on the doors of City Hall which depict the history and trades of the town. One showed an engineer working with a propeller – a reference to the firm Boulton & Paul Ltd, a general manufacturing firm which built aircraft and airships among other things.*

Talking to the art school caretakers about the doors later that week I was told how Boulton & Paul Ltd had won the contract to construct the frame of the fateful R101 airship in the 1920s, then the largest aircraft ever built.** One old boy recalled being held aloft as the ship flew over Norwich on a test flight.

'The whole city stopped to watch it circle and pass. Everyone was out in the streets.'***

Maybe R101 was circling and passing through my mind that night because the conversation about GET YOUR HAIR CUT, student work, and the roof came to rest on me, suggesting the construction of a large-scale airship above the bar. That would be brilliant, we agreed; and then went back to staring into space.

---

* 'Other things' including stove grates, portable bungalows, wheelbarrows, dog-kennels and glasshouses, steel-frame barns, engines for small boats, military camps, wooden sports pavilions, schools, churches, transmission towers, pylons, kettles, sausage machines, agricultural machinery, iron gates, fences, wire netting, and looms.

** R101 had twenty-seven miles of tubing, eleven miles of bracing cables and 65,000 nuts and bolts.
Despite R101 being beset with technical difficulties during both her construction and air trials, the decision was taken to press on and fly to India.
In 1930, en route to Karachi, R101 crashed killing forty-eight of the fifty-four on board – ending British airship construction in the twentieth century.

*** He recalled this vividly, which was surprising since the flight occurred in 1929, meaning he'd have to have been pushing eighty in 2007. He looked very good for eighty, I must say – and still working! Amazing stuff.

. . . . .

A week passed. I knew Rob had probably forgotten about our conversation and I still had every opportunity to forget it too and walk away, but the seed was sown and the space was there, waiting. I couldn't look up any more without seeing the negative space of a large, ominous airship hanging there, goading me.

. . . . .

A month into the winter term I had drawn and researched to a point where I'd some idea of the airship's size. I wanted the balloon to loom in a big room and as such it would have to be large. Six metres long, perhaps; over a metre in diameter. Also, it would have to be light so as to hang from the trusses without causing damage and, most importantly, look right. If weighty and over-engineered it would look wrong, I knew – it had to appear to float. Wood and paper, then – flexible, strong woods covered in paper like a kite.

However, it became clear that there wasn't the space for me to build it in the art school workshops. I remember I sought out a technician and we paced the airship out; too big. Not that there seemed a surfeit of students making massive wooden things; not that there seemed much being made at all – the wood workshops seemed principally employed to make canvas stretchers and the main wood of choice appeared to be 'ply'.

My rough notes about the 'springing/laminate potential of beech and birch' were met with polite concern. I was pointed towards the birch ply and chipboard.

'That's not really wood, though, is it?' I asked the technician.

I think he took that rather hard.

I decided to let it lie.

Within a week it wasn't the woodwork which concerned me as much as the people coming out of it to ask why I, a student on a two-year part-time writing MA, wanted to build things at all.

•　•　•　•　•

I am writing this introduction a couple of years after the events I'm describing and it's strange to think now but my idea of an art school can't really exist any more. The new fee system introduced after my time in Norwich has brought an end to the idea of studying with an open mind 'just to see what happens'. I don't think you can really do that if you're paying £30,000.

The notion of value has shifted and the vocational is king once more. To pay out so much 'just to see what happens' seems decadent; the fees will surely cost out those unsure of what they want to become, or looking for an adventure.

Jarvis Cocker expressed the idea well:

> 'As much as I wanted to study something, I went to Saint Martin's because I just wanted to get out of Sheffield. I just looked at the colleges and it said, "This one is on Charing Cross Road", so I thought, "Great, three years in Soho. Summat's going to happen." And it did.'*

To arrive in a space and be inspired to make art by its fabric and atmosphere – if I'd been asked what my ideal of an art school was before I arrived in Norwich, that would have been close . . . but maybe we've moved into a post-impulsive airship epoch.

------

* Jarvis Cocker, the *Guardian*, 27 November 2011.

Today, all government funding cut, I note the school has closed down my course and moved towards a more logical, verifiably employable roster of subjects – the abstruse hinterlands of Fine Art and Sculpture squeezed in favour of the more honest fare of Fashion, Graphic Design and Animation; a white sea of Macs sweeping all before it.

But let's return to the winter of 2006 and the wood workshop where I'm not going to work and look around. There are tools here. The ones on show are old and battered. The better ones are locked away, we're told, because otherwise they'd walk. Security is a problem and the technician cannot be everywhere at once, so the available kit walks and the rest is kept hidden.

Paranoia permeates the space and I feel bad for the technician, who's doubtless doing his best but he's under pressure and having to take on responsibilities beyond his original remit. In this context it's reasonable to suppose that writers on part-time MAs talking about ambitious zeppelin projects would be given short shrift. He has to be there. He's put upon. He's busy. I bet he had people in there 'talking' all the time. Time wasters, charlatans, and opportunists – out to nick the shiny G-clamps, light-fingered magpies with asymmetric haircuts. Bastards to a man!

Now, it's all very well writing this down with hindsight and retrospect and all the other tools available after the event – indulging in a bit of the third person to suggest a distance between now and then, the school and me, the technician and me – but it's important to say that I didn't help my cause. I don't like confrontation. Hate it. I felt plywood wasn't the way to go and should have stood my ground, but it was much easier to smile along and nod and agree we should order a load of it and then run away; it was the hiding for the next two years which proved tricky, especially since the wood workshop stood at the entrance to one of the main buildings at the school and I knew I'd upset a man with a large collection of hammers.*

· · · · ·

In early 2007 I travelled down to Henley-on-Thames to ask a pair of boat builders how best to construct an airship.

En route to London, the previous week, I'd spoken to my father at length about the project and he'd suggested that to question received wisdom, to experiment, fail and learn, was the point of a degree. Better to fail on your own terms than be led astray and compromise:

> 'You know, you'll spend ages building it out of the wrong stuff to please someone else, it'll go wrong and you'll end up smashing it up with an axe, or something . . .' he pronounced near Heston Services, adding, 'You've made your bed now anyway.' **

---

* With this in mind, my earlier assertion that 'paranoia permeated the space' might seem disingenuous but I'd like to point out that, whereas the birds who took the clamps and screwdrivers were thieving, I was indirectly bolstering the flow of ply into a workshop which loved ply and mainly dealt in ply. Lovely ply.

** My father is a craftsman and has a great deal of experience with wood and plaster among other materials. When I was eleven months old my parents moved to the Greek island of Spetses where my father was part of team that built a 54-foot replica of the *Argo*, the ship on which Jason and the Argonauts sailed in quest of the Golden Fleece. He used traditional methods, materials and tools, overseen by master shipwright Vasilis Delimitros, and when the ship was complete the adventurer and writer Tim Severin put to sea with a crew of twenty to row and sail in the oar-strokes of the Argonauts – a voyage of 1,500 miles.

Vasilis was a tough, brusque man by all accounts but my father speaks of him with great affection. He knew boats and he knew wood. I still have a model boat the old man made for me – built of *Argo* off-cuts, electrical tape and string.

The first time I met Severin, I'm told, I was terribly sick on his shoes.

. . . . .

Colin Henwood and Richard Way know about wood and their knowledge is deep. At our first meeting we sat in the shed at the heart of their yard and talked around the airship – unpacking each possible solution, weighing the ways it could be done. This took quite some time since it turned out I had many options – different woods, fixings, joints, glues; each with their own character and peculiarities.

Their enthusiasm for the project, my doodled sketches and the mooted materials spilled out along tangents and into stories about craft.

At that first meeting, Richard spoke of his work with wood and boats, his tools and concerns, with a love and mesmeric intensity that affected me deeply and has subsequently shaped this book. He put the idea in motion that people who love what they do, are immersed and consumed by their work, are wont to speak about it with an engaging and infectious generosity. There was no cynicism when he spoke, just a simple clarity of thought, of process and labour, and this was to set a pattern for many subsequent exchanges I was to have; in fact it's largely due to Richard's enthusiasm and lucidity that I went out and sought those exchanges at all. I'd taken along a rudimentary Dictaphone to record our chat – and it was to be a chat, a casual meeting for which I'd made no notes other than rough drawings and annotations in my journal. I suppose I imagined I'd be there an hour or two. But two hours turned into four, and lunch, and as dusk fell we three were still talking. I didn't want it to end, it was such a pleasure. When I got home I transcribed the tape and happily listened to the day over again.* Below is a little of our

---

*This enjoyment of transcription was not to last, however.

conversation, beginning with Richard describing his daily
routine:

'I start at half past seven during the week and finish
at six o'clock. I used to work much longer. My first
experience of boat building was working at a time
when there was much too much work and not enough
people so we used to work through till ten o'clock at
night or one o'clock in the morning and that went on
month after month so I got very used to terribly long
hours. You can't do that when you get to my age, it just
becomes too exhausting.'

What age were you when you started?

'I was twenty-one. It was tiring but at that age you
can do enormous amounts of work and still get up the
following morning and do it again. Young people are
always half out of control anyway, aren't they? (Laughs)
I discovered shortly after I started that I much preferred
using tools that had been used before. It wasn't a conscious decision to begin with but . . . I can feel a lot
through my hands. I've got a very delicate sense of feeling and just felt that new tools were very sharp, all their
edges were very sharp, and I much preferred buying
old tools that were quite worn but still very usable.
You always buy some things new because you want
the full length of a long paring chisel, for example, but
gradually I've swapped over all the ones I bought new
for older ones I've found. It didn't become an obsession,
thankfully, but I decided that I liked knowing about
tools, so I read a lot of books and I used to buy tools
when job-lots came up at local auctions, and sometimes
I'd get them from people I knew, so that meant I'd tools
that reminded me of the man who owned them before.

I'll pick a tool up and think, "Ah, that's Pat Wheeler's – the old boy who lived in the village." It brings a picture up in my mind which is rather fine and it's nice to know that your tools have done other work, you know; generations of work.

At home in my workshop, I've tools that are centuries old – Georgian chisels, things like that, and they're absolutely magnificent. I've got Georgian wooden planes, braces, and drills, extraordinary things . . .'

At this point Colin pointed ruefully to Richard's toolbox – a blanket box on caster wheels – a hefty laden chest:

'As you can see, Dicky hasn't brought very many tools with him today . . .'

And as we laughed I became aware that the scope of my project was opening out, alive in the room, after so many

months of being closed down. I was engaged with people who knew what they were doing. The spectral airship flew here too – more than that – buoyed by enthusiasm, it lived.

For the next few months, every chance I got, I travelled home to Bristol to build the ship of my imagination – 200 miles from the art school bar as the crow flew.

The body of an airship is a collection of variously sized hoops fixed together with cross braces – dirigibles generally have a keel like a boat, their skeleton frame distinguishing them from blimps, which are essentially bags that use gas pressure to maintain their shape.

To start with I set about making twenty hoops of various sizes – each as thin and strong as possible, each formed of three or four layers of beechwood. Beech has a fine grain which lends it a strength and flexibility suited for shaping and moulding – for this reason it is used a great deal in furniture making. I built up a laminate sandwich of wood/glue/wood/glue/wood around circular template formers, each a slightly different diameter – clamping each complaining lath length tight until it set, before adding the next.* My first efforts were fairly awful but gradually I learnt what I was doing and the hoops began to take a more uniform, circular shape.
Successful rings were laid out on the floor like ripples; pear-shaped failures were taken outside and burnt.

---

* Ply: noun (pl. plies) – a thickness or layer of a folded or laminated material.
Yes, all right, but my hoops were made of radial, ring laminates as opposed to the vertical laminate sheet of plywood. A thin plywood ring would have no strength and would snap when compressed . . . raining debris and death down upon unsuspecting students out for a pink gin, in the worst tradition of unreliable airships which kill people.

12

While laminates dried in their jigs, I moved on to the nose and tail. Again, this was trial and error and the thought that it was all going to fall apart or bow (and then fall apart) was never far from my mind; but I was fathoming the beech and coming to respect its toughness. Once layered up and glued into shape it was steadfast. The material didn't lie. When I botched I couldn't blame the beech, which often called my bluff; refusing to be undone – wood and glue having become a sturdy third thing – hoop or half-uncoiled mess.

Four tailplanes were measured and marked on board, sawn up, sanded and slotted together – aerofoil ribs fixed at regular intervals looking beaky and svelte.

The dust was flying from the bandsaw blade, sketched revisions and tea stains filled my notebooks, and solvents daubed my boiler suit and stunk out my hair. At the end of each day, on the train journey home, I'd peel PVA from my hands.

The nose cone went together fairly quickly with a similarly slot-oriented approach to the fins – the profile of the front

dome built up in segments to form a pointy jelly mould, a hollow cupola built around the smallest of my beech hoops; a card skinned nib.

An assembly frame was made on which to build the kit of bits. Thin stringer laths were cut to fix across the hoops and form the rigid frame – skeleton cigar . . . late nights listening to the radio, sugary tea and pencil shavings – ticking off the parts lists until early summer, when I packed up the airship like a pasta tangram into a Volvo Estate.*

My MA, meanwhile, was going well. I was writing strictly relevant pieces for my course and moonlighting with zeppelins the rest of the time.** As the first year finished and the long summer break between the first and second year stretched ahead, I was setting out my kit in the union bar, ready for the build.

Up went the frame with its central jig. On went the hoops, held by spars. Everything was clamped and cable-tied at this point since nothing was straight or square.

This part of the project was time-lapse filmed for posterity and the early footage shows me deploying tape measure and spirit level with enthusiasm. Lying on my back beneath the fuselage, head scratching, wandering off, wandering back with tea and a pencil, losing and hunting for the pencil, making notes, fiddling with string; like Buster Keaton . . . that was week one.

---

* By this point I'd been working on the zeppelin for three months with the aim of getting it built and suspended in the SU bar over the summer holidays – a September deadline.

** Nearly all the tutors and technicians at the school were brilliant and many went over and above to help me. Some of the help was covert when it fell beyond the perceived and permitted remit of my course – it was there the tensions lurked – but I was more than accommodated in the main . . . they were certainly not all miserable jobsworths, some of them were only too pleased to assist me build a tangential rogue airship.

Week two saw the keels* glued into place and the tail cone taking shape.

Week three was a bit of a write-off since I spent much of it undoing laths stuck into place under the influence of Guinness Export. The wrong place. Wonkily.

The nose was fixed in week four and the rest of the stringers followed. Because of the ship's size, lath strips had to be seamed together at intervals with scarf joints, the two lengths cut with a taper and joined to form a continuous span. The scarfs were positioned at intervals so as not to create weak spots in the frame.

Week five, the tail fins went on; the central spars were cut and removed. The ship was carried off the stage and hung from its top keel for the first time, swinging slightly on its new jib. The team of bar staff who'd helped me lift and relocate it stood back.

'Bit big, isn't it?' said Rob, looking warily up at the beams, and it was true; away from the stage and out in the room the airship did look massive.
'Don't worry,' I reassured him, 'I've done some maths and it only weighs as much as your legs.'
This seemed to settle him down.**

. . . . .

---

* Two keels – one top, one bottom – to run and strengthen the airship down its length since it was to be suspended and stressed from above; a backbone. Keels, like the hoops, were laminated but their timbers were thicker and gently curved like lazy bananas.

** Approximately 27.3 kg.

All the time I was building the airship, especially in those final weeks, I was distracted. A couple of years later, Stewart Lee nailed the feeling:

> 'You often don't realise that you're working on some-thing in your head until it's formed – you might have had something that you thought you were doing for fun or was just interesting to you but suddenly you realise that it's all adding up into the shape of an idea.'

Now built – out of my head and over there, causing Rob to fret about the beams – I saw the airship as a manifest preoccupation.

It wasn't just an airship built on a whim; it was a reaction – an elephant in the room – everything the art school seemed to be turning away from;* a large, ambitious, crafted wooden piece of work which mirrored and celebrated the building around it, inspired by the ghosts of the city. I believed in the fabric of the bar and school and wished to celebrate that. The building was benign, inspiring and positive; it was the people at the top who concerned me.

Looking down the beech laths at the scarf joints, I felt the calm assurance of the materials and saw the influence of Richard and Colin in Henley-on-Thames and my father back in Bristol. The airship had put me in touch with them and articulated their knowledge better than words. The process was a language, lucid and succinct. It had an integrity.

I had faith in the wood and glue.

---

* A white elephant airship in a bottle – one of the reasons the SU dirigible was built on-site from a kit was that it was too large to go in through the front door – never mind up the turret. The pieces were hoisted in through a high window shortly after arriving in the Volvo.

On 15 August 2007 I made the following note in my diary:

> Today the bar paid for a set of ropes and pulleys and hired a scaffold tower.
> I keep finding notes I've written about 'People who know what they're doing.'
> I work here, in this room. The airship is site-specific.
> The room is the space I respond to.
> Does this happen to other people?★

. . . . .

The scaffolding tower was assembled one weekend shortly before the start of the new school year. From the top it was clear that the eaves were a lot higher than they seemed from the bar far below. Three of us scaled the gantry to hang ropes and thread the pulleys and shortly afterwards the airship was winched into the air for the first time accompanied by a blast of 'When the Levee Breaks'.★★

It was up.

From beneath, its lines merged and intercut the wood of the roof, putting me in mind of Orozco's *Mobile Matrix*, a suspended whale skeleton,★★★ and as the concentric graphite circles drawn on those bones radiated out, overlapped and distorted, so the beams moved through the cage of beechwood

---

★ I knew there was more to it than an airship in a room but was groping for equivalence, a bridge to a kindred process.
There is something winningly naive about my notes from this time; the idea of going out and asking creative people I admired to explain to me what I'd done was forming and while this book didn't turn into that, my notebooks record that it might.

★★ 'When the Levee Breaks', *Led Zeppelin IV*, Led Zeppelin, 1971 – Drums!!!

★★★ *Mobile Matrix*, Gabriel Orozco, 2006.
Graphite on Gray Whale skeleton (196 x 1089 x 266 cm)
Biblioteca Vasconcelos, Mexico City.

above our heads now. The few of us there in the moments after it was raised walked up and down below as the airship swam.

Later I sat on the stage at the back of the hall and looked at it for an hour or two, watching it settle in the ropes. It was up; unpapered and naked for now but that could be addressed over time.

But the important thing, as Rob pointed out, was that the stage was now freed up for the pool table because, say what you like about arty kids in an arty bar, they loved their pool: 'You know, given the choice between an arty airship and pool . . .'

Luckily such a nightmarish choice was never forced upon them.

The new term started and I went back to my MA, papering the airship on Sunday mornings with tissue paper donated by Habitat.★ I was helped in this task by Virginie Mermet, a brilliant French girl.★★

We'd arrive early and open all the windows to ventilate the stale ale air before making tea and lowering the airship down. Tissue was cut into strips and applied with aircraft dope – a varnish that tautened and strengthened the paper as it dried while giving us headaches and mild hallucinations.

★ My friend Joseph worked at Habitat and managed to get me a large pack of the white tissue which they used to wrap items at the till point. I'm sure he ran it past his managers first but, if not, the firm's gone into receivership now and he's become an art teacher in Leicester, so it's probably fine.

★★ Virginie had built a giant mouse wheel on her Fine Art course the previous year and invited all the top brass from the school to come and run in it with her. Their letters of excuse and refusal were framed next to the wheel at her final show. It was truly brilliant. She also worked in the union bar. After the airship was finished I heard that she'd helped crew a tall sailing ship across the Atlantic before walking down to Mexico from New England; quite true, I'm sure. She was that kind of girl.

During these mornings we'd talk about ideas of artists and space and listen to Klaus Nomi.* Virginie was of the opinion that all artists create and respond to a space, be it site-specific sculpture like the airship or an environment attuned to making work. We spoke about photographs we'd seen of Francis Bacon's studio and Roald Dahl's shed, concepts of theatre and atmosphere; the idea that a resonance of creativity can remain in a building long after the people have gone and the function altered.

Kitchens, boat yards, studios, halls, sheds, rehearsal rooms, cellars, theatres, roofs, gardens, landscapes, vehicles – inspiring and facilitating artistry.

---

* I didn't know a lot about Klaus Nomi but we'd always listen to that same album of Virginie's – Nomi's debut. A Fritz Lang hybrid of Max Wall and Freddie Mercury, he gazed with haughty indifference from the monochrome sleeve – an operatic New York synth vampire with Cadillac shoulders.

Some spaces must bear witness to a process while others stimulate it – become steeped in it. While some buildings evolve over decades into a perfect working environment, others are built for that purpose from scratch, others will be a compromise; some permanent, some fleeting, some known about and public, some private, even hidden.

That night as an experiment, I wrote a few pages about the broadcaster John Peel. Under the heading ATMOSPHERE, I recalled my second-year house at university; Thursday night, a large cold bedroom where the living room should have been. A desk, a set of shelves, a dicey gas fire, a bed, a wardrobe. I'm sat at the desk in a thick jumper, illuminated by a balanced-arm lamp and the flicker of a radio set handed down from my mother – bought during the three-day weeks of the seventies because it could take batteries.
I'm listening to John Peel.
Thursday was not a pub night, Thursday was the night John broadcast his programme direct from his Stowmarket home, Peel Acres. Thursdays were sacrosanct. I remember taping Mono, The Black Keys and Four Tet sessions, listening with my finger hovering over the red button on the deck.

My diary of 13 May 2004 records that John played four session tracks by The Izzys and I enjoyed them very much. He opened the show with the greeting 'Hello, brothers and sisters, and welcome to Peel Acres' – very much the spirit behind those Thursdays; he was welcoming the audience into his home, where he sat playing tracks he thought we might like to hear – something new. Something by Jazzfinger or The Fall, say; the jet-wash of Part Chimp or The Izzys in session covering Richard and Linda Thompson.
Amazing to think how intimate it all felt – a man in his house in conversation with the world but broadcasting to you. A public service.

I remember the quiet of my room then, the crackle of the radio and the feeling of connectivity.

John Peel died in October 2004.*
In 2008 I wrote to his wife, Sheila Ravenscroft:

> 'Perhaps the most interesting spaces grow up and around the person working within them. The longer this project** goes on, the more I think of John's programmes from Peel Acres and recall the way the atmosphere of his studio seemed to percolate out into my room; the wonderful conversational way he had of speaking, how it fostered a world and set of associations that continue to inform what I'm writing today.'

•   •   •   •   •

In his book *Waterlog*, Roger Deakin describes a seemingly impossible swan dive made by a market-worker in the 1920s from the copper turret of the Norwich art school, over Soane's St George's Street Bridge and into the River Wensum.
A friend lent me the book towards the end of my degree and I

---

* I remember exactly where I was.

I was queuing for coffee in the interval of a Heidegger seminar.

John's picture kept appearing on the rolling news of a corner television. There was no sound but I stopped and watched it, waiting for the headlines to roll around again, stomach sinking.

Afterwards I went to the library and sat; just sat staring blankly out of the window for a couple of hours.

Later I sought out my logic tutor, Peter Green, to talk about it. He was brilliantly humane.

** 'Project' here refers to the airship, which had led on to the idea of a book or, at least, the idea of investigating working space and creative practice further . . . I used the word *project* a lot in 2008 as a general term for whatever the airship, this *thing*, was becoming.

raced through it, drinking up the words on water, wild swimming and landscape. A few minutes after discovering the Norwich nosedive passage, I was stood on the same bridge, text in hand, eyes skyward, trying to join the dots – turret, bridge, river. Copper, sky, Wensum – but the orbit did not fit. I went back to my work on the airship, disbelieving – imagining the lad Goodson arcing, plunging head first and arrow-like – aiming at the water, his eyes brim-full of bridge.

I returned at lunchtime but the bridge was no thinner than before.

Did Roger Deakin stand here too? I wondered. Did he weigh the thing up?

Waterlog and Deakin's subsequent book, *Wildwood: A Journey Through Trees*, suggested a course beyond art school.

Writing in 2010, his friend Robert Macfarlane described him as

> 'a film-maker, environmentalist and author who is most famous for his trilogy of books about nature: *Waterlog*, *Wildwood* and *Notes from Walnut Tree Farm*. I say "nature", but his work can perhaps best be understood as the convergence of three deeply English traditions of rural writing: that of dissent tending to civil disobedience (William Cobbett, Colin Ward), that of labour on the land (Thomas Bewick, John Stewart Collis), and that of the gentle countryman or the country gentleman, of writer as watcher and phrenologist (Gilbert White, Ronald Blythe).'[*]

I had a lot of questions, had gone off piste with my MA to fill gaps in my heuristic knowledge and in so doing become

---

[*] *Roger Deakin Remembered*, Robert Macfarlane, the *Guardian*, 8 May 2010.

convinced that something was amiss and the answers lay elsewhere, in the heads and hands of people at work.

Roger Deakin walked out to meet the people who knew – who swam, worked wood, dwelt and engaged with the land. Meeting with people in the spaces where they worked and lived, he found communion and kinship. Perhaps I, in light of the Beechwood Airship, could do the same and find some resolution . . . because the postmodern doublethink of the art school seemed a very lonely thing – a vacuum occasioned to funnel and mould the kids in a system where 'all aesthetic judgement is entirely subjective.'*

Such a cheap trick! A spiteful closing down of the cosmos and, I couldn't help but think now, having clashed against the axioms of the institution, that their dogma was self-serving and unfit to underpin a job of work in the world beyond their walls.

I knew of graduates turned out as graphic designers with almost no knowledge of its history – the roll-call: Brody, Beck, Oliver, Saville, Kare and Scher passing without a flicker – set up to be a caricature with no depth to their knowledge beyond a syllabus which ticked the school's boxes – eggshell graduates who'd only been pressed top down.

But then, perhaps this does the tutors a disservice, perhaps it wasn't their fault – maybe they were under pressure to deliver a certain sort of course – perhaps the onus should be on the student to broaden their knowledge. Shouldn't a degree be all-consuming? The past and present insatiably mined out, the future dreamt, the vocation so pressing that each new contextual source is gorged? But I knew from my own encounters that students were being dissuaded from going too far away from their prescribed course remit. Peregrination was not encouraged, cross-course collaboration

---

* See footnotes on pages 413 and 494.

dissuaded – at an art school! Surely that was wrong or was I being unreasonable?

No. You need more. You need enough rope to either hang yourself or create something great. And sometimes you need to get out on the road and discover it, physically seek and experience it for yourself – whatever that is.
Take risks. Get your hands dirty.

Bill Drummond's totemic GET YOUR HAIR CUT and the MAKE SOUP that replaced it seemed a good place to start. Where did he work? I wondered.

The final weeks of art school found me serving rowdy in-temperance to student types on weeknights while Sundays passed in quiet concentration, Virginie and I lying side by side on the floorboards of the SU bar: papering the airship, strung out on psychotropic varnish fumes, listening to Klaus Nomi.

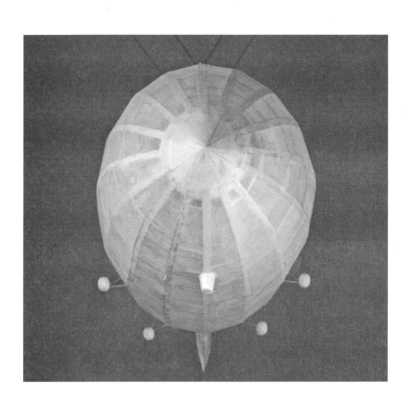

BILL DRUMMOND (1953–) is a Scottish artist, musician and writer who came to prominence in the 1980s with his band The KLF. He achieved notoriety after burning one million pounds in cash as part of his art project the K Foundation. He is the author of several books and is the founder of countless art, music and media projects as well as the writer of two solo albums.

BILL DRUMMOND

St Benedicts Street, Norwich
Summer 2007

I'm building my airship in the Student Union; a month to go
before the autumn term and the hall is empty. It's early and
brilliant sunlight pours down from the cinquefoil windows
above me, flooding the low stage where I work.

I enjoy being here out of hours. I have the run of the building
from as early until as late as I like.

Most of the student art and canvases have been stored over
the summer – to be hung up again once the bar reopens – so
the white walls are bare except for one large red and yellow
canvas which looms to my left as I look down the room:
MAKE SOUP.★

I like MAKE SOUP. It greets me every morning with bright
clarity and purpose. The framed text beneath it reads:

★ MAKE SOUP replaced GET YOUR HAIR CUT on the SU wall shortly after I
returned from Bristol with my kit of airship bits. Further information on all of Bill's
work is available at his website: www.penkilnburn.com.

29

NOTICE

Take a map of the British Isles.

Draw a straight line diagonally across the map so that it cuts through Belfast and Nottingham.

If your home is on this line,

contact soupline@penkilnburn.com

Arrangements will be made for Bill Drummond

to visit and make one vat of soup for you,

your family, and your close friends.

I appreciate the simplicity and generosity behind this venture. I like soup, for one, but also I like the sense of quest, the bold colours, the aesthetic of the large stark letters – four and four, MAKE SOUP – the fact Bill will rock up and physically make you literal soup with his actual hands.

I look on Bill's Penkiln Burn website and find that there are many more canvases of the same size and style – PREPARE TO DIE, SILENCE, DRAW A LINE, 40 BUNCHES OF DAFFODILS, STAY – each with an attendant story and aim.

I ponder what a BLOODY GREAT AIRSHIP canvas would look like; three words, one above the other. I sketch it in my notebook.

•　•　•　•　•

March 2009

Bill's workshop is a grey unit with a roll-shutter front, solid and anonymous on a ring road industrial estate . . . outside

Norwich.* As the shutter rises it reveals a stacked interior. I follow him into the space, stepping over piles of books and magazines, around walls of filing cabinets and heaped boxes into a clearing with a large canvas suspended upside down on a stretch of bare white wall – ⊥ᴉǝɥ⊥. White on red. Bill rummages in a cupboard and emerges with a handful of bungee leads, picks the canvas up and makes his way back out to the Land Rover, before climbing onto the substantial roof rack to secure it there. I ask what happens to his older, redundant signs; Bill says he paints over them.

Rather than the portentous figure I'd been expecting, Bill seems a quiet, thoughtful man – far more tolerant and humorous than I'd imagined. On the drive back into town I think over the disparity between the Bill with the reputation for dark shenanigans that I'd read about in preparation for this meeting and Bill the enthusiastic instigator of spontaneous choir The17 because it's the latter who's sat beside me now, imagining aloud waking up tomorrow to find all recorded music had disappeared.

•   •   •   •   •

Later that day – Norwich Arts Centre

A dark hall. Set up on a stage at one end is The17 canvas collected this morning. On the floor down the middle of the

---

* Bloody Norwich!
Of all the places to have a workshop. Bill lives in London but commutes to Norwich to make art – which accounts for the presence of his pieces in the SU, admittedly but . . . What are the chances!?
To add insult to injury I'd moved back to Bristol before I discovered this and had to travel back to meet him . . . Norwich: just when I thought I was out, they pull me back in.

room runs a white line, bisecting the eighty or so chairs on which people are starting to sit, filing into the gloom from the light outside. Shuffling to a seat while their eyes adjust.

Between the seats and the stage is a table.
On the table sit a laptop and an Anglepoise lamp. The lamp is the only light in the room and the room – once a church – is large, with a high black vault and pillars that mark out the nave and frame the stage and table.

More chairs fill, more shuffling, low whispers.

Bill appears and walks to the front to a scattered applause and sits down to face the audience.

'Hello,' he says, 'my name is Bill Drummond and you are The17.'

Thereafter the audience, myself included, are told the story of The17, how it grew from the sounds in Bill's head as a child and his lifelong love of choral music; how Bill tried to fight the music, which welled while he drove his Land Rover, tried to ignore it, but how he found it swirled and coalesced with other ideas he was having about the way music in the twentieth century – recorded, manufactured, sold and now ubiquitous – had lost touch with time, place, event and performance . . . how he'd sought to write these feelings out in under a hundred words; how he got it down to ninety:

SCORE

1. IMAGINE

Imagine waking up tomorrow morning
and all music has disappeared.
All musical instruments and all forms
of recorded music, gone.
A world without music.
What is more, you cannot even remember
what music sounded like or how it was made.
You can only remember that it had existed and that it
had been important to you and your civilisation.
And you long to hear it once more.
Then imagine people coming together to make music
with nothing but their voices, and with no knowledge of
what music should sound like.

The music they would make is that of The17.

pb Poster 128 (Printout version) 2006

Bill sells us the idea of The17, seduces the room. He sits in
his circle of lamplight before the red canvas and reads out
ALL RECORDED MUSIC and his sonorous Scots tones
reverberate around the building, then he moves to another
score, IMAGINE, and begins to form us into a choir – no
previous musical experience necessary – to create a new
music. Year zero now.

NOTICE

ALL RECORDED MUSIC HAS RUN ITS COURSE.

IT HAS ALL BEEN CONSUMED, TRADED, DOWNLOADED, UNDERSTOOD, HEARD BEFORE, SAMPLED, LEARNED, REVIVED, JUDGED AND FOUND WANTING.

DISPENSE WITH ALL PREVIOUS FORMS OF MUSIC AND MUSIC-MAKING AND START AGAIN.

YEAR ZERO NOW.

The17 IS A CHOIR.

THEIR MUSIC HAS NO HISTORY, FOLLOWS NO TRADITIONS, RECOGNISES NO CONTEMPORARIES.

The17 HAS MANY VOICES.

THEY USE NO LIBRETTO, LYRICS OR WORDS; NO TIME SIGNATURES, RHYTHM OR BEATS; AND HAVE NO KNOWLEDGE OF MELODY, COUNTERPOINT OR HARMONY.

The17 STRUGGLE WITH THE DARK AND RESPOND TO THE LIGHT.

jb Poster 59   2003

I can't tell you much of what happened next because it would spoil the inherent mystery and magic of The17 as a uniquely immersive happening, but it's enough to say that the choir, led by Bill, made sounds that swelled and filled the space, more moving and beautiful than I had ever expected and when we filed out of the building, blinking in the light, we were all grinning and buoyant and wanted to do it again.

•　　•　　•　　•　　•

Later still that day – Rob's front room*

There is only one chair in the room where we later convene to talk. Bill sits on it. I sit on the floor. At this angle he appears even taller than he is – which is very tall.

The room is full of Bill's work. About ten framed posters lean or hang on the walls having migrated from the art school bar.**

As we entered we passed two large canvases, GET YOUR HAIR CUT and MAKE SOUP. Since I last saw them in the union bar I've read, watched and researched the Drummond canon, spoken to fans, friends and collaborators and come to appreciate the extent of Bill's range . . . and it's fair to say MAKE SOUP is not the work that defines him in the public

---

* I had planned to speak to Bill backstage or in a dressing room at Norwich Arts Centre.

The first idea proved impossible because 'backstage' at Norwich Arts Centre consists of a wall behind the stage and the dressing rooms turned out to be full of a highly strung ladies choir rehearsing for a concert.

This resulted in the nightmarish situation of having to find somewhere to speak to Bill with Bill there . . . because he was there and ready to begin an interview I was meant to have organised.

Luckily, Rob from the SU bar lived next door to Norwich Arts Centre so we went round there and knocked. I'd no idea if Rob would be in but it turned out he was and that he didn't mind Bill and me sitting down for an hour in his front room and was happy to make us a cup of tea and pretend that this was normal.

Had Rob not been in I don't know what would have happened; perhaps I would have pressed on with panic-eyed cheer in search of other venues, the atmosphere darkening with each hopeless mile until we reached the black North Sea . . .

** I believe Bill first started lending work to Rob having met him socially and discovered that he ran a bar in an art school with large expanses of wall. Every couple of months he'd deliver some more canvases and Rob would put them up, storing the older work at his flat – wrapped up in the shed, propped on the mantelpiece, hung in the lounge, in the kitchen . . . accidentally amassing a shrine.

Bill drops into Rob's depot every so often to borrow work for shows and projects.

consciousness. No. That'd be THE MONEY;* an event chronicled in a film titled *The K Foundation Burn a Million Quid.*

I begin by asking if being Bill Drummond is sometimes a hindrance to work like The17.

'It is something that I think about. Not all the time but . . . and I'm not the only person this happens to, it happens to most people that have done certain things. It casts a long shadow. I can feel that stuff I've done in the past will cast a shadow over whatever I do from here on in and there are times when that can get to me and it has influenced, to an extent, the way that I work. I have evolved ways of working where my name might not be attached to something.

It just so happens that piece thing behind you there, 40 BUNCHES OF DAFFODILS, that very thing, I've been doing that for about nine years now – I did it last week in Southend – and it's got nothing to do with me. I go out in the street, I'm just a man, I've got a box of daffodils and I hand them out. There is no explanation. I don't go out there to explain what it's about. I do it and some people say, "What's this about? Is this some sort of promotional thing?" and I say, "No no, I just want to give out forty bunches of daffodils."'

Do you like that anonymity?

---

* *The K Foundation Burn a Million Quid*, Chris Brook (Ellipsis Books, 1997).

Blurb: 'In the early hours of 23rd August 1994, in a derelict boat house on the island of Jura, the trustees of the K Foundation, Jimmy Cauty and Bill Drummond, burned £1 million in cash – money from a previous Cauty and Drummond project, the KLF.'

'I know what you're saying. I don't know. I think I live a pretty unsociable life so I don't get into situations much where these conversations can happen. I'm usually so focused or wrapped up in what I'm doing at that moment . . . Even when I'm being interviewed by a journalist, they don't seem to ask those questions or maybe they tip-toe around them but then, when they write up their piece . . . it's there. Maybe the first third of the feature will be a potted history of Bill Drummond. They feel that, if they don't put all that in, whoever is reading the piece won't know who this person they're writing about is and I don't know if that's because I've never particularly gone out to have a large profile as a personality, maybe they've got to give that history to say, *"Look, this person has been working for quite a long time in some sort of way and there's some sort of thread here that leads through to where he's at now . . ."* I don't know.'

You've always pursued that thread with a strong work ethic; is that linked to your Scottishness?

'It is that, it's very much that; that's the background I come from, that's the attitude. I've never been drawn to decadence. I've never been drawn to that thing of "the wild artist", it just doesn't interest me. The work ethic is . . . it's not work for work's sake. I get wrapped up. I get driven. The big motivation is that "life is short". I've got a lot of things I want to get done. I could die tonight, that's always there; and I'm always excited by what I'm doing. Exploration. The next thing.'

Do you see a pattern or progression in your work?

'Usually, I can look back on what I've done – or look into myself – and see a theme. It's almost always like I'm gnawing at the same bone or scratching the same wound. The17 this afternoon and "Doctorin' the Tardis" – in one sense they're a million miles apart, in another sense they come from a very similar place.'*

·   ·   ·   ·   ·

You often relate your ideas and journeys in a very character-istic first-person style when you write – often in retrospect, often in the form of a diary or log.

'Yes, although some of the time I cheat. Sometimes I write in the present tense although it's been written after the event and I'm aware, in the sense that all writing is lying, that I'm telling a story so I'm leaving out a percentage of things in order to tie a thing together

---

* 'Doctorin' the Tardis' was a single Bill made in 1988; a novelty song composed of other pop tunes mashed up together. A trashy Frankenstein's monster of a number one, it was followed by a book, *The Manual (How to Have a Number One the Easy Way)*, a step by step guide, a set of golden rules, to make a number one record with little or no money or musical aptitude.
Just as The17 celebrates a unique music that exists only in the moment and space of conception, *The Manual* sought to strip out the illusory romance of the pop industry process and the elitism of 'us and them' – that democracy again; no artists, no audience, just us.

'It was an excuse to say a lot of things I wanted to say about how the industry worked. It was an excuse to go out and say, "If you want to do something, go and do it! Don't wait to be asked, don't wait for a record company to come and want to sign you or a management company. Just go and do it." Also, it was saying: "If you wanna have number one . . . you can have it. It won't make you rich, it won't make you happy, but you can have it."'
– Bill Drummond speaking in a Norwegian national radio interview in September 1991

so that it has a beginning, a middle and an end, and I will do that unconsciously. I don't set out to do it but somehow I've learnt to do that. Sometimes I look back and think, "I've just learnt these tricks," and sometimes I try to break free of that – I can see my own clichés.

I'd like to think I could write a proper book with one whole story, like a novelist does but I guess, for a successful novel and definitely a successful film, you have to have something that happens in the first ten minutes or the first X amount of pages in a novel that sets something up: *Something has now happened that changes everything* – you've got to get to the end for it to resolve itself, that's what takes you through. That doesn't really happen with my things.

You mentioned earlier that your writing is episodic, Dan. That's what my stuff is and that's what will stop it from ever crossing over commercially, I think. That's the reason people can maybe get so far with one of my books and then go, "Okay, I get the picture," you know? There's no plot, it's not going to go anywhere particularly.

'When I was eighteen I read *On the Road* by Jack Kerouac – huge influence on me; that and Henry Miller is what got me wanting to write.

When they brought out the scroll of *On the Road* a couple of years ago I reread that and it was weird. I'm now, you know, quite a bit older than Jack Kerouac was when he died – he was young when he wrote it – and it's only now that I realise "but there's no story here, there's nothing!" He could have cut that book off at any point, it has no conclusion.'

Has that influenced the way you see your role as a raconteur?

'It was never a conscious thing; it wasn't until me and Z, Mark Manning and I, went to New York to do *Bad Wisdom** and we became like a double act, reading and telling the story, that I started learning how to actually talk to an audience. I knew I didn't want to do it with a microphone. I knew I wanted to keep it as intimate as possible but I was aware that a craft was being learnt – it was an act to a certain extent but I knew that it also had to be for real. I know that, every time I go out and tell a story, like with The17 this afternoon, which I've told who knows how many times, I've got to somehow reach down into myself and make it real, in the same way as an actor has. Now, the last thing I ever wanted to be was an actor, but I know that's what I've got to do and that has now become a big part, to use a cliché, of my practice as an artist; to get out there and tell stories and make it work, draw people in.

'There's another thing to this too. My dad was a minister in the Church of Scotland and in 1963 we did an exchange. He took over a church in a small town in North Carolina and the minister from that church worked at my dad's church in Scotland. We went and lived in their house for three months and they came and lived in ours. Then, in 1993, we went back. It was

---

* *Bad Wisdom: The Lighthouse at the Top of the World*, Bill Drummond & Mark Manning (Creation Books, 2003).

Blurb: 'Having exhausted (and been exhausted by) the young man's religion of rock and roll, the authors undertake an epic journey to the North Pole to sacrifice an icon of Elvis Presley. Two very different accounts emerge as the pilgrims venture into the frozen wastes at the top of the world.'

'A monumentally sane project carried through, blood and hair, by madmen'
– Iain Sinclair

just for a week or so but my dad was asked to give the sermon in the church there. Now, I grew up seeing my dad give sermons every week, as a kid, and I didn't think about it, you know? "He's just my dad." When I was very young I'd be off into Sunday School by the time he got to the sermon . . . anyway, my dad was asked by the regular minister to come up and give the sermon, "We have Reverend Jack Drummond here . . ." and he got up out of the pew and started walking backwards down the aisle and started talking straight away. He got to the front and started going into it and I thought, "My dad's got an act!" It had never crossed my mind (snaps fingers) and he was really good at it! He had them in the palm of his hand and the guy afterwards, the minister, said, "God, if I could roll my Rs like you, I'd be able to charge X amount more as a visiting preacher!" (Laughs) Which in this country, especially in Scotland, would never be said but that's how Americans think, and I really learnt something from that. It's not that I'm trying to imitate my father at all . . .'

But it's in you.

'It's in me. And I realised I must have taken that in from a very early age – to get up and stand in front of an audience, no amplification, no band. You know, you're not hiding behind the loud sounds of your guitar or the drums, or everything else, it's not even that you're hiding behind a tune. It's just you and those people there and you've got to communicate something and leave something behind.'

You don't think of yourself as a writer, though?

'No. I've written books but I'm not a writer. I've made records but I'm not a musician. I can pick up a guitar or sit down at a keyboard and play some things but I don't think of myself as a musician, never have done. I don't think of myself as a writer, don't think of myself as a painter . . . I went to art school by accident and I fell in love with painting. I was pretty good at painting too. That's what I thought I was going to do and then, while I was there, I rebelled against the whole thing. Maybe I realised I wasn't the genius I hoped I would be but I also thought, and this is going to sound arrogant, "I don't want to spend the rest of my life attempting to make things to sell to rich people." You know, one-off things.

I was then beginning to read, as I said, Kerouac and Miller. I liked the idea that with writing you could buy the paperback, everybody could buy the paperback and it was the same everywhere; and the same with music – a seven-inch single. I wasn't thinking of getting into pop music at that point but I thought – the example I gave myself at the time and remember writing about is that Andy Warhol's seven-inch of "Penny Lane" by The Beatles is no better or worse than my version. I liked that democracy.

'So, I walked out of art school, walked away from painting and thought, "Well, I'll write. To do that, I'll have to go and live life and do all sorts of jobs, go all over the place." It's not like I just wanted to sit down and write novels about relationships and all that kind of stuff. I wanted to get out there into the world and live a life but I realised after a while that I wasn't really a writer. I don't know at what point it dawned on me but I was actually doing everything with the head of somebody who'd gone through the British art school system circa early 1970s and that's still the overriding thing. So the storytelling, doing the posters, coming up with a way of allowing myself to do the paintings all comes from that.'

You say 'allowing myself to do the paintings' and you do often seem to structure work around a dogma or set of rules – allowance and denial.

'It's not like I'm "into denial" like some sexual or perverse thing . . . It's like when I was making three and a half minute pop records; there's no point making them longer than three and a half minutes. The way that these things are communicated to people is via radio, initially, and radio stations don't want to play anything longer than three and a half minutes. If it is, they start fading it or talking over it. Also, with a pop record, any record, any recorded music, you can only have it within so many megahertz – you can't have really high sounds or really low sounds because it can't exist on a piece of vinyl or an mp3.'

You see a beauty in restriction?

'Yeah. Like, with oil paints – not that I use oil paints now – you know that this colour and that colour, they can't mix chemically – so you're always aware of it.
Doing the posters over the years, I always thought, "Trim it down. Trim it down." Whereas they started off a lot wordier and there wasn't much difference between the posters and the writing in the book.'

Are you happy with the term 'artist'?

'I'm never happy with that at heart, no, but anything else I try to come up with, it doesn't work. There was a time when I thought, "No, I'm a poet, that's what I am, just so happens I don't use words . . ." and I tried to convince myself of that but I knew it was even more pretentious and would need even more explaining. There was a period when I was reading more poetry than I was looking at or thinking about art . . . I don't know, saying you're an artist has always had, maybe should have, that pretension. "Oh, you're an artist are you? That what you think you are? You're an artist now?" Pop record making was only (holds up thumb and index finger) that much of my life. There was a lot before and after that.'

The advent of The17 seemed to coincide with a shift in popular music away from the single voice to a more choral sound.

'I think it's a zeitgeist thing. I think I'm just part of a . . . this didn't come into The17 book but I could have started from another point of view:
I buy an iPod. Theoretically, I can have every piece of music that I have ever wanted to listen to on there and I can listen to it when I want. So I get all these tracks and I start flicking through, this one, this one, this one – that's just me though, jaded – but then I notice my thirteen-year-old doing the same thing, "flick, flick, flick, flick", or she hears something on an advert, likes it, types it into Google, downloads it – whoosh, she has the band's whole everything. She doesn't know what decade they're from, where they're from but she's got it all and maybe listens to it for a week and then it's gone. Bang.
Next week it's something else.

'Something has vastly changed, really hugely changed. When I was a kid, to have an album cost you quite a bit of money. You invested in it. When you got it, if you didn't like it, you accepted there were maybe only two tracks you liked but you worked at it and you ended up liking it, learnt to like it – that's not going to happen now, it's different and I'm not saying anything's better or worse, it's just changed. What's happened since the whole downloading thing has kicked in big time is the live side – going to see the act live is far more important; last year with Leonard Cohen over here – whole generations said, "We've got to go and see Leonard Cohen."

It doesn't matter if they buy the album . . .'

It's the event.

'The event, yes. Look at the rise and rise of the amount of festivals. It may be a bubble that's going to burst but it's now about time, place and occasion – all of those things that I'm dealing with in a different way with The17 – that is what people are going for. It's no longer contained within the recording.

Some people now, people more of your generation, fetishise vinyl and it's young people who are buying into a want, a need for music to be more solid, the sleeves bigger . . .

So those are all reflections of that thing. Of course I hear Arcade Fire and Fleet Foxes and I love it but that's just me, that's because of my age and the way it reminds me of things from other times.

I didn't bring it up this afternoon but I know, over the years, any time I've heard choral singing music my ears have gone out to it and that'll be because I sang in choirs as a kid.'

Perhaps part of the magic of singing in church as a child is that you're unaware of what you're singing about.

> 'It's just the sounds, yes, and I've read recently how – I can't remember the composer – he wanted less words, more long vowels and more harmonies because that's what's really being communicated. That's what has the power in religious music. It's not the words, it's the sounds, it's the voices.'

Are you finding that many members of The17 are being affected by the experience?

> 'I don't know. I don't know enough people . . . I'll go and do something like today but I don't know what the long-term effect is. I've got no idea.'

• • • • •

**Stoke Newington, London
March 2010**

Bill is sitting on his roof – the roof where he writes, weather permitting.
It was here, surrounded by the ambient noise of outer London, that he wrote much of his book about The17*.

———————————

* *17*, Bill Drummond (Beautiful Books, 2008).

> Blurb: 'THIS BOOK IS ABOUT
> Music, uncertainty, sitting on a ledge, night trains across Russia, Bill Drummond, drunken mercenaries on the North Sea, starting over again, a classroom of thirteen-year-olds, getting everything done before death, art, a river full of headless eels, girl pop, waking up to find all music has disappeared and a choir called The17.'

Earlier in the day, when I expressed concern that the portrait we're here to take might look contrived, Bill patiently pointed out that, since he wasn't in the habit of writing on his ledge with other people looming over him, it was contrived whether I liked it or not and we should probably just make the best of a contrived situation and not worry about it. So we do; Bill with his notebook and tea, Lucy and I teetering precariously above the guttering and the drop, trying to frame the shots.★

We speak about Lady Gaga. Bill loves Lady Gaga; loves her complete ease and ownership of pop. She has compromised nothing, he says, she has created a whole universe and now straddles it, unsurpassed.

Bill tells us that, for a few weeks last year, he and fellow ex-KLFer Jimmy Cauty were in agreement that the only thing which would tempt them back to pop music would be to work with Lady Gaga.

'Jimmy said he was surprised she's not telephoned us yet.'

•　•　•　•　•

After leaving Bill's house, I'm struck by the thought that the way he records and narrates his work, however unreliably, may be a stratagem to buttress and bolster its shape – for himself as much as the layman. His world of mad doings only

---

'I can't wait to hear the music that is being made in 100 years from now. These notions keep me awake at night with excitement.'

★ Photographer Lucy Johnston agreed to document the conversations and work-spaces I encountered while working on the book and so occasionally accompanied me on jaunts to places like Bill's roof.

lines up in retrospect when viewed from the justified head-lands of *17*, *How To Be An Artist* and the other written records of his work. His books are accepted histories of a lifetime of tangential missions into the unknown and he takes such care to define the narrative path because he knows the chaotic abyss that lurks either side of his stated methodology.

Even the story that there's no story – no meaning behind a decision – *'Nothing to see here'*, is a sleight of hand way of working.

He generates the story and embodies it, but sometimes his stories are not enough, the wilfulness of his acts too great to be constrained within the books, films, music and state-ments he makes in their wake – as with THE MONEY – and long shadows threaten to swallow him up . . . but he writes and talks his way out of it, making something new from the fallout; forms a new plan; invokes a new dialectic and moves on.

RICHARD LAWRENCE (1958–) is a British letterpress printer based in Oxford.

He started printing at school in 1970 and bought his first press (a Heidelberg platen) in 1976. As well as commercial printing work, he teaches letterpress and linocut courses at the St Bride Foundation in London.

RICHARD LAWRENCE

Widcombe Studios, Bath
2008–2011

Returned home to Bristol from Norfolk, I found myself in a post-MA slump. Unsure of what to do next, I began working on a house renovation, returning life to a wreck, digging retrospective foundations where the Georgians hadn't seen fit – claggy mud, army boots, two pairs of trousers, early dark starts, insipid rain . . . it wasn't much like art school. 'Well, at least I'm still working with my hands,' I'd think, dubiously. After a couple of months, around Christmas 2008, my father told me he'd met an interesting Bath-based letterpress printer who worked with a lot of old kit. I'd written nothing since talking to Bill (I'm not sure I'd even listened back to the tapes). Something about coming home had stumped me and I wasn't sure where my idea for the book was headed. So I'd stopped. But something about the idea of talking to a printer brought thoughts of the brilliant time had in a Thames boat yard back to mind. I'd known very little about boat building but the craftsmanship and enthusiasm I'd discovered in Henley had inspired and re-energised the whole airship project – my MA too, perhaps – so I telephoned the printer, Richard Lawrence, and asked if I could talk to him about his work. He wasn't keen, explaining it would likely be very disappointing and tedious for me since what he did was in no way arty, but we arranged to meet in any case after I'd explained that few things could be as disappointing as digging footings with a spade in the freezing cold.

Stood beside the River Avon, Richard's workshop was a single-storey building with a pitched roof made of corrugated iron but held together with moss.
Mist from the river hung level with the gutters.
I remember the hefty padlock on the garage door was green and its long-term knocking had worn away a hollow in the wood behind it.

The first thing I saw once inside was a print of Fleet Street being consumed by fire and flood – one of a series of linocut visions by Stanley Donwood, an artist with whom Richard had worked for several years; the inky nous to the Donwood dash.*
At the time of my visit they'd recently finished work on a project called Six Inch Records and remnants of the printed sleeves and card inners were piled up on the printshop's central bench.

Once sat with coffee, Richard explained the division of labour:

> 'I do this because I love the machinery and am fascinated by the process of squashing ink onto paper. It's nice if what you end up producing looks nice but that's

---

* Stanley Donwood (1967–) is a British artist and writer, known for his work with the band Radiohead.
His chapter follows next, after Richard's.

not actually why I do it. (Laughs) I mean, obviously it's a lot more satisfying to produce something that looks good; and it really doesn't take any more effort to produce something that looks good than something that looks bad.

Against which it's very interesting dealing with Stanley. (He points up to a drying rack of prints) Those posters are very obviously made up of broken old wood type. If I had my printer's hat on I'd go through and replace all the letters that are wonky and fiddle until it all printed solid and so on but that's not what he wants, he wants it to look like that. That's why it's printed on brown paper. (Laughs) It's rubbish!'

You're the technician and Stanley's the artist, then, but where's the tipping point do you think? What is the difference?

'In my case, the difference is that I do not have the artistic skill to produce an image that looks nice. So the tipping point between art and straight printing is probably the ability to produce a printing surface that is considered a piece of art. Recently I've fallen back on this theory: "I am someone who knows how to put ink on paper" . . . but it's very interesting, this distinction between craft and art.

Printing is a design skill, a practical application of common sense.'

Editorial common sense.

'Exactly. It's a very difficult dividing line and there's an enormous amount of expediency in what I do which I don't think people appreciate. That's something that Stanley is very good about, actually – he'll have a vague idea of what he wants but then quite happily bend it or, you might say, be inspired by what's available. That's the essence of all the typography that I do. I have an idea of what it would be nice to do and then I think, "Well, what have I actually got with which I could do it?"

'Somewhere along the way I spent some time at Reading University doing a History of Printing, Design & Typography degree and one of the things that people there say – and it's very much the way I feel, working with letterpress – is that letterpress is extremely good training for typography and design simply because of the number of things that you can't easily do. You're constrained in all sorts of ways and you're made to work with what there is. It's a very interesting exercise.

'A few years ago I had the order of service to do for a funeral and there was a lot of copy in it, a lot of words, and I found I'd only enough of one typeface to typeset the whole thing. You're then confronted with the problem of how to distinguish all the instructional headings for the congregation, delineate between hymns and pieces of text and, armed with one size of one typeface in roman and italic you can actually produce something that is extremely . . . I mean, "functional" makes it sound boring but you can produce something that works extremely well and looks good, having started with one option.
If I'd been doing it on a computer it would have been very easy to have as many sizes of type as I wanted and as many fonts but it would have been less thought out – that's the other constraint with letterpress, if you're typesetting a lot of material, doing it by hand, it takes a long time and you can't, at the end of it, say, "Oh, I think it would look better if it was a half a point bigger,"

and click a button. It doesn't work like that. You have to decide before you start what you are doing. It inspires you to plan.'

• • • • •

There are three presses in the printshop proper. An Albion hand-press stands in a corner with an air of solid menace. Next to this a black and chrome press runs the length of the workshop wall – shrouded by a greenish tarp. ORIGINAL HEIDELBERG CYLINDER. 1958. Wheels, handles, dials and levers poke out at intervals, like Dalek punctuation.

To the right sits HEIDELBERG 1965, a smaller machine which Richard now starts and lets run. As the paper in the feed is fed up to the hinged ink jaw – the myriad movements are crisp and hypnotic – I realise the noise is taking me back to my childhood and the top-left-hand corner of Wales.

'Pish ti'coo; Pish ti'coo; Pish ti'coo; Pish ti'coo . . .'

Ivor the Engine reincarnated as a press* and, indeed, all the presses here are substantial, locomotive-like apparatuses – sat still and quiet now but potentially very loud and powerful. Richard resembles a lion tamer sat in their midst.

> 'The thing that puts a lot of people off owning one of these is the sheer size – it weighs almost exactly a ton. Like all letterpress machines, you need an inky surface and a piece of paper and you squash one against the other. That's it. That's printing.
>
> This press achieves that by running ink rollers over the surface, and the really clever bit of this machine is the feed mechanism which, rather ingeniously, can suck just one piece of paper up, deliver it to the gripper-arms which then rotate, carrying the paper.'

He hands me a newly printed sheet, the slight indentations of the pressed type just visible if I hold it up at an angle to the light.

> 'Most of the trick to running this is knowing how to make it pick up one sheet and not two and not none. What you get good at, after a while, is looking at the pile and listening to the noises the press makes so that, if it does do something wrong, you can very quickly figure out why. You can adjust the number of suckers turned on, you can adjust both the height and strength of the blow that comes through the pile, you can adjust the angle of attack of the suckers, you can adjust how

---

* Ivor the Engine was a small tank locomotive who belonged to the The Merioneth & Llantisilly Railway Traction Company Limited in the top-left-hand corner of Wales. Created by brilliant animators Oliver Postgate and Peter Firmlin, Ivor's adventures on the BBC made a deep impression on my childhood.

fast the pile is driven upwards and, depending on the thickness of the paper, what height it's picked from. By adjusting one or all of those things, you can get it to pick up one sheet of anything you want – from very thin paper right up to beer-mat board. Have you ever made balsa wood aeroplanes? They're done on these, that's how you print and cut out the pieces for the kits – die cutting. (Rummages through a box file on a shelf by the sink) That's a cutting die and that's what it does.'

Richard puts a rectangular piece of wood on the bench. A maze of metal blades project up from it, surrounded by small, close-fitting blocks of foam.

'The important bit is the shaped cutting rule – it's quite sharp. If you imagine pushing the die into a piece of card, it would tend to stick in it, so the foam is there to push it apart again.'

Are fold-lines made in the same way but with blunt rules?

'Yes, the folding rules are rounded on top and very slightly lower than the ones which cut. These are made in Bristol. If you ask people, "What's printed the most?" the bulk would say newspapers or books when, in fact, it's packaging material. Cereal packets win hands-down. The vast majority of printing around the world is for packaging and along with packaging comes boxes and for those you need die cutting.'*

---

* Several months later I visited the premises of A. Stevens & Co. in Yeovil, Somerset (Est. 1896).
The company produces high quality packaging including hand-made presentation boxes and folded cartons – much of if cut and manufactured on Heidelberg presses and other amazing vintage machinery: the Vickers 'Empire' Stitcher and the Samuel

Rooting through another box, Richard pulls out a block comprising two interlocking parts. A piece of paper or card placed between these matched male and female dies* will emerge embossed – the design pressed through the page. This is blind embossing, he explains, 'blind' because it is an inkless process, the pressure of the press moulding the material into a relief – the definition wrought by the light.

The examples of the practice that he proffers have a wonderfully tactile quality. Fingertips trace the contours of a set of Stanley's bears – stamped into a furrowed map for a Six Inch Record outer, a linear Braille-scape.

I hadn't considered printing presses being put to work 'dry' in this way. The technique seems so elegant. I ask how Richard cleans his type and presses down.

'White spirit. You can use paraffin but it leaves a slightly oily residue behind.

One thing I run into which irritates the hell out of me is that the whole letterpress printing thing has been taken over by "creative" people, artists and such, some of whom have, what I consider to be, absurd ideas about safety. There are aspects of this which are clearly very unsafe – don't stick your head in a moving press; don't take a handful of lead type and eat it, all that sort of thing – but a lot of people, particularly Americans, are terrified of solvents . . . and you can get inks that,

---

R. Parry/Stokes & Smith Co. Model B motorised duplex blade cutting machine (Serial No. 908) and the Andrews & Suter motorised corner cutter (with foot operation).

A. Stevens & Co. have produced boxes for the MOD to the same pattern for over eighty years, I was told; generations of the same family making up the same box on the same machinery.

* Male and female halves of an embossing set mesh like gear cogs – the male convex, the female concave.

instead of being based on linseed oil, are based on soya oil; you can use cooking oil or soya oil to clean down the machinery afterwards, you *can* . . . but it leaves it in the most foul, sticky, gunky condition – if you know what you're doing, washing a machine up with white spirit, you'll perhaps use two fluid ounces.'

Can you tell me a bit about your inks?

'Oh, they're all boring old linseed oil based inks – you take linseed oil and boil it, then grind pigment into it. I don't personally do that, there's an ink making company in South Wales who treat me extremely nicely. I started using them some while ago. I asked them, "Could you possibly, maybe . . . ?" and they said, "Oh yes, not a problem," and now they produce six different pots of bespoke colours for about £20 apiece which was about a third of what I'd expected to have to pay. I subsequently looked them up on the internet and they turn out to be Britain's major ink producers – they're the people who supply Fleet Street – so what they're doing piddling around producing pots of obscure colours for me I've no idea; but I love them for it.'

Richard crosses over to a shelf, takes a lid off a tin and holds it out. Inside the ink resembles emerald engine grease – sickly, fat and viscous.

'Here is a tin of green that I bought the other day.'

He up-ends it. Nothing happens.

'I could probably leave it upside down for an hour before any came out; but some inks are thinner than others. White is a problem.'

He opens a tin of white and lays it sideways on the bench. An ominous bulge begins to form, like angry custard.

'As you can see, it's almost able to flow. White is a notoriously difficult colour to work with because white, as a pigment, is lousy and getting enough of it into stuff is very difficult. That's why, if you ever see white type on black in a magazine it was almost certainly printed black onto white paper rather than the other way round.'

How is white ink made?

'It's usually titanium and other stuff – aluminium oxide sometimes, depending upon what you want. Most of the pigments are inorganic chemicals.'

Gone are the days of beetles for blue and suchlike?

'Um, mostly. (Laughs)
I don't know what some of the pigments are that they use. Having said that, I bought all these tins of ink for the same price and some had noticeably less in than others because the pigments involved were just that bit more expensive. To this day, a kilogram of blue will cost you more than a kilogram of yellow.'

•   •   •   •   •

At this point we pause for more coffee and a Penguin biscuit. Richard sits framed by a stacked tower of drawers that rise floor to skylight, each one partitioned into myriad cells – packed with an unseen type, filed away; dormant words.
Tall, bearded, an L.S. Lowry figure in jumper and gilet, he seems quietly amused by most things – I suppose he's what people would call diffident, but actually I think it's another facet of his economy – he's not one for small talk, reserves judgement. There's nothing superfluous about him – he's lean. A spare man.

'It's actually quite rare to find someone who is interested. As you've probably worked out by now, I'm interested in the technicalities of it. That's what I get excited about.
The images are great and it's nice working with people like Stan but it's the whole business of "How does it work?" that actually excites me.'

Do many people track you down because you work with Stanley?

'No, thankfully not, somehow it hasn't happened. He's very fair about giving me billings on things that I have helped him with but no one seems interested in me,

for which I'm eternally grateful. But then, I've been to one or two of his launch events and he seems to have a habit of wandering around, not actually telling people who he is.*

Having said fiercely that I'm not an artist, I'm actually a scientist by training. I spent the best part of twenty years working for a publisher in various editorial functions producing maths and science books. I like printing because I can understand how it works – if this bit doesn't work it's because that bit isn't connected to the lever that makes it wiggle . . . and I can then do something about it. I'm very happy with this lot and if something goes wrong I can fix it.'

---

* This is later borne out at the Six Inch Records launch.

Where did you get your presses?

'Well, the Albion in the corner came from an artist, a genuine artist, who made linocuts and worked at the art school at Banbury. He was getting on to retirement and needed to get rid of it so he advertised in the back of a magazine that I read and I bought it from him.'

Can it be taken apart?

'It can to a certain extent, yes, but the main casting remains unfeasibly heavy and awkward to move; and while nobody knows what Gutenberg's press looked like, it was probably very similar – except of course that his was made out of wood rather than metal.
While letterpress continued they were very useful, practical things – they made excellent proof-presses. So, rather than locking something up in a machine forme* and all that – particularly on very large printing machines, terribly tedious – you could ink these by hand and print a sheet or proof very quickly.

'The 1965 platen came from a printer in Oxford who was closing down. He'd made it to the age of eighty-something and his second replacement knee didn't really take to it so he decided it was time to retire. I'd got to know him and, when it came time for the mach-ine movers to come and take this away, he suggested

---

* A machine forme is the frame into which movable type is locked once composited into words and lines of text. The forme presents the letter faces at exactly the same height so as to form an even surface which, when mounted in a press and inked, can print onto paper.

that I had a word with them. They were essentially taking it away to recondition it and sell it on – probably for die cutting and blind embossing and that sort of thing. I think I gave them about £400 for it and they took it out of his workshop and dropped it at my house a mile up the road. £400!'

What is it worth now?

'£400!' (Laughs)

Really?

(Still laughing) 'There's a limited market for them; a limited number of people who know how to use them. This 1958 Heidelberg came from a private press in Marlborough. I'm very lucky to have got it. They used it very little but kept it in very good condition so it hasn't done many miles.'

It looks in amazing shape.

'The longevity of these machines is mind-boggling; if you look in the back of trade magazines you'll see "Heidelberg, six colour – only 70 million impressions." If you look after them, oil them and replace the odd bits that do wear out they just go on and on. The one I had before was from 1940-something and it was a little rattly but, if you treated it with a small amount of care it would work absolutely fine. The one I used at school was built in 1920-something – that was definitely on the wrong end of rattly but still worked quite well.'

I imagine Richard using the old school press. I wonder what he was like as a child. He seems to embody a stoic enjoyment;

a half-amused smile of concentration on his face. The flat smell of ink on his hands.

> 'It's interesting to see the reaction of people who do come in here. I've had quite a few in who used to work in the printing trade and they say, "Ooh, wonderful! The smells of ink!" and so on, and some people get excited by all the curiously shaped lumps of machinery and some get excited about all the bits of woodcut and type and I sort of understand that but what excites me is that "It's machinery! It works! I can do something with it!"
>
> People get a bit put out, frightened even, when I don't react in the right way; when I don't get enthusiastic about the "incredible texture and quality" of something . . . but I'm a creature from a mechanical world, really. That's what excites me.'

STANLEY DONWOOD (1967–) is a British artist and writer, known for his work with the band Radiohead. Since 1994 he has produced all artwork for the group in collaboration with lead singer Thom Yorke. He has also written the short story collections *Slowly Downward: A Collection of Miserable Stories* (2005), *Household Worms* (2011) and *Humor* (2014).

STANLEY DONWOOD

Derelict dance hall, Bath
March 2009

The first time I met Stanley Donwood he was not in his element. Hosting the simultaneous launch and closure of his record label, Six Inch Records,* at a trendy London bar he stood apart from his guests; nipping outside for furtive roll-ups whenever possible, eschewing the venue's lava-lamp paint scheme and 8' egg-shaped isolation booth latrines.
When he had to interact and address the crowd to introduce a band he stood onstage uneasily. A pregnant cough. A pause; another cough before breaking into a run-up of 'Um . . . er . . . OI!'
The night wasn't his idea, I suspected.

----

* Six Inch Records was a record label set up by Stanley in 2006 – 'An exercise guaranteed to lose money.'
Three six-inch records were released in editions of 333, costing £6.66 pence each – 999 records in total.
The label was designed to be dissolved after all the albums sold, which they quickly did, resulting in the launch party also being the wake: 'The launch went quite well; I sacked all my artistes, sacked myself and purchased possibly the most expensive round of drinks of my life.'

He's not a man for the spotlight, Stanley.

He's much more likely to be the man taking apart the spotlight with a spanner . . . or a hammer.

He has the air of a man in a spot of difficulty; a man who'd much prefer to be elsewhere, perhaps.

He's not even really called Stanley, you know; not even that's right.

'I've got a rubbish pseudonym. "Stanley Donwood"!? Rubbish.'

I approached him at the trendy launch and introduced myself. Yes, I'm the chap with the airships, we establish, and he's the chap with the bowler hat and the pseudonym; no, it wasn't his idea.*

• • • • •

Stanley Donwood, whoever he might be, is responsible for Radiohead's** aesthetic, artwork and labyrinthine websites. Millions of people have his work in their homes, hundreds of thousands would recognise the pointy-toothed bears that have become something of a trademark. He has accidentally become very popular and his work is in demand. He is adept in many media, constantly evolving and adapting. He exhibits all around the world. He has won awards.***

---

* Richard Lawrence had been good enough to pass my details on to Stanley after our meeting at his printshop in January, so Stanley was aware of me and my zeppelin by the time we met.

** Radiohead are a band from Oxford, England. Formed in 1985.

*** Among numerous other prizes and plaudits, Stanley has won two Grammy Awards – Best Recording Package, 2001, and Best Boxed or Special Limited Edition Package, 2009:

'I'm not really into that sort of thing. I went once . . . it was awful.'

He's not sure how he feels about any of this, preferring to keep a low profile and not give interviews . . . for a long time people assumed he was an alias of Radiohead's singer, Thom Yorke; but he isn't.

'That'd be nice, though. I'd have better hair.'

Stanley's studio is an old dance hall. Where once it thrummed to the tunes of the day, it now echoes, abandoned and cavernous. The floorboards creak, the windows are cracked and icy, ivy grows through the frames. The only light in the place shines feebly – up a flight of wooden stairs that groan – a small office with a workshop beyond.
He beckons me in and shuts the door, apologising for the extreme cold.

'All studios are cold. It's the law.'

Is it always so cold?

'Yes.'

And you always work here?

'At the moment, yeah. I paint in a barn in Oxfordshire as well but that's a bit more rudimentary than this, it's . . . well, it's a barn. There's a wood burning stove so when that's going it's quite nice but most of the time it's like being outdoors.'

Do you work with other people? I mean, will members of the band chip in?

'Oh yeah! For instance, with *In Rainbows*★ I'd have whatever stage the artwork had got to cycling on all the computers around the studio and the band would say, "Oh I like that one and I like that one." So, over time, I could say, "Right, so that's where it's going." We'd all talk about it and come into a sort of creative consensus about what was working well.

It was evolving as the music was evolving . . . and no record label! We were all working towards a deadline which became more concrete as time went on because we'd got things to manufacture, we had to book the factories to press the records and all that kind of thing, and all anonymously.

If the next thing works in that sort of way, that would be great. I'm sure it won't because they're never the same.

Hail to the Thief,★★ the one before, that was me in my barn with huge paintings around the walls, working on several at the same time, and the nice thing with that

---

★ *In Rainbows* is Radiohead's seventh album and was released in 2007.
The band self-released the record online, allowing people to download on a 'pay what you want' basis.
A limited edition 'discbox', designed by Stanley, was made available towards the end of the year. The large hardcover box opens out to reveal the album on CD and two twelve-inch vinyl records, a disc of additional tunes and photographs and a book of printed artwork and lyrics.

> '*The Killer!* The first record packaging you could actually kill someone with! At least, I think you could kill someone with it if you hit them in the right place . . . that's probably not the first thing I should have said about it, is it? This is why I don't do interviews.'

★★ *Hail to the Thief* is Radiohead's sixth album and was released in 2003.
The artwork features paintings of road maps, which included lyrics from the album. The maps were painted in the bright petroleum colours Stanley had encountered on road signs in the LA area where the album was recorded. A special edition foldout map version was produced.

one was that I'd got this rubbish CD boom-box thing in there with me and the band would come into the barn in the evening – which is across the way from their recording studio – with the latest whatever-they'd-done on CD and play it and, because the barn's all wood and vaguely insulated with plywood, it just sounded really cool! So they would come over to have a beer and listen to what they'd done. Outside, away from the brilliant speakers, to hear it more as it was going to be heard.'

• • • • •

Stanley has a record player in one corner of the room. While we talk he plays a selection of well-thumbed punk and post-punk records – Bauhaus, Magazine and Sex Pistols. Cold as it might be, the studio is a den, stuffed with collected ephemera; test prints and clippings on the wall, an old piano, a screen printing table at the back with tins of ink and paint stacked behind; a painty carpet and a painty sink. Above a wide window overlooking a courtyard is written:

FIRE EXIT
BASH SIDE BITS OUT WITH HAMMER
PULL WINDOW OUT AND BE
VERY FUCKING CAREFUL

Stanley puts the kettle on and I unpack some of the Radiohead records I've brought along as reference.
He returns with tea as I place the *My Iron Lung* EP★ on the table.

★ The *My Iron Lung* EP was released by Radiohead in 1994 as a stopgap between debut album *Pablo Honey* and 1995's *The Bends*.

'Oh God! (Turning it over in his hands) I can't remember this at all! This was the first thing though . . . we had all this footage Thom had shot on tour and we ran it through his telly and took photographs of it. I liked the men standing around for their meeting – they were Osaka businessmen, I think. Lots of legs, yes . . . we didn't really know what we were doing.' (Laughs)

You don't generally do interviews, do you?

'Not loads, no. I prefer to do them over email really 'cos I feel rather inarticulate when I'm speaking – lots of "ers" and "ums" and "hmmms". Whenever I've done it, talked to someone for an interview, I always feel like such a twat afterwards. I think, "Why did I say that? I should have said something else."'

Bill Drummond told me he wasn't happy being called an artist for a long time. Was that an issue for you?

'I don't mind saying I'm an artist now. I used to say I was "sort of an artist" but as you go on you meet people, grown-ups, adults, and they say, "What do you do?" and you can't really get away with that so I just say, "I'm an artist" and it covers everything.
"Commercial Artist" I quite like. That's what graphic designers used to be called; artists for hire. I don't mind being for hire! (Laughs)
In a different world I'd be painting pub signs; doing something useful. I want to be, you know, a bit useful, because I'm a Jack-of-all-trades, master of absolutely none.
I'd love to be actually good at something, you know? Do one thing. That would be great!'

Richard Lawrence is very good at one thing.

'Richard is, yes, and I think this is why I get on so well with him – because he says, "I'm a technician. I'm not an artist."'

He does! Your relationship seems very complementary in that he's the practical print mechanic, able to make your ideas about lino, text and printing happen pretty quickly.

'He really can, yeah. I wouldn't be able to work those bloody machines, they terrify me!
When I went to art college, the first people that I connected with were the technicians. There was a guy called Tony who was the print technician and we got on straight away; he was a real local boy from Devon and while all the tutors were talking about stuff from their sixties educations which had nothing to do with what I was about, he was someone who actually knew what he was doing and how to do it – that was much more interesting to me.'

Were you working as a 'sort of artist' before you began work with Radiohead?

'Not "working", no. I was officially a job seeker – £39.70 a week. That was alright for a while. I was a clandestine artist – not a spray-can artist, I didn't have the means. I had a paint pot and a brush.'

Then you got the call.

'Yeah, "Do you want to have a go at doing a record sleeve?" and I said, "Yeah!?" I didn't know how to do it. I know how to do it now because I've done it lots of times. I've learnt on the job, as they say . . .'

I want to ask you about the bears; they're your bears, they were on the Six Inch Record sleeves, but they're Radiohead Bears to most people.*

'I've been working with them for ages. I'll use my stuff in their stuff. It's hard to separate; I mean, it doesn't separate – I do their artwork. Their artwork is my artwork.

The bears began when my eldest daughter was quite little, about one, one and a half – they wake up devilishly early in the morning and you're in this weird state, it's dark and there's nothing to do but make a cup of tea. I used to draw stories and tell them at the same time. I was telling a story to do with toys, abandoned toys . . . it's really bad when I think about it, luckily she couldn't understand . . .'

Was it a bit dark?

'It was a bit dark, yes – all the toys that are discarded by adults, sitting in this attic, got really fed up and so these cute teddy bears came down and ate the grown-ups . . . scary bears who'd started off nice and then became (bares teeth and howls) "Grawww!!!"

And that was it, it was just a drawing that was in a sketchbook and then I drew a load of them marching down a dark alley and then I started using them with Radiohead – the website first and then on a t-shirt and then it turned into all sorts of things.'

---

* See photograph of Stanley's bear blind-embossing set in previous chapter.

Around the time of *Amnesiac** I remember you put out a very scribbly poster of bears flying through a city and people looking up concernedly . . .

'That's Thom's drawing. He drew that; that was weird that one. At that time there was a lot of faxing back and forth "Phish, pheee, phew"; he'd send a fax, I'd draw on it and send it back, but that particular drawing of the flying bears, I'd done one at the same time – we did them on the same night, it was really weird – without telephoning or anything like that. We were both having some sort of mental flood or storm or something. I remember it intensely; drawing like mad

---

* *Amnesiac* is Radiohead's fifth album and was released in 2001.

with a biro, almost going through the paper with it. I think I scanned and faxed it to Thom and he scanned what he'd done and sent it back and they'd both been done at the same time and they were pretty much of the same level of biro intensity . . . that happens quite a lot with us, we work together a lot and do this thing of swapping where I'll do something and then say, "You do something" and he'll do something and say, "Now you do something", so we'll pass it backwards and forwards. We've painted large canvases where one person will do something until the point where you think, "I'm finished" and then the other person would go along and "Shhhhhhh" do something to it. We'll basically fight over the ownership of the canvas until one or other of us owns it – which is a hard thing to do but, you know, you'll get to a point where you think, "Right, that's mine now, I've got it." It's like fencing but with a piece of artwork.

We've done it remotely with fax machines and lately with emailing.'

Do similar battles happen with the band musically, do you think?

'I really don't know. I hear them making music and some of the stuff for *Kid A*.* (Laughs) . . . I mean, *Kid A* is apparently quite dark but earlier versions of it were really dark – much more upsetting really . . . they got rid of some of the bits, some sections and sounds which were just too much but I . . . I'm a sloganeer, I'm into sorta like "BAM BAM BAM!!!" but they're into a more musical art thing, something that will last

---

* *Kid A* is Radiohead's fourth album and was released in 2000.

and something that will work in different situations, so certain things they did, I said, "That's brilliant! You've got to keep that!" but they decided, "No, it won't work in time. It works now but it won't work in a year's time . . ."
I don't have the same level of quality control because, I mean, with the way that I've worked with Radiohead and so on, there's five of them and Nigel.'*

Six?

'I would say 5 + 1 rather than 6.
With the artwork there is me and Thom, which is very different to 5 + 1. We're 1 + 1, which, compared to 5 + 1 . . . what comes out of that is very different. I mean, obviously, we don't go ahead with stuff if the other members of the band aren't comfortable or happy with it.'

Has that ever happened?

'No . . . although I've gone wrong a few times.
With *In Rainbows* I was going to do all this architectural stuff with the software that's used to create optimum car parking spaces . . .'

The 2006 tour posters and merchandise were grey, I remember.

'Yeah. "Any colour so long as it's grey." All the t-shirts were grey – it was possibly one of the most insulting

---

* Nigel Godrich – producer, sound engineer and longstanding Radiohead collaborator.

things I could have done. Immediately afterwards we set up in Tottenham House, this decaying stately home near Marlborough, to work . . . and I'd been there for two days or something – had been obsessed by this book *The Long Emergency* by James Howard Kunstler★ – was in this dreadful nihilistic state, preoccupied with car parks and all that sort of thing, thinking, "There. Bam. Right. This is how it's going to be" . . . but they were playing the music and it was the most organic, spiritual, sexual, sensual, beautiful thing that I'd heard them do and I realised that what I was doing was completely wrong and that my head, my mind, my response, had gone awry.'

How did the *In Rainbows* artwork evolve then – the discbox and the 'pay what you want' aspect of the digital release?

'They'd been thinking how to put the new record out. The idea of people paying what they wanted for it was a bit of a reaction to the way that people who like music are treated by the record industry – if you can imagine such a thing as this overarching authority: "The Music Industry".
They treat people like, if not actual criminals, potential criminals. All this stuff – targeting people who

---

★ 'James Howard Kunstler's *The Long Emergency* may be destined to become the *Dante's Inferno* of the twenty-first century. It graphically depicts the horrific punishments that lie ahead for Americans for more than a century of sinful consumption and sprawling communities, fuelled by the profligate use of cheap oil and gas. Its central message – that the country will pay dearly unless it urgently develops new, sustainable community-scale food systems, energy sources, and living patterns – should be read, digested, and acted upon by every conscientious U.S. politician and citizen.'
                                                        – Michael Shuman

download music for nothing, what happened to Napster.* It was a reaction to the way the industry assumes
people are going to steal music and has created a legal
and software mechanism to prevent that. So there was
this idea, "Okay, let's put the record on the internet and
say you can pay what you want for it, pay what you
think it's worth – and some people won't pay anything,
some people will pay something," which was a bit of a
gamble, really. A huge gamble.
So the band and management said, "Okay, let's do it
for nothing," and, to me, "Can you make us something
that's worth about forty quid?" and I thought, "That's
quite a fucking challenge!" (Laughs) "How can I make
something that is essentially wrapping paper worth
£40?" because, you know, I'd been doing this thing
with EMI and they were principally releasing compact
discs – horrible, clattery boxes which I hate and have,
to my mind, really degraded what record packaging is.
When I was a kid growing up, I would buy records
because I liked the sleeves and I would spend ages
looking at the sleeves and poring over the sleeve-notes
and the lyrics.'

---

* Napster was a pioneering peer-to-peer file sharing internet service that empha-
sised sharing audio files. Napster ceased operations in mid-2001 having run into
legal difficulties in regard to copyright infringement.
Debate continues as to whether file sharing is bad for the music industry or stimulates
the sales of both physical and digital music. The leaking of Radiohead's *Kid A*, weeks
before its official release, led many to support the latter view since, in spite of being
downloaded by several million people, the record topped charts around the world
– this an album of so-say 'difficult' ambient electronica, jazz and processed vocals.

'The cool thing about Napster is it encourages bootlegging; it encourages
enthusiasm for music in a way that the music industry has long forgotten to
do. Anybody sticking two fingers up at the whole fucking thing is wonderful
as far as I'm concerned.'
– Thom Yorke

You'd made unusual sleeves prior to the discbox, though: the *Hail to the Thief* foldout map and the *Amnesiac* book . . .

'Yes, but they were always "Special Editions" and I had to really hassle the record company to do it. They really didn't like doing it. The people that I dealt with first off were great but there would be people higher up who'd say, "Well, you know, can you reduce the number of pages?" It was always very hard to get it done.'

Without compromising the idea away.

'Exactly. It was always a question of "How far can you push them?"
Kid A sounded to me like a message left on an answerphone that you received too late to do anything about, but *Amnesiac* was something else, it was something found when clearing a house, something in an attic, an old book in a drawer, a fragment – something left behind, the meaning of which had been lost.'

The *Amnesiac* book always struck me as fraught, as you say. Cross-hatching, layered detailing, out of focus, pixellated images – so much work in it, yet its meaning is a mystery; lost and unloved, like the toys in the attic.

'I spent a long time in London working on it. Walking in London and reading books about London. I found this book called *The House of Dr Dee* by Peter Ackroyd* and he mentioned Piranesi,** who I'd never heard of,

---

* Dr John Dee was an eminent English astronomer, explorer, mathematician, occultist, alchemist, philosopher and adviser to Queen Elizabeth I. He is often cited as the inspiration for Marlowe's Faustus and Shakespeare's Prospero.
There has been a recent resurgence of interest in Dee, who seems to be being reclaimed and rehabilitated as an English folk hero of sorts. Damon Albarn's *Dr Dee: An English Opera* opened as part of the Manchester Festival in 2011 – the opera having begun as a collaboration with Northampton writer and magician Alan Moore. *London Under* by Peter Ackroyd (Vintage, 2012) is also chock-full of meticulous research and labyrinthine tales of subterranean London, past and present.

** Giovanni Battista (also Giambattista) Piranesi 1720–1778. Italian artist noted for his etchings of ruined Rome and complex imagined prisons. In 1750 Piranesi published *Carceri d'Invenzione*, a series of sixteen prints depicting cavernous subterranean vaults with soaring staircases and fantastic machines.
Thomas De Quincey described the prisons in *Confessions of an English Opium-Eater*.

'Many years ago, when I was looking over Piranesi's Antiquities of Rome, Mr Coleridge, who was standing by, described to me a set of plates by that artist . . . which record the scenery of his own visions during the delirium of a fever: some of them (I describe only from memory of Mr Coleridge's account) representing vast Gothic halls, on the floor of which stood all sorts of engines and machinery, wheels, cables, pulleys, levers, catapults, etc., etc., expressive of enormous power put forth, and resistance overcome. Creeping along the sides of the walls, you perceived a staircase; and upon it, groping his way upwards, was Piranesi himself: follow the stairs a little further, and you perceive it come to a sudden abrupt termination, without any balustrade, and allowing no step onwards to him who had reached the extremity, except into the depths below . . . But raise your eyes, and behold a second flight of stairs still higher: on which again Piranesi is perceived, but this time standing on the very brink of the abyss. Again elevate your eye, and

so I went out and found out a bit about Piranesi and I started copying Piranesi's drawings with a biro because I wasn't quite sure about copyright. Peter Ackroyd, Iain Sinclair and Stuart Home . . . Michael Moorcock's written some brilliant books about London. *King of the City** is fantastic! (Begins turning the pages of the *Amnesiac* book) God, yes, and the bull . . .'

The Minotaur?

'Mmm, Mithras, labyrinthine structures and the idea of a city being a maze or a prison – Piranesi's imaginary prisons . . . I would get the train up to London for the day. I did it again and again, doing something that I've since found out Bill Drummond does, which is to write a name or a word across a city and then walk the letters . . . but I was trying to make a film as well and I did make a film in the end, to do with the bull. I think I went a bit mad, to be honest. I think I developed an obsession, looking back; but this idea of bulls . . .

---

a still more aerial flight of stairs is beheld: and again is poor Piranesi busy on his aspiring labours: and so on, until the unfinished stairs and Piranesi both are lost in the upper gloom of the hall.'

* *King Of The City*, Michael Moorcock (Scribner, 2000).

Blurb: 'The death of Princess Di heralded a spring clean of the soul. And the dirt we wanted off our coffee tables was the kind of salacious exposure tabloid paparazzo photographer Denny Dover had made a fortune out of. Now he's out of work and moving to the godforsaken wastes of Skerring on the south coast of England to lick his wounds. A former rock star and existential maverick, this East End lad-made-good lived it up with the best of them. But his childhood friend, hugely wealthy magnate Sir John Barbican-Begg (deceased, allegedly) is resurrecting events from a past littered with dysfunction and greed, sex, rock and roll and a ton of drugs. Denny's life encapsulates the fevered underground of a London teeming with contradiction and ambivalence, subversion and rage.'

Smithfield Market and Smithfield Fair and its ancient past of bull running. I imagined that the cattle would be taken there, then they'd have this ritual thing where they would drive a bull down to the Thames and kill it and have some sort of horrible sacrifice thing; something to do with bridges and the little beaches you get on the Thames . . . and I made a film.

There was me – I wasn't filming, I was directing – and there were three guys with cameras and an actor whose name I cannot remember . . . Graham? He was a proper actor and he was dressed as a City gent, you know – suit, overcoat, briefcase – and the idea was that he would come out of Farringdon tube station and walk through Smithfield and then down Giltspur Street – I'd mapped all this thing out and written a screenplay and everything!

He would be possessed by the spirit of the bull and become like the Minotaur almost, and descend into a type of madness. So we were filming him walking along, walking faster and faster and looking behind him and then, outside the Old Bailey, he stood against a wall, freaking out, and then start throwing his clothes off and chucking his briefcase!

'We were filming all this on the hoof and because we just had little handy-cams people couldn't tell that he was being filmed, you know?

We got down to the River Thames and the City of London Police came and stopped us. Apparently they'd been filming us with CCTV all the way down, filming us making a film – except they didn't know we were making a film, they had no idea what was going on. Thankfully this was before all the terrorism stuff, otherwise I don't know what would have happened. The police wanted to confiscate all the cameras and I had to say, "Right, no. You're not confiscating anything, we've stopped," and then we just filmed the last bit where the Minotaur gent walks into the Thames. Just about managed to get away with it.

Then the film got made but I lost it! (Laughs)

It's one of those things. No one's ever seen it.

I guess all that became R&D for the *Amnesiac* book. Funny how all that condenses down into such a little anecdote.'

• • • • •

I want to ask you about the thing underneath *Kid A*.

(I take the *Kid A* CD from my bag and begin to take apart the case)

'Oh, the thing underneath!?'*

Yes, the hidden thing underneath!

'That was the record after *OK Computer*, yes** – I hate jewel cases, as I've said, and I took one to bits and was looking at it and I realised there was this tiny gap and thought, "You could put something in there . . ."

They had to hand-pack them, apparently – it couldn't be done by a machine. So I think that annoyed the record label . . . again.

That was really tough, that record; really tough for everyone. It was forced out, really.'

---

* The 'thing underneath' is a booklet of writing and artwork that was concealed inside the case of early editions of *Kid A*. Many people would not have discovered its existence until long after buying the album, I imagine; if at all.

** *OK Computer* is Radiohead's third album and was released in 1997.

You took a lot of people with you, though, with *Kid A* and what followed.

'Not a purposeful thing.'

What do you remember of that time?

'The time? Um, I kind of . . . I don't really remember it in the same way I remember childhood or something. I think it was over the course of about two years but *In Rainbows* was about two years and that was bliss compared to that.
I was not very happy, I don't think.
OK Computer had been so successful, everything a band could want – number one record, good reviews, lots of sales, blahdy blah . . . I think they were worried about turning into U2 or something. You know, doing another *OK Computer* and turning into a huge, Simple Minds-esque stadium rock band – the weight of success hung extremely heavy.'

For you as well? Did you feel that?

'Um, no. No, because I was even more anonymous then than I am now but . . . (thinks for a minute) I really can't remember it too well – it was just fucking hard. (Brightening) I'm very proud of it. In fact, it's difficult to choose my favourite but I think, because it was such hard work, I think that was a really good one – and I really liked the music as well, that was when I really connected with them, musically, although that started with *OK Computer*.'

What was it about *OK Computer*?

'I remember Thom screaming in an outhouse . . . they were recording out in this stately home, the first stately home of many, and he was screaming in a shed in the middle of nowhere with a mic and a line running all the way from that little shed, all the way into this impromptu recording studio; I thought, "That's it."'

Do you work with a sense of 'I need to make an album cover'?

'No, I don't really. With all the albums I've done, the cover has been the very last thing – usually, almost a snap decision. The cover for *Hail to the Thief* was a big painting, a metre and a half square, and it was hanging up in the studio and it was not even going to be a part of the record artwork. It was the first one I did in that style and size and, because it hadn't got words from the record on it, it was sort of outside of it all.
We were just sitting down and saying, "Which one should we put on the cover?"
"Why don't we use that one?"
And suddenly it was obvious that it was the cover. The same with *Kid A*. The night before we had to decide I did loads and loads of printouts and stuck them round the kitchen with tape. There were loads of different titles as well. Loads of different titles. And we had them all up. Stuck onto all the cupboards in the kitchen. "Okay, there's a cover in the kitchen somewhere, you've gotta find it." (Laughs)
And luckily they chose that one and, I mean, this is my memory, but I think partly the title was because it looked so brilliant in that typeface – BD Plakatbau.
We had other titles with different typefaces.'

You seem to strive to avoid a recognisable style with your work.

'Yes, I wouldn't want to do the same thing twice anyway. I think that would be boring.

Someone like Vaughan Oliver, who did all the sleeves for 4AD* – Cocteau Twins, Pixies – and they were all different but they were all his, and I've always wanted to work in a way where you couldn't tell it was the same person doing it.

I had a fantastic compliment with *In Rainbows* when someone said, "Oh, did you do that?" Which was great! It's so totally unlike what I've done before; all abstract . . . and lovely in its way. Pretty. I became very interested in velocity – ink and velocity, paint and velocity and what happens when you throw or squirt pigment at a surface. I was squirting stuff out of needles and I found them quite frightening to use, needles, they're very spiky . . . and this was a direct response to the music after that strict architectural drawing, and what happened was that I was working in this decaying stately home and I knocked over a candle and it poured a load of molten wax onto a piece of paper and I was really taken with this, and it was at the same time I was working with these needles so I began to work with these ideas of spurting and dripping and melting which seemed to fit very much, for me, with what the music was. I found that record an extremely sexual record, very sensual.'

They'd been threatening it for years.

'Exactly. (Deadpan) It's the long-awaited happy album.'

---

* 4AD is record label started by Ivo Watts-Russell and Peter Kent in 1979. Between 1982 and 1998, graphic designer Vaughan Oliver and his team at v23 created all sleeve and promotional artwork for the label, developing distinct visual identities for the 4AD stable of bands while maintaining a distinct label aesthetic.

It was pretty chipper.

'Yeah! Molten wax, squirting stuff out of needles, spattering . . .'

It's all there, for goodness sake! It's all there!

'There it is!' (Laughter)

So is the new thing always the most exciting thing?

'Yes. To do the same thing you've done before . . . why would you do it again?
There's no point in repeating yourself. I mean, in a way, what I've been doing recently with *Hartmann the Anarchist** is repeating myself. I've done that, but I haven't illustrated a book before and I love a bit of lino, I do. I love the physicality of carving it out, but I don't want to do the same artwork I've done before . . . it's easy to draw the same picture you've drawn before.

---

* *Hartmann the Anarchist*, Edward Douglas Fawcett, (Bone, 2009).
Stanley made six linocuts to illustrate Bone's republication of *Hartmann the Anarchist* in 2009.

> Blurb: 'Dirigibles, Zeppelins, Airships, Blimps – whatever you want to call them there's no doubt these inflatable monsters of the sky exert a deep fascination for fans of aviation and modern-day "Steam Punks" everywhere. Well, this book is where it all began!'

Hartmann the Anarchist was originally published in 1892, when Edward Douglas Fawcett was sixteen years old, and has been out of print for more than 100 years. In it, Fawcett's imagination creates 'The Attila' from a wondrous new form of lighter-than-air metal, canvas and ships' rigging and has it piloted by Rudolph Hartmann, one of the most fiendish villains in literary history, raining pitiless death and destruction from the skies on Parliament, St Paul's and the City. Just twenty years later, Fawcett's apocalyptic vision came true when German zeppelins bombed London.

If I tried to draw an *OK Computer*-style picture now it would be really easy; and I could do it better than before, you know, "better" in inverted commas but . . . it's horrible to look back on stuff. It gets easier after a while, when it becomes history.'

The recent past isn't any good?

'No. There's a difference between memory and history, isn't there – the difference between, "Oh yeah, I was just doing that a little while ago, I remember that . . . oh God!" and when it becomes history and you can look at it in a more even way. I can look back at most of my stuff when it's got into its history phase and quite like it. It's alright . . . but maybe that's to do with working in this periodic way with capsules and projects because of the Radiohead thing. "Here's the record – Phoosh!" It's clearly delineated between one record and the next.'

Do you think you'd work like that if you didn't work with the band?

'No idea. I've been working with them since I was twenty . . . four? And I'm forty now . . . but, you know, I'll still wake up at night and think, "I should be doing this" or "I should be doing that" or "What can I do to make that better?" I don't like it. I'd rather not have that happen.
I always feel envious of people who have a job and when they get home they don't think about their job any more, but maybe that doesn't exist. I always felt envious when I was cycling back from college, seeing people in their cars driving back to their homes on a housing estate somewhere – driving their car which

looks the same as everyone else's car, parking it in front of a house that looks like everyone else's house but somehow they know it's theirs . . . they'd park their car and they'd open the door and they'd close the door of their car, "Ker-chumph", and open the door of their house, "Kru-ch-ch", and in they'd go in and that would be it . . . but I've always sort of known that . . .'

Not for you?

'Well, it's not been possible for me to be able to hate my job! (Laughs) That's the thing; people hate their jobs. I don't hate my job, I quite like it. I hate it sometimes but it could be worse, oh yes!'

•   •   •   •   •

It's late now and the dance hall beyond the office is dark. We take a break from talking for the tape and I go off to find the toilet. My Dictaphone records cars passing and the creaking of the building and Stanley pottering about with tea and wine. It records the moment he accidentally spills wine over my notebook and then, to compensate, closes it to leave a Tyrian butterfly over my notes. After a long procession of echoey footsteps I re-enter the room, unaware of the mishap. Stanley doesn't mention the turn of events and I don't discover it until I get home.

•   •   •   •   •

Old Bond Street, Bath
Saturday 12 March 2011

I bump into Stanley in a stationers and he invites me to the pub. He is working on something big, he says, biggest thing

94

he's ever done. The project's tentacles spread worldwide . . .
but he can't tell me anything about it. It's all set up and in
place, though. Ready to go at the press of a button.
Yes, it's to do with the band.
It'll all kick off soon, yes.
He'll explain more in a bit when he's allowed.
We drink up and he cycles off.

Brick Lane, London
Monday 28 March 2011

So, *The King of Limbs*,⋆ a Radiohead album, has been put out into the world digitally with a 'newspaper album' to follow, whatever that is. Very mysterious.
The artwork features colourful paintings of trees fronting dark woods beyond, strange multi-limbed creatures and lurking, vaguely glimpsed monsters.

I'm in Brick Lane, in a long queue of people that snakes back several hundred metres from a Rough Trade record shop.
Stanley has made a concomitant newspaper that is to be given away at noon today around the world, apparently. All the noons.
Information is somewhat scarce yet here we all are in the queue, and there's a buzz; something's up.

⋆ *The King of Limbs* is Radiohead's eighth album and was released in 2011.
The album shares its name with an ancient oak tree in Wiltshire's Savernake Forest.
As with *In Rainbows*, a limited edition version – in this case a 'newspaper album' – was released a few months after the music itself became available digitally.
A free newspaper, *The Universal Sigh*, acted as eccentric, counterintuitive promotion, as Stanley explains:

> 'I went up to London to talk about and show some of the newspaper albums and that was odd. There were four journalists around this big table. I laid it all out . . . and it was like *Dragons' Den*!

> 'Hi everyone, I've invented this newspaper album and it's essentially an album wrapped in a newspaper. I call it "The Newspaper Album".

> 'And they'd say, "Well, I'm out."
> "I don't see the point."
> "Why not just put a normal album out?"
> "Why would you do that!?"
> "Have you done any publicity?"

> 'Well, no, we thought we wouldn't. Hang on, you'll like this . . . what we're going to do, we're going to put out a *different* newspaper that's not this one at all and we're going to do that for free . . .'

96

A strange website has appeared with directions to this place and a warning reminiscent of the fire escape instructions above Stanley's studio window:

IMPORTANT NOTICE:
This newspaper IS NOT the newspaper that accompanies the Newspaper Album version of *The King of Limbs*.

This event WILL NOT be repeated.
This event IS NOT a live performance by Radiohead.

I am here to experience the physical, tactile event of being given a newspaper and leafing through it to see what I can see . . . I imagine Stanley will be still cycling around Devon or somewhere and the last I heard the band were in LA so it's a bit odd to turn the corner and find him and Thom Yorke dressed up as barrow boys in flat caps and braces, proffering copies of *The Universal Sigh** newspaper.

---

* *The Universal Sigh* was a newspaper produced in 2011 as part of the release of Radiohead's album *The King of Limbs*:

Website blurb: 'The Radiohead album The King of Limbs will be available for purchase in all good record stores everywhere on Monday 28th March, except in the United States of America and in Canada, where for reasons beyond the purview of this writer it will be available from Tuesday 29th March. On VINYL! On COMPACT DISC! As a DOWNLOAD!

'To commemorate this momentous occasion, Radiohead have produced a newspaper which will be given away, free, gratis, without cost to the consumer by accredited vendors from a multitude of locations WORLDWIDE! In the USA, in the Netherlands, in Belgium, Poland, Germany, Austria, in the Czech Republic, in Spain, Portugal, Sweden, Ireland, France, Italy, Slovakia, Finland, Greece, Norway, Lithuania, Estonia, Russia, Hungary,

'Socialist Worker!'
'Sooo-cialist Worker!?'
'Socialist Worker, sir?'

• • • • •

Derelict dance hall, Bath
July 2011

The last time I saw you was just before the *Socialist Worker* debacle.

'Oh yes . . . I was a bit scared because I didn't know where it was happening. I got to Liverpool Street and then walked round and round the queue. I felt like a hyena circling a herd of wildebeest. It was a good day! It was the most orderly and polite London mob I've ever experienced.

There was quite a lot of fuss and I was very pleased because we had this big meeting before we began with all the record company people who were to act like this big distribution network for the paper, and the publicity plan was to give out a newspaper in sixty-one cities around the world, simultaneously, for free, that mentioned neither the band nor the title of the album once. They took a little persuading but I think it worked. It got into every real newspaper. It was sufficiently stupid to even catch the eye of the *Sun*:

'"Read all about it," says Yorke, miserablist.

Australia, Latvia, Iceland, Romania, New Zealand, the UK and a load of other places around the globe, our dedicated teams of newspaper delivery people will be handing out copies of THE UNIVERSAL SIGH to anyone who wants one, until we run out!'

'"Professional Gloom-monger Thom Yorke was today spotted in London's Brick Lane handing out an incomprehensible art project . . ."

'And then I went home and then I had a cup of tea and thought, "That was alright! I can begin to forget all about it." Which I almost have.
It was fun though. We both wore flat caps and everything.'

Was *The King of Limbs* newspaper album designed around the same time as the *Universal Sigh*?

'No, that was from the year before; September or something, and it went through lots of redesigns. Imagine setting up a newspaper and publishing the first issue, all that tweaking, changing . . . because there were going to be loads of sections and a little A5 magazine; lots of different sections, one black, white and red like an old-fashioned tabloid . . .'

We spoke about these things obliquely before, I suppose, down the pub.

'Yeah, though it's weird; when I was doing all the *King of Limbs* stuff it was all I was thinking about, but now it's quite hard to recall . . . but I just thought it was really nice how the newspaper album turned out and the prints were quite rough, with mistakes and holes punched – so valueless, you know? So ephemeral. If you want to keep it nice you've got quite a job on your hands.'

Keeping it out of the sunshine . . . because it's on the way out already.

'Exactly. Self-destructing record packaging. I won't get a Grammy for that one, I'll tell you now. (Laughs) They won't appreciate such irreverence, the Grammers.'

I see you're cutting some wavy lino in the other room.

'Yeah, meteors or fireballs, Vorticist waves; it's taken a long time . . . it's not just waves, you know! They're the easy bit, they're like a little treat for me after doing all the buildings. I did the downtown financial district and all these modernist blocks and they're really boring to do, but the nicer stuff takes a long time so it's a bit of a trade-off really.'

Is this for Atoms For Peace?*

----

* Atoms For Peace are a band formed by Thom Yorke in 2009 in order to tour and expand upon the music of his first solo album, *The Eraser*, which was released in 2006.

Stanley's artwork for *The Eraser* marked his first engagement with linocutting and depicted London being consumed by fire and flood:

'That was great fun actually, *The Eraser*, funnily enough because it was quite easy.

Thom. Nigel. Me. (Laughs)

It was quite fast, really; quite quick to make.

There was a big flood down in Boscastle in Cornwall after which I started drawing. I had a book of medieval woodcuts from the *Nuremberg Chronicle* and I started drawing them – fallen cities and floods. The cover of the record wasn't going to be the artwork, originally. We were going to do this thing that was like a kit. Do you remember the Nuclear Power No Thanks badge with the starburst sun? I was going to do something like that. The record was going to be like a kit so you could assemble your own campaign. Nuclear Power No Thanks . . . It was going to be called Atoms For Peace or something like that.

I did all this stuff and I had the little badge with the kind of little Whiz For Atoms logo and stuff – which only ended up on the record's centre label, I think. I don't remember.'

'Yes. I hope so. It is at the moment.'

A lot of your Radiohead work seems cloak and dagger. You're wrapped up in these projects but can't discuss them.

'Yeah, I know, it is weird – very internal, all of us very locked in. I didn't over-listen to this record either. I mean, I listened to it, obviously, I couldn't avoid hearing it a lot, but I wanted to try and keep it as something I could enjoy later rather than being sick to death of it – because I usually get really enthusiastic and listen to it intensely, which is great for the year or so it takes to do the artwork but after that . . . no.
I've recently just about been able to listen to *OK Computer*. I really over-listened to that.'

How does that situation arise? Do you put it on?

'In shops? It makes me slightly uncomfortable for some reason when I hear Radiohead music in shops. I don't know why. I don't know . . . because in my head it's still quite a secretive thing and then you think, "Oh no! Everybody knows!"'

Where does this bunker mentality come from, do you think? I mean, other bands are able to embrace it.

'I know! Able to "Live The Dream!" We're congenitally unable to live the dream. That's it. That's what everybody wants to do, don't they?
I don't know what the secrecy thing is about really . . . perhaps it gets out of hand.'

It's a bit late now, perhaps, on album number fifteen.

'Is it!?'

Not really, no. (Laughter)

'No, it's about eight or something . . . I'm supposed to be getting the lino stuff finished because that's supposed to be being exhibited around the time the Atoms For Peace record comes out.'

Can you tell me that? Surely that's supposed to be shrouded in subterfuge.

'I can't live the dream!'

A while ago you mentioned painting a series of portraits in oil. What became of them?

'They ended up being the trees for *King of Limbs*! I was going to paint naturalistic portraits of the band because I looked at Gerhard Richter's paintings and they were really good and I thought, "I'll do that," but, of course, I'm not Gerhard Richter; I couldn't do that. It was not possible. Where he managed to get all these great blurred effects in oil paint, mine turned into mud, it was awful; very depressing for about three months . . . and then I started painting trees in oils in Oxford . . . and it all came about because of the way cathedrals used to be all different colours inside. Apparently all the vaults and tracery used to be painted really bright colours before the Puritans came along and painted over them white. All Northern European ecclesiastical architecture is based on the forest – being in glades, being in a sacred grove – they would paint their cathedrals in the brightest colours they'd got, absolutely beautiful. Going into a cathedral would have been like entering into an illuminated manuscript forest and I just thought, if all the trees of the forest were all different colours, how beautiful it would be . . . and that's how *King of Limbs* came to be.

There you are, a rare moment of articulacy! You should put it in a special box with red arrows pointing to it.'

JENNY SAVILLE, RA (1970–) is a Cambridge-born artist. Her visceral oil paintings and drawings of the human body are often realised on a massive scale and have appeared in exhibitions at the Royal Academy of Art, Gagosian Galleries and Norton Museum of Art, Florida. Her work has featured on the covers of two albums by Manic Street Preachers – *The Holy Bible* (1994) and *Journal for Plague Lovers* (2009).

JENNY SAVILLE

Brewer Street, Oxford
26 January 2010

In light of Stanley's eclecticism, I wrote to Gagosian, Jenny Saville's gallery, and asked if I might have an audience with her since she seemed to represent the other end of the spectrum: a lone figure singularly preoccupied with painting flesh and the figure – solid, tangible, massive adipose studies of the body in oils.

The last I'd read, she was working in Sicily, so the approach was a bit of a punt since I wasn't sure how I'd get out there even if she agreed to see me. However, it turned out Jenny had recently relocated to a studio in Oxford, so any thoughts of a Mediterranean adventure were quickly replaced with the more prosaic reality of a day return ticket because, to my surprise, she did agree to see me.

So one freezing Tuesday morning – satchel packed with a wine-stained notebook and a fickle Dictaphone – I caught a train.*

---

* My notes from the journey recall the air was bitter and a hard frost covered the ground. It was dark outside and the carriage was still and muted – bleary people in a

• • • • •

Jenny Saville's studio is in a quiet shaded lane that belies its central city location. A two-storey building; grey-fronted and anonymous.

Lewis Carroll wrote *Alice's Adventures in Wonderland* at Christ Church College, two minutes from here. My rabbit hole is rather unprepossessing – an ashen door with a burnt-out intercom. I clatter at the letterbox and wait, stamping my feet in the cold.

Descending footsteps. Jenny opens the door and I step in. To my left is a room of large, briefly glimpsed drawings and charcoal pieces.

A set of stairs before me. We go up and Jenny makes tea.

The first floor is spacious and open plan, lit by large windows and greenhouse-like skylights. The walls are white. In front of the walls are paintings.

At the top of the stairs is a three-metre-high work of a new-born baby, the umbilical cord snaking back to a splayed vagina and soapy legs. Along from this is a trolley stand stacked with books – magazines, newspaper paint swatches, photographs and journals. Notes, clippings and articles are stuck up on the walls while other torn-out pages are filed out on the floor – creative 'compost' as Francis Bacon dubbed it.*

------

surgical interior – reflective surfaces, severe metal and halogen. At Didcot I changed trains and looked through the catalogue of a Palermo show of Jenny's. The sky began to lighten as I fumbled through the images and attendant Italian captions and articles I could not understand. I remember squinting down at the text in the dawn and it occurring to me that I must look very odd – red-eyed in the cold, apparently hunched and tearful over pictures of pre-op transsexuals.

* Paragraph 1, xiv, *Francis Bacon; Anatomy of an Enigma*, Michael Peppiatt (Constable & Robinson, 2009).

Empty cigarette packets, turned to display pictures of cancer and disease – bad teeth, laryngeal tumours, black lungs – are lined up on a dado rail.

Below the packets is a radiator that bears a painterly impression of Jenny's bottom – a Rorschach test pattern.

The studio, as well as being large, is freezing and Jenny explains she can only work for an hour or so before she starts to seize up. The radiator is where she warms herself and takes stock:

> 'This is where I stand, as you can see. I find that a cigarette is a perfect space to stand or sit and analyse what you're doing – the length of a cigarette.'

Opposite the radiator are several explorations of a single subject – a face with a mangled mouth; eyes closed, taut waxen skin lit from below, rising from a writhing, exploded mess. There are three versions of this piece, a large charcoal drawing, a mostly monochrome painted scheme – some patches of intense red and peach/pine – and an enormous black and white painting, streaked and leaking, the running paint visible below the surface layer.

None of the three is explicit about what is going on with the mouth, the wound is elusive and seemingly out of focus – a flayed moment of abstract expressionism – a de Kooning maw.

The finished piece, *Witness*, has recently left the studio for a London show in honour of J.G. Ballard. I've just missed it:

> 'I think that show's a brilliant thing to do because he was going to write my catalogue notes several times and I've got a lot of faxed letters from him – these great rejection letters from Ballard. (Laughs) Whenever I was asked who I'd like to write the catalogue I would always say, "Ballard. J.G. Ballard," but first his partner was ill and

then he was ill and then he wrote a fantastic summary of my work but didn't want to write the catalogue – I've still got that. Everyone I've told about it has said, "Oh, you've got to publish it" – letters from Shepperton. I've got a really good interview with him that I taped off the radio. It's from just after he wrote *Cocaine Nights* and he's talking about the internet. Claire Walsh, his partner, was telling me how they used to watch a site where you can see the migration of swallows, a camera follows them. That was his favourite thing to watch.'*

---

* J.G. Ballard lived in Shepperton from 1960 until his death in 2009. The sage of the future possible sat before a suburban typewriter.

In his autobiography, *Miracles of Life*, he wrote of being drawn to the place because of the nearby film studios 'which gave it a slightly raffish air' – and there he remained. One day, some years ago, I walked around Shepperton for several hours looking vaguely for his house, although I had no idea of his address. Looking back, I think I was exploring the space to prove it existed; tracing out patterns on an unseen map; listening for a hum like that of a distant fridge; swivelling my antennae like a moth.

We sit down on a pair of paint-specked chairs and I ask about the studio, how long she's been here, and the differences between here and her previous workspace in Palermo, Sicily.

'In Palermo I had the guts of animals outside my studio window; the stench was amazing in the summer. That has an effect on the way you think about making work. When I first walked in here there was blossom on the trees and it had an airy feeling. I haven't wanted to overload it so far, it's quite pure for me to have a space like this with only the work and a few things up – normally the floor is a cascade of books, but they're all still in boxes so I've quite enjoyed having a clearer head. I've noticed that, when I have a lot of reference material around, I tend to work a certain way, so I've tried to switch that around a bit and see what happens.'

Did you ever find yourself trying to get reference material into the work because it's around you?

'Oh yeah, I collect a lot of bits of paint, like that thing there (points to a paint-smeared newspaper). I've got hundreds and hundreds of those, trying to get an effect of flesh – burnt flesh or when you slide one colour into another – they become like a word-coupling or a musician putting sounds together – it all eventually feeds in.

I used to go to the Hunterian Museum in London, part of the Royal College of Surgeons. I was a member of the Pathology Society there and they used to have a room for surgeons to practise new types of operations; so there was always a room which had corpses and I used to go in and wander around; and what I loved was that each head was wrapped in a plastic bag, a Sainsbury's bag or a Tesco bag – obviously it depended upon what part of the body the surgeons were working on – the last time I was there they were working on something to do with the spine, but all the heads, bagged up. There was something so everyday about having a Sainsbury's bag over your head at the end of your life.'

Jenny leads me to a table of paint tubs, each different, numbered and labelled.

'I've mixed these for a new piece. Because I work on such a large scale and on quite a few things at the same time, I make a series of tones and spend days studying one colour and mixing a large amount of that, shifting it so that I've got a core tone that can be moved around.'

Have you got huge vats of paint somewhere?

'Big tubs of white, yes, and I use kitchen knives, big old-fashioned things to mix with. I think the maximum I've ever made in a day is six or seven tones. That (points to paint on a glass-topped table) will be, for example, a side cheek and a panel of the neck, so I'll mix up two tones to go near each other – one to move your eye right back and the other to pull you forward. It started as a way of painting more abstractly, but now I've got certain tones that I know are going to do a job in the painting. Once I've got those, they'll shift and move around. The process came out of trying to keep something fluid in a larger scale.'

Do you see these paint tones as 'movers' rather than colours, then? You see them in the context of the actions they'll perform, pushing and pulling the eye – a sculptural, kinetic thing?

'I started doing it because I thought about it as a sort of human paste; making big pots of liquid flesh. It's like composing – painting is like playing music, I think; so certain notes I've already keyed and I know that, if I shift it, say, "Plus cerulean blue to the left, plus cadmium red deep to the right," I know that that's going to move the tone in a certain way and I write that on the edge on the pot and I'll keep it and I'll get maybe six or seven pots and then I'll do a session and I can be much freer with the actual painting because I know they'll do the job.

If I want real space behind an ear, for example, I'll work out exactly "more cold red, more ultramarine" so that tone behind the ear will literally shoot back and do what I need it to do.'

You've always drawn and painted bodies?

'Always. I've always done that – anybody who would sit for me. My best friend at school was interested in French literature and she would come and read and I would do paintings and drawings and sculptures of her. Instead of revising at home, she would revise on my bed while I was doing drawings; the human figure has always been something I've been immediately drawn to.'

Were you always drawn to the viscosity and physicality of these materials too – the oils up here and the charcoal down-stairs?

'Yes. I don't mix my mediums much. I use linseed oil and genuine turps in the paint and that's it. I know the strength of the paint I want and language just develops and develops. I look at other artists – I look at a lot more abstract painting than figurative – I look

at very old figurative painting by the Old Masters and I look at abstract work from the last century. Abstract Expressionism; de Kooning's are probably the paintings I look at most because they feel so incredibly modern, but he had to be abstract to get to what he wanted to get to and I don't want to be completely abstract. When he tries to paint figures later on they become quite hilarious and monstrous and cartoon-like and I don't want to go to that level. I want to find a way, a space to keep – not a tight realism but something very precise and serious about the body. I want to do that but also keep the abstract qualities of paint so that I've got those two things constantly rubbing next to each other.'

• • • • •

The first piece of Jenny Saville's work I encountered was *Strategy (South Face/Front Face/North Face)* that was used as

114

the cover of Manic Street Preachers' 1994 album *The Holy Bible*. I remember listening to it in the art rooms at school – scrutinising the cover triptych, liner notes and lyrics – a symbiotic body.

Jenny collaborated with the band again recently, the painting *Stare* fronting *Journal for Plague Lovers*, an album written around lyrics left behind by disappeared member Richey Edwards.*

'The first time I did the Manics thing, I was living in Glasgow. I'd just done the show at the Saatchi Gallery and Richey Edwards called me up and we had a conversation about anorexia and I wasn't initially keen on doing an album cover but then, after talking to him, I really wanted to do it because we had a lot of interests that were similar – about technology and the body, writers we liked – and he faxed me the lyrics to "4st 7lb" and I read that and said, "I'll do it. Use the triptych, you can have it."

I didn't realise it was going to become this incredibly cult album. People still ask me to sign that album cover when I give talks about my work; there's always someone, in America or wherever, who brings *The Holy Bible* album along.'

---

* Richey Edwards was lyricist and guitarist in Manic Street Preachers. He wrote the majority of the lyrics on the band's 1994 album *The Holy Bible*.

A contradictory man – robust, verbose and fiercely intelligent; distant, fragile, anorexic with a propensity to self-harm – he vanished in February 1995 on the eve of an American tour. Never found and was declared 'presumed deceased' in November 2008.

Manic Street Preachers continued on as a three-piece, had number one records and sold millions of albums.

The album *Journal for Plague Lovers*, composed entirely of lyrics Edwards left behind, was released in 2009.

Later that year, I ask Nicky Wire of the Manics about working with Jenny:

> 'She's been so good to us, really. Amazing. I was really intimidated to meet her when she came to see us play *Journal* at the Roundhouse. You know, intimidated in a nice way but . . . I was so impressed with her and actually more intrigued and indebted afterwards.
>
> I feel a correlation with her in the sense that, for me, she's by far the greatest modern British artist but sometimes she's not seen that way because she's never been associated with Tracey Emin or Damien Hirst, even though they sprang up at the same time; she's out on her own. There's something inside her that's like "Oh, fuck the rest of you."'

I was in the Roundhouse for that *Journal for Plague Lovers* gig and recall Nicky dedicating a song to Jenny, who was in the crowd, with the words 'She's taken a lot of shit for this cover and I don't know why' – a nod to the hysterical reaction of several supermarkets to the *Stare* sleeve; removing it from shelves, covering it up or refusing to stock it altogether.

> 'I didn't know it was going to get the publicity that it got,' she says when I ask her about it. 'I was shocked by the supermarket scandal because it's quite a straight painting really. I thought it was interesting the way people reacted – "There's blood on the face!" Sorry, you're made of eight pints of it, what's so damaging about that?
>
> In Italy the relationship with death is much closer. We've sanitised all those things. We don't wash our parents' bodies before burial here whereas in the south of Italy they still do that. I feel that's the way the culture's moved really, we haven't learnt to deal with

death. We're all so paranoid about prolonging our lives for as long as possible . . . I think we're going to have a lot of tubular humans.'

• • • • •

Standing among these paintings, it strikes me that Jenny's work, like J.G. Ballard's, is ultimately concerned with the inter-zone between life and death. The work on the walls crackles with this enquiry, the energy worked into them, bunched and potential beneath the viscous skin.

Close up, the paint is meted, cut and spread – the movements caught and frozen; plains of colour conjoining and colliding. I point to the red swipe of an inside ear.

These moments of raw colour, there are scrapes of blue on the nose and cheek of *Stare* that seem to up the ante of reality and abstraction at one and the same time.

'You can push the limits of it because you've got, say, this blue; the blue is there but I've pushed it, made it more extreme, but you can only go to a certain level of that and still keep a realism. You can go too far and have to come back – that's what takes the time because . . . (digs out a three tone swatch) here we are, I know I can put that, that and that in any combination and those two will swing your eye over and the third will be a background – when I'm actually painting I can start to run things through that; they're what give you the extra heightened reality.

The artists I like always can combine and move the nature of the medium they work in – be it paint, music or whatever. Radiohead are so good, they have such a good musical craft that they can push it so even something like the Shipping Forecast, they're able to take that

117

and move it. The people I like understand the nature of the material they work in and the nature of life; it's the combination of putting those things together, melding and mixing, pulling it all in, that I respond to.

I used to have stacks of cookery books because I found photographs of cookery and food were really luscious. I collected a lot of things like that – fashion magazines because they always soup-up the body, they make the mouths more luscious, give the eyes more shadows – you can take elements of that, hyperbolic fashion shoots which twist reality a certain way and, if you've got the right eye, you can take all that and do something very interesting with it that's not just superficial. It can be anything; the stain left by a dropped Coca-Cola on the floor – this human presence that's been left on a pavement.'

You often have spatter and workings beneath your paintings – tea stains like scar tissue, paint running out of the frame.

'A lot of that's from Velázquez. I've got a picture somewhere where he shifted the edge so that most of this surface is literally raw, and Bacon did that too – raw canvas he then drew on top of. I like the idea that the material of the canvas itself becomes part of the image – you're not just using the surface as something to cover up. You see the stain where I've painted this here? The oil that's gone into the paint has gone into the paper. I've tried to replicate that in paintings so many times because I think it shows a sort of present. You see where the paint has slightly lifted off the paper there?'

You're celebrating the process, then, embracing the canvas for what it is and the oily paint likewise.

'I'm trying to get inside the mechanics of what paint is.
I want paint to do something that only it can do. I know
how to slide paint; how to put it on dry. I go through
phases of wanting to use a lot of oil and slide the whole
thing, really wet and then other times see the benefits
of dragging dry paint over dry paint – the way it picks
up the light slowly.'

The paint projecting to meet you.

'An unkempt surface. We live in a time where a lot of
things are hermetically sealed – I like it when I activate
a surface and that surface is unique, it can't be repli-
cated in any way. I think that's very human, that interest and need.
I was reading recently about Leonardo drawing a
mother and child, how it took him two years to do it.
Today, hardly any artist working, apart from Frank
Auerbach probably, spends two years making a drawing. Our ability as humans to physically move faster
hasn't changed from Leonardo's time; if you've got
one stick of charcoal or Conté crayon or whatever,
the ability to make a drawing hasn't really shifted, so
I think it's interesting that art's shifted according to
the necessity for human speed – maybe that's why the
majority of art now isn't made over a long period of
time.'

Is your work exceptional in regard to the time you spend
on it?

'Yes, I think so. Lucian Freud, Frank Auerbach – there
are artists about who spend a lot of time on work. I
don't think there are a lot of people who'd choose to
spend a lot of time on their own in a room, to be honest

– not like this. I can spend three months mixing colours. Just mixing colours. Every day. And that's before I've even got going. A lot of people don't want to spend their days doing that.'

But you do.

'I realised that I wanted to do this very young. I knew I would be labouring over making one piece and that what I wanted to do took a long time and I felt a kinship with people like Auerbach who goes to the studio every day, the same thing. It can seem very dogmatic but at the same time you have to stay in that painting space – if you want to make paintings you have to be in front of a painting by and large – unless you're Jeff Koons and you get eighty people making them – if you want that one-on-one, Bacon-esque battle with the surface, you've got to stay inside a room . . . and you don't really need a lot of other stuff around you; you need a bit of human contact so you don't go mad, but actually it can be just a coffee with someone, a conversation on the telephone – enough contact so you're linked but not so much that it consumes and distracts you. The Van Gogh letters at the RA recently were really interesting for that reason because Theo offered exactly the valve you need. Vincent just needed to get it out, to say, "I'm not completely isolated; I'm making this work and this is the progress," and his brother would say, "Okay, great. Send me some drawings." It was enough, a long piece of elastic so Vincent was out there but he wasn't totally on his own.*

---

* *The Real Van Gogh: The Artist & His Letters*, The Royal Academy, London, 21 January–18 April 2010.

'I used to get frustrated about painting, the fact that you'd make one painting and it's just one and can only exist as that, whereas a lot of my friends were doing photography, what seemed a more versatile medium because it could exist in all different places, but now I feel completely different about that; I like that you make this singular object and it's almost like a human performance – the trace of it. When you make a painting, every single bit of that process is in the document that's left. It's like speech almost, a collection of speech, so over the year of making a painting you've got a year of collected experience on the surface and that, for me, is an incredible document, and so to experience the work properly you have to see it in the flesh.
The Van Gogh show was incredible to see. The work that you've looked at in books a lot and think you know very well – some things are a bigger scale than you thought they were and the drawings are suddenly alive in the flesh.

'The experience of having your body in front of the piece of work, I think that's an entirely different thing from a reproduction, obviously.
If you stand in front of a great de Kooning you literally stand where he made that work. You can't do that in another medium – you can't do that with music. Even in writing, when you read a printed book, it

Blurb: 'The Royal Academy of Arts presents a landmark exhibition of the work of Vincent van Gogh (1853–1890). The focus of the exhibition is the artist's remarkable correspondence.

'Over thirty-five original letters, rarely exhibited to the public due to their fragility, are on display; together with around sixty-five paintings and thirty drawings that express the principal themes to be found within the correspondence.'

transforms you and takes you somewhere else but you're not actually in the creative moment, and I think painting is the closest you can get – apart perhaps from performance art – the closest to creation, if you like.'

•   •   •   •   •

How far do you look ahead and plan your future work?

'Work comes out of work, I think. I've got certain aims as to where I want the work to go – this marriage between abstraction and realism, this space that oscillates between those two things. Certain artists couple that and make a dialogue between them. I'm not near it. I'm trying to get near it but I've learnt from doing paintings over the years that that's a journey you have to accept. You can't get there easily; you make jumps and then plateau a bit and then make another jump and then you've got to ride the plateau and when it starts to go, that's when you've got to be brave and really push. Sometimes I'll be in a painting session and I'll completely trash the painting.'

Do you then try and get it back to where it was or work on with what you've got?

'I work with what I've got. I know I've got to ride it – you're in a game at that point and you've got to try and pull the strings because I try to make marks and each mark is like the way you play a note – you have to decide how you're going to play it – but when you're really on form or you're really in it you don't even think about the way you're playing it, you just play. Sometimes you're just awful and you say, "None of this works," but then, often, you can turn a corner and, because it

really doesn't work, you'll make a huge leap because, "Fuck it. I might as well try this and this." You do two or three things and then suddenly you think, "There's something in that."
The mixing of the colours beforehand gives you the ability to get to that space.'

You're grounded by that.

'I know I've got a sort of safety net. If all else fails I can scrape it all down and just panel-in that tone and it will smooth that side of the neck, or whatever, but the best bits of my paintings usually come out of mistakes. A sort of desperation; it's like driving and getting lost, not having a map and going another way and then, suddenly, you've got to the place you wanted to get to but you've gone by a different route.'

•　•　•　•　•

The ground floor of the studio consists of a single open room stretching from concertina doors at the front to multi-paned windows at the back. Jenny's drawing studio takes up about a quarter of the floor space – a curtain of clear plastic sheet hangs down to divide this portion off and contain the warmth of two electric fan heaters which buzz and tick beside us now as we stand, surrounded on three sides by large charcoal drawings of mother and child. Inspired by Leonardo da Vinci,* each cartoon is over-drawn to depict multiple scenes, like a triple-exposed film – the figures frozen in three acts. My eyes pick up and follow a line, a leg or a hand, and then

---

* Specifically, Leonardo da Vinci's *The Virgin & Child with St Anne* and *St John the Baptist*, also known as *The Burlington House Cartoon* (1506–08).

recognise the rest of the drawing to which it belongs before skipping over to another detail or action. It's quite disorientating and in these moments the babies seem to be multi-limbed and flailing . . . and I realise, standing there, how quickly I've taken for granted how mind-blowing Jenny's work is because I'm describing it as disorientating and hypnotic when what I should be telling you is what it's like to stand with an artist in the space where she creates work that I imagine would delight the pillars of the Renaissance. It's shock and awe. It's awesome and very moving . . . and I don't want to jump ahead and spoil the end but I wasn't able to revisit Jenny after this meeting and that aspect of this chapter – it being a unique four-hour encounter – means the details are rendered rich and vivid in my mind. We got a lot done, talked and walked around before the work, peered close where the paint became a livid landscape and smelt of sour gummy turps and stood back where the apparently disparate shards and pocks of paintings focused to form these remarkable wholes. We drank tea. We spoke about Duncan Jones's film *Moon*, W.G. Sebald's *De Emigrés* and I told Jenny about G.K. Chesterton's essay 'A Defence of Skeletons'* and then it was over and I was back out on the street and everything was prosaic by comparison for a long time afterwards, the focus and colour lost – as if I'd been drinking tea with a phoenix and now had to go back to rubbing two sticks together.

But I didn't know that yet as we stood downstairs among the drawings.

---

* 'One would think it would be most unwise in a man to be afraid of a skeleton, since Nature has set curious and quite insuperable obstacles to his running away from it.'
– 'A Defence Of Skeletons', *The Defendant*, G.K. Chesterton
(R. Brimley Johnson, 1902)

'I've used drawing a lot but never really wanted to exhibit them, whereas these are different. I'm trying to make something where you can read several things all at the same time and it's really from looking at the internet. You don't have one stream of information now – not one and then another – it's many things that exist and are seen together. You'd never get that from these drawings but that's where my thinking came from; you can see the workings of ideas.'

The draughtsmanship is brilliant. Are you self-taught or did you get a lot from art school in this respect?

'I went to a very traditional art school. Life drawing every night from seven until nine. Thirty-six life drawings a term – whether you painted abstract, whatever you did. Obviously I liked it because I wanted to paint the figure.'

I've read that you teach, is that right? When did that start? Is it useful to you?

'I used to teach a lot more. I used to teach at the Slade, UCL, but I really prefer the school of Eileen Guggenheim in New York – a graduate figurative school. Warhol bankrolled it quite a bit at the start. You can go and do a class on how to paint like Velázquez, you can do sculpting directly from the figure. It's very traditional but you learn tangible skills. I do a workshop there that I was taught when I was at art school; a tutor showed me how to mix colour and he made me make a painting with squares – mixing a tone and putting it down so you make a space invader figure. Each square had to be a tone. It forces you to think behind a shoulder – "How do you make tone a piece of space? How do you decide what that tone is going to be?" There are no lines, just tone, and so I pass that on and they really struggle for about three days and then, after about the fifth day, they start to make progress because they're then allowed to make half-squares, triangles, so you can do the edges of shoulders until, finally, you get something . . . I always say to them, "You're not making art. This has nothing to do with art. This is an exercise in looking."'

Articulation.

'Yes! It's about articulation. There's not a lot of instruction in art schools now. People are quite ashamed of having skills, actually. I've always thought, "I want to show off as much as possible!" (Laughs) I don't really see why I should be apologetic about that. I want to articulate. I think that, if you're intent on doing something, then you need to be able to articulate how to do it and . . . you know, the amount of students I've had who've painted a broken hand or foot that they can't articulate and have constructed a philosophy around that painting to justify it because they can't do it. I think that's part of the big problem with painting: there's been a whole construct of "bad painting is good painting". I find that annoying.'

Jenny trails off to a glum shrug. The fan heater clicks and whirs. The plastic sheet walls whisper and we stand there in silence for a moment.

Is most of your current work about pregnancy?

'No. I'd like to mix it up a bit. I don't really want to do a "Mother" thing. I've noticed from looking at art history that the notion of mother and child is very much a fantastical idea but it's fucking visceral, giving birth; it's unbelievable. You have a body coming out of your body. That is weird.'

I've always thought having a baby must be incredibly scary – this thing growing inside you, getting bigger – the amount of horror films based around that premise.

'*Alien.*'

Eraserhead. Videodrome . . .

'What struck me most about *Miracles of Life*, Ballard's last book, was that he talks about this baby arriving that's a new life yet looks like it's been there for centuries – such an ancient, animalistic thing. That was quite a shock, I didn't know how I'd feel but you are absolutely an animal in that moment . . . it was very close to painting and, it's technical but I had a difficult birth; after my daughter was born a surgeon had to come and remove part of my stomach and all the placenta by hand – literally grabbing handfuls of placenta out of my body and putting it onto a table next to me. I was looking at that and, in that moment, I was in a Francis Bacon painting. I thought, "I am never going to make paintings in the same way again." It was incredible – seeing the inside of your body being pulled out. I could feel the surgeon's hand at the top of my ribcage – while his arm was inside me.'

James Herriot stuff.

'Really like that, really profound; an incredibly intense moment. I've worked under medical light before, the feeling of medical light – so all the colours, the greens and the reds, are very intense, but at the same time I had just become a mother so I had just given birth to this little girl and I had all this going on at the same time. I saw painting everywhere.'

Did you feel detachment or absolute presence in the moment?

'I think I shifted between those things constantly. I remember thinking, "Look at that, Jenny; you've got to take that in, you've got to hold and watch that, that's amazing. Look at the colours in that!" At the same time my aunt's holding my daughter and I was asking, "Is she alright? Is she okay?" You know, "That's my daughter! Isn't she beautiful!"
I have noticed in life that I've had times where I've had a conscious feeling of trying to hold a moment, visually, because I've known it was important; even at a very young age.
I remember riding on a merry-go-round and seeing another little girl who'd cut her legs open because she'd fallen off her horse and I was going round – sitting with my dad on one of those golden horses that go up and down – getting snippets, coming round again and getting another snippet.'

With a jolly pipe organ soundtrack.

'Exactly. I remember thinking, "That's really powerful," because everyone was looking and then you couldn't see. I wanted to get round and see again. That's very much the kind of animal/human – wanting to see something but being worried at the same time or repulsed. I remember the scene so vividly. I was obviously tuned-in to that way of thinking even then because I knew that it was important, visually important to me, and I

understood the mechanics of it and I must only have
been four or five.'

I remember slamming my fingers in a car door when I was
very young and my dad – in the way dads do – bought me a
Crunchie chocolate bar to make it better. So now, every time
I see a Crunchie I have that memory and a slight twinge,
a feeling of pins and needles. I remember looking down at
the dent in my fingers, squished right down . . . that moment before the pain hits. You get a split second of perfect
clarity.

'Yes, exactly, and I think that sometimes I paint with
that in mind. That moment.'

•   •   •   •   •

Normally, of course, these are just the sort of conversations that might make you change seats, carriages or trains if it came unbidden from the lady next to you – unless she'd introduced herself as a surgeon or a butcher, say, and you'd kicked off with 'So . . . evisceration and the films of Nicolas Roeg, eh?'

Yet I'm fascinated in Jenny's company and engaged to an extent where any weirdness, macabre connotations or squeamishness could not be further from my mind.

The incredible intensity of the few hours I spend with her will remain with me and, looking back, there was a saturation about that morning – the colours and the images, the source texts and the photographs . . . yet, at the heart of it all was this quiet, contained lady in painty tracksuit bottoms, hair held back by an elastic band . . . 'But she was so bloody normal,' I'll later recall, then, almost in the same breath, 'She was one of the most brilliant, uncanny people I've met.'*

We break for tea and I ask about Jenny's childhood, how she came to be here, when she discovered who and what she wanted to be, her formative years.

Did you spend a lot of time in your bedroom?

'I would say so, yeah. I lived in lots of different houses and went to lots of different schools and so art became something that was a constant for me. I just always remember making paintings or building things and I read a lot about other artists. I visited Cézanne's house

---

* Interviewed in 2011, gallerist Pilar Ordovas – Christie's Director of Post-War & Contemporary Art in Europe for thirteen years, Director of Gagosian Gallery for two – spoke of having visited the Louvre with Jenny and getting 'to see Monet through her eyes'.

when I was sixteen because I had an obsession with Cézanne and I knew pretty early on what it took to be an artist – reading about the life of Van Gogh when I was about twelve, things like that. My uncle was an art historian and he ran courses in Venice and Florence so I'd spend summers there and would join in all the art history courses. In the Frari in Venice, there's an enormous Titian altarpiece of the assumption of the Virgin and I can remember sitting in front of that and saying, "One day I'm going to make paintings as big as that." It wasn't a joke. I was absolutely serious. I didn't really know who Titian was but I learnt about him and Tintoretto and eventually I owned it through that knowledge. I knew that was going to be my life. I didn't even consider that that wasn't a thing that women had done. It wasn't even on my radar. It was absolutely my life – there was my life: I was going to be in dialogue with these people who had done this stuff. I think the naivety of my desire helped me. That's just what I did and my mother was a teacher – she was my teacher actually, when I was very little – so the classroom, when all the kids left, was mine; so she'd be doing what-ever she did and I'd just be making things or drawing and that continued. It was my language from a very early age.'*

---

* At a later date, going through my notes and recordings, I find an amazing para-graph which seems to go some way to crystallise Jenny's thoughts about being a woman in the modern art world:

'Gagosian Gallery, where I had my first solo show, hadn't had a show by a woman; it was a big macho gallery. Now that landscape has shifted completely because there are so many women artists that everybody knows about, but when I was growing up there weren't really. If you said, "Okay, name British female artists" . . . Elizabeth Frink, Barbara Hepworth, Bridget Riley, maybe Paula Rego – I knew a little bit about her – but that was about

Your vocabulary to communicate with the world.

'Absolutely. I mean, I admire writers greatly. I don't find the precision in words that I do in paint. I find paint's the way I can hold all the contradictions of life. I can't begin to use words that way.'

Interesting then that a lot of your catalogue essays are very cerebral and penetrating in that way – John Gray, for example, one of the most acute and steely writers I know.

'I love his writing. *Straw Dogs* in one of the best books written in the last twenty years because it's incredibly precise; to be able to go through that amount of infor- mation . . . the relationship that he's got with humans as animals is something that I've had in my work, that I've felt, since I was much younger. I give it to everybody, that book.*

---

it really. There wasn't a Tracey Emin, a glamorous big-time artist who everybody knew about. That landscape has changed but women still don't command the same prices as men. I'm incredibly fortunate that mine sort of do, but there aren't many of us that do in proportion. I mean, Rachel Whiteread was as proportionally big an artist, if you like, as Damien and her prices never went anywhere near the same level as his. I can't really say whether I make the work I make because I'm a woman, or whether my instinct for a certain type of imagery is the way it is because it just is. I've never known anything else.'

* *Straw Dogs* cropped up in conversation with several of the people I interviewed including Nicky Wire, Stanley Donwood and David Nash. It was J.G. Ballard's book of the year in 2002:

'This powerful and brilliant book is an essential guide to the new millennium . . . A clear-eyed assessment of human nature and our almost unlimited gift for self-delusion. A deeply provocative and unsettling book.'

One passage on page 77 seems particularly prescient in relation to both Jenny and the thought processes behind this book:

'I'm interested in fictional, constructed ideas of the self – *'If I had this procedure, I'd be more myself'* – that's just a myth, a mythical thing. You have this fictional idea of what you want to look like or could look like, need to look like, to be more wholly you. It's an artificial construct and I found that very interesting when talking to patients in New York; they felt that they were inhabiting their body more by having this artifice . . . and that's not a modern phenomenon but the idea that you can re-sculpt your flesh, I thought that thrilling.

I wasn't making a moral judgement with the work, which a lot of people thought I was; I was fascinated with the need to do it and what the mechanisms of that were because I've often been interested in the space between things. I'd say the biggest thread that runs through my work is "the in-between".

If it's a transvestite or a transsexual, you're in-between – a floating gender. You aren't fixed – and that movable boundary I found an interesting place to operate. A free space.'

That's the word, I suppose, operation. A surgical gaze.

'Yes, I would say so, and I've painted quite a few things where you're not quite sure whether the body is alive or dead. I've often tried to find images that have that – one eye left open or a face that's completely mauled. When I paint it, I want it so you have to work to piece

---

'Our fictive selves are frail constructions. The sense of I is dissolved in trance and dreams, weakened or destroyed in fever and madness. It is in abeyance when we are absorbed in action. We may forget it in ecstasy or contemplation. But it always returns.'
– *Straw Dogs*: Thoughts On Humans & Other Animals, John Gray
(Granta Books, 2002)

the head back together again, so you've got a moment of crisis, as a viewer.'

There are very few things more arresting or off-putting than to have your gaze met by something 'other' – familiar yet alien.

'I suppose so, but by the time I've done them I'm so involved with them that I don't see them with fresh eyes because I've done the journey . . . I think I've developed the withdrawal of personality, the opposite of what portraits have been aiming to do for centuries. I try to show the personality of whatever trauma or alteration is of the body.'

The crash site. The aftermath.

'That's it, I'm not trying to show the personality of the human being in the way of "the eyes being the gateway to the soul" – it's not that.'

But I think you can have both together. I remember John Hurt talking about how he cried reading the script of *The Elephant Man* because of that feeling, the glint and purchase of recognition – the body, the man behind the trauma.

'That's the thing: when you get people that work well – even an artist like Velázquez, his Pope painting in Rome, he doesn't illustrate. Velázquez isn't like Caravaggio. Caravaggio, however great he is, for me, he's a bit of an illustrator. Velázquez doesn't illustrate. He builds in paint. He's in that moment where it's more real than real because he uses paint so well, and people like David Lynch do the same thing, I think. Something like *The Elephant Man*, it's not you but it's the hyperbolic you, but he has enough realism in it that it brings it to you; so it's in you and out of you at the same time, and that's quite thrilling because it unlocks sensations that you know you've got but don't often have the facility in life to think about or experience.'

• • • • •

Jenny leads the way into the larger room beyond, pushing through the plastic sheets,★ revealing a space dominated by multiple versions of the painting *Stare*. The faces gaze out, each with a dazed expression somewhere between "Have I left the gas on?" and "I've just cut off my thumb." The expression lives in the moment of a child's confusion – the split second between the fall and the tears, the crash and the blood.

I tell Jenny I'm amazed she's able to redraw and repaint the same image over and over – each individual yet retaining an essence.

'I know that mouth back to front now. Each one; but I'm quite pleased that I'm finishing them because I've painted this head an awful lot of times now.'

The textures here are really meaty.

'They're all going to be shown together. I became interested in video phones a few years ago and early MSN messaging; you'd see somebody break apart and pixellate, leave part of their flesh over there and you'd

---

★ The sheeting is similar to that in cold stores and abattoirs, although this similarity will only occur to me later.

try with your eye to get the head to come back together again.'

Where did the source material for *Stare* come from?

'It's from a medical book that I had a long time ago. I use Photoshop a lot to shift the colours around so I did a blues and greens version and I did drawings of it – it had everything I needed. It had a mouth that I love, a landscape map-face, one ear that almost holds up the painting so you can shift the head.'

The ellipse of the shirt is great.

'Exactly, it's a good rocker at the bottom. So it's got a lot of elements to it – the shadow of the nose – a lot of things where you can get good shapes going, so really it was an indulgence being able to concentrate on the paint, being allowed to make these landscape figures.'

When you're preparing a show, do you arrive with some paintings or do people know what's coming?

'I don't have a lot of people coming into the studio because I like to get the work the way I want it before I show it.
I have the link to the gallery, the person who looks after my work, and I talk to them regularly – a few times a week – but I've tended not to have somebody coming in to say, "I'd like to show that and I'd like to show that." There's nothing like that. They say, "Are you going to be ready in September?" and I always push it. I'll say, "I don't know, I'll tell you in March." And then, in March, I'll say, "Can we go for Spring next year?" They're used to me and I know that there is an elastic

level that I can get to but, once I've made the commitment to that show date and said, "Okay, let's do that,"
they book the trucks and then I know I've got to get it
done.'

I saw a film of trucks coming to take the panels of David
Hockney's *Bigger Trees Near Warter* at Tate Britain recently.

'I've had guys have to have cups of tea in my kitchen
because I've said, "I'm not ready, you'll have to wait a
bit."'

Hours or days?

'I get them to take the paintings piecemeal so, say it's
eight paintings, they'll take three first and then they'll
come and get another two and then another two and it
goes like that for about six weeks.'

Is that to get them out of the space or so you won't fiddle
with them?

'So I can't fiddle. I can't juggle them all at the same
time, but in one case the last truck was coming to pick
up the last two and I only let them take one. I said,
"The other one's not done," but the whole show was
pivoted around that piece and I didn't have a lot of
work so it wasn't as if you could leave anything out.
The person at the gallery had to find a military airbase
in Scotland to fly the last painting to New York.
I had a taxi outside my studio door and then I went,
covered in paint, to Heathrow and got changed at the
airport and the painting went to the airbase.'

Was it on a military flight?

'It was a cargo flight that went out of a military base. It was the only flight that was going – the other ones had to go to Frankfurt first because they were too big to go in a regular cargo plane. I know what the biggest size you can get on a cargo plane is because I've pushed for the canvas stretcher to be as big as it could go . . . but I'm not so dramatic as that any more. I used to love the drama of that, you know (mad staring eyes), "I need more time! Arrrgh!"'

I'm an artist!

'Exactly. "I'm not ready! You can't have it!" The gallery person is freaking out because they're going to get killed for not getting that painting on the truck, and they are also tied by "But we need to respect you because you're an artist . . ." so you've got this bit of elastic where you're pulling "Arrgh! I can spend another night on the nose . . ." Then you get to New York and everything arrives, or you get there and they're still locked in customs and you're going, "What the fuck!? Where the fuck are they!?" It tends to always work out in the end . . . but I don't know if that's really the best way to make art. It's okay when you're in your twenties and you've got tons of energy and don't sleep for two weeks at a time but I think, once you get a bit older, it's much better to let the work generate itself together. But I know of people who, I mean, Giacometti couldn't let anything out of his studio – for years he wouldn't let anything go.'

·   ·   ·   ·   ·

I think of Rothko exhibiting in his Bowery studio and then to the book Jenny published with Rizzoli whose pages were filled with images of her own workspace – glimpses of mirrors, ladders and platforms. Is Jenny still up and down scaffolds? I wonder.

'I am but I haven't worked on anything huge for a while. In Palermo I built a second floor on wheels. It had a palette table, the whole thing at different levels, but what I really want is to buy a studio and have a hole dug in the floor so I can let the painting down and up because I find that when I paint on a scaffolding I don't paint as well because I can't walk back to look. I like being on the ground. I want an inspection pit!
I've tried painting sideways but you get a slightly wonky head, so now I make the effort to go up and down a ladder. It's a lot, though, up and down for every single mark.'

Do you have to think more in terms of landscapes when you're painting sideways?

'Yes, or an abstract painting. Thinking of space and the ways things work in space. I've tried multiple ways of working – collapsible scaffolding, second floors, ladders . . . ladders in the end are the things that I like but I don't have the same desire to make enormous paintings. I'll make paintings the scale of that wall, but it's an enormous emotional job to make a painting on that scale, getting it to work. I suppose my equivalent of that is having seven or eight heads on the go at the same time, which is what I've got going on with these *Stares*. I'll probably come back round to large work again but, you know, I've got two babies now so . . .'

You're busy.

THE BEECHWOOD AIRSHIP INTERVIEWS

'Yeah. To do that was pretty gruelling, physically. Maybe I'll do another one in a couple of years but I like this current scale. It's a good scale for me.'

It's still relatively massive, you know! (Laughter)

'I do get kinda shocked. I saw a painting I did called *Hyphen* – my sister and myself, heads, and I loved making that painting, I really flew. I was at the top of my game and had a great studio in London – I'd forgotten the paint was so thick, you know? I was trowelling it on. Everything is quite precise, I get the paint in the right place, but I don't think I could make that painting now; not in the same way. I remember the studio had fantastic lino floor tiles from the sixties and I pulled them up, they were bendy. You could get the paint on and literally go like that with it (mimes smearing paint up and over with a lino squeegee) – sort of like plastering but it gave the same feeling as when a plastic surgeon pulls the flesh, so I was getting a tension and able to use the paint in a sculptural sense on the surface.
I'd ripped up all the floor tiles in that studio by the end.'

• • • • •

I heard on the radio the other day that Philip Glass was still driving a taxi at forty-one. You had your break quite early on – no time spent in the wilderness working up your practice. How has that shaped your development?

'Well, it wasn't the great easy ride that people sometimes imagine.
It's seen that I've always had money but I was making shows in New York absolutely broke – eating an orange in five days, scraping out paint from old tubes – be-

cause everything I earned went on studio rent. You work for two and a half years on six pieces, and you're not selling. The money just goes. It's draining to work like that.

It's nice to make a complete story "from Saatchi Gallery to Gagosian in New York" – a very singular ladder, but it's not actually like that.

'I made this very big painting called *Fulcrum* and that I nicknamed "The Bitch". I couldn't get it working. I spent more than eighteen months trying to get the figures together and the paint the way I wanted. It was a gruelling act of faith to keep at it because I should have probably trashed it but I'm a bit stubborn like that, I keep going but, yes, I suppose I don't know what it's like to have years in the wilderness, that's for sure. I've been extremely lucky like that. I came out of art school and had a commission to make work for the Saatchi Gallery; that was the lottery ticket that I got.'

But you also had the pressure of being a high-profile and recognised artist from the very beginning. Lots of pressure. A very steep learning curve.

'But when you're young, I mean; I had no fear. As soon as Charles said, "Okay, do whatever you want with the space," I just knew "I want this 21-foot triptych, I'm going to make it in three panels and it's going to be like this." My God! You know? Who else is going to buy that kind of scale of work? The dream that you've got of making such pieces; most people don't have the finance to follow that through because they've got to do the nitty-gritty stuff of selling drawings or whatever, and I was extremely lucky in that sense: I wanted to make those big works and I could do it. And I did.

I was very quiet about it, though. I mean, I left art school with a lot of friends and a lot of people were getting really broke and having to get part-time jobs. Hardly anybody knew that I was going to show at the Saatchi Gallery, I didn't tell anyone. I just worked in my studio for two years. Every day. Trying to get the work the way I wanted it, and then I was quite shocked by the level of press that was generated by the Saatchi Gallery. I left to go and work in America a few weeks later.'

Was that exposure one of the reasons for that?

'I was very relieved to do that, yeah, because it's never sat too well with me, being known. I don't know how actors can live like that because their persona and their body is known, whereas I work very quietly in my studio. I was lucky that it happened when I was very young so that I could understand the mechanism of it and realise that, when you go back in the studio, it means jack shit. It doesn't make you a better painter. The investment by other people – to show at different galleries, have exhibitions with amazing artists – that does help because it raises your game. I've just done a show with Picasso, Bacon and de Kooning in America and you're there, accepted as part of this canon of art. That makes you . . . you lift yourself.'

I can see Jenny beginning to itch to get back to work, so I thank her for her time and am about to switch the tape off when I recall something else I wanted to cover related to her Rizzoli book, which featured shots of scrapbooks, lists and notes for her work. Is that an ongoing process? I ask.
In response, Jenny walks over to the back room, footsteps echoing around the space, and shows me an A4 sheet pinned to the wall: 'Heads', 'Burns', 'Bodies', 'Babies', 'Blown Up Mouth' . . .

'I've had a third of those for about ten years. They'll come up again or I'll look through a scrapbook and find some other ones.
"Botched Suicide" – I like the tragedy of that.'

She gestures to a row of what look like crime scene shots of, well, botched suicides; although most of them look pretty successful to me. It's hard to imagine people getting up and walking away with no intestines or only half their head. Dead people who got that way in violent hurry.

'"Black Teeth" – I've had "Black Teeth" on there for years. "Albino" – I've got lots of albino photographs, I've just never got round to making the painting. "Patch Head" – patches of shadow on top of a head. I photograph lots of people all of the time and I've been doing these photographs recently of women in baths of water with shadows on the water. You know when you fly and you look down over the sea and you see the shadows of clouds on the sea? It's got that sort of sense.

I have images that I collect and images that I create – where I get the model and I set it up and do a photographic session. I have that stream of my work and I have images that I just find. This is quite a barren studio for me at the moment. If you come here in two years it'll probably be absolutely loaded with images.'

We're stood by a back window now. Photographs of people in baths hang from a dado rail. I walk back to look again at the pictures of violent death but am intercepted by shots of burns victims and babies without legs.

'I keep them in here because I don't really want my children to see, so I keep them away. I've got a lot of images of babies like this. Depleted uranium. It's having a huge effect on people who've been in Iraq. It's on the outside of weapon shells and it affects the gene pool for generations; people who've been in Iraq, servicemen, have gone back to America and their wife or girlfriend who's never even been to the area – it's affected their child.'

I point to the violent deaths further on.
And these?
(Peering closer) These people have really gone for it, haven't they?

'She (pointing to a girl with half a head), that was from a love affair. I started to research what cultures had more suicides than others and discovered that

suicides rise in countries where there are more high-rise properties built. Japan didn't have a huge suicide rate until they built high-rise buildings and then a lot of death by high-rise occurred.
(Pointing to another)
That is someone whose stomach was driven over in Brazil.
(Man in a pool of scrambled egg entrails)
I'll only use the colouration patches of that. So it's about trying to get the sense of it. If you think about food, that also looks like food.'

Jam or treacle or something.

'Yes, blackcurrants or whatever.'

Scrambled eggs.

'It's the marriage of all those things together.
I tend to have six or seven things bubbling – photographs, sketches, ideas – and I will put them up, wait, and see what I think about them. You have to see if you can unlock them.
Downstairs I've got sketchbook after sketchbook of things I've collected over the years.'

We cross back into the warmth of the radiator, to the table where we originally sat. Jenny roots out a book of clippings and sketches from beneath it.

'Some images suddenly become interesting as a way to work or suggest something that I didn't see before. Every now and again I'll go through a lot of them.'

How do your sketchbooks work? Do they travel with you?

'Oh yes, they travel with me. (Begins to leaf through one) Notes. Babies. Photographs of pretty mistakes and I've got other books of colour collections. Colour combinations. It builds up over time.

That (a torn-out page from a medical textbook) will disappear off and then turn up in another sketchbook because I'm tidying up. (Flicking through) This is from a restaurant review and that mouth there, I love the isolation of that mouth. I think I'll probably use that mouth for those *Stares* downstairs. (A picture of two fighting dogs) "Dogfights". I've got a huge collection of dogfights; where the mass of flesh is interchangeable – there's something about human relations and divorce in that. Pictures of de Kooning's studio. My daughter being born . . .'

I know you don't do many interviews and wanted to ask before I go, why you agreed to talk to me?

'Because you sounded quite different from everybody else. I don't know, it wasn't overtly self-promotional in that it wasn't about "The Art World" because I get a bit fed up about Young British Artists and The Art World. I was quite interested because it wasn't just artists but creativity in a general sense; I thought that was interesting.'

* * * * *

Leaving Oxford after five hours in Jenny's company, the sky was blood and flinders. The setting sun all arterial reds draining to luminous vermilion and lavender.

At some point near Didcot I tuned into the recollections of an elderly man a little way down the carriage whose father had been an Italian officer in the Second World War and taken part in the last recorded cavalry charge – a night-time sabre breakout against Yugoslav partisans in 1942. As I listened to the story of the battle, my eyes swam out of the window and my mind spun back to the photographs of fighting dogs I'd seen earlier in the images compost of Jenny's studio floor . . . and I remembered something Jenny said about having had dinner with the artist Richard Long in Rome:

'He's a nice man, Richard Long. I liked him right away, very down to earth – which makes sense with all his walking. His studio is whatever walk he takes.'

And I thought of the line Jenny had made in her studio by walking back and forth between her paintings and the radiator, over and over again.

• • • • •

I fully intended to revisit Jenny to take photographs of her space but it never quite happened. She disappeared back into her world of work and the lines of communication petered out . . . and then the Brewer Street studio, Rorschach radiator and all, was demolished to build student accommodation.

Nothing remains today.

DAVID NASH, OBE, RA (1945–) is a Surrey-born sculptor known for his work with wood and living trees. He has exhibited and worked worldwide, with solo exhibitions in the UK, Spain, Switzerland and Japan.

In 2012 he began a working exhibition at Kew Gardens, London.

Wooden Boulder, a peripatetic work, and *Ash Dome*, a many decade-long collaboration with a group of living trees, are among his best-known creations.

DAVID NASH

Capel Rhiw, Blaenau Ffestiniog
5 August 2009

Walking up from a Maentwrog campsite, along the A469; in the gutters, hugging the low stone walls built flush to the road. All sorts of things have been used to build and fix the walls and fences, I note: wire, iron brackets, railway sleepers, blue brick and slate – black and bright in the wet. It's an over-cast morning but I make good time, reaching Rhyn-y-sarn and its chipped red phone box after a quarter of an hour, crossing the Afon Teigi and bearing north-east up the hill towards Coed-Penguern, tramping through the long grass of the verge that slaps at my boots and makes everything below the knee sodden.

I'd been working on a building site for several months by this point, writing in the evenings and at weekends. Wet feet were not unknown but the recent memory of a younger lad standing helpless in a trench as it slowly filled with concrete – raking madly about him as the inexorable grey mass rose, rose up, threatened and then, with terrible inevitability, began to fill his wellington boots – was enough to make me wince now and count myself lucky.

On days such as that, returning home to discover a letter or email in response to an interview request was a wonderful thing, and so it was when I received a message back from David's assistant, Sabine:

'Dear Daniel Richards,
    On behalf of David Nash I would like to thank you for your letter in which you express your interest for David and his work.
    David would have time at the beginning of August and be pleased if you could come then (if possible in the week of Monday 3rd except Tuesday).
    I look forward to hearing from you.
        Kind Regards,
            Sabine Schlenker'

That's the sort of email that leads to jigging about the kitchen and banishes the image of tearful chippies with lime-burnt calves.

•   •   •   •   •

A couple of miles further on, a low sun is beginning to burn off the mist. Above Ty'n-y-cefa, I pass a lorry pulled up in a lay-by. The driver stands beside his cab, warming his hands around a mug of tea. As I draw level we nod good morning and he asks if I'm going far. I say I'm on my way up to Blaenau and he tells me about how, when younger, he walked extensively in Brecon – not now though, not for many years.

Arriving early at David Nash's chapel, I sit on a low wall opposite and reread his chapter in my rather foxed copy of Roger Deakin's *Wildwood*. I'm anxious to pick up threads from Roger without repeating him since it's largely due to his account of David that I am here – *Waterlog*'s connection back to the art school buildings, the beechwood airship and its resultant questions having led me to North Wales.

I ring the bell and I am met by Sabine, who leads me through the olive-green front doors and into the hall beyond. We walk among the running woods, columns and hewn works. Capel Rhiw is stacked with sculpture, very much as Deakin described – 'a congregational throng'.
A frozen crowd of Ents,* a charged and dancing mass, a silent paused conspiracy.

David arrives shortly afterwards. He's smaller that I'd expected and seems composed of a bunched energy. He shakes my hand and laughs while explaining I'm half the age he imagined. I tell him about my walk and the *Beech Throne* in Bristol Museum which I explored as a child; set opposite a slate circle by Richard Long – my first introduction to Land Art.

Left alone while David catches up with Sabine, I amble around the balconies and cold boards of the hall, making notes as I go:

A chair of sapling pieces with all of the shoots left on – a branching chair-form visible within a ball of twigs.
Wheeled toys. 'Nash, 83' in pencil. Rough-hewn rolling sticks.
A throne like a miso spoon.
Massive burnt toast.
Black domes.
Rough ladders.
Squid pieces, tied around the top – eight wedges driven up under the head to make eight legs.
A comet – clean shooting stem and black burnt ball.
A red flash – fast moving. Yew, cut at the top – like a 30s train poster.

---

* J.R.R. Tolkien named his tree creatures 'Ent' after the Anglo-Saxon for giant.

A wooden bench topped with a stone cube, sphere, and pyramid.

A collection of balls, tufted, axed-off. Coconut textures.

Charcoal puts your teeth on edge when you touch it. Burnt wood is like sastrugi – ridge edges cut sharp.

Crack & Warp columns – an amazing amount of delicacy, each chainsaw laceration a centimetre or less.

A vertical cross the size and bulk of railway sleepers with metal, possibly copper, set around it. The metal is green and lichen-like. Frosty to the touch.

I discover a side room filled with drawings and charcoal works – the largest charting the course of the *Wooden Boulder*, quarried from a tree high in the Ffestiniog valley and then left to make its way down through the streams, river and estuary to the sea, which it did in the subsequent decades – sitting, sticking, rolling and resting for years at a time, becoming a part of the landscape, before being buoyed off again by the next spring flood; on and further on again. Always on.

A smaller boulder on the floor, carved into planes like a football, surprises me when I reach down to touch it and find my fingers meeting cast metal. It looks so woody but rings hollow to a knock from my knuckles.

David returns and points to a reproduction of the sapling-ball twig chair.

'The original's upstairs but it's incredibly fragile. This is actually a better sculpture than the wood one, I think.'

Does bronze still flex and snap, like wood?

'Well, if you "bend" (emphasises the stress of the wood by lunging as he speaks it) it will bend and then snap, whereas wood would just "phut" because it's so dry. The original is thirty years old.'

Have you always made editions of your work?

'I made Wheelies and ladders and little running pieces as multiples – that was before I had a gallery – I'd do a show in an alternative space like the Arnolfini in Bristol and make 100 Wheelies, as I call them – wheels on sticks – and sell them for £3 each; £30 in today's money.

'I have a huge show coming up at Yorkshire Sculpture Park next year and there's that big Longside Gallery. It's going to be a full retrospective including new work made especially for it which I'm engaged with at the moment and so a lot of this will go there.' (Gestures around the hall)

Will this be your first retrospective?

'Well I've done exhibitions called Survey Shows because I tend to tell stories with my shows; there's a
narrative within my work. Have you read the Roger
Deakin story about the boulder?'

Yes.

'He tells the story of the boulder very well but there
was one thing that was wrong. He sent me a draft but
then put an end on it after I'd sent it back with correc-
tions. He described me rowing up and down the river
looking for the thing, well that's just ridiculous! We did
do a couple of boat journeys – one looking for it and
another filming it floating – so that's where he got the
idea from but he wanted to add a romantic touch to the
story . . .'*

You're off in the estuary somewhere . . .

'I searched the estuary when it disappeared for about
six months. Not every day by any means but I did make
a concerted effort to check every creek, every nook
and cranny of the estuary and, when it wasn't there,
I assumed that it had gone to sea. And then I made a

---

* *Wildwood* was published shortly after Roger Deakin's death in 2006. Looking
through his archive at the University of East Anglia in 2010, I discover a book
of notes and sketches made during and after his meeting with David. He clearly
struggled with the chapter's ending, rewriting it several times. One entry reads:

'In the end one finds oneself struggling to write about Nash because he is
the only one in full command of the necessary language: he speaks wood.
You're left in the end with the fact of sculpture. That's probably why he
chose it as an art student instead of painting, which is where he began.
You're left without words at all; just the fact of sculpture.'
          – *Wildwood: A Journey Through Trees*, Roger Deakin
                              (Hamish Hamilton, 2007)

film of its journey using my archive for which I made
an edition – a box with prints – and then, a year ago,
it turned up in the estuary again! It was still there but
had got sucked down into some soft sand, caught up in
a tree that had also been sucked down, some branches
of which came up above the water – it's tidal, you see,
so . . . I looked there twice because a friend of mine, he
told me to look; he thought it was there and we went
there and it wasn't, you know? It was not there! Five
years later it's come up, so I've had to add that onto
the film now . . . I loved the idea of it having gone out
to sea.'

Is it very near here?

'Well it's tidal, so it would go right out near the sea, get
picked up by an incoming tide and taken right back up
– five kilometres each way. It would go up as far as it
could and then the tide would turn and it would lodge
itself somewhere.
Let's go and have some tea.'

We walk through a door in the end wall of the chapel into
a kitchen and tea is made, after which we climb some stairs
to a set of rooms used by David as an office and occasional
classroom. There are blackboards on the wall and large
windows look out over one of the huge slate-tip mountains
which tower around the town.
An incline plane cuts up the slope to a decrepit winding
house. A zigzag stairway runs beside – the path the miners
climbed to work each morning.

I note that this chapel feels very substantial and 'together'
compared to the fragmentation of the slate tips outside;
almost Cornish – a solid granite building.

'There were twenty-six chapels in Blaenau, not all of them as big as this but some of them were; three were strict Baptist, Calvinist. Each major quarry built their chapel for that denomination where their people were expected to go. There were more seats than there was population, actually, but this one was a Methodist/ Calvinist and it was an independent and very popular with the shopkeepers and other people who weren't affiliated with a quarry. Between 1830 and 1860 it was rebuilt three times, not on the same site, it moved because it wasn't big enough – and the bit that we're in now was a school room.

When I first came here on my own I was living below here and I built a mezzanine and had a bed there and a hot water tank and a back boiler from an open wood fire. I lived here for about three years on my own in this little bit – the big chapel I couldn't really handle, it was just too big a space but the school room was a beautiful size for living and working in.

Now, let's get down to what you're doing so we can be more specific. You're writing this book . . .'

Yes, my first book and quite an odd book; a reaction to an art school, an investigation of how people work; process and materials – the conversation between the worker and the thing worked – I think you'll understand what I mean by that, since you'll have a conversation with a piece of wood or a living tree and then the wood goes away and thinks about it.

'Yes. That's exactly how it is.

When I was making things like this, in 1967 (shows me a picture of an early tower which looks like a nest/ scaffold pylon), it was coloured wood – demolition beams and planks, that sort of stuff, and I was making

158

them very crudely . . . that's one of the squares (hands me a small box on a dowel from a shelf in the corner). See how badly made that is?'

It looks stapled.

'Hardboard, yes. I banged the nails over to act like a staple. Anyway, it was very philosophical and meta-physical and there were all sorts of reasons why they were like they were – I was trying to go from earth to the heavens through these vertical stages and this was representing the head, heart, guts and legs – so that was in my early twenties. Then I made a radical change and I reduced the whole thing to that (points to another picture, a linear totem-like tower).
It's going up but it's flowing down as well – that was the big step, those two.'

A streamlining.

'Yes. An old art teacher of mine, I sent him pictures of all these towers and a great arch – I'd built what looked like a village, a stage set – and he said, "It's much too complicated. The great artists, as they get bigger they get simpler . . . I'm not sure what you're doing." (Laughter) And I've always been a great fan of Brancusi, more for his way of life than the actual ob-jects, but then I began to look at the objects more and realised how profound they were in their simplicity, what he said about simplicity, how you had to earn it, that simplicity for simplicity's sake is meaningless, that you simplify things to make them clearer . . .'

Like Turner sketching ships towards the end of his life.

'Or Picasso; Picasso could put down four lines for the legs of an acrobat on a ball and you can tell the age of the acrobat, the balancing motion, incredible.

So I realised the whole thing was in my head, the idea, and I was making materials do this thing to represent something in my head, so the materials didn't have any say in it. I realised that what I did could only be as much as what was in my head, and that wasn't very much. I needed something to lead me, teach me and when I started working with unseasoned wood, I felt the presence of a kind of wisdom that was external to me. I had a moment where I felt it actually addressing me, and obviously there's a dialogue; there's my will – my intelligence – but there's this wisdom and deep intelligence, wordless intelligence which you can feel.

'I love going into the different trees, the personalities of the different species of tree. Having had the opportunity of working all over the world, particularly in the Northern temperate zone, which is where you get oak all the way round. In Japan and America there's white oak, which is pretty much the same as our oak, but birch is really different in Finland, here and Japan, incredibly different. In Okada it grows so slowly that it's as heavy as oak, really dense but with a slightly silk quality to it; sawing it, cutting and carving it is an absolute delight. In Finland it's a holy wood – sacred, pagan; and they use it in their saunas and do a lot of furniture making and house building, they really revere it. Working with birch in Finland, I just naturally felt this reverence for it but in Britain it's treated like weed. The wood has all those qualities in it but it's amazing how the approach and appreciation of the culture seems to impregnate into the substance and material.'

Do you find opportunities in chance meetings with trees? The piece is there, you're just finding it.

'Oh yes, then I've got the right piece of wood! If I've had my idea and I'm applying it and just trying to make the tree give me that, then I very rarely have the right piece of wood. The idea is in the wood. (Pauses) Ideas . . . that's a sort of lightbulb moment when you have an idea, a true idea. A lot of ideas are very old but they look for refreshment; and there are good ideas and bad ideas – an idea wants to be and it's chosen you or me to make it happen, and the material is usually less flexible than the idea; ideas can often be realised in many ways. That was quite a revelation to me when I realised it because the idea has no molecules, it's seeking molecules to incarnate.

'I've done seminars and master-classing around ideas – "What is an idea?" The usual meaning involves "how to do something" and problem solving, but the essence idea is something else; you don't get many of them. When you're younger, you get a load of them and you get much more happenstance. That happens more at your age than mine. I'm just sorting things out now, going back. When I built that tower I remember somebody said to me, "You get loads of ideas when you're young; just bung them in, sort them out later – you've got the rest of your life to sort them out." Really, what I'm doing in the chapel and with the installation out there is just that. They're individual pieces, autonomous on their own, but they speak to each other when you put them together as a congregation or in a museum show and, being a showman, I love to make a show! The idea of having an audience, people I don't know, I don't know who they are – you get that particularly in a museum because it's a public space; a commercial gallery is something completely different because galleries are there to make money, they make money for me and they make money for themselves and they have to go targeting clients and collectors; that's who the show is directed at . . . but it's got to make sense. When I've let the gallery do a show without me being there, using the stuff that they've got, it's been awful. Bits. Didn't make sense at all.'

No story.

'No story. No linking. No anchors to pull the space down or arrows to lift it up in different directions. Richard Long, whom I'm a great fan of, he got picked up by the commercial world straight away but has been incredibly strong in his ethics. A friend of mine was an artist in residence at Southampton University; they had a gallery and invited Richard Long to come and do a show. He looked at the space – which had a big window in it – and said, "Hmm, four tonnes of chalk. Can it take four tonnes?" because he saw the light and the length of the space and the fantastic possibility of

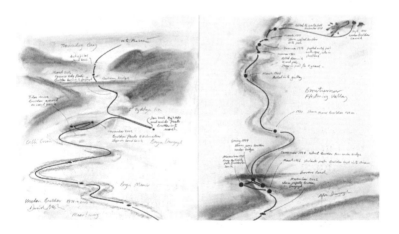

using that material . . . he didn't have a studio for a very long time, Richard, he was travelling; so he'd get asked to do a show and the galleries were his studios, so he'd make his shows in the gallery by saying "I want that material and that and that," and getting people to help him gather it and get it there.'

You've a strong association with this place, Blaenau Ffestiniog. How did you come to be here?

'My father's parents were from Shropshire and he was a pharmacist, studied pharmacy at Manchester University, then he got a chemist's shop in New Town and then Montgomery, which is very close by. He was an inventor, an entrepreneur and in New Town there was a big mail order outlet – which is still there, incidentally, a big department store – so he made stuff for them, anything they wanted. He bought up a lot of redundant wool mills and made ginger beer in one and powdered toothpaste in another, massage snake oil in another . . . He was very successful. He bought up a lot of army boots from the British army after the First World War and sold them to the Turkish army and made a lot of money.

'Most of their lives were spent up here, apart from a period in London when he opened a department store in Regent Street with a partner who swindled him, he went bust; but my father was mainly brought up outside London. He went to school near Brighton so he and his four brothers went to private/state/private school depending on what the family fortunes were and then, during the Second World War, they moved to Harlech, which is near here, as an evacuation place. Then, just after the war, with what little money he had left, my grandfather bought a huge house with forty-four acres in Llan Ffestiniog, near here. The house had all this furniture from when he'd had all these other houses down in London, silk curtains like rags, torn . . . very threadbare carpets but they were still living in a sort of grandeur and opulence but it was just like a stage set, worn out. There were fencing foils hanging on the walls, an old pistol on a sideboard, huge paintings – he used to deal in paintings in Regent Street – massive paintings with great gilt frames, just what was left, filling up this house in Llan Ffestiniog.

'So, for me and my cousins, it was fantastic. And there were some houses on the estate, the forty-four acres. My dad bought two of them, sold one and made a holiday house of the other. That was also an evacuation house because he was convinced we were going to have a war with the Soviet Union – this was in the late forties. I can just remember coming up here when I was very young, three or four years old, and him buying that place because my mum and older brother had moved nineteen times during the war, he was an infantry officer. So he was determined that wasn't going to happen again – it would have cracked Mum up – so we had this house and we liked being here more than Surrey. All my nature experience happened more substantially and deeply here. Weather. Gales. Rain. Gales that would pick our dustbins up and twirl them round the garden like tornados. Endless games of Monopoly when it was raining . . . I've known the Dwyryd river where the *Wooden Boulder* went in since I was a little kid.*

---

* Transcribing this section of our conversation, I was strongly reminded of my friend

'So there is a deep connection but not necessarily with the culture of the people, much more with the land and the weather. I didn't realise it at the time but we were living in an English bubble; we had our English friends and English things so, while there were people living here who we bought things from, I don't think we had any attitudes about them and we weren't aware of attitudes towards us either.

My father connected with quite a lot of people up here because he bought some other houses and was doing holiday lets and so worked with builders. He was very good with people but had a blind English middle-class thing; because he had Welsh origins he felt he was Welsh, but his thinking was English . . . so that's how I got to be here.

Where was I going to be when I left college in London? I've always been a planner, I realised I didn't want a mortgage, I wanted to get away from the south of England, away from the middle class and Blaenau

---

Alec Cumming – a painter from Norfolk who'd been Student President during my time at the art school.

His work is abstract but has definite landscape qualities and we've spent long evenings talking in the various hypothermic studios and garret spaces he's occupied around Norwich in the years since we graduated.

I think he's rooted in East Anglia, whether he'd accept that I don't know, but even the work he's painted most recently in India shows traces of these flatlands, buried inflections, subconscious palette choices – the landscape in and through him.

I see Sandra Blow's influence, shades of Roger Hilton and John 'Kyffin' Williams, but mostly I see Norfolk in the flat plains and colour choice; the reed avenues of the Broads, the sedge beds which stretch along the coast; the dune embankments which rise to check the sea. While there is rarely a given perspective in his painting or a recognisable cast of objects to locate and orientate the viewer, a sense of looking on and into something imbues it in a palpable, seductive way.

I plan to follow his work and continue our conversations for as long as I'm able because, like the *Wooden Boulder*, I feel he's off somewhere exciting and unknown and I want to see where he ends up.

Ffestiniog is really not that. I wanted to live somewhere foreign – to be an exile, a romantic idea, and the most economical way of being an exile was to come back to live here . . .'

You were quite young at the time, weren't you?

'Yes, it was '66; I was twenty-one when I bought the first cottage and I got a local grant to put the roof back on. It was there I built that first tower on a flat space where a pigsty used to be. The rest of the garden was almost vertical. It was in a fantastic position.'

You went back to London after that.

'Chelsea, yes. I was here for two years and then this place came up for sale. Before Chelsea I was trying to get into the Royal College because one of my teachers at Kingston had a good connection and thought I was the right sort of person to go there, but he wasn't there when the interviews were going on so . . . anyway, there's a story about it; I didn't get in the first year. Also, I'd made a decision while at college not to apply while still a student to do the diploma exam because I'd noticed people were very distracted from their work by all this application to go on being a student. I thought I should test myself and make the best show I possibly could, which I could only do, I felt, if I wasn't distracted by thinking, "Royal College, Slade next and then I'll try for the Royal Academy . . ." So I didn't get into the Royal College and was actually on the point of quitting Blaenau and going back to London and then this place came up for sale, initially for £50.'

You haggled them up?

'Well no, one of the gypsy families here wanted it for the scrap iron; wanted to pull it down and sell the slate and the granite so they went up to near £200 and I got it for £200. I had to sell the cottage but I had this huge building! And then I got a place at Chelsea, a one-year postgraduate course which had been started the year before.'

That was quite a crucible, wasn't it? A lot of people went for that course.

'Yes. There was one in Birmingham, one in Manchester and one in London and George Fullard was the Head of Sculpture and he just let me have my head – I'd been out for two years and I was hungry because I hadn't had time, I'd been earning a living by doing odd jobs. I knew what I wanted to do, I wanted to build these towers and so he told the technicians, "Give him whatever he wants." The other students were thinking, mainly, while I'd decided I needed to better my technique so that was one of the reasons to go back to college. They'd asked me, because they knew I'd got this place in Blaenau, "Why do you want to be here?" and I'd said, "To improve my technique," and I wanted to develop my discipline so I was getting up early, cycling into Chelsea – there when they opened, there until they closed, and there on Saturday morning when they'd open for a few hours. The caretakers were fantastic, we had such good fun with them.'

If you make friends with the caretakers, you'll be alright. I found that in Norwich.

'They run everything! I had the most fantastic year – the full twelve months, it wasn't just three terms. I built four towers – three at Chelsea and one as a commission for someone.'

Were they becoming streamlined at that stage?

'No, they were still pylons; coloured things, coloured constructions but I was getting disenchanted with painting colour on, colouring the space.'

Was that transitional, the painting of the wood? When I was researching your work I saw that you'd painted a great deal before that time.

'Yes. Well, this is one of mine – '67.'

David fetches down a print from a shelf. It's brightly coloured and abstract yet with discernible figurative forms in it. It reminds me of Futurism, Kandinsky, de Kooning's *Excavation*.

'Bosch, all sorts of people. Gorky . . .'

Kandinsky.

'Oh, absolutely Kandinsky, yes. Kandinsky was very interested in making sound visible and I've had a lot of moments when I've heard a sound and seen a form or I've heard a sound and felt a depth of resonance and then when I began to study Rudolf Steiner. His whole Eurythmy – which is an art of movement – is about making sound visible. He and Kandinsky were quite close.
Back here, after Chelsea, I tried to keep working and always be doing something. My problem was that I was anxious all the time about whether this was the right

colour, the right length, the right thickness . . . I felt like I was putting anxiety into the form. I felt colour as a skin wasn't real or working so I tried staining and then I thought, "Simplify everything. Go with the natural colour of the wood." How could I take the anxiety out of the process? So I tried "making" in the simplest way possible, with just wood.

What's the most basic way to shape this substance? An axe; metal edge on a length so you could hit it and chop it.

There was an ash cut down in the field opposite. It wasn't very thick, a foot or so, and I bought it for a pound and the guy put it over the wall with a JCB and I rolled it into the front of the chapel. It already had a rounded end from the axe so I propped it up and, with my axe, I followed the curve round and cut through – cut a V, rolled the log, cut it, rolled it and, when it came off, that was the object. And I loved it, I loved doing it but I wasn't confident that this could be art because there was no intellectual argument for it.'

It was an emotional exercise.

'I was trying to solve a problem. It's interesting, a lot of my work, like the *Ash Dome*, came from a problem. The problem for the *Ash Dome* was "How do I make an outdoor wood sculpture that doesn't rot? Something of the place – not made elsewhere and plonked."

The problem I had with Land Art was that someone like Richard Long – walking, making, photographing, walking away and leaving it behind – would come back with the result but the things he'd left no longer seemed necessary. I wanted to make something to start and evolve. I had all these questions and so the idea that "Wood doesn't rot if it's alive, when it's a tree" occurred; and it would come together over a very long period of time and it would need me to stay with it for it to happen. So I was answering my questions to myself and that resulted in the *Ash Dome* . . . but what we were talking about then was the problem solving – addressing a problem and finding a form that leads to a solution. There's something about art that I'm uncomfortable about; I don't really like outdoor sculpture, most of what I see, and I've realised the reason is that most of it is trying to resist the elements rather than engaging with them. So the *Wooden Boulder* and *Ash Dome* engage. The *Wooden Boulder* is the cycle of a tree – coming, becoming, growing or dead, going, reintegrating. We borrow wood out of that cycle; if you put it back into the cycle it'll go back into rotting down into the general humus. The *Ash Dome* is coming, the *Wooden Boulder*'s going.'

You're using your tools to alter the trajectory of your material, then, drawing out what it is and can be within its natural cycle rather than seeking to radically alter or deny its nature?

'Yes. Exactly so.'

For a long time you used hand tools to do that, making a point of leaving your tool marks.

'The marks of the tool, yes. I don't like polished wood. My eye bounces off it. If it has some tool texture – my eye doesn't bounce off the floor here because I'm taken in by the black cracks – that takes me inside, into the form and my eye doesn't run over the surface. If it's a smooth surface your eye slides, at least, mine does, whereas it can linger on a textured one. It's to do with speed of eye and how you read an object – which is

largely from outline and, because we want to understand, we look for clues as to what something is. We
read the physical world with our physical bodies, we
read things in relation to ourselves whereas, with this
painting here, while I know how big the picture is, the
actual subject could be any size . . . hand tools!'

Yes.

'Axe. An axe is a wedge. The most primitive way of
dealing with wood is splitting it, wedging, and then
there's cutting it – a wedge cutting across the grain so
you've got to sharpen it. Instead of pushing it so as to
split you put a handle on it to cut. I had axes like golf
clubs, a bag of axes; hand axes, different shapes. They'd
give me a difference of texture as well. (Ruefully) I was
good at sharpening them, though . . .
Now I've got a fleet of saws so it's pretty much all saws,
but I learnt wood through the hand tools. I had a six-
foot saw that I'd do big cuts with but it would take
me ages. I learnt a whole rhythm, right from my toes;
working alone because there are very few people that
you can work with for a long time on a saw.'

Was that when you forged your relationship with wood?
That time.

'That period, yes. I'd already got into art but I was
making art from outside, from the history of art:
Brancusi, Kandinsky . . . these were the mentors that
I had. I was having ideas and then trying to make
art out of that. The change was that I began to get
inside the material and make the art come out from
inside, coming out of the material. That was a fundamental change.'

Where did you get your fleet of axes? Richard Way, a boat builder I've spoken to, told me he likes to have tools passed on from people he's known – living and dead – so that he can carry on. Was that the same with yours?

'Yes. Some of them were junk shops, some were new – I've got a French axe I bought in France in '71, still got it . . . I hate anyone else using it! But I don't use them very much now, the axes, for getting bark off perhaps but it's mainly the saw. That's partly a sort of laziness but it's also knowing . . . they were a revelation to me, you see, because I had this principle of only making the art with the hand tools – that was part of the point of it – block and tackle and levers . . . (thinks) I've still got it in me, that trying to do it in the simplest way, economy of means, but we had this wood fire in the house and sawing wood for that was a pain in the arse so I bought a chainsaw because I could afford it; to cut firewood. Not to make sculpture. I had a pile of firewood to cut up and within an hour I had a sculpture – a cube on a rough board and then three legs and I'd bored holes and put the legs in. It's in the Guggenheim Collection in New York! We're trying to borrow it back for the Yorkshire sculpture show.'

And that was the first piece you did?

'Yes. I realised it was this amazing tool – like all the wood tools I was using amalgamated – and the fact I could push in and through and down like a jigsaw! Amazing. Then, a few years later, I had a big lime tree and the end wasn't straight; I wanted to straighten up the trunk so that it could stand flat, so I cut a thin slither off and it went on the grass. It was hot, summer, and an hour later I noticed that this thing had come up like a bowl, the sun having dried the moisture from the top and the ground having kept it wet underneath so there were two different radiuses, this longer than that, so it had had to bend. That was the beginning of the cracking and warping work.'

●　●　●　●　●

We walk down to David's workshops, which stand in the old goods yard of the railway station. Here, stood back from the man-made slate moraine that hems the valley head, the worked nature of the landscape becomes apparent. It's a scarred place, industrially redefined.*

David opens up the furthest shed. En route we pass a massive chunk of tree, sawn into a rough sphere.

'That's yew and it's grey because that's what happens outside.'

Is that oxidation?

'Well, it's pollution really. Every raindrop has got dust inside, rain forms around dust. It used to take two years for something to go grey outside – I did a little

---

* Several years ago I discovered a catalogue from Tate Gallery, Liverpool (published in 1988 for the collection display, 7 September 1988 – for three years) entitled *Modern British Sculpture*.
David's entry concerns the oak piece *Flying Frame*, 1980, but what's written could apply to much of his work, workshops and environment:
'This "Flying Frame" is related to tables and cubes in that the angles created by natural branch growths are incorporated into a geometrical structure. The rough woodcuts (usually administered by a large axe) betray Nash's straightforward relationship to his raw material and a workmanlike sense of economy in both time and motion. The idea of a frame, and the sculpture does indeed frame a landscape of view.'

experiment in the seventies. There was a big volcano in America, St Helens, which put up billions of tonnes of dust and a year later wood was only taking six months to go grey outside. It's man-made pollution as well. (Pauses) Very rarely do I import wood in from abroad but for Yorkshire Sculpture Park I need some really big wood so I'm using some Californian redwood.'

Is it a problem shipping massive hunks of wood here?

'There's money and then there's the carbon footprint. I think I've got a lot of credit in the bank from the early days, carbon-wise, and I'm spending a bit of it at the moment. I do have a truck to bring things up from my base in Sussex, but that's money. Money can move things and make things happen.

In the early days I always went to the tree and made what I could, what I could lift away and do what was feasible with the location – if it was downhill, all the better. Then I started working with the idea of the wood quarry where I have a tree and I quarry it for sculptures. I'd do that in Japan or Australia because there were budgets there and I could get a crane in to help me . . . so as time went on I was able to do bigger things, but I'm at the limit. What I want to do now is deepen the work; I don't just want to make more of the same.'

Is this something that you've been thinking about for a while?

(Unlocking a door) 'I've always seen it as very independent – I see the work as a whole being not just an ongoing, running thing. This Yorkshire Sculpture show, that's the show. There isn't anywhere else in the world that I could do this show, not that I know of . . . after that, I don't think the work's going to change as such, I'm still working from the same principles; I want to do less but do less better.'

We walk through to the room where David stores his saws and other tools.

'Now, this'll interest you. *Cracking Box*, you know about the cracking boxes? They started from the tool. (Reaching down a large and lethal-looking crank screw from the wall) I was in an ironmonger's in Dolgellau – a two-inch bore. I love the tool. It cost a lot of money for me back then, but I felt I could make these holes with it – so I had this before I made a cracking box, but I would have never thought of making a cracking box until I had this so the tool led me to the piece.'

Did you find that when you first got a chainsaw too?

'What the saw could do? Yeah, but then I was pushing what could be done with the saw. You can do these incredibly fine lines. I can make pieces rather like a razor blade when wood is fresh – it could be done with a chisel but it would be so precious whereas here it's like drawing. The tool is a line of cut.'

The saws are lined up in order of size from small hedge-trimmer to monolith-slayer. David points to the largest.

'In America, where I work in an amazing woodyard – all ethically sourced wood – there's an astonishing guy, Evan Shively, who's got a saw with a nine-foot chain! Redwood is a relatively soft wood so you can use saws with that.'

You must spend a lot of time on maintenance.

'Yeah, we do. There's a place ten miles away who do all my maintenance – calibration and things – but I do the sharpening and Alan, who comes up some days to help me, he sharpens too because we hit nails, hit shrapnel in the old oaks; a lot of fence wire and other stuff that's disappeared when the tree's grown around it.'

I've heard that's a problem for people using wood from the Balkans.

'Shrapnel, yes.'

What sort of size was the first chainsaw?

'That sort of size (small to medium). That was the size I had for years. In '79 I bought that size (larger), this one (massive) I don't really use myself; Alan uses it. Alan's big. I'm not really big enough for it. I've got another set of saws in California and another whole set of tools in two big boxes that can be sent to wherever in the world I'm working – vices, gas burners, masks, boots, branding irons, whatever I need.'

We walk back out into the yard.

I wanted to ask you about Dutch elm disease, because you'll remember the elm but it's a tree I've never really known.

'We can go over to a big elm piece actually, over here.'

We walk over to one corner of the yard and a roughly balled mass that puts me in mind of the Lunar Module sat squat, silvery and unassuming on a pallet. It seems to bristle with latent menace – like a massive fist.

'This tree probably died in the eighties but remained standing up. It fell over recently and I've got a bit of a problem here with rot, which I'm going to carve out. The whole thing is going to be much more jagged when I'm finished, I think. I was going to use the surface in relation to the curve but it's this rather dull colour . . . elm's not nice as a colour and so it might be partly charred; there's six tonnes in there. (Unlocking another workshop yard) This room is a kiln with underfloor heating and a dehumidifier. Over there is a piece of red eucalyptus from California that is drying out, crack-ing. I need a bigger kiln really, a lot of the cracking and warping wall pieces hang in here and we put the fans on and turn up the heat and humidifiers.'

I'm sure they don't know what's hit them!

'Ha! No! Poor things. If you cut, say, beech, lots of cuts – beech, birch, hornbeam, a lot of woods have got within them the fungi to start breaking them down when they're dead. If I just left the beech cut in an ordinary room there'd be enough water left for the fungus to work and you'd get white moulds but, if I bring it in here the fungus can never get going on the surface because it's never wet enough, I'm sucking it dry. I can do that here whereas otherwise they'd rot.'

Do you know the way things will go? Can you look at a piece of wood and think, 'That's going to go so and so'?

'I know it's going to crack but I don't know where and sometimes when I want them to crack on the front they'll crack on the sides so I just go with it . . . unless it doesn't work and then I don't go with it.'

We pass into a larger third shed with a forklift truck in the centre.

'This is a tool that's pretty much indispensable when working on scale – moving bits about, getting the big things into the kiln with it. This is more of a finishing room although there's a lot out at the moment in a show up in Kendal, Abbots Hall, and a lot is already in Yorkshire or coming back from a big museum show in Germany.'

David turns to a large red monolith of redwood, cut to bisect the hairline strata of rings.

'There's a thousand years of growing in there, approximately. This again is from the woodyard in California.

I'm going to have it on the wall at Yorkshire as a millennium block. Can you see the wide annular rings when it was very young? And then look how tight they are when they get out there. I've actually got to count them but I'm reliably told that it's about a thousand.'

The first thing I think of is *2001: A Space Odyssey*.

'Oh, the slabs? Black obelisks, yes. I remember seeing that in the sixties.'

It's very powerful just as it is, isn't it?

'Yes, just the fact of it.'

We step back out into the yard, lock up and then we go back to the chapel where David makes a pot of tea and we speak about the plywood of de Havilland Mosquitos unravelling in humid climes,⋆ the weathering of Norwich gateposts and the giant dented girder in the Tate Modern gift shop which absorbed me almost as much as the Rothko exhibition upstairs at the time – the dent was so violent that I stood there

---

⋆ The de Havilland Mosquito was a fast British twin-engined fighter/bomber aircraft of WWII nicknamed 'The Wooden Wonder' because of its plywood and balsa laminate construction which, as well as being light, proved very tough and robust. The Mosquito was revered by aircrews and feared by the Germans for its speed and ability to fly beneath radar. In 1943, Hermann Göring wrote:

'It makes me furious when I see the Mosquito. I turn green and yellow with envy. The British, who can afford aluminium better than we can, knock together a beautiful wooden aircraft that every piano factory over there is building, and they give it a speed that they have now increased yet again. What do you make of that?'

However, late in the war, the casein-based glue used to bond the wood layers was found to crack when exposed to the extreme heat of theatres in the Far East – causing a number of planes to unravel.

gazing at it for several minutes while other people walked around me to buy postcards and tote bags.

'I love stories offered by the physical world. (David puts the teapot down on the kitchen table) This table was part of a big sculpture I made at Chelsea. Before that it was part of a big sculpture in the courtyard at Chelsea – it was at an angle, a table with a black sort of pig-head shape. It's been in several sculptures but became a table in the early seventies. You see I've had to add a block there? A dog that we had chewed through the leg, took her six months to get through it . . . it's the erosion of objects that I really love. I saw a biscuit tin in Italy that had been used to feed hens for many, many years and it was pecked so that it was pitted. It was just a fantastic object that had obviously taken decades to form. And there's a scaffolder here who uses a wheel-barrow when they're dismantling scaffolding, throws the clips down into the barrow so the barrows get buggered up and last about a month. I was praising him, praising the shape of his barrows; I said, "I'd love to have a bunch of those hanging on a wall!" He was completely nonplussed.
Erosion is marvellous; especially human erosion.'

David goes to answer a phone call, and I drink my tea and ponder which Sherlock Holmes story it was that dealt with the human erosion of Watson's doorstep. Later I look it up – 'The Stockbroker's Clerk':

'Your neighbour is a doctor,' said he, nodding at the brass plate.

'Yes; he bought a practice as I did.'

'An old-established one?'

'Just the same as mine. Both have been ever since the houses were built.'

'Ah! Then you got hold of the best of the two.'

'I think I did. But how do you know?'

'By the steps, my boy. Yours are worn three inches deeper than his.'*

Later, sat in a hut that resembled an upturned coracle, I gaze out over the four acres of woodland where the *Ash Dome* lives. The day is clear and a brisk wind whiffles the trees so the dappled light shimmers on the ferns and grasses that grow thick and lush on the ground.

After lunch, David drew me a map of the wood's location and layout, resting on a sculpture in the chapel to do so:

---

* 'The Stockbroker's Clerk', *The Memoirs of Sherlock Holmes*, Sir Arthur Conan Doyle (Penguin, 1965).

'There's an avenue of oaks you'll walk up. *Ash Dome* is here. There's a lime and a sycamore wall. A line of bendy larches here. Two arcs of ash. The hut is here. Behind the hut, here, is a group of seven by seven in a square – I'm growing a rhomboid, an uneven square – seven rows of seven trees, seven feet apart . . .'

The *Ash Dome* itself is a wonderful revelation. Walking up from the road through the oaks, it emerges, camouflaged in my peripheries, a ring of dancing trees: spiralling round and up towards the sky. I walk around them, noting the mosses and lichen flecking their papery bark.

The way the trees have been trained round, the many cut joints healed over with green scar tissue, suggest a hundred elbows – although elbows make for a jaunty dance and these trees twirl with a delicate grace. They seem to be moving very fast while furnishing the place with a stillness. It feels very ancient.

I stand before *Ash Dome* for some time, taking it in; enjoying the shadowplay and subtle movements of the pale trunks and delicate higher shoots.

After exploring the rest of the living work around me I settle in the shelter.

At length a distant whistle rouses me – a sound from across the valley that I heard while pitching my tent the night before: the rhythm of a train high in the hills.

I determine to find the source so set off down towards Maentwrog, crossing the bridge and turning off up the hill. I leave the road for a bridle path and zigzag my way up steepening slopes beside a stream in clouds of pollen and heather fug, heavy earthy smells. I follow tractor tracks through an evergreen wood and across a stile, coming out onto a ridge overlooking the valley floor.

DAVID NASH

The path I've joined leads up towards a cottage sat in the lee of the hillside. In front of this run narrow gauge railway lines, crossing the small side-valley on a curved, dry-stone embankment. When I reach the tracks I see a platform, little larger than the bench upon it. A painted sign reads 'Coed-y-Bleiddiau, Wood of the Wolves'. The last Welsh wolf having died nearby, legend has it.*

I hear the huffing of a distant train and, looking down the tracks, see a red locomotive approaching. I hold out my hand and am pleased and surprised when the train begins to slow and draws up before me, the engine crew grinning.

A guard opens a carriage door for me and I climb aboard. As the train sets off I ask how much it will be to travel down to Porthmadog but am told not to worry, he's never picked anybody up from this station before, it's not even on the map, apparently.

We steam above the Dwyryd river and down to the estuary where the *Wooden Boulder* may still be hiding; through ancient woodland and cuttings, over dry-stone ledges, slate embankments and bridges; past houses, overlooking washing in back gardens, slowly descending towards the sea.

---

* As well as the wolves and the wonderfully unexpected platform, later research revealed a darker secret history to Coed-y-Bleiddiau. The remote house, far from any road, was originally built for the Superintendent of the Ffestiniog Railway Company who'd travel to work on the first train of the day and home on the last. Later it became home to several interesting people, including Sir Granville Bantock, composer and conductor, St John Philby, father of the spy Kim, and William Joyce, better known as Lord Haw-Haw of 'Germany Calling' infamy.
Elgar dedicated a *Pomp & Circumstance March* to only one of these men, but perhaps each waved a hand to hail a train to Porthmadog in his time.

183

On the journey I think of David's charcoal drawing of the boulder's path from tree to stream to the river and the sea, blackened and gleaming, bobbing and drifting with each salt tide. Its course was drawn out in Blaenau and now I'd tracked it on an old slate train, passing it perhaps – although who knows where. Somewhere it sits in the landscape, among the marshes, coming and going, at once still and in motion like the swirling *Ash Dome*.

The engine whistles again, clanking and clattering beside cemeteries and workshops before swinging out right and on to Porthmadog Cob.

A few months after my visit to North Wales I wrote to Richard Long to ask if we could meet to talk about his work. In truth I didn't really expect a response since I knew he isn't fond of talking about his work, drawn instead to the empty, stony deserts of the world; to mountaintops or Dartmoor tors; making his work alone – encountering the landscape as David does the wood.

Long has described the moor as his natural workspace:

'I've done a lot of work on Dartmoor.
It's relatively flat and treeless.
I've called it my prototype landscape.
It's very powerful, you know, being alone on a mountaintop.
I've made my work out of those wonderful experiences.
It's art that can be made in solitude so, in a way, it's like a one-to-one situation with a place . . .

'People are not the subject of my work; but that's purely because the work is not about all that social interaction. The work is probably about the landscape or it's about making a line or a circle of stones.

'There are many Dartmoor-like places all over the world; it's almost universal but it's also very particular. I guess it's my studio.'*

With this in mind, I thought, it might have been best to address my letter to 'Richard Long, Dartmoor', like a child writing to that other elusive rover, Santa Claus.
So it was a surprise when a handwritten letter, in pencil, arrived a few weeks later. He was sorry to disappoint, he said, but wasn't keen to talk since he'd 'no talent for that type of thing'.

A lovely note, it only confirmed my image of him and drew me back to Roger Deakin's comment about David Nash 'speaking wood' and the simple fact that the only dialogue of lasting matter to both Nash and Long is action – cutting wood, placing stones, walking paths, training trees – less talking, more motion out into the world.
A journey can be a work of art.

---

* Richard Long, speaking in a short film about Dartmoor made to coincide with his 2009 Tate Britain retrospective, *Heaven and Earth*.

MANIC STREET PREACHERS (1986–) are a Welsh band consisting of founding members James Dean Bradfield, Nicky Wire and Sean Moore. After the disappearance of lyricist and guitarist Richey Edwards in 1995, the band decided to continue as a trio.

Since 1992 they have released twelve studio albums to international acclaim and chart success.

MANIC STREET PREACHERS

Faster Studios, Cardiff
May 2010

> 'Every reckless claim or promise the Manics ever made contained the launch code for its own heroic or unheroic failure.'
>
> — Taylor Parkes, *The Quietus**

● ● ● ● ●

Wales had opened out of my peripheries. After the previous four studio visits, David Nash's space had shown the possibilities of landscape as venue and inspiration for work.

I returned to Blaenau Ffestiniog a few months later to revisit David and take pictures with my friend Kev – driving from Norfolk on the night of the Summer Solstice so the sky was never wholly dark.

We spent £50 on petrol at Thetford and nervously watched the fuel gauge for the rest of the trip, having little money,

---

* 'There Are No Horizons: The Holy Bible at 20', Taylor Parkes, *The Quietus*, December 2014.

listening to the two CDs we'd brought on rotation, *The Holy Bible* by Manic Street Preachers and a compilation made for the trip. Funny how a soundtrack sharpens recollection; I recall Magazine near Northampton, 'Archives of Pain' playing as we passed beneath multi-storey junctions in Birmingham, The Velvelettes on the Migneint Moors – sheep skittering away in the headlights – 'Never Stop (Discoteque)' by Echo & The Bunnymen spitting from the car's tinny speakers as we wound our way across Snowdonia in the dawn.

When we reached the Blaenau outskirts we found a lay-by and crawled into sleeping bags in the boot.

It was already very light outside. 3 a.m. – we'd made it in under five hours.

When we awoke, I found I could not afford breakfast so we pooled our coins and sat on the tailgate of the car to eat sad Special K from paper cups with our fingers . . . agreeing that this was not how we'd envisioned our lives turning out – a world of empty bank accounts and borrowed milk.

We parked up beside David's workshop compound and walked into the yard. Three lengths of greenheart lay on trestles in the main work shed. Lignum vitae, the densest wood – formerly part of a sea defence somewhere on the South Coast. David worked with a freshly sharpened saw, shimming the wood golden again, strimming away the surface layer; blackened by years submerged in saltwater.

Sand, he said, busts blades like nothing else.

Heavy dust streamed behind the saw, massing on the floor, too dense to cloud.

While this went on, Kev climbed around to shoot the scene on a borrowed camera – wiry and lithe in a pink t-shirt, suede trainers without socks and paint-spattered combat trousers rolled up above the ankle, in contrast with David's armour, mask and boots.

Driving back through Snowdonia we saw the landscape illuminated. The previous night we'd caught dark glimpses and impressions of rock faces, misted peaks and valleys, but this time around the scenery shone in the sun, a very pure and starkly beautiful part of the world, almost Alpine.

Super Furry Animals were playing as we hit the first dual carriageway and our speed increased for the flatlands.

• • • • •

As this book grew, it changed. As I wrote and travelled, a sense of quest began to build – my initial celebration and challenge of the art school manifested in the airship, I met the boat builders then sought out Bill Drummond because the work of both parties seemed tied to zeppelin . . . but then moved home and met Richard and Stanley and it was only really after that, having explored their symbiotic link with craft and art, expedience and creative experiment, that the book began to gain momentum and a shape in my mind.

The jump to Jenny Saville from Stanley seemed logical in light of the latter's perception of himself as a Jack-of-all-trades – Jenny being an astonishingly accomplished master of one – after which, having visited Jenny's Oxford base, I approached David Nash as somebody who works in landscape – a practitioner of both site-specific and roving art. Which brings me back to the words 'momentum and shape in my mind' because that shape, or perhaps *path* is a better word, isn't obvious or terribly logical. Sometimes oppositional aspects link the interviewees and chapters here, sometimes it's similarities, sometimes it's a matter of coincidence and chance connections which fired me to write a letter.

In the case of Manic Street Preachers, who I'd wanted to approach in any case due to their relationship with Jenny Saville, the catalyst was a quote I read in a newspaper interview with the musician Richard Thompson, in which he described the internal landscape he carries inside him, where his songs live. That idea set me thinking about landscape and nationality and seemed a perfect bridge to explore ideas of what it was to work in Wales and what it was to be Welsh, ideas of inner and outer landscapes (as opposed to *workspaces*).

At this point, in this way, I began to take charge of the direction the book was headed in. By consciously taking a theme or image from one conversation as a link to the next, every interaction informing and framing the subsequent encounter, I felt I'd regained control of the project's trajectory. Perhaps I'd been doing it all along but now, having recognised this strange chain reaction of knight's move dodgem logic,* I felt hugely relieved and able to carry on exploring the common ground between apparently unconnected artists and disciplines, their methods, motivations and habitats, as well as notions of 'Art for Art's sake', which seemed to be becoming common themes.**

· · · · ·

---

* *Dodgem Logic* is a magazine edited and published by the Northampton writer and magician, Alan Moore. The magazine's manifesto reads: 'Colliding Ideas to See What Happens.'

** What had I thought I was doing until this point? I'm not sure – but just because it was vague doesn't mean that I wasn't taking it seriously. I was driven by a conviction that what I was writing had worth and I really enjoyed spending time with the people I interviewed. I enjoyed the process of writing too – although I hated the transcribing – but even this felt formative. It took up all my time when I wasn't working on building sites or behind bars.

Had I had a more focused editorial end in sight I might not have explored the tangents I took which ended up bearing fruit; had I taken a more journalistic attitude I don't think all the people I approached would have agreed to speak to me. It was my curious status as an odd proposition which opened doors.

If the idea of 'Art for Art's sake' became central to the book, then perhaps this can be traced back to my writing, which grew from a belief in 'Book for Book's sake', itself born of 'Airship for Airship's sake'.

'There is an inner landscape you carry around with you and that's where your songs live. For me, it's fifties or sixties suburban Britain, I guess. And I very much keep in touch. I open my laptop and there is the *Guardian* on the home page. In my car I've got the World Service and *Test Match Special* ...'

– Richard Thompson*

. . . . .

Faster Studios, Cardiff
February 2011

Faster Studios is housed in an industrial quarter of Cardiff near a brewery and the docks; a unit in a square of two-storey brick workshops set around a courtyard. The place has a worn feel, the edges taken off; a site of graft and gravel.

When I reach the body of the Manic Street Preachers' kirk, I find the three members surrounded by thousands of postcards they're in the process of signing.
The scene encapsulates a part of the Manics ethos and ethic so perfectly. They've agreed to sign the cards so they're bloody well signing them, properly – RSI and permanent marker fumes on a wet Wednesday afternoon.

Bassist Nicky Wire bounds over to shake hands and enquire about my journey down. Tea's made and we descend to the 'studio bunker' – a recording and rehearsal room with a beast of a mixing desk next door.

---

* Richard Thompson, *Independent*, 11 April 2010.

'This place has become incredibly important to us, almost like an extra instrument. It gives us a lot of inspiration; just being here together in a room.'

We sit on black sofas beside the desk console and Wire starts by asking how my meeting with Jenny Saville went – Jenny having texted to vouch for me in the interim.

'You went last year? Did you do a good session with her?'

Really great; about four and a half hours in her studio. We discussed *Lifeblood*★ in terms of some of de Kooning's more challenging work. (Wire cackles with delight) I said, 'I like it. I don't care that some people say it's their Tin Machine.'

'Ha! Tin Machine.'★★

She said she loved de Kooning similarly; not all of his work but you've got to stick with an artist. 'You can't trash them; they're just making jumps on to somewhere else . . .'

'I still think "Song For Departure", "I Live To Fall Asleep", "Cardiff Afterlife" and "1985" are wonderful, especially the lyrics in "1985". We did a lot here; we

---

★ *Lifeblood* is Manic Street Preachers' seventh studio album, released in 2004. Colder, perhaps more distant than anything else they've done, it divides opinion. I like it.

★★ Tin Machine were a hard rock group featuring David Bowie as a member – but billed as 'Tin Machine' rather than a new Bowie project or incarnation – which formed in 1988 and disbanded after two albums.
They're invoked here as an (admittedly lazy) example of trying something different which perhaps isn't very good.

didn't own it at the time and it was a shit-hole – one decent room and a decent desk. There was nothing upstairs, just rats. It was a tip. We did a lot of rehearsing here and a lot of songwriting.'

What was the plan behind that album? I know you don't like talking about it much.

'We had a disastrous run: "So Why So Sad" as a lead single, "There by the Grace of God" for the Greatest Hits and "The Love of Richard Nixon" – three songs that just don't sound like Manic Street Preachers.'

You've said when your mother first heard 'The Love of Richard Nixon' on the radio she didn't know it was you.

'She didn't! I remember Jo Whiley playing it for the first time on Radio One and you could just feel the confusion.
I think we were trying to tear down the things we'd always done – words like "Passion" and "Commitment"; we were scared of those words. We knew they turn you into Springsteen at his worst. But then we looked back and realised that even *The Holy Bible** isn't actually a cold album in a lot of ways, it's as passionate as you can get about misery.'

You couldn't call it anaemic.

'No. You couldn't.
I think the general idea with *Lifeblood* was to sound like a different band and I'm all for that – if you go

---

* *The Holy Bible* is Manic Street Preachers' third studio album, released in 1994.

back to *Satanic Majesties*,★ Keith Richards said it was
a complete disaster but the next song he wrote was
"Jumpin' Jack Flash".
I always go back to when we did the Millennium
Stadium then released *Masses Against the Classes* –
which was so fucking raw – that going to number one.
You can hear the vitriol and I remember thinking at
that time, "If there is such a thing as a Knebworth
moment, that was ours."
From then on, for at least five years, we tried to . . .
and if I was "an artist" I would be really serious to you
and say how we went through trauma by trying to be a
different band, which did happen, it's just . . .'

It's interesting, though, you're using the vocabulary of the
artist and talking about this fraught dialectic process but
you're clearly very hesitant about crossing that line and
identifying yourselves as artists.

'Yes. I'm really scared of it. I think it stops you actually
connecting with an audience and sometimes with yourself because you're connecting more with your view of
what an artist should be – wilfully obscure rather than
trying to connect with your true self, which for us has
always been wanting to reach millions of people – but I
think we've reached a point where we kinda realise that
that can't happen any more . . . you know, since *Send*

★ *Their Satanic Majesties Request* was The Rolling Stones' psychedelic album – self-
produced, rambling, patchy, 'a bit Sergeant Pepper' – it doesn't really hold together
or sound like the band's hearts were in it.

'I liked a few songs, like "2000 Light Years", "Citadel", and "She's a Rain-
bow", but basically I thought the album was a load of crap . . . I was never
hot on psychedelic music.'

– Keith Richards

Away the Tigers* we've had a blast, a brilliant blast, but we know this is it, really; from now on it has to be more self-indulgent – we will change our sound and we will be slightly different people on record.'

Another year zero?

'Yeah. The last phase . . . and that's not even being overdramatic. I never thought we'd have this good a time – to be on our tenth album and still be so centred in the culture is brilliant . . . (thinks for a moment) But it would have been interesting, I mean, Richey had really deep, brilliant pathos, severe humour beyond belief, but towards the end – I don't think he saw himself so much as an artist but he was becoming one. The kinda comedy element had taken over – from the fabulous disaster of Malcolm McLaren's Pistols** that had changed. It would have been unbelievable to see what band we could've been. But I do think – and this might not sit well in your book – that that's probably the difference between us and people who consider themselves artists because, for me, as a rock and roll band, the minute you consider yourself an artist you're fucked. You're basically making records for yourself, you know? And we might be reaching that point soon

---

* *Send Away the Tigers* is Manic Street Preachers' eighth studio album, released in 2007.

** Malcolm McLaren (1946–2010) was manager of The Sex Pistols among other punk and post-punk bands and one of the first to fully recognise the potential of 'fabulous disaster' – embodied by the Pistols bassist Sid Vicious whose lack of musical ability was no obstacle thanks to his good looks, charisma, attitude and onstage ambience of simmering violence. A magnet for the audience; the punk spirit personified and a big influence on the young Manics – Wire and Edwards acting predominantly as band spokesmen, performing mainly aesthetic roles onstage during the early 1990s.

but, to be really vital . . . it's like Björk. She just makes records that nobody listens to now; same with Tom Waits – it's just a load of noise.'

Yet one of the reasons I wanted to talk to you is that you're a band of so many schisms. You're like a box of schisms.

(Laughs) 'There are a lot of schisms.'

There was a great article by John Niven recently in which you said you don't want to be defined by the past and yet . . . (Wire begins to laugh) You know!? That's the currency of the band, isn't it? Unasked for but, blimey, there's some history there.

'We don't want to be defined by the past but we go on about Richey at every gig!'

You just won't shut up about him, will you!?

'I know!'

Manic Street Preachers – a schizophrenic dichotomy; alienating and galvanising in equal measure. Influences worn proudly, self-acknowledged hypocrites, cultural magpies, damaged idealists, liberal hardliners, collaborative outcasts, global localists, cerebral reactionaries, pragmatic visionaries, self-defeating saboteurs.

While the shaded areas of the Manics' career Venn diagram are rendered in Technicolor, the outer reaches are cold and desolate indeed.

Bitter-sweetness pervades.

Wire speaks of having 'a Bill Drummond moment' before the release of *Journal for Plague Lovers*,* wanting to bury the tapes in the ground.

This is not the straightforward trajectory of a band focused solely on commercial success, their ambitions have always lain elsewhere.

Wire recalls the band working on a cover of 'Fight the Power' by Public Enemy,** the four teenage Manics in the front room of James's parents' house:

---

* *Journal for Plague Lovers* is Manic Street Preachers' ninth studio album, released in 2009.
All lyrics on the album were written by Richey Edwards:

'All thirteen songs on the new record feature lyrics left to us by Richey. The brilliance and intelligence of the lyrics dictated that we had to finally use them. The use of language is stunning and topics include *The Grande Odalisque* by Ingres, Marlon Brando, Giant Haystacks, celebrity, consumerism and dysmorphia, all reiterating the genius and intellect of Richard James Edwards.'

– Manic Street Preachers website, March 2009

** Public Enemy are an American hip hop group who formed in New York in 1982. In 'Fight the Power', rappers Chuck D and Flavor Flav spell out the need to fight abuses of power over a bed of layered and looped samples, a sound pioneered by the band and production team The Bomb Squad.
'Repeat (Stars And Stripes)' on the Manics' debut album, *Generation Terrorists*, was

'We wanted to make a defining cover version and, listening back to it, it's actually really minimal and interesting because there are no chords as such . . . this would have been 88/89.'

Globally defining, you sense; their sights having already been set beyond Blackwood, Wales, Europe, off any extant map towards legend – promising to sell 16 million copies of their debut album *Generation Terrorists* and then split up in an early interview, espousing a world view that brooked no distinction between high and low culture; unswerving in their quest to exist apart at the heart of the charts and public consciousness – slash and burn polemics married to indelible, grappling-iron melodies.*

There's a quote by Antonio Gaudí which the Manics deployed on the sleeve of 'A Design for Life', which may crystallise the ideas behind the band's evolution around the time of *The Holy Bible* and their first collaboration with Jenny Saville:

'The creation continues incessantly through the media of man. But man does not create . . . he discovers. Those who look to the laws of nature for support for their new works collaborate with the creator. Copiers

---

produced by The Bomb Squad and the lyrical vitriol, social conscience and use of samples in their songs has been a feature throughout their career and often inspired journalists to pun on these apparent aberrations – 'It Takes a Nation of Millions to Hold Us, Bach' one such travesty.

*   'Our first album was an attempt to find answers from Public Enemy, Guns N' Roses, McCarthy and The Clash . . . I don't think we're original but I think we're unique.'
– James Dean Bradfield, Mojo, December 1996

do not collaborate. Because of this, originality consists in returning to the origin.'*

• • • • •

When I met with Jenny, she spoke about her first conversation with Richey.
What is your memory of the first collaboration with Jenny?
She remembers Richey faxing through the lyrics to '4st 7lb'
– was he in charge of that?

'I remember the day vividly because we both bought the *Independent on Sunday* and in the magazine was a special on Jenny Saville – the first time we'd been exposed to her – and we both phoned each other up and said, "Those paintings are amazing." It was a sort of psychic thing that me and him had.
I remember the image that we all looked at and thought, "Wouldn't it be brilliant?"'

---

* 'Antonio Gaudí (1853–1926) was a Spanish architect and designer.
Inspired by the Pre-Raphaelite and Arts & Crafts movements, Gaudí became a leading exponent of Catalan Modernismo – steeped in the landscape, his native Catalonia inspired many of the organic forms for which his work is known.

The deployment of quotes by Nicky Wire on Manic Street Preachers' record sleeves, merchandise and set lists is a recurrent and distinct feature of their process, a way of focusing the message and mind-set for both the audience and band themselves.
I remember following a t-shirt bearing the lines 'Life can only be understood backwards; but it must be lived forwards – Soren Kierkegaard', to a concert at the Brighton Dome.

The quotations by Taylor Parkes, Richard Thompson and Sylvia Plath which bookend this chapter are a nod to this tradition.

The *Journal for Plague Lovers* set list to The Roundhouse gig of 30 May 2009 is grounded by Jenny Saville:

'The way women were depicted didn't feel like mine; too cute. I wasn't interested in admired or idealised beauty.'

I do remember Richey had a phone call with her and said how brilliant she was because she was giving it to us for free as well – which she's done with both albums, which is amazing.

I mean, with *Journal for Plague Lovers*, she offered to paint us a brand new painting!'

Did she?

'Yeah! I felt like saying, "Well, if we can have it . . .

"'I tell you what, we'll put it on the back. We've got our heart set on the other one but if you want to paint us something new for the back, that'd be grand . . . if you're not busy. (Laughter)

"'Could you bring it down!?"
She was amazing to work with on *Journal* as well. I showed her the picture via email and then she came back with another suggestion of a blond boy, but I just thought the other one echoed Richey; and then she offered to paint something completely new and said, "You can have it for nothing."
I just remember being in Rockfield and thinking, "Right, we're working with Steve Albini, Jenny Saville's a part of our heritage." Jeremy Deller had just won the Turner Prize and he did a video for us and an exhibition and I thought, "If all that were attached to a band like Radiohead that'd elevate them even further . . ." but, with us, you know, some amazing things have happened but all that's slightly undervalued really because, I guess, going back to what I was saying to you about the considerations of being an artist; being deeply sarcastic and working-class to the core has probably worked against us in those terms.

The dichotomy of being aware but humble, yet driven to go out and shout, *"Look at this! No one else is doing this! Come on ... but don't make a fuss ... but, then again, don't forget about it because we reserve the right to bang on about it until someone notices ... but only a bit."* (Laughter)

'Yeah! Being Welsh, I do think that's what comes out in us. I think it's a Welsh thing ... (ponders a while) maybe not; I'd say West Wales is slightly more bohemian but I think, generally, in South Wales we're very much like that. That romanticism – like when we left, as a people, you know? We never made a big deal of it.

There are no parades in America despite Pittsburgh being full of Welsh people who dug all the mines. New South Wales is the biggest state in Australia. The Prime Minister of Australia is Welsh; we just don't make a show of it. It's not a lack of pride, it's just a deep-rooted pathos.'

That pathos runs deep; deepest, perhaps, through the disappearance of Richey Edwards and the band's subsequent decision to continue as a three-piece.

Richey had written three-quarters of the lyrics for *The Holy Bible*, the last album he worked on – a musical return to the darker, formative influences of Wire, Siouxsie and the Banshees, Magazine and Joy Division; lyrically laden with images of suffering, nihilism, regret and death.

If Orwell's picture of the future consisted of a boot stamping on a human face, forever, moments of *The Holy Bible* were a sonic equivalent; astonishing, brilliant, troubled and brooding. The band toured the record exhaustively around the UK and Europe and were scheduled to take it to America when Richey vanished.

In the months that followed as the remaining Manics attempted to come to terms with the loss they found themselves faced with what to do next – the prospect of beginning again and the question of whether they could.

The song 'A Design for Life' was the result.

Nicky Wire

'That song really was crucial in helping us to stay together as a band. We hadn't written a thing since Richey disappeared. It was originally written as a two-page poem. One side was called "The Pure Motive" and the other side "A Design for Life". I gave the whole thing to James and he cherry-picked the bits he thought would work best. Pretty quickly he had an epiphany. He called me up saying, "It's Ennio Morricone, R.E.M. and Phil Spector."

It was the first thing that clicked after Richey disappeared. On the face of it we were really stoic and Manics-esque, thinking we'd just plough on, but in reality we weren't doing anything. Those lyrics were the first thing that poured out that I thought were good enough to give to James.

We went into the place we recorded *The Holy Bible* – this shitty studio in Cardiff – and the three of us played it together and it just fell together so naturally. James already had the whole thing worked out in his head, he was singing the string parts. He knew he wanted a cinematic, broad sweep to the whole thing.

The song was definitely inspired by what seemed to me at the time as a flippancy, what I perceived as the middle classes trying to hijack working-class culture. That was typified by "Girls and Boys", the greyhound image on the *Parklife* cover.* It was me trying to say, "This is the truth".'

---

* *Parklife* was a 1994 album by the band Blur.

205

James Dean Bradfield

'I remember being given the two lyrics by Nick. We'd come to a total standstill since Richey had disappeared. There was a long period of shock where we just couldn't do a thing. I just really needed something to occupy me. Deep down I wanted to know what it was like to write a song as a three-piece. That was the most daunting task facing us at that point – how would it work? I remember being incredibly nervous when the first proper set of Nick's lyrics arrived five months after Richey disappeared. I didn't actually start writing anything for a few days after they came, which is strange for me as I usually start pretty much the second I've torn open the envelope.

I remember atomising the two lyrics. It felt like there was a thread running through them both; they shared the same anger and what I thought at the time was the same sarcasm. They both had truly amazing lines. From the time I organised the whole lot into one lyric, I think it was one of the quickest tunes I've ever written – it came fully formed in just ten minutes. By the time I called Nick, I was pretty sure I was onto something brilliant. Up to that point, we were genuinely in limbo. That song was a door opening for us, showing us a way out.

The most bizarre part of the experience, apart from Richey being missing, was having people coming up to me in the street saying, "I love that song, it's amazing, what a great first single." That happened a lot, people saying they knew nothing about us. People were incredulous when we said we'd been going for years, they all thought we were some new upstart Britpop band. That was really, really strange.'

Nicky Wire

'We got to the Brit Awards and I remember thinking, for once, "This is the fulfilment of everything," because Richey was still so much on the record as well. I think it's our best record. I don't know if it's my favourite, probably because I've played it too much – that mixture of underground and overground, you can only do it once in your life, you know? Coming from *The Holy Bible* and going into something bigger . . .'*

Both 'A Design for Life' and its parent album *Everything Must Go* peaked at number two in the UK charts. Three other singles from the record reached the UK Top 10. *Everything Must Go* remains the band's most commercially successful LP to date.

• • • • •

You used a number of Richey's lyrics on *Everything Must Go.*** Was *Journal for Plague Lovers* put together from a different set of writing that he left behind?

'No. It was all from the same source, the difference was that he had heard "Kevin Carter", "Small Black Flowers" . . . "Small Black Flowers" was the last session we did with Richey. It was at House in the Woods studio just before he disappeared. We did "No

---

*This section of text was kindly donated to me by Robin Turner, writer and friend of the Manics, and was first published in the Best British Songs edition of *Q* magazine, April 2011.

** *Everything Must Go* is Manic Street Preachers' fourth studio album, released in 1996.

Surface All Feeling", "Small Black Flowers That Grow in the Sky"; James actually played him some of "Kevin Carter" – but I can't remember if that applies to "Elvis Impersonator" or "Girl Who Wanted to Be God". I don't know if James had started work on them, see, because Richey was always giving us lyrics.'

Do you write and send things to James in the same way now?

'The basic premise hasn't changed since me and James wrote our first song at the age of fifteen. The main thing has always been that initial spark of a lyric.'

Has your recent work as a songwriter changed the way you write?

'As a rule, my songs come very simply and naturally and that's all down to my solo album which gave me the confidence to pick up an acoustic guitar; and that's helped me write more straightforward lyrics, undoubtedly. I can shave the edges off when I'm writing songs myself; the flow of a vocal, it's definitely helped. Obviously, you can always be wilfully awkward but that's something I've always tried not to do because Richey was . . . (laughs) he wasn't awkward by choice, it was just that he was trying to cram so much in.'

He'd give you an essay as opposed to a précis.

'Yes, but then there's so many odd bits; when me and him sat together writing "La Tristesse Durera" in the studio – which was my lyric and title – he added a lot of good stuff to it as well and I guess that breaks loads of rules because it's pretty accessible. You know, we sat down and wrote together a lot. Those are the bits I wish I could remember more.

I always remember us sitting at the desk in my room doing "Motorcycle Emptiness", and there's quite a lot of me on "Faster" but the key lines are definitely Richey's. I still think it's the one time we can look at ourselves and say we've been truly unique. I do. I think there's never been a record like it before or after – the bravado in the lyric is amazing really: "I am stronger than Mensa, Miller and Mailer." The bravado to say that is so obviously Richey. "I know I believe in nothing but at least it's my nothing" is just a brilliant advertising line.'

A pure manifesto.

'Yes. A manifesto of the self.
I might be doing a memoir so I've been going through all my archives and I was thinking I could use all that stuff – letters from me and Richey and everyone but it's just . . . too much! (Laughs)
I mean, I had a brilliant childhood, I loved it! I loved my mum and dad. I don't know where this rage comes from. Speaking for myself I think it was because they gave me such an environment just to learn; there was a sense of anarchy but not in a bohemian sense because there was discipline. We were imbued with a slightly naive and tragic romantic version of rock and roll because everyone we were drawn to had a completely destructive side. (He looks towards the bust of Aneurin Bevan which sits on top of the mixing desk) That's changed now because I think we've formed into something more social and political, but I look back now and every time we wrote a letter to each other there was a picture of Béatrice Dalle or William Burroughs or Jack Kerouac or Ian Curtis, you know? It is imbued with something we wanted to be; we were only fifteen!'

Jenny spoke about a mind-set of not having moved far from drawing in her bedroom as a child.

> 'The bedroom boy aspect is something you could almost say has held us back but we still exist there, absolutely.* If there were a Thought Police we'd be lifers because the amount of insanity that we still have to filter between the three of us . . . you know, some of it just deeply wrong, but that is what being trusting friends is all about; it's through that we get to a coherent structure that we think is important.
>
> There's a brilliant piece in Dorian Lynskey's new book, *33 Revolutions Per Minute*, the history of protest songs and for some bizarre reason he chose "Of Walking Abortion" because he thinks of it as "the protest song which eats itself". He says it's different from all other protest songs because, while everyone else has a world view that humanity can end up doing good, *The Holy Bible* is written around the idea that humanity is predominantly evil . . . and I think you can apply that to the band sometimes. Unless we go through a process of serious argument . . . utterly honest to the point of not being very tasteful at times. You can see it in our interviews at the start; that's why we sometimes came across as so tacky and blunt. We were just talking like we did in our bedrooms to interviewers. I don't feel burnt by that, I feel it was our own fault, but the cartoon character element of that, in the beginning, was us being in our bedrooms. We didn't change at all.'

Is that a physical space where you still work, as well as a psychological one?

---

* It's interesting to note that the artist Jeremy Deller, another Manics collaborator, lived at home into his thirties – another bedroom boy.

'I still think the prime movers for me are hotels and my bedroom back home – being surrounded by stuff, my millions of photos – and the TV, which is vitally important to trigger my imagination.

Stationery is almost an aphrodisiac; like Kubrick, I am obsessed. I've got a massive collection of hotel stationery because I love the feeling of those individual sheets of paper and I have a lot of ideas on planes because I always think I'm near to death. "You Stole the Sun from My Heart" was totally conceived on a plane. Travel is important . . . (Pauses) Going back to Radiohead, one thing I do share with Thom Yorke, undoubtedly, is that incessant chatter. More than James or Sean, my head is always filled – not just with ideas but chart positions, sales, things to do. It's very rare I can stop apart from being in a hotel room. I find my mind de-cluttered there and a lot gets written – although almost everything is finished at home.'

Do you need a completely different set-up to write an album as accessible and melodic as *Send Away the Tigers* as opposed to the darker *Holy Bibles* and *Journals*?

'It's utterly different. I think there are three mind-sets; there are the two you've mentioned and then there's something in the middle like "Motorcycle Emptiness" when we've tried to do both. It's a pretty mad idea to write a six-minute song with a three-minute guitar solo about the decay of youth and civilisation; and the same with "Tolerate"*. I'm so proud of "Tolerate" as a lyric.'

---

* 'If You Tolerate This Your Children Will Be Next' was a Manic Street Preachers single of 1998 inspired by the Spanish Civil War – specifically the writings of George Orwell and accounts of Welsh volunteers who fought in the International Brigades against Franco's fascists between 1936 and 1939.

'The Everlasting' too, perhaps?

> 'Yeah. I love that first line: "The gap that grows be-
> tween our lives / the gap our parents never had." The
> idea that, in the old days, you didn't have time . . . but
> there is a syntax I've learnt; it'd be wrong to call them
> tricks but there are certain lyrical conceits which work
> in music – that work in terms of being pop. Certain
> rhymes. Certain ideas, you know? The idea of home
> will always work. Soul.'

• • • • •

While Wire has always been band propagandist-in-chief,
capable of firing off a dozen slanderous missives before
breakfast, James Dean Bradfield is more restrained. He con-
siders each question I ask through a haze of cigarette smoke
and, where Wire was quick and reactionary, with him there
are long pauses. The two deploy their minds in quite different ways and, as such, complement each other – the band's
division of labour having been marked from the earliest days:

Richey & Wire the sloganeers.

Sean & James the engineers.

The former writing the headlines, the latter oiling the presses. The former's agenda focusing more on a Pulitzer Prize than learning to play their instruments, the latter honed their craft.

ROCK 'N' ROLL IS OUR EPIPHANY: CULTURE,
ALIENATION, BOREDOM & DESPAIR*

LIBRARIES GAVE US POWER / THEN WORK
CAME AND MADE US FREE**

I KNOW I BELIEVE IN NOTHING BUT
IT IS MY NOTHING***

Until recent times James was the main tunesmith, writing music around the lyrics he was given, turning sprawling diktats into something for radio and, more than that, anthems for a generation – songs of mass communication.

I tell him about Wire's thoughts on the band's bedroom boy bunker mentality and he grins.

'You're more interested in ley lines, yeah?'

Several people I've interviewed have spoken about workspace and environment being key to their work. You've built a den here at Faster, and I remember demos for *Everything Must Go* labelled 'Nick's House, 96'.

Are there still specific places where you write?

----

* 'Little Baby Nothing', Manic Street Preachers (Colombia Records, 1992).

** 'A Design For Life', Manic Street Preachers (Colombia Records, 1996).

*** 'Faster', Manic Street Preachers (Colombia Records, 1994).

'I think it changes in periods of your life, you know? The places that I write now . . . I have a flat in Cardiff – because for years I was living in London, I always had a small flat in Cardiff and . . . – I'm not quite sure if I'm an atheist or an agnostic – but for somebody that has no connection to the spiritual or religious world I'm very, very superstitious. I think there was a point before *Send Away the Tigers* when I was trying to write some tunes and nothing was working and then, for some reason, I was in a corner of my Cardiff flat and the guitar was propped up against the wall and an idea came into my head and it was a really, really good idea – something that went on to be part of the album in an indelible sense – and it really kicked me off; and it's pathetic but it's that spot; I've still got the flat and it's that spot that I still return to write. I write there.

Now, that's a very precise answer to the question but there is a spot in the flat where I actually sit against the wall and write and there used to be a spot here in this studio, at the front; and I'd been through a period of not being able to write anything – what you might cornily call "writer's block" in terms of being able to write a tune – and I still return to that spot, which is just under the front window upstairs. So they're the two places mostly that I write because I've had really incredible luck in those places, previously, but before that it was spots in my parents' house and a rehearsal space in Cardiff called Sound Space which has now been knocked down. There was always a spot there where I always used to go to write.

So, like I said, for somebody who has no religious beliefs or connection to the spiritual world . . .'

You have your own ley line.

'Yes, it is a bit. I remember Ian McCulloch of Echo
& The Bunnymen talking about ley lines and something called The Crystal Day in Liverpool where the
tour itself was a series of events and the shape of the
tour was a rabbit's head or something, you know* . . .
and another thing that affected me when I was young
actually was that I went to read a guitar book in Blackwood library, it was called *The Book Of The Guitar*, or
something, and it was talking about guitarists and how
they approach it and stuff. I was about sixteen years
old and there was a quote in there, Keith Richards said
the first spot he found where the guitar made sense to
him, when he was young, was at the top of his parents'
staircase where the echo was just right and he felt as
if the world was still, just in that moment. It just made
sense that you had to isolate yourself from "the world
outside" et cetera and you had to find that spot to
actually be true to the idea that might come to you. I
don't know why but there you go.'

We were talking about 'Faster' earlier – the way it was written.

'One of the most important factors about "Faster" is
that Nick came up with the title, "Faster". And that's

---

* 'Bill Drummond (manager of the group) encouraged the Bunnymen's self-
mythologising. They revelled in majestic follies such as The Crystal Day, on
12 May, 1984, when fans joined the band in a 24-hour 'happening' in Liverpool: apart from a choir recital in the Cathedral, and a gig in the city's most
exclusive concert hall, participants had to eat at the group's favourite café,
Brian's Diner, take the Mersey Ferry, and attempt a mass bicycle ride in the
streets, along a route that Bill had mapped in the shape of Echo, who was now
re-cast as a mystical Rabbit God. Another time, bored with tour routine, he
planned an itinerary for the boys that took them from New York to Iceland,
from the Outer Hebrides to the Albert Hall. He joked they were following a
global ley line that ran through Mathew Street, and was widely believed.'
– Paul Du Noyer, *Mojo*, July 1997

215

such an amazing springboard for ideas, I think, just that title. Titles always kick me off completely. It's never changed; whether it's been Richey's lyrics on *The Holy Bible* or "Motorcycle Emptiness", which was Nick and Richey together, 50/50, or whether it was "Design For Life", which was just Nick on his own; I've always approached a lyric in exactly the same sense, which is that I decode it first – and there's an anticipation and build-up because Nick or Richey would tell me on the phone or they'd tell me face to face, they'd tell me the title: "Motorcycle Emptiness", "Design For Life", "Faster", "Archives of Pain"; and I'd start imagining how the lyric might look; the shape of it, just on the page; the syntax or whatever. The build-up to it is almost like a boxing match or a rugby match. I feel the walk-up and then it arrives – usually through the post, which is great because it comes usually with lots of collage on the inside and all that . . . and then I sit down with it, after all that build-up – which is quite important to me – I sit down and I decode it, because obviously I'm singing somebody else's words so I always feel the need to catch up with the shortfall of understanding, I suppose . . . and then, once I've decoded the lyric to my level of intelligence (laughs), then I just start writing. I pick up the guitar and I just look at it, I just look at the piece of paper in front of me – and it's got to be at the right height and it's got to be at the right time of day and it's got to feel right and that's nearly always the same for me. I'd say that, in our history, ten per cent of the time it's been different. Ninety per cent of the time, that's my experience.

I've just got a real deep-seated fear of letting the music take control. I've got a deep-seated fear of it just being for the music's sake.'

Because you want it to be a conduit for the words?

'Yeah. I dunno, we set up with so many rules and dic-
tums at the start that I find it hard to go outside of
that box, I suppose; I just feel that, if there's a slight
sense that a tune's come first – which it has a couple of
times – then there's a slight sense of betrayal of what we
started out trying to do.'

Because the guiding principles for each tune are in the lyrics.

'Yes. I mean, we've done some instrumental pieces
where obviously it doesn't matter, but even then I've
written to a title, whether it be "Horses Under Starlight"
or . . . um . . .'

'The Vorticists'?

'"The Vorticists"! That's the one. Yeah, that's the one,
so even then the title is really guiding me but I suppose
there was this thing at the start where we felt, in the late
eighties and early nineties – late eighties especially – we
felt as if there was just a lot of music for music's sake.
No loaded gesture! (Laughs) We needed more loaded
gestures . . . and even though I listen to stuff like that
for inspirational purposes and I actually get off on it I
don't want to be part of it somehow; but it would be
interesting to see how we'd turn out if we did let the
music be the birther. On the next record I'm interested
in trying that kinda thing out.'

I was talking to Wire about the different approaches the band
take to melodic pop music and being led by wanting to connect on the radio as opposed to *The Holy Bible* or *Journal for
Plague Lovers*, which take no prisoners. Does that make sense?

'Yes, it does make sense. But even with something like "Archives of Pain", I still have the basic rule that if I go to bed after writing a tune I want to remember the tune in the morning without recording it. I read a quote by Paul McCartney when I was young, he said, *"I could usually tell if something was good when, if I wrote something, I could remember it the next day."* So, yeah, you might not be looking to get the A-list at Radio 1 with "Archives of Pain" but you still want it to stick.
With "Archives", I felt there was a disjointed nature, something there which an audience might not expect because it was saying, "Yeah, we are on the libertarian side of things and we come from a hotbed of what you might call traditional British socialism in the valleys et cetera but do not be mistaken, we're not tokenistic and wet when it comes to retribution and justice."'

Because the left goes right the way around.

'Yes. There's a great tradition of authoritarianism in leftist politics, you know, and it was just saying that most people, whether they come from a socialist background in the sense of our parents' generation or not, want retribution when harm occurs against them. It's not a right-wing point of view . . . and I felt that our audience – if Richey were asked, "What is this lyric about?" – the audience would be jarred by the answer.'

A defence of capital punishment.

'It is, yes. In the right circumstance.
I think his argument was that people, the Tory Government, didn't give a fuck about what happened to people within a community when their lives were marred by somebody who had no sense of community whatsoever.

218

The lyric was saying, "It's an isolated gesture, your justice, sometimes, when ordinary people's lives were being absolutely destroyed by people who had no values" – so I could sense that disconnect, perhaps, and straight away when I was writing the tune I felt as if I was slightly walking out of time when I was writing it; I felt as if he was reaching for the outer margins of what people were expecting from us – so that hit me off my stride and therefore, I think, it affected the music (sings the opening riff), it's loping towards some kind of truth and then, at the end, it unleashes its righteous fury. Now, if that sounds like "method tune writing" or if that sounds stupidly pompous and suggests I've internalised something just for the sake of it, that's how it made me feel at that point. But, then again, it's strange: I've been writing with the same lyricists all my life and they've made me feel a million different things.'

• • • • •

Looking back through my notes now I see I've written 'a plurality of convictions / Christopher Hitchens-like', and I think the comparison holds; the aspect of foreign correspondents, gimlet-eyed left-wingers pouncing on the lazy-minded, and bugger the party line, with a forthright defence of war, or Nixon, or *Strictly Come Dancing*.
Pity the poor saps, sloping into shot with a wonky grin for a handshake who find themselves blindsided – chewed-up and spat out with a bloody nose and sad, kicked-puppy eyes.

Wire spoke to me about the gig the band played in Havana in 2001. Fidel Castro★ was in the audience, it was to be the

---

★ In 2001, Manic Street Preachers played a gig at the Karl Marx Theatre in Havana, apex of a plan doubtless hatched in a Blackwood bedroom. A writer, unnamed, 'did a piece on us when we went to Cuba and it was so fucking drippy and liberal . . .' he trails off, deflated.

> 'The reason I sometimes watch Fox News is because I get bogged down in liberalism, I really do . . . and I've spent half my life being a communist, in my head, if you know what I mean, yet there's a part of me that just cannot take that much soft-hearted liberalism. It's not that I agree with the other side, even. I just can't take it. I mean, Obama's first month in power was a fucking disaster; his staff were being done for tax; he didn't even sign the inauguration properly – imagine if Bush had done that! He would have been pilloried as a complete fuckwit who couldn't even sign the inauguration. I can't ignore shit like that.
> For the past two years I have actually scarred myself thinking, you know, if me and Richey were saying now what we did in 1990 we'd be on Sky News every day! There must be a gigantic gap in the culture if we – me in particular – are still a voice . . .' and he trails off again, but this time with a grin.

* * * * *

National Treasures: The Complete Singles was released in October 2011 and lodged straight in the Top 10, spurred by a swarm of ecstatic reviews. The public clearly aren't bored of

---

Cuba – the first time a western rock band had performed in the country. Fidel Castro attended and met with the band in their dressing room before the concert. Wire warned him that the gig would be loud and Castro replied through a translator, 'It cannot be louder than war, can it?'

either Manic Street Preachers or the tunes they've written in their twenty-year career – many of which they still play live.

I ask James about the way the band approach their back catalogue:

You still play the key parts of the solo to 'Motorcycle Emptiness' as they sound on *Generation Terrorists*; you still seem thrilled by that composed piece.

> 'I think I'm more thrilled by the audience's reaction to it sometimes, to be honest, because I've played it so many times.'

Do you feel bound to keep it the same?

> 'I feel the need to put the signature motifs in and then I can drift off. I used to hate it when I'd been waiting to hear a song by a band live that I'd never heard live – say I'd go and see The Waterboys and want to hear something like "Rags". Perfectly. I hated it when people reinterpreted the songs! I couldn't fucking deal with it!' (Laughter)

It's in waltz time!? Great.

> 'We're guilty of doing it; we did it to "Faster" once and it just didn't work. You've come along to hear that song and . . . Simple Minds have done it to a certain degree – early Simple Minds is holy sacred ground up, for me; until *Sons and Fascination* – and I've seen Simple Minds play some of those songs since and it just breaks my heart.
> So, at the bottom of that question is that, if something is like a Roman candle exploding in your mind when

something touches you musically – I mean really, really connects with you – when you go and see it you don't want it reinterpreted. You want to hear snatches of what originally caught you and then you can drift off a bit . . . but I do feel the need to represent what and why people initially liked us.'

I was talking to Nick about how the band make seemingly left-field counter-intuitive decisions but are fearful of being seen as too indulgent or calling themselves artists or artistic. You're musicians making records for an audience, he said.

'I think, the way the culture is going these days, it's very hard to be in a band and think of yourself as an artist. When I think of what an artist is I think of Mishima,* when he wrote his tetralogy, or Goya, somebody like that who dedicated themselves to series of paintings or writings . . . but, you know, the words "art" and "artist" are very different things! (Laughs) They really, really are . . . I just know that it's something different, being in a band.

I've got a friend who I grew up with who's an actor, and every day is a journey towards finding out whether he can still do the job, because it's just him on his own, but with us, if one of us is at a low ebb then the other one is ready to come up with an idea – there's a collective thing, this communal spirit about being in a band if you are all equal participants in it. The only thing that comes close to it really is an ensemble piece in theatre

---

* Yukio Mishima was the pen name of Kimitake Hiraoka (1925–1970), a Japanese author, poet, playwright, actor and film director, who committed ritual suicide by seppuku after a failed coup d'état. Nominated three times for the Nobel Prize in Literature.

or sport, you know? It's really strange . . . when you think you're fucked somebody comes up with something to save the day; whereas, when you're on your own doing something, if you're fucked you're fucked – you've just got to go away and find your inspiration in a panelled room with a desk in St Petersburg like Pete Doherty said . . .'*

Do you feel compelled to work every day?

'No. If I come here I feel compelled to do something, but I shouldn't have to break for dinner and I shouldn't go home if I don't want to. The hours should be free to do what the hell you want with it and hunger is not something you should really care about. Life outside, whatever that be, family – people I love more than anything – you've got to try to block that out completely . . . it's a purely selfish thing. The hours should be absolutely free and I do believe that, once you go past midnight, there are ghosts and you've just got to try and catch them and, you know, I don't believe that when I say it but I absolutely *feel* that it's true. When I hear myself say it I think, "What a pile of fucking wank," but I do completely believe it because, if you've found the right place, beyond twelve o'clock . . . post-midnight in a place where I love working, there's an

---

*   This quote derives from an interview with Pete Doherty and Carl Barat, bandmates and founding members of The Libertines, speaking at a point of crisis – 'Despite it all, Carl and Peter are still bound together. When asked what they hope for the future their answers are strikingly similar. Pete says he'd like, "A desk, a desk of my own, and a room of my own . . . maybe in St Petersburg." Carl alludes to Ernest Hemingway and says he'd like, "A desk in a well-lighted room."

– *Mojo*, July 2004

inevitability about being able to do something; that's what we've found here. It's been amazing.'

* * * * *

'I want to taste and glory in each day, and never be afraid to experience pain; and never shut myself up in a numb core of non-feeling, or stop questioning and criticising life and take the easy way out. To learn and think: to think and live; to live and learn: this always, with new insight, new understanding, and new love.'*

– Sylvia Plath

---

* *The Unabridged Journals of Sylvia Plath*, Ed. Karen V. Kukil (Anchor Books, 2000).

1. MOTORCYCLE EMPTINESS
2. YOUR LOVE ALONE IS NOT ENOUGH
3. NO SURFACE ALL FEELING
4. YOU LOVE US
5. TSUNAMI
6. LA TRISTESSA
7. FASTER
8. IF YOU TOLERATE THIS
9. LITTLE BABY NOTHING
10. AUSTRALIA
11. YOU STOLE THE SUN???
12. OCEAN SPRAY
13. STOP IN THE NAME OF MOTOWN JUNK
14. EVERYTHING MUST GO
15. DESIGN FOR LIFE

"THE WAY WOMEN WERE DIPICTED DIDN'T FEEL LIKE MINE; TOO CUTE. I WASN'T
INTERESTED IN ADMIRED OR IDEALISED BEAUTY" JENNY SAVILLE.

DAME JUDI DENCH, CH, DBE, FRSA (1934–) is a Yorkshire-born stage, film and television actor renowned for her work with The Old Vic Company, The National Theatre, RSC and her central role as 'M' in the James Bond film series. The recipient of an Oscar, eleven BAFTAs and seven Laurence Olivier Awards, she is one of the most critically recognised actors of all time.

DAME JUDI DENCH

Wasp Green, Surrey
May 2010–September 2011

I'm sitting with Judi Dench in her kitchen. I realise that's a bit of a leap from sitting with the Manics but there it is, I'll explain in a page or two – until then you'll just have to trust that there's logic at work and good reason for it.

I'm sitting with Judi Dench in her kitchen and she's telling me stories. She's very good and does all the voices. In this story she's in the bath, it's late and the water is chilly. She'd like to get out of the bath but she can't:

> 'It happened on *Amy's View*; I was having such diffi-
> culty with the lines that I asked Richard Eyre to
> release me from the play because I was so frightened I
> wouldn't ever learn them. I came home in such a state
> and Michael* said, "Just run a bath. Go up, get into the

---

* Michael Williams (1935–2001). English actor and Judi's husband for thirty years. They met in the early sixties while both at the RSC – with whom Williams worked for fourteen years – appearing frequently on film, television and radio.
I first became aware of his work listening to Radio 4's Sherlock Holmes productions in which he played Doctor Watson.

bath and decide to learn three pages. You do not get out of the bath until you've learnt the three pages."
Of course the bath starts to get cold; that doesn't half sharpen you up!
But that is good and it's nearly always at night, of course, and that's very good – just before you go to sleep.
The tenser you get, the more worried, the less receptive you are.'

I ask what made *Amy's View* so difficult and she sighs.

'Well, David Hare is always difficult. Always.
Gambon* said to me at the time, "Oh, when I did *Skylight* somebody was sitting in the front row with a prompt copy." I said, "That's no comfort to me at all, Michael."
He's always difficult to learn. *The Breath of Life* was difficult to learn. Once you've learnt it, it's absolutely wonderful but there's something about the construction of it that's hard; it's like Oscar Wilde, the grammar so

---

Apparently he, like Judi, was quite small:
How tall are you?
'Not tall. I'm five foot one and three-quarters (laughter) and Michael wasn't much taller.
Michael and I once met Martin Scorsese and, afterwards, said, "Oh wouldn't it be wonderful to be directed by him!? He's so much smaller than we are!"'

* Sir Michael Gambon, CBE (1940–). Irish-born actor, trained at RADA, who made his professional stage debut in a 1962 Dublin production of *Othello*. He went on to audition for Laurence Olivier at the new National Theatre Company, going on to play in productions at the National and Old Vic for three years before moving to the Birmingham Rep.
A bastion of British theatre, huge in voice and stature, Gambon is strongly associated with the plays of Shakespeare and Beckett and, more recently, Albus Dumbledore in the *Harry Potter* films.

perfectly constructed, but we don't do that any more when we're speaking in everyday life . . . I had a line in *The Importance of Being Earnest* when I was at The Vic,* this must be 1959, and I couldn't learn it. I could not learn it at all. I have subsequently never forgotten it and it is this:

"It is always painful to part from people whom one has known for a very brief space of time. The absence of old friends one can endure with equanimity. But even a momentary separation from one to whom one has just been introduced is almost unbearable."

I've never forgotten it.'

Before *Amy's View* you could learn lines just like that?

'Michael once said to me, "It's a form of osmosis with you, learning lines," because he would always come home and sit in the kitchen and learn lines but I never did that, ever. Ever, ever, ever. Never.'

You never sat in the kitchen to learn?

'I wouldn't be learning at all. I'd be going about doing my stuff because I had a facility for being able to some-how know it on the hoof.'

Really?

---

* Established in 1818 as the Royal Coburg Theatre, The Old Vic theatre sits south-east of Waterloo Station in London.
The repertory company based there in the early sixties formed the core of the National Theatre of Great Britain upon its formation – the National Theatre remaining at The Old Vic until new premises were built on the South Bank, opening in 1976. The theatre underwent complete refurbishment in 1985 and 2003 – the rooms where Judi rehearsed in the late fifties, for example, are gone.

'Yes. But David Hare is very difficult, for me . . . Shakespeare is very easy because of the rhythm. Very easy indeed. I could do the whole of *Twelfth Night* for you now, just now, everybody's parts, and *The Dream* . . . partly because I've done the plays so many times but, you know, some are more difficult than others . . .'

Outside, wisteria is blooming and tapping on the window while birds scoot on the pond – although I suspect it may be a moat. Inside, Radio 4 murmurs and we drink tea.
There's a stillness, although that might have something to do with Judi's voice and presence; the way she fixes you with her bright blue eyes and speaks with such life.
She's small with white puckish hair – so interested it's re-markable; like an ageless precocious child, ebullient and funny; Björkish – the sort who make their own weather.*

'You must have a sense of irony, Daniel, a sense of absurdity. That's why I love actors so much because there's a childlike quality about them. Not child-ish, childlike, because actors are always wanting to learn something. Good actors never think they know it all. Good actors are always trying to find some-thing and always being challenged and, in a way, there is something childlike about that. I don't know how to talk to people who are in what I call grown-up jobs . . .'

---

* I mention Björk to Judi and she relates how she was at the Oscars ceremony where the former came dressed 'in' a swan and laid an egg . . . 'Ridiculous! Quite ridiculous.'
I pointed out that a recently issued stamp depicted her in a somewhat similar Cygnus pose – Judi as a black swan Lady Macbeth. This got short shrift:

'Don't be silly, Daniel. I'm clearly summoning up a demon.'

I wonder for a moment how this book rates as a grown-up endeavour . . . ricocheting round, spurred on by audacity, coffee and the fumes of an overdraft. Childlike absurdity abounds! I'm as surprised as anyone that it's happening and as curious to find out what'll transpire next – which isn't to say there isn't a plan! No, there's definitely a plan, it's just that it's protean and changeable and driven by hunch and whim – so it was that, post-Manics, I decided to investigate the nature of performance: performance and acting as discussed by Bill Drummond and Jenny Saville previously; the difference between performing music and drama; the nature of playing a role and acting, and so I wrote to Dame Judi Dench – because she's a brilliant actor – and asked if I could see her for lunch and ask about it; and she said yes. So last night I slept on a friend's sofa in the Barbican and this morning I was picked up by Dame Judi Dench at a Surrey railway station. And that's how I got here, talking about grown-ups and absurdity and the high-wire mixture of wide-eyed enquiry and deep-seated fear which impels Judi's work:

'Lack of desperation – terrible. Lack of fright, lack of desperation. How do you get through that? I don't know. Sometimes – I've thought about this quite a lot lately – I obviously have a kind of dread of setting anything in stone – you know how everything is so fluid. That's why I don't really like watching my films because, once you've done that, it's in formaldehyde on a shelf; it'll never change. You look at something and you think, "Why the hell did I make that choice?" That's what's so lovely about the theatre, you don't ever set it in stone, it's completely fluid all the time . . . and uncertain.'

Dangerous.

'It is dangerous and you'll think, "I'll try this," and it may not work, you know?'

But then there's tomorrow!

'There's always tomorrow! Tomorrow I might do it in a different way or the audience might signal something to which you respond.'

You have a Tannoy in your dressing room, I understand.

'I do. I'm in touch from the moment the audience start to come in.
It's quite tricky not having a Tannoy, to just walk down and *suddenly* be met with that . . . and you may come in in three-quarters of an hour or you may come in in four minutes but, if you've not had any of that kind of feedback earlier, it seems to me that there's some of the story left out – your story for that evening, I mean – your actual process.
I have to link in because the audience always makes it a different thing.'

When you're onstage you're in character; how are you off-stage?

'When I played Lady Macbeth, people used to say, "Do you carry that part home with you?" Carry the part home with you? I mean, at Stratford I'd be playing Lady Macbeth in the afternoon and Beatrice in *Much Ado* at night so there's no question of carrying it over, no question at all – comes off with the costume, it really does . . . but what people don't realise is that – you know how you go into biology at school one day and there on some tar is a frog, pinned out? That's just exactly how I always feel at the end of a play, and therefore the moment somebody comes in through the door you know within three seconds what they thought of it, whatever they say or don't say, you just know . . . because you're that pinned-out frog.'

Does that strength of feeling start to build during rehearsal?

'During rehearsals I would talk about the play but I wouldn't outside, simply because it dissipates the intensity of the process, for me, when I'm rehearsing.'

What form does that process take? Is it different every time?

'I don't know! I suppose it's the same structure in that you learn the lines and have to hear what everybody's saying and know that some people aren't necessarily speaking the truth – that was a note that Peter Hall* gave me:

'"Don't believe everything that everybody says about you in *Antony and Cleopatra* and, at the same time, don't think that you've got to play the whole of a part in one scene."

---

* Sir Peter Hall, CBE (1930–). English theatre and film director who founded the Royal Shakespeare Company at the age of twenty-nine, serving as artistic director for the next eight years.

'In 1960 the 29-year-old Peter Hall formally took charge at Stratford-upon-Avon and set about turning a star-laden, six-month Shakespeare festival into a monumental, year-round operation built around a permanent company, a London base and contemporary work from home and abroad. Looking back, it is difficult to realise just how radical Hall's dream was at the time; or indeed how much opposition there was to the creation of what became officially known in March 1961 as the Royal Shakespeare Company.'
— *State of the Nation: British Theatre Since 1945*,
Michael Billington (Faber & Faber, 2007)

'Which is the most wonderful note, because you do, you know . . .'

Especially with such iconic parts.

'Yes, it completely overwhelms you, but "Just play an aspect of the person" is a wonderful note.
I remember Harold Prince said to me when I did *Cabaret*, "Don't ever stop using the voice that you speak with in order to use another voice to sing," and that stood me in incredibly good stead because, you know, I know the notes and can keep on the notes, nevertheless, I haven't got a singing voice – my singing voice is the same as my speaking voice, sounds like I've got a cold . . .'

But it is your voice.

'But it is the voice and it is the same person who carries on singing, who speaks and carries on. That was a wonderful note too . . .
(Brightens, excitedly) I don't know what one would say to an opera singer. There's that wonderful bit in *Turandot* where Liù is being tortured and she goes (sings) "Whoa-hoo-hoo-hoooo!" and you want her to scream. I don't want her to make that funny noise, I want to hear a real scream of pain. So that's the difference because they have to sing in a proper way. So that's a kind of opposite.
I saw a wonderful production of *Billy Budd* a week ago today at Glyndebourne that Michael Grandage* had

---

* Michael Grandage, CBE (1962–) is a British theatre producer and director. For ten years, until 2012, he was Artistic Director of the Donmar Warehouse, London. He is currently Artistic Director at the Michael Grandage Company.

done, my God they all acted so well! Not only did they sing it wonderfully but they really acted up a storm; it's lovely when you see that.'

Is the process of film very different to theatre?

'Well, it is very different because it's not necessarily in order and it's up to the editor, really. You never know – well, I don't – good film actors do but I don't – whether a film's going to be any good or not. I would have put money on the fact that *Nine** was going to be absolutely wonderful but it seems that it's been completely ignored, really.'

So much of this is dependent on how a film is marketed and pushed, though, isn't it?

'I don't know. I've no idea. You have more of a feeling with a play in the theatre because you see it in its entirety ... but a film is not like the theatre – (to herself) it's not like the theatre at all, of course – and you don't know how much of you is going to be left on the cutting-room floor ...'

I suppose you've that much less control.

'Oh you do, you don't have any control about it really.'

The Glyndebourne production of *Billy Budd* was his debut opera production.

* *Nine* is a 2009 film directed and produced by Rob Marshall. The screenplay was written by Michael Tolkin and Anthony Minghella, based on Arthur Kopit's book for the musical of the same name, itself suggested by Federico Fellini's semi-autobiographical film *8½*.
Despite a strong cast, chock full of A-list types, the film didn't get great press or reviews upon its release. It was nevertheless nominated for quite a lot of prizes, including four Academy Awards.

Does that cause you to be especially discerning about what you do?

'No, no, you just kind of do it and have to really trust your director. Many directors will go on until they get what they want, and that's wonderful . . . you just hope that you've served it up and they haven't gone home and said, "Well I had to stop at Take 22 because I wasn't getting what I wanted," or "Somehow I'll make it work," or . . . you think of all those kind of things and it's hard; it's very, very hard, I think, to see it as a whole.'*

---

* Between 2010 and 2013 I interviewed the film maker Gavin Rothery several times about his process.
Gav is the writer and director of the films *Archive* and *The Last Man,* and was Concept Artist and VFX Supervisor on the 2009 motion picture *Moon* – made with his friend, the director and writer Duncan Jones.

In the course of many conversations at his Hampstead flat, he explained the massive amount of work which goes into getting a movie made. In the end I amassed and transcribed over 20,000 words but couldn't fit them into this book; they're the beginning of another great book in their own right, though, and I hope to pursue this idea further in the future.

His description of how you go about making a film once you've written a script is particularly relevant in the context of Judi's thoughts on the difficulties of seeing a movie 'as a whole' from within:

Where do you go from having a good script?

'It depends where you are with the money. Ultimately the money will decide whether you're making a film. You can write a script but if you've no money you're probably not making a film. You could get some friends together and make something but the odds are, if you don't have any money, you're not making a proper film . . . without wanting to demean making a film with no money . . . you're not going to get Sam Rockwell turning up unless you already know him, without any money. You're not going to get a stage at Shepperton and all the things that you need to properly make a film . . . you need a lot of people's time and a lot of resources.
So, if your money's in place, you can get everything going. First thing is to get the script, then the script becomes the bible and template for what happens next.
You'll hire in your heads of department and they'll all take the script away

and break out of it what they need. Somebody like me, doing all the design work, obviously needs to be in there as soon as possible to get stuff moving. Sooner or later you'll have some dates forced on you, such as, "We've got a really good deal at the studio between here and here so that's when we'll film." All of a sudden you've got the first day that you have to be in there with a completed set and a camera crew ready to shoot. Things like that make you go, "Shit, that's three months away. Let's get on the phone."

So, first thing you do is hire in your heads of department. You've got your actors that you're after, your Director of Photography, your Production Designer, first Assistant Director and their AD team – all these people who need to get everything done. Usually the heads of department will bring a team with them – your Director of Photography will bring a team of lighting engineers and sparks and everybody else they need. Sometimes a producer on a project will know a lot of people they want to work with and they'll be pulling people in from here and there, or you'll hire the head of a department and they'll bring people with them; people usually prefer to work like that.'

Did you always have Sam Rockwell in mind for *Moon*?

'Duncan wrote *Moon* for Sam, to give him a sci-fi film. We'd been trying to make a sci-fi film for years and it was all really fortunate that it wrapped together and we could actually do something with Sam in mind, really cool, but that was no guarantee . . .

Someone like Sam can be cast in a film like *Charlie's Angels* where he gets paid loads, he doesn't need to do *Moon*. But Sam wanted to do it and it was lucky that he had the connection to Duncan already so we could get to him and chat because when you give things to agents, you never know if it's passed on.

It's the agent's job to leverage and negotiate, that's what they're there for, and one way that works is that they don't agree to anything until the very last minute. We didn't get a "yes" from Sam until . . . well, we were on the phone saying, "Come on, please tell us you're doing it, we've got to sort ourselves out," and at the last minute he said, "Okay".

That's agents, but there you go.'

You're going to get a lot of sleepless nights when all this sort of thing's going on.

'If we'd not got Sam we'd have had to find someone else and we were already building the sets! It's like *Timecop*, you know? When they get in that time machine and go down the rail really, really fast towards that concrete wall. (Breaking off to pursue a tangent) That's a great example of terrible design in a film; why put that wall there? Why not just have a rail that goes on for about two miles?' (Laughter)

Back to the Future, similarly. Always driving towards a wall or into a gorge.

'Get on the motorway! (Drinks tea thoughtfully) I've got an ambition to own a DeLorean.'

It hasn't got any easier?

'It's got a wee bit easier, a little, little bit easier but only because I've now done quite a lot of films.'

So, when you look at a film, you look to see who the director is first of all?

'When it's given to me? Mmm, I'd be easier in my mind if I knew who the director was. I hadn't met Rob Marshall for *Nine* before; he asked me to do it and I went to meet him and I instantly knew that he was somebody I wanted to work with, absolutely instantly . . . and, of course, if you do know somebody well, there's an ease about it. I mean, Richard Eyre; I've done a lot of things with Richard Eyre and I know him. I'd be able to say to Rich, "Should I not do so-and-so?" You know? Whereas I might be quite frightened of somebody who I'd not met before and not have a rapport with them until we actually started working.'

Do you find people come to you because you're 'Dame Judi Dench'?

'I hope not. I hope they're coming because they think, "This is a good part for you." I hope they think, "She might bring something to this". . .'

Do you find yourself being offered things where you have to say, 'No, I've done this before'?

'Yes. I've just done that recently. I did a film called *Notes on a Scandal* where I played a terrifying lesbian teacher who falls in love with another teacher; I've been asked to do another part which is really very like that. Well, you know, having done that (voice takes on a manic, pleading edge) I want to do something else!

"Have you not got a play about an Afghani woman who comes over here and learns how to walk the tight-rope and, before the end, turns into a dragon before our very eyes in the third act? Or . . . something else?"'

The shining eyes again, always the next thing. I'm sure Judi has never entertained the thought of refining her craft down to an end – what would be the point? Why end when you could begin every day? Why repeat and hone one element when you could be, every day, exploding out along a multitude of curves and discovering more – it's the only sensible thing to do.

With this in mind, I'm aware I mustn't duplicate daft questions. This is an opportunity to ask something new. I find myself mentioning my concern later over tea and Judi is quick and kind enough to reassure.

I'm sure you must be asked the same questions so often, like a loop.

'Yes, I know that well. You get that a huge amount.'

How much 'media shindig' do you do?

'I don't do any.'

You manage to avoid it?

'I do as little as possible, absolutely as little as possible. They do these ridiculous things now called EPK,* you do it on every film.'

Sounds painful.

'Yes, it is painful actually; you sit in a chair and then they ask you questions like, "Why did you do the part?" and these are all things that are tacked onto the end of DVDs.'

Extras.

(Whispers) 'I. Hate. It.
I feel so stupid doing it . . . and, anyway, I don't think it's any business of anybody's why you do the part or what you feel about it or how you approached it. I loathe all that, but it's mandatory, all those things like being interviewed; you have to do a certain amount . . . but I don't enjoy it.
It never used to be the case, you know, you'd go and do a film; you'd have your own private process that you went through but you never had to talk about it.

'If Michael and I were working separately on two different things – or even when we were working on the same play – we'd get into the car to come home and we'd never speak about it. Never ever. If I were working on something at home I would never speak about it to Michael or to Finty or to anybody because

---

* An EPK/Electronic Press Kit is a pack of supplementary information, media and bonus features assembled, written and recorded to grease the launch of a film. A film EPK might consist of biographies, trailers and clips, high resolution press photos, and specially recorded Q&A interviews with cast and crew.

it's like a pressure-cooker, you know? Fsss!!! (A noise like a steam valve) Immediately you let that little cap go, some of the pressure goes out of it.'

At this point Judi's daughter, Finty, telephones with news from The Globe, where she's been reading for a part. Judi's been expecting the call, checking her watch sporadically and asking me to keep my fingers crossed. She leaves the room to take the call.

(Returning, buoyant) 'It went very well! Very well! They were lovely and got her to read lots of parts and said, "Can you sing?" Well, we'll keep our fingers crossed, that's what we have to do. She was pleased about the way it has gone so that's excellent.'

They didn't give her an answer?

'No. They're not going to give her an answer for quite a long time because they're cross-casting with *Henry IV*.'

Always tricky!

'I'm going to get us a drink, Daniel.'

Judi leaves again to fetch drinks and I stand by the large windows, alone in the room. Outside a moorhen japes on the moat, hooting, skimming backwards and hand-brake turning in front of three baleful ducks who sit on the bank and mutter in the drizzle.

Judi appears at my elbow and I tell her about the moorhen.

(Handing me a vase of champagne) 'Oh yes, he lives on our pond. The garden is lovely. It goes down to a paddock and then a meadow – I'm so sorry it's not very nice out, with the wisteria on the back it's so beautiful . . . Anyway, cheers, Daniel. This is what we need. This'll turn the blue litmus red . . .'

(We drink. I make a mental note to tell everyone I know about this day over and over again for ever.)

'Not very warming but better than a poke in the eye with a burnt stick.'

Very true. Is it burnt for you? It's sharp for me.

'Sharp, burnt, yes. Either's pretty rough . . .'

The telephone rings again. It's Sammy's school, Judi's grandson. Three minutes later she's back:

'Ten past three he's allowed out – I was so frightened about doing that; I had to ring the school and say, "Can Sammy come out of school early tomorrow at ten past three?" but my heart was in my mouth . . .'

Why was that?

'Oh, it's talking to authority and asking for things – standing outside the Headmistress's door . . . the worst thing of all is when you're going through customs and you've absolutely nothing to declare. I walk through and I'm absolutely scarlet with guilt. I have absolutely nothing in my bag . . . that must go back to school, mustn't it? It must go back to authority.'

The phone rings again. It's Tim Piggott-Smith. Judi says she won't be a moment.
I wander outside to talk with the moorhen.

• • • • •

I wanted to ask about your recent work with Clint Eastwood.

'In Los Angeles, yes. *J. Edgar*,★ it's called. I played his
mother. I had a fortnight, though I wasn't needed all
that time because he hardly does any takes at all, Clint.
He'll do one; he might do two. He doesn't like you to
think about it, you know, just do it. Wonderful. Very
quiet, the set, and he says (low Clint whisper), "In your
own time," or he says, "Okay, Amigo," and then when
you get to the end of the scene he says (barely audible
whisper), "Stop. Print." And he walks away.'

Does he expect a great deal of preparation from his actors
because of that speed?

'Well, if he does he doesn't give any sign of it. I said at
one point, "Really? Is that it?"
He said, "Yep. Why?"
I said, "Well, um . . . shall I have another go?"
"Why?"
"Well, you know, there might be something else."
"Okay. Don't think about it."
"Okay."

'Don't think about it. He doesn't like it to be analysed
at all.
Legend doesn't do him justice. He's an adorable man.'

★ *J. Edgar* is a film directed by Clint Eastwood which focuses on the career of FBI
director J. Edgar Hoover and was released in November 2011.
Judi plays Anna Marie, Hoover's mother.

Do you do a lot of work on accents for something like that?

'Mmm. They sent me some tapes. Clint said his grand-mother was from New England and she barely had an accent. Barely. So that was good.
She was a monster, Anna Marie; certainly didn't approve of the fact Edgar was gay . . . a monster, but that's good – good stuff to deal with.
And we weren't in a studio, we were on location in a house and that was good too, something very real about it . . .'

Is it usual to get sent a pack of information about someone you're to play?

'No. I mean, I didn't have one with Iris Murdoch* but because I was a huge admirer I knew about her before I played her. What I didn't know about was the whole business of Alzheimer's, but Jim Broadbent's mother had had Alzheimer's and so had Richard Eyre's, so I had a completely one-to-one relationship with it and that was really useful.

'I went once, while John Bayley** was away, and looked at the house in Oxford and the car in the drive. That was good; anything that you can feed into your

---

* Dame Iris Murdoch, DBE (1919–1999). British author and philosopher, best known for her novels about political and social questions of good and evil, sexual relationships, morality, and the power of the unconscious.
Judi played Iris in Richard Eyre's 2001 film of the same name.

** Professor John Bayley (1925–2015). British literary critic and writer.
From 1956 until her death, he was married to the writer Dame Iris Murdoch. When she was diagnosed with Alzheimer's disease, he wrote the book *Iris: A Memoir of Iris Murdoch*, later made into a film.

picture-book memory, you know – that's what you have to do if you're an actor, you have to watch things and there has to be part of your mind that can take a quick snapshot of something without being detached from what you're watching because sometimes it's a scene of grief or ghastly things that have happened to you or happened to your friends or to people you know . . . I don't know if you do it consciously but it's something that you just have to notice because you might at some point have to use it.'

Alright then, I'll ask my naive question that I've noted down here and written 'Naive!' next to.

'Be naive.'

Well, here goes. How much personal experience of what you're doing do you need when you're playing a part?

'Experience?'

Well, for example, there is a certain steeliness in some of your work, incredibly cold, but, at the moment, chopping that cucumber, that isn't there.

'Well, no, because that's nothing to do with me; that's an aspect of me that is sometimes required – like an aspect of anger or, I mean, I've never actually murdered somebody or even incited somebody to murder but I can understand that, when you come to doing *Macbeth*, how – through love of somebody – all you want is for that person to get his desires and therefore, out of love, you urge him . . . you know, I have never done that but I understand the motive.
(Eating a piece of cucumber)

I'm not remotely like M. I'm not *remotely* like her. I don't understand any of those things, but my job is not to make you think, "Gosh, that's very unlike her," but to think, "My God! I wouldn't want to cross her!" A certain steeliness, yes. That's not me, though. It must be an aspect of me, though.'

Have you ever been involved with something where you're out of your depth in that sense?

'Oh, masses and masses of times . . . but people always say, which I don't like, they say, "Do you like that character?" It's not a question of liking. It's never a question of liking or disliking, I'm just trying to be a person . . . and if you haven't actually experienced something that you have to experience in a play then you have to perhaps have observed something, you know, it's like everything – it's part of your training isn't it? You have to have something very, very watchful in your make-up because if you haven't actually experienced something yourself then sometimes you have to rely upon something you've observed.'

When you met me at the station, earlier, you said I'd done something funny which you might use at some point.

'I saw you come out and glance up at the sign, "Alright, right station?" I absolutely watched you do it.'

In that way you can read somebody's mind by observing their behaviour?

'Absolutely. You have to. It's the great eye and the great ear – you have to be able to observe things, otherwise you're lost.'

Earlier in the year, I found myself lost on the overpasses of the Barbican. Senseless and cold; all bandsaw towers, sheer walls and long drops. The stairwells and lit windows across the way looked warm and inviting, like an ocean liner passing out of reach. I'd been wandering for half an hour and not seen a soul in the weird quiet – muffled sirens, the far-off sigh of the city, the buzz of a moribund strip light.

Sure there was something to it, something warm inside the concrete, I kept walking but couldn't find a way into it that night and escaped to Goswell Road.

I think of this now as I look through my notes and find a black and white photograph of Judi and Zoë Wanamaker onstage together.

I have this photograph of you in *Mother Courage*.*

'*Mother Courage?* Yes, that was at the Barbican.
Good fun! It was hard – the set kept breaking down . . . so, at the end when she's meant to be pushing the cart and going off by herself, I had to go off with two or three stagehands pushing it as well; that kind of blew it, for me.'

The magic was tempered somewhat.

'Yes, this picture of a woman pushing a cart off to the war with a lot of friends!
Zoë Wanamaker stole the whole thing as my mute daughter, of course. Wonderful. Gosh it was hard work; hard work but enjoyable, hugely enjoyable – except that I don't like the Barbican.'

---

* *Mother Courage and Her Children* is a 1939 play by German dramatist and poet Bertolt Brecht (1898–1956) – often cited as the greatest anti-war play ever written.

Funny old place, the Barbican . . .

'Well, it's not fish, fowl or a good red herring is it? It's
nothing. Terrible. You have to get in through the stage
door with a number. (Grimacing) Oh, it's ages since
I've been back there because I just don't want to go back
– a kind of concrete hell. There's nothing kind about it.
No kindness, no curves (with despairing horror), oh
God . . . when you think of all those wonderful theatres
that are made of wattle and plaster, or somewhere like
The Vic – they're, you know, so kind; so forgiving and
so all-embracing.
Have you ever tried to meet anybody at the Barbican?'*

Have you ever tried to get out of the Barbican? (Laughter)

'You can't get out of it, you can't get into it without
a number, you can't meet anybody inside it . . . you
should never, never ever have a stage door where you
have to get in with a number.'

Are you as discerning about theatres as you are about plays?

'Well, Theatre Royal, Haymarket – that is such a beautiful theatre; a wonderful backstage that's beautifully
kept by Arnold Crook, absolutely beautiful. That makes
it very attractive but, at the same time, if somebody
said . . . but, I mean, no, it doesn't really matter; ideally

---

* Now, we're quite obviously slagging off the Barbican here, and it was in the
balance to be cut but saved by a friend's anecdote about avant-garde theatre artist
Robert Wilson, standing in the midst of the Barbican complex and asking, with sad
exasperation, 'Where's the fuckin' door!?'
(While we're at it, see also The Guggenheim in Bilbao.)
The labyrinthine Barbican door issue seems to be endemic.

I want somebody to offer me two plays that will run in repertoire. Heaven. Heaven! And, if possible, four plays, so I don't do the same one every night. That's what I like best.'

That's how you started your career?

'Yes, at The Vic, and they were all Shakespeare – playing a part in one, walking on in another, playing another part in another, walking on and understudying in another . . . it was wonderful. Wonderful and of course it kept you so much on your toes, so invigorating and – you couldn't for a second get complacent in any way or think, "Oh well, it's only that . . ." You were really up to the hilt in every performance.'

Do you have certain places that were key to your practice?

'Yes, there's The Vic, of course, my first job was at The Old Vic, in *Hamlet*, oh, I learnt such a lot – coming out of three years of training and then going straight to the kind of place that you couldn't have learnt better, where you could make any amount of mistakes because you were given small parts – well, Ophelia, I was given – and you watched your principals who you were understudying and you had a chance to really look at other people and that's terribly important. That's the way you learn . . . being part of a big company, there's no substitute, I think. I just love it.'

How long were you part of that company?

'I was there from '57 to the middle of '61, when I went to start work on *The Cherry Orchard* with Michel

Saint-Denis and Sir John* and Dame Peg** and everybody, and then, during that season at the Aldwych,
Peter asked me to do my first season at Stratford – that
was '62.'

That was the RSC?

'That was the RSC, yes, and it was during my time
there that Peter formed the two-year plan, you know;
that you were contracted for two years and you played
the Aldwych and Stratford . . . we used to go up and
down the road three times every other day – there was
no M40 then. *Penny for a Song* at the Aldwych then
back to do the *Dream* at Stratford then back down
to rehearse for something else . . . it was wonderful. I
loved it.'

That was the first time you'd been in *A Midsummer Night's
Dream*?

'Well, school first then '62 in Stratford with Peter
– Titania in the *Dream* and Isabella in *Measure for
Measure.* That was that season. (Quietly) Oh, heaven.'

---

* Sir John Gielgud, OM, CH (1904–2000). English actor, director, and producer.
Achieved early international acclaim for his youthful, emotionally expressive Hamlet
which broke box office records on Broadway in 1937. He was known for his beautiful
speaking of verse and particularly for his warm and expressive voice.
A founding RSC cast member.

** Dame Peggy Ashcroft, DBE (1907–1991). English actress.
In 1934 she played Juliet in a legendary production of *Romeo & Juliet* in which
Laurence Olivier and John Gielgud alternated in the roles of Romeo and Mercutio.
When she first played Beatrice with him in 1950, Gielgud found her performance 'a
revelation – an impish, rather tactless girl', while a teenage Peter Hall observed in her
'English containment and decency, contrasted with a wild passion'.
A founding RSC cast member.

You played Titania again, recently – Titania as Elizabeth I.
Was that a very different experience?

'Totally different. Peter said, "We have to find a way
to make a sense of that," and the sense was that she,
Elizabeth I, must have seen that play – she might well
have gone to it or it was done at court – why should we
not approach it that way?'

The Faerie Queen and courtly love . . .

'And Essex and everybody, yes, it made a wonderful
sense, I think. Peter wanted Elizabeth I to be watching, but what I longed for was that I should have come
in at the beginning with my back to the audience so
that they were all a part of the court, sit down and
the play begin and then, suddenly somehow, come in
with Oberon, who would have been Essex, so you'd set
that up. She should go up into the play and then when
the girl playing Titania came in I should have gone
up and . . .'

Pushed her in the face! (Laughter)

'That's what I longed to do! That's what we longed to
do but then we thought, "Well, that sets up a whole
other thing," so we devised a mime of just taking the
script . . . (pauses, thinking – suddenly steely-eyed and
sharp) but in actual fact it was wrong to take the script
from the girl who played Hermia, it was wrong. It
should have been from somebody who you never saw
appear.'

A person never seen again.

'They're never seen, quite right, but you can't mess it up too much . . . but it was just enough to establish what was happening.'

Perhaps more than anyone else in this book, Judi's work and process is reliant upon others inasmuch as film, theatre, television and radio are large undertakings. Troops of actors, teams of writers, directors, producers, camera crew, set builders, dressers, stagehands, fixers, gaffers, runners, caterers and the rest make work possible. She moves constantly in a peripatetic whirl from venue to venue, set to set, country to country as part of her job; a constant jostle of riposte and rejoinder.

Her conversation is well populated by friends and colleagues; remembered tales, jokes and anecdotes.

It's perhaps no surprise she's so comfortable and good with people, since people are her life, characters real and fictive; understandable too that her kitchen is such a quiet haven.

'I love coming back here, I just love it . . . we sold our house in Hampstead when Mike was so ill and he loved it here.

We lived in the most beautiful little house. Do you know Hampstead?

You go along Church Row and there's Hampstead churchyard that goes up a hill, Holly Walk, and you go up this little hill and there was a gate that said Prospect Place, number 1, 2, 3 & 4; and we were the last one. Beautiful little house, tiny. I bought it for £14,700 – which was a lot of money for me then – when I did *Cabaret* in 1968. I loved it.'

At the end of our first meeting I suggest visiting The Old Vic theatre with Judi since it was so important to her early career, and she readily agrees, but it turns out to be very difficult to schedule.

I walk around it on my own later in the year. Climbing the steps to the stage door – past a hatch with a stage doorman in it.

It's labyrinthine inside with a lot of stairs and white corridors. I explore the dressing rooms, high up on the third floor. A wooden lift with mirrors.

'Did you have anything specific in mind?' I'm asked, but I

don't. I wish Judi was there to explore and tell me stories, root me in this space; but everything's changed since the sixties, my guide tells me. Two refurbishments, the rehearsal rooms moved; Judi probably wouldn't remember this, although she might recall that.

Strangely quiet, a theatre without actors or audience. Flat. No, not flat, in fact of all the spaces I've visited this one seems to be asking the most of me; it feels charged – an echo chamber awaiting the eloquence of action but standing mute alone onstage I felt hollow, sensed the empty pull of the pit, pinned by the lights.
Not an actor, not in company, just stood before the abyss. This is a recurrent dream of Judi's:

'I'm standing there, all dressed up, and whispering: "What do I say now?" It's awful, really, but it's the big fear. The one that never goes away.'*

• • • • •

Back out in the sunshine I ponder The Old Vic while walking round its arrow footprint, tapering to where Webber Street and Waterloo Road run into The Cut. The bricked-up bulls-eyes in the arches either side would have once shed light into a rehearsal room, I guess, and I imagine the scene, the energy – an intense crucible of feeling and story.

A photograph of Samuel Beckett in a trench coat by some bins suddenly jumps to mind** . . . maybe we could photograph

---

*The *Observer* Magazine, 14 October 2012.

** The photograph in question was taken by Paul Joyce behind the Royal Court Theatre in 1979.

Judi by the bins out the back, I think. Maybe that would speak more about the itinerant nature of things . . .

• • • • •

A month or two later, back at Wasp Green, Lucy is talking about Samuel Beckett while she takes Judi's picture:

Lucy – When I die, that complete works of Beckett is coming in the coffin with me. It makes me sad to think I'll die and won't be able to read them any more.

Judi – Quite.

Lucy – I do love him.

Dan – I don't know, it would be a very Beckett twist to discover you weren't dead and had time to read after all.

Judi – Yes, that would be very like Beckett.

Dan – Did you ever meet Samuel Beckett?

Judi – No, never. Never ever. I've never been in a Beckett play. I was asked to do *Happy Days* and I'm afraid, Lucy's never going to speak to me again, I turned it down.

Lucy – Did you not like it?

Judi – Well, have you read it? Have you seen the first page of it?
The whole of the first page is exactly what she's doing. 'Something in her left hand, something in her right hand. She looks to the left, she looks to the right, she moves . . .'

Lucy – All stage direction.

Judi – Exactly. I can't do that; that's something I just cannot do. I just can't do it because I don't know where I slot into any of it, do you know? So I didn't understand it. I mean, I didn't understand what my role in it was.

• • • • •

There is a scooter café on Lower Marsh, a stone's throw from The Old Vic, a coffee haunt tucked below the knotted rails of Waterloo's throat where the ancient whoosh and wallop of the espresso machines jostle with the clatterbox trains outside.

I'd imagined taking Judi there after the theatre expedition and selling her on the superb hot chocolate they make, so reminiscent of school custard, and she'd either be enchanted and converted or dismiss it as filth (I find it splits an audience like liquorice or Marmite . . . or Morrissey).

The day after The Old Vic business I went back, drawn back like a witness to the scene of the accident, and drank hot chocolate on my own – overlooked by the disinterested girl behind the bar and the even less interested cat across the way – reading *Notes from Underground*. Here is Dostoyevsky's man in full vent: mankind, he observes, is constantly forging new paths and revelling in the tangential since 'the main thing is not where it leads but rather that it just goes somewhere . . .'; and this rang true with my experiences of the book so far, there had been a discernible itch for the next thing. Judi, Bill, Stanley, Manic Street Preachers, all seemed to pursue a trajectory into the unknown, the last thing a bridge to the next. Dostoyevsky again:

'And might it be that he loves destruction and chaos (indeed it is indisputable that he sometimes loves them very much) because he is instinctively afraid of achieving his goal and completing the structure he is constructing? How do you know? Maybe he just loves the structure from a distance, and not at all from close up; maybe he only loves to build it, and not to live in it . . . perhaps, like a chess player, he loves only the process of achieving his ends and not the ends themselves. And who knows (one cannot guarantee it) perhaps the sole end of mankind on earth, for which he strives, is the perpetual process of achieving, in other words, in living and not in attainment itself . . .'*

The reprised ideas of aiming oneself towards a perpetual process of becoming, together with the need for spins into folly, struck me as comforting – here was the root of Judi's disquiet at being trapped on film, perhaps, for a finished thing is dead while theatre is about rebirth, each night a new chance to start again – 'Begin afresh, afresh, afresh!'**
And so, while the dark vacuum of The Old Vic still haunted me – together with the hawkish spectre of Beckett by the bins – heckling that I'd lost my way, found out and wanting . . . I found the tortured failings and flailings of Dostoyevsky's subterranean consoling now in the sense that surely it would have been more foolish not to try, not to flail and get out of my depth. The point was that I did not know the answers. Better to career off widdershins and embrace the tangential, rather than dictating the pace and course; best to be naive and keep on . . . and I recalled Geoff Dyer in his D.H. Lawrence odyssey, *Out of Sheer Rage*, meeting a lady in her nineties who'd delivered the post to Lawrence as a little girl:

---

* *Notes from Underground*, Fyodor Dostoyevsky, trans. Natasha Randall (Canongate, 2012).

** 'The Trees', *High Windows*, Philip Larkin (Faber & Faber, 1967).

'And it was not surprising, I reflected when we were out in the street again, for I had not asked Salvatore's mother anything. Even though she had known Lawrence I had said nothing to her except "Buongiorno," which should have been "Buonasera." How nice it would have been, how authoritative, if she had said, "Mr Lawrence he was very nice, molto simpatico," something like that. Spoken by a woman who had actually known him, this otherwise unexceptional observation would have carried more weight than anything I had ever read about Lawrence in dozens of memoirs. This was as near to Lawrence as I was ever likely to get and I hadn't asked her anything, partly because she was old and tired and I was too respectful, but mainly because it had simply not occurred to me to ask her anything and now it was too late.'*

God, how awful! How that would have haunted me, the inertia! The torturous torpor of doubt, you know? 'Who am I to . . . ?' No. Shut up. Get on with it. Or don't. The worst that you'll do is make a fool of yourself – at least it would make a good anecdote.

If I held back for fear of seeming foolish, I thought as I spooned custard skin off my teacup, I'd never do anything at all.

---

* *Out of Sheer Rage*, Geoff Dyer (Canongate, 2012).

I only discovered Geoff Dyer's writing towards the end of this endeavour and was so pleased to find a kindred, if infuriating, spirit. *Out of Sheer Rage* is a brilliant book about the torture of writing, procrastination, the 'obstructions we all experience in settling down to work'.

His description how he built the book really struck a chord:

'There was no plan to frame this book, to hold it in shape. I started in the middle with one or two images and am working my way outwards, towards the edge that is still to be made.'

• • • • •

I want to ask . . . you keep getting awards.

'Oh, please . . .' (Laughter)

I wanted to ask about it, in all seriousness, because it must be a bit odd.

'It's unnerving when it's a "Lifetime Achievement" award. You think, "Oh, that's it, is it?"
I'm going to be made a fellow of the British Film Institute the week after next, and I'm going to Czechoslovakia to get something. So that's lovely . . .'

Does it feel strange?

'Well, it does feel quite strange. It does feel very strange; you think, "But I'm still running the race! Don't give me a prize for getting to the tape yet."'

You and Alan Bennett under glass.

'Oh God, don't . . . "National Treasure" – it's the kiss of death, isn't it? Dreadful. Some old museum that nobody goes to; there we are, stuck in, under the glass. Nothing moving. Horrible. Sounds so musty. Don't like that. Not right at all . . .'

People writing letters of complaint when you swear on-screen and suchlike.

'Oh, for goodness sake, why? You know!? What has it got to do with . . . why?
My job is not to be me! My job is not to be me in any

262

form. Why would I want to do a job to promote who I am? I don't want to do that.'

Speaking of things you don't do; let's say, having just come offstage at Glastonbury with your band . . .

'Me? Is this me? Well I wouldn't do that because I don't like that kind of music but, yes, okay.' (Giggles)

The applause is so much that you're compelled to return and perform an encore. What song are you going to encore with?

'I wouldn't be doing it in the first place! (Laughing) I would no more go to Glastonbury than I would fly to the moon! Sorry about that . . . there you are. No, I can't do that. Can't be at Glastonbury.'*

Yet I'm sure many people would think of musicians and actors playing to large audiences as being similar in many ways.

(Rhetorically) 'Well it's not, is it? In the same way that people think that standing up in a pulpit is related. I'm not going to do that either.'

Do you think there are many misconceptions about what you do?

---

* What music do you like best?

    'I love the Beatles; I loved the Beatles and there are many things now I like but not many that I love.

Transportative music.

    'Jazz! That's classic music, you know? Brilliant. When I was in New York I used to go and see Kid Ory, Count Basie – I was wooed by Jerry Mulligan – Miles Davies, I loved that.'

'I think it's because you're considered rather effete if you don't want to talk about it – that thing that all actors want to be loved; I simply deplore that. What we're trying to do is tell a story to an audience and hope that, in the process of doing that, you might change their – well, hopefully, ideally, change their outlook on something or make them very angry or cry or be pleased or laugh a lot or talk to the person next door or feel better when they come out of the theatre than they did when they came in or, maybe, feel worse.

You're trying to tell somebody's story, you know?'

You're a conduit.

'Yes. It's not me. There's a wonderful story that David Dodimead used to tell about playing Lear at the Sparrow's Nest, Lowestoft; he came on and these two ladies who were always there – always in the front row – one turned to the other and said quite audibly, "David's not looking too well this week." (Laughter)

And even if I were to say that it's the mystery of what it is that we do . . . there is no mystery any more because people have to know every single thing. They have to know why you're doing the part, what attracted you to it, why you're working with those people, what you think of that director – it's nobody's business! It's nothing to do with what one does the job for, nothing at all . . .

'Some nights something completely takes off, and if you knew what constituted that feeling on that evening you would do it every time but you can't because you don't know what it is. It's something to do with an amalgam of all sorts of things – being too tired or not being tired, being hungry or not being hungry, being in the theatre early or getting delayed – it's many, many, many things but sometimes the magic thing is that it happens and it happens throughout the whole company, it catches . . . it is a kind of magic and you can't quantify that in any kind of way.'

It would ruin it to pick it apart. You don't always want to know how they've disappeared the elephant.

'It absolutely ruins it. I don't think you do want to know how the man puts the person in the box and saws right through it. Why should we know that? I can't imagine doing the EPK for a magic show – we want the illusion.'

CALLY CALLOMON (1956–) spends a certain amount of time within the music industry in order to earn enough money to ride, restore and research ancient bicycles.

Having started out as a musician, he went on to work in A&R and was Creative Director at Island Records throughout the 1990s, working with Tricky, U2, PJ Harvey and Nine Inch Nails among many others. He currently navigates Bill Drummond and manages the estate of Nick Drake.

CALLY CALLOMON

Marlinspike Hall, Walpole, Suffolk
17 August 2010

Writing in a caravan.

Nothing to do but write.

A week alone to write while house-sitting for Cally. Left in charge of the chickens and this van in the woods, green bicycle propped by the door.

Birds fuss on the tin roof above me; landing, dancing, taking off – drumming, tapping, clacking feet. Cars swish out of sight on the Halesworth Road.

At night the poplars roar.

I met Cally through Bill Drummond. Cally is Bill's manager – which, on paper, looks akin to Rupert Bear managing Sparta Praha but seems to work remarkably well in reality.

Yesterday I spoke to Cally for a good five hours. We sat in his office, took a tour around his house, outhouses and sheds; examined his collections of vintage bicycles and cars, motorbikes, box files, comics, records, signage, baths, and books; the 1930s Parisian bar he's built in his cellar, the reinforced floors, the dentist's chair in the bathroom . . . the man collects on an epic scale and has amassed a palace of interesting things, 'resource' of amazing scope – but didn't it all seem vaguely familiar, I puzzle later in the van – something about fried eggs?

Graphic Designer, Engineer, Director, Executor, Archivist, Manager, Cyclist, Chameleon, Comedian, Corinthian and Caricature . . . I wonder, does he sleep?

Above the caravan's bay window runs a line of smaller die-cast caravans – the start of infinite regress, a Russian doll convoy. Looking around, I see that the bookshelves are stocked with volumes on gypsies, canals and circuses, the caravan life, a 900-piece jigsaw of a canary-coloured cart to while away wet afternoons . . .

A moth edges above me to inspect the galley light. A downy grey-brown creature with hair-sprung trembling legs.

18 August

Transcribing, writing things into shape, staring out into Suffolk, making tea on the gas stove. Ideal.
Here I am in a caravan out in the nature, just me. Nothing to do but write; write and consider writing . . . mainly the latter as it turns out.
I sit in the moment of 'about to start writing' for a long time, listening back to tapes of conversations I've collected about creativity . . . I sit there, stalled. Inert. The world's most unproductive writer, neither writing himself nor transcribing the thoughts of prolific virtuosos.

26 January 2010

Jenny Saville – Is there a space where you always write, then?

Dan – At the moment I write in the kitchen. There's no heating in the house apart from the AGA so I write next to that with the cat for company.

Jenny – Do you keep regular hours?

Dan – I try, yes. I work half the week on a building site and the rest writing at home. I've taken to wearing two pairs of trousers in the kitchen, I find that helps.

Jenny – Do you know Cy Twombly? I suppose he's the last American Abstract Expressionist still alive. He works in a place called Gaeta, between Rome and Naples, and he's about eighty-two and he must be a multi-millionaire – his works sell for millions – but he still works in an industrial unit and, in order to get warm, he has his car running outside the studio; he works for a while then goes and sits in his car for a bit.

He should get a caravan, I think; save himself a fortune on petrol.

A caravan. A week. Nothing to do but write.

Undisturbed quiet to focus the mind – not too hot, not too cold, 'just right' to write – 'I mean, why shouldn't I write here?' I ask the trembly moth. 'There's nothing here to stop me.'

I have my books, I have a good pen, I have my Mac – and no internet to distract me – no building site hovering in my peripheries. I'll brew up and set about it, I think. This Suffolk caravan is just the thing – better than a cold kitchen.

A caravan. A week. Nothing to do but write. Great.

But then I go back to staring, half listening to the tapes, distractedly tinkering with the same three sentences, thinking about Cy Twombly sat in his car – what sort of car? Did he have the radio on? Was the driver's seat covered in paint? – staring out of the window or down at the caravan's carpet . . . which rings a bell. Carpet. Didn't I record something off the radio about carpet, a while ago? Carpet and process?

'He would come out of his study, take hold of the carpet sweeper – which was right next to his study door – and start sweeping the hallway . . .'

Carpet.

'The carpet sweeper served a very important function. Daddy had a routine – he would get up quite early in the morning, have breakfast, always do the *Times* crossword and then settle down to write at his typewriter for the morning and, as a way of pausing, he would come out of his study, take hold of the carpet sweeper – which was right next to his study door – and start sweeping the hallway for, I don't know, a few minutes . . .'

J.G. Ballard's carpet.

'And then go back to his study and do a bit more typing. He'd come out again half an hour later and do a bit more – maybe a couple of hours later he'd come out again, do a bit more – so I think, in a sense, the use of the carpet sweeper was really a device to stop and reflect on what he'd been writing.'*

I look at my notes, those three mangled sentences – pulled apart distractedly as cats bat mice – and I shudder and agree with the ghost of J.G. Ballard's carpet sweeper that, yes, this is shambolic and I really must get cracking; that transcription

---

* Fay Ballard, *Front Row*, BBC Radio 4, 10 February 2010.

is the writing equivalent of laboriously mixing paint before the painting proper can begin . . . that the drudge has to come before the fun stuff.

'I've only got a week to really crack on,' I think, glumly. Then I cycle to Southwold instead.*

Cally stands before his bicycles. A racing penny-farthing with slender sharp front forks, a hammock saddled Pedersen with a silver welded frame – one particularly hefty example was

---

* Two encouraging extracts from the writer Bernice Rubens's obituary:

'She wrote every day, declaring, "I feel unclean if I don't write." She worked in an attic room – her "hole in the sky"– with her desk set up beside a grand piano and a cello. She once explained: "I do a nice sentence, then I think, that deserves a little tinkle on the piano. I do another sentence and then I have a go on the cello."'

'Writing was her life but it wasn't an uncomplicated relationship. She said once: "I don't love writing, but I love having written, if you know what I mean".'

– *Independent*, 15 October 2004

designed to be parachuted into Normandy over the shoulders of the invading SAS, who were doubtless pleased when those plans were shelved in the run-up to D-Day.

Dressed in an apron, hair swept back, work boots, turn-ups, shirt sleeves rolled, every inch the artisan, he runs me through the cycle's evolution, illustrating each advance with reference to his collection, many of which he's built or restored to exacting specs, all operable and ridden – if he doesn't use a bike, it goes, swapped or sold on; utility exemplified, form and function fused.*

Over in his office I am shown some more 'resource'. An annex from the main house, the interior of this solid double-decker shed is stacked out, a massive cache of 'stuff' and 'things' and 'data' . . . an asset battery: floor to ceiling, stowed, boxed and catalogued. Resource is the panacea. Resource is anything and everything that could be of use. Resource is the very thing you do/might/could/shall want. This is Cally's brain manifest:

---

* Some of the greatest musings on fusion and bicycles were expressed by Sergeant Pluck in Flann O'Brian's *The Third Policeman*:

> 'The gross and net result of it is that people who spent most of their natural lives riding iron bicycles over the rocky roadsteads of this parish get their personalities mixed up with the personalities of their bicycle as a result of the interchanging of the atoms of each of them and you would be surprised at the number of people in these parts who are nearly half people and half bicycles.'

I let out a gasp of astonishment that made a sound in the air like a bad puncture.

> 'And you would be flabbergasted at the number of bicycles that are half-human almost half-man, half-partaking of humanity.'
>
> – *The Third Policeman*, Flann O'Brien (Harper Perennial, 2007)

How much time does Cally spend 'leaning with one elbow on walls or standing propped by one foot at curb stones'?

'This is where a lot of the design resource stuff is. Upstairs I've got folders and folders full of clippings; every time I read a magazine, if there's something in it that I like, I cut it out and file it under subject matter.'

When did that start?

'When I was at art school, because at art school they had filing cabinets with Hands/Faces – resource material really for being an artist. If you were doing a piece of advertising and you needed a hand holding a book, you'd either get someone to hold their hand and you'd draw it or you'd find a picture of a hand and copy the picture because if you were in advertising you had to hand-draw visuals with magic markers to say "This is what the advert would look like" and, because it was a graphic design course, they tried – rather humorously – to do visuals quickly. Some people were brilliant at it but I was absolutely hopeless so I thought, "Well, if I just collect all this stuff, I'll be able to collage it together and it will have a nice quality all of its own." That was 1974/5 when I started to collect and I've had this enormous amount of stuff which has followed me round: articles about fairgrounds, articles about outsiders. I've got a file that's just called "Nutters" (laughs). If I read an article in the *Evening Standard* about some guy who died while hanging off his roof, that would go in there. I don't know why . . . it's partly resource, I do dive into it now and again but I sometimes think – I had to go through a file at the weekend and I thought, "I forgot I had all this stuff." It does work as stimulus, I suppose, but I think, "What is going to happen to all this when I die?" That's a silly thing even to think about, you know . . . it burns. The danger is that you start feeling that it's an important collection.'

You don't think somebody else would want it?

'No. They won't. There are some bits that people might want, and when Island's fiftieth anniversary happened this year and they had an exhibition I went through all my Island Records files and I found tonnes and tonnes of stuff that Island hadn't kept – because I loved the record company and part of loving the record company is collecting the record company, for me. It's all the ephemera: programmes, packing tape that had the Island logo on, things like that.*
My memory is not good, never has been, so everything is filed under headings . . . but sometimes I forget that boxes exist; I was a member of the Sherlock Holmes Society of London so in there (points up to a file) will be all my clippings from papers and magazines. I don't know if I'll ever look through it again, but there may come a time when someone will want it and I'll give it away or I'll need it again; I don't see the point of throwing stuff away. My dad came round at the weekend, we were doing the family tree, and he's got boxes and boxes of photographs and old family paintings and he was going through them, organising all the photos in eras, and he came to me with a box of photos and I said, "What are these?" And he said, "Well, these are all the ones where I don't know who they are or they're

---

* Cally started out playing drums in various bands before leaving to work at a record company designing album sleeves and 'to manage Julian Cope amongst others' as well as releasing records on his own label. He then worked as an A&R man for Warner Brothers, later moving to Island Records to become Creative Director – recently revamping their Kensington High Street offices, paying tribute to the company's heritage, employing such visual treasure as a graffitied Trabant bonnet from U2's *Achtung Baby* album cover and Bob Marley tour photographs on a bright trompe-l'œil corrugated iron background – harking back to Island's Jamaican roots.

boring or they're swaps so we can throw them away,"
and I said, "I'm not throwing these away!" And he said,
"Oh well, you bloody keep everything, you – what's
the point in keeping them?" (Holding out the photographs for me to see) Well, look, there's a picture of my
grandfather and my grandmother at Kew I can't even
begin to explain to him, my dad . . . (Reaching around
behind him) I've got some of these books, maybe you
know them, they've become quite popular – anonymous or found images. There's just something about
a lot of these images that clicks (turning to a random
page). That's wonderful, isn't it? Beautiful. Someone
caught in a street – maybe in New York or maybe Paris
. . . the anonymity of it all is just fantastic. This book
is one man's collection of found photos and when I
first discovered it I thought, "Someone else has been
doing it!" Because I've got books of found things –
photos that I've particularly liked or drawings – (gets
down another book, one of his own, and opens it
out to show a crumpled doodle) that was on a train,
someone's screwed it up – I think they'd drawn a picture of the ticket collector . . . (leafing through the
scrapbook) I don't know who the people are, what
the story is; letters that I've found . . . (reads from a
dog-eared page) "I have enclosed a few snaps. I am
not quite so fat as this one." Brilliant. I get them from
car boot sales, wherever . . . (reading out another find)
"Please park further up drive so that others can park.
Peter."
I've got a whole file upstairs of "Angry/Annoyed", you
know? "What kind of fucking parking do you call this?"
Stuff like that. People give them to me now.'

· · · · ·

I see the influences of so many things in Cally's house and work, but something that stands out is the collaged Pop Art influence of Peter Blake and Richard Hamilton.*
I peered into Peter Blake's studio once, I tell him. It was full of elephants.

'I love Peter's work. I like it when he's less direct; odd bits pieced together; when you don't know what it's about. When I was at art school we were blessed with fantastic visiting lecturers – Tom Philips, Mark Boyle, Richard Hamilton, yes. It was great; and I just thought that was normal and that's what always happened – I didn't realise it was so unusual . . . and we published books when we were at art school! Mark Boyle – who's very like Bill in a lot of ways – he decided he was going to get a project together that his family would carry on after he was dead. He got a map of the world in the ICA, got a hundred people in and they threw a hundred darts at the world and each one of the holes was a site – so some of them would hit England, say, so he'd get a map of England, another hundred people to throw darts and all of those would be sites in England. Perhaps one landed in Hertfordshire so he'd get a map of Hertfordshire, a hundred people, a hundred darts and one might land in St Albans and he'd work out where it had landed and go to that place in St Albans with a metre square which he would throw and, wherever it landed he would do an exhaustive field study of wherever that was; road, water, scrub, street. His pieces are one metre square casts and exhaustive studies and

---

* Sir Peter Blake, CBE (1932–) and Richard Hamilton (1922–2011) – British painters, illustrators and collagists. Early exponents of Pop Art; one Beatles sleeve each . . .

the project is called *Journey to the Surface of the Earth*. He, in my view, has been incredibly influential . . . I've got his first book somewhere but I can't find it to hand . . . so when I look at Richard Long studying the surface and bringing it into a gallery I see echoes of Mark Boyle's work. He would come in and give us a lecture at art school. I used to love it; I thought, "This is what art should be about – an adventure in minutiae – arcane and idiosyncratic." I didn't realise at the time that there wasn't that much of it about, we just seemed to have a lot of it because our head of course was Peter Schmidt and his best mate was Brian Eno . . .'

Was this in London?

'Watford. That's how I first met Brian Eno. I knew about him from Roxy Music but he had left and this is what he moved back to later on, art school, so he would come in as well. It was amazingly adventurous and exciting and funny. You wouldn't get away with that now, unfortunately, at art school because they've become institutions.'

It seems so odd that you manage Bill Drummond. Aren't you polar opposites in your approaches to almost everything?

'Bill is a puritan. He's hard on himself. Loathes nostalgia. I'm interested in why he hates it so much – it's a conversation I really want to have because he's so very hard about it. It's a bit like how Julian Cope* used

---

* Julian Cope (1957–) is a British musician, poet, author and a world authority on Neolithic culture – 'with a noted and public interest in occultism and paganism'. He came to prominence in 1978 as the singer and songwriter in Liverpool

to say "I hate hippies." I think it was because he didn't want people to think that he was one. I don't know why . . .

'Nostalgia is seen as a bad thing, just as being middle class is. I don't know the answer. I'd like to formulate one; I find it fascinating because, when I design Bill's stuff, I work with him on the words and the way that the things look – we've touched on nostalgia and he's been very definite: "No, I can't have that. It looks too much like a pastiche" . . . I'm really happy with the cover of The17 book, but it was partly governed by Bill saying, "I will not have nostalgia." You know, it's great working within rules in that respect and I think people do resort to nostalgia as a cheap way of getting some-where; "Remember this? Well, we're going to give you *this*."

But I'll give you a good example of barbed nostalgia and that's The Bonzo Dog Doo Dah Band. At a time when people were being psychedelic and acid-drenched, the way The Kinks and The Bonzos referred back to British eras fascinated me because the Americans didn't do that; there was no mixing. The Bonzos took psychedelia, music hall, 1930s show tunes, and The

---

post-punk band The Teardrop Explodes – Bill Drummond was the band's producer and manager:

February 1979 – Liverpool's Zoo Records release the seminal debut 'Sleeping Gas'. It becomes Single of the Week in the rock press, being compared to 'Louie Louie' and '96 Tears'. The band's third live show is a performance of 'Camera Camera' on Tony Wilson's Granada Television programme *What's On*, transmitted from Manchester. 'Sleeping Gas' is produced by mentors Bill Drummond and David Balfe, who subsequently insinuate themselves into roles as manager/publishers of both Teardrops and The Bunnymen.
– 'Story of the Drude', www.headheritage.co.uk

Goons and put all of it together and I thought that was so amazing.'

19 August

Exploring the caravan this morning I discovered that nearly every item of possible resource bears a ticket:

1. Circus Box, Mark Copeland, 2002

ANTAR ARCHIVE

'From actual travelling show.'

SOURCE – Greenpeace Fair
PURCHASE COST – £10.00
PURCHASE DATE – Sept 4 05
FILE DATE
VALUE RATING – A (B) C

2. Wild Wales, George Borrow, 1955

ANTAR ARCHIVE

SOURCE – James Hayward 2nd hand books, Halesworth
PURCHASE COST – £4.00
PURCHASE DATE – Jan 2001
FILE DATE
VALUE RATING – A (B) C

3. A Gypsy Brownie, H.B. Davidson

ANTAR ARCHIVE

SOURCE – Edinburgh Children's Bookshop
PURCHASE COST – £10
PURCHASE DATE – April 07
FILE DATE
VALUE RATING – (A) B C

4. Treehouses of the World, Pete Nelson

ANTAR ARCHIVE

SOURCE – Strand Books, NY
PURCHASE COST – £25.95
PURCHASE DATE – June 05
FILE DATE
VALUE RATING – (A) B C

5. The Circus of Adventure, Enid Blyton

ANTAR ARCHIVE

SOURCE – Cratfield Car Boot Sale
PURCHASE COST – 25p
PURCHASE DATE – May 03
FILE DATE
VALUE RATING – (A) B C

'What a story! Exciting, mysterious, and with lots of laughs – for which Kiki, the world's best-known parrot, is mainly responsible.
Jack, Lucy-Ann, Philip and Dinah (and Gussy, a most peculiar "guest") have the adventure of a lifetime. You must read about it – about a travelling circus, a castle with secret passages, midnight escapades, and thrills galore!'

20 August

'It's important that "it having been done before" should never put you off. If it did I would never do any sleeves at all and I have to say that sometimes to bands: "If we're going to work together we have to agree to never use 'it's been done before' as a reason not to do it again" – and it's quite easy when you talk to musicians because

you can say, "If that's the case, can I go through your album and say, 'That's Scott Walker, that's The Beatles . . .'?" You still find that people say, "Oh, that's a bit like The Smiths," and I'll say, "Oh, wow! Is it? Great." Some of it's just in the soup.'

Scott Walker hangs on the wall of Cally's kitchen – re-imagined as an automata diving suit spaceman, copper tanks and mouth-gear, goggles and bands. That first morning Scott loomed behind Cally as he spread jam over his Marmite toast – because he'd hate to miss a new combination, he explained – sat eating breakfast in his nest, his trove, implement repository – resource, resource, resource . . . and then it hits me, FRIED EGGS! That image I'd been searching for, the Heath Robinson breakfast machine – the swivelling Bunsen burner train set apparatus from *Chitty Chitty Bang Bang*. Marlinspike Hall. Here's where it all ends up; the tracks run down from Fleming's windmill, past the flying car and the sweets that toot, through Nutwood, the Tour de France and footage of the moon landings, filtered, bounced round this magpie mind to now, where, over breakfast, Cally, mouth full, muses, 'Very few people but especially the tax man understand what a graphic designer does . . .' – as well The Man might scratch his head when faced with Cally and ask, 'Are these steam-powered eggs, you know, safe?'

'His house; there is his life's work,' says Bill Drummond when I ask him about Cally later. 'Working with people like me, the record covers, that's just to pay the bills.'

•　•　•　•　•

On my last Marlinspike night, I cycle out, past fields of cross-hatched stubble broom under a red sky, making a final few-mile circuit of the hall, letting the week sink in.

I think of my kitchen in Bristol, the place I normally sit to write – recalling its long oak table, the benches either side, and the mirror behind – frame stuffed with postcards and photographs, pressed down between the wood and glass.

The mirror itself is flecked with rust, the foiled back peppered.

Once it hung in my great-great-uncle's barber shop up on Regent Street in Clifton and generations of Clifton College school boys would have sat before it to be cropped – all those faces; all those eyes.

My father likes to think he'll one day catch his father, uncle or grandfather looking back at him and, of course, whenever he or I gaze into it, we do . . . but it's dark now so I fumble at the bike to engage the elderly dynamo and find it sends an odd vibration through the frame and seems to make what shallow hills I tackle harder, but the little candle-power the headlight has illuminates the road enough that I feel reassured.

Emerging from a shallow holloway near Marlinspike I see a pale owl, milky, moonfaced, drifting. I watch until it merges with the northern sky and passes into night.

SHERYL GARRATT (1961–) is a freelance journalist and editor. She currently writes for the *Telegraph*, the *Times* and *Vanity Fair* among others – having started writing for the *NME* as a teenager. Sheryl edited *The Face* from 1989 to 1995 and the *Observer* Magazine after that, during which time she worked with the photographer Jane Bown.

SHERYL GARRATT

Deal, Kent
January 2011

I'd not been to Deal before but it seemed very nice. Shingly. Quiet. A clear cold morning, the winter sea a frosted sweep, rapt anglers on the concrete pier.
Boots crunch. Collars up. Dragon breath.

Deal is where Sheryl Garratt lives and I'd caught a fast train down to see her because of a magazine interview she did with Björk in which Björk rarely featured. Sheryl spent most of her stay in Reykjavík wandering round talking to tangentially connected Icelanders, building a pointillist picture of Björk in her absence. (I thought it was brilliant, obviously, although the commissioning magazine weren't initially enamoured, apparently . . .)*

As we walked along the Bauhaus pier to the café at its prow, Sheryl told me about the way she works, the hows of interviewing and stratagems to get transcribing done – the

---

* The Björk article was in *Word* magazine, July 2003.

main one being to do it in public: 'I always think you look a complete idiot if you're in a café with a laptop, not working.'

When we reached the café it was closed so we turned back to the shore for tea and toast. After so long working on this odd book – I was still on the building site and working in bars* – it was good to meet a writer and kindred spirit. Much of what she said rang true, particularly the idea of working freelance:

> 'I know I don't want to work in an office again. I've found I am weirdly suited to a routine but it has to be my routine and it has to be a routine that I can break at any point.
> Earlier this week I did a day of really solid transcribing – the thing about my job I hate more than anything.'

Me too!

> 'Everyone does. I've tried paying other people to do it and I've realised it doesn't work, but the other day I was transcribing and the sun suddenly came out; it had been raining all day and it was such a joy to be able to stop. I walked right up to Sandown Castle, up there, and back again along the sea. I could take two hours out and choose to work until ten that night instead.

---

* The book had now taken on a talismanic quality in my life. Rather than a distraction *from* my day jobs it had become the justification and reason *to carry on with them.* My main focus now was to finish the book and get it published in the hope that it would lead me somewhere else – off the building site and out of the bars. Having said that, despite the fact that by this point I'd been working on it for several years – despite my life being in limbo – there strangely seemed no rush. I found that I was willing to carry on until the book felt finished, for the good of the book, if you like . . . of course, I assumed someone would publish it shortly thereafter.
This proved to be an error.

I love that about being self-employed. I love being in control of my own time. I've got deadlines but what I do to meet those deadlines is up to me.'

Yes, this bit – the conversation – is my favourite part of it. The transcribing afterwards is tedious. I know I'll listen to this piece of the tape, back at home, and be pleased I don't have to write it out.*

'Yes, it's sad when you listen back and you're actually relieved that you stopped to go to the loo or that the waiter has brought over another coffee – a couple of minutes you don't have to type out. I hate that part of the job but, you know, I love my job. Last week, for instance: the Pet Shop Boys are doing a ballet at Sadler's Wells and I love the Pet Shop Boys and I've interviewed them many, many times and I thought, "Oh, that'll be interesting," so I did it and it was, but then I was offered the chance to go and watch the choreographer work and it turned out to be the most magical day! Watching this man create something out of nothing with two dancers; and it started off really clumsy, mechanical and emotionless but by the end of the three hours I sat there they'd got this beautiful, emotional, flowing piece and to watch that be created, that's the best job in the world; and that was completely unexpected.'

Yes, I've found that, the things which stick are the unexpected tangents and connections . . . Jenny Saville and I kicked around the idea of a website which cross-referenced the listening, reading and viewing recommendations of artists and others – their lists – favourite books, plays, songs and artworks. So

---

* Although I did, of course, gnashing and miserable.

maybe you'd click on a title or a name, 'Johnny Marr liked this so . . . oh look, so does Sarah Waters.'
If I did it with John Gray's *Straw Dogs* I'd get Jenny Saville, David Nash, Stanley Donwood, Manic Street Preachers – the readers might seem disparate but their interests overlap.

'Really creative people, I've found, are interested in all sorts of odd things. If there are strands, and I must have interviewed hundreds of people over the last thirty years, it's that they are passionate about what they do, that they have a playful streak and that they're interested in all sorts. Tunnel vision when they're on a project is very important to get the project done, but then you always find the musician interested in architecture – interviewing Neil and Chris last week, I came away with three books I wanted to read immediately and an art show I was desperate to see, just from talking about music with them.⋆ I think that all people who are really good at anything creative are very open to other stuff – obsessions other than what they're known for . . . I'm always interested in where people's ideas come from – Mark Quinn was really interesting for that. When I went to his studio, the whole place is about "what would happen if you tried to take a photograph of popcorn exploding?" . . . "what would happen if you took something really small and made it huge?" It's all playfulness. It's about sitting in the British Museum and looking at all the statues without arms and thinking, "If these came to life they'd all be terribly disabled" – that's how he ended up doing the huge monumental marble statues of disabled people, through thinking about how people would react if the Venus de Milo

---

⋆ The Pet Shop Boys are Neil Tennant and Chris Lowe.

came alive – everyone would avert their eyes because she's got no arms. That's what led him to make that statue in Trafalgar Square of Alison Lapper.

Jonathan Ive, the guy who designs all the Apple Mac stuff, the mouse design came from looking at a drop of water on a table . . .'

How do you approach your journalism? Do you have particular working methods or patterns?

'I read voraciously, but I think most people who write will do and I'm sure whole phrases come from someone else. I think my writing is very simple. I don't think it's particularly interesting, it's very simple and it usually takes its voice from the person I've interviewed.

One of the compliments I really enjoy is "that sounded

like me" because, you know, when you have a four-hour conversation with somebody and you have to distil that down to 3,000 words there's a lot of editing that goes on; and I think, if you can still get something where the person can read it and recognise themselves . . . I'm always really pleased if that comes across . . . but Stephen King's *On Writing* is brilliant . . . I haven't really got any great original thoughts, no, isn't that terrible? With me, I think I get more inspired by seeing a good film or, especially, music than I do from writing. All that writing does, to me, is tell me how bad I am, do you know what I mean? Sometimes I'll think, "Hey, I'm pretty good," and then I'll read two lines in a David Leavitt short story that's said something I was struggling to write in five paragraphs a month before . . .' (Laughs)

I think writing is a great leveller, in that respect. I've struggled hugely to write this book – distracting myself, prevaricating, doubting its purpose and value and point . . . but I've kept on because I think, really, the only way to discover all that is to finish. But building the airship was like that! Maybe I'll always be like that, whatever I do!

'I think there is a degree of bumbling in any creative endeavour and as you get older you realise the pattern. I always think, "Oh God, I don't think I've got enough to write this," and then I transcribe it and get really depressed because there's not anywhere near enough and there's hundreds more questions and research I could have done; then I'll put off the writing, clean the house . . . and then suddenly I write the thing . . . but that's just part of my process – and I know people who do have that routine of getting up at a certain time and starting work and I wish I was like that; I wish I could work nine till three and get my work done but I'm not like that really, it just comes in bursts. But, sitting down and starting is the most important thing. It sounds really obvious but nothing happens unless you start.'

•   •   •   •   •

As it turns out, *On Writing* is very good. Subtitled 'A Memoir of the Craft', it has at its core a set of practical suggestions to help a writer write – from fundamental grammar and style guidance to the fact you should aim to write every day in a room with a door that you shut – 'The closed door is your way of telling the world and yourself that you mean business; you have made a serious commitment to write.'*

The second foreword is very heartening:

> 'This is a short book because most books about writing are filled with bullshit. Fiction writers, present company included, don't understand very much about what they do – not why it works when it's good, not why it doesn't when it's bad. I figured the shorter the book, the less bullshit.
> One notable exception to the bullshit rule is *The Elements of Style*, by William Strunk Jr and E.B. White. There is little or no detectable bullshit in that book. (Of course, it's short: at eighty-five pages it's much shorter than this one.) I'll tell you right now that every aspiring writer should read *The Elements of Style*. Rule 17 in the chapter titled Principles of Composition is "Omit needless words." I will try to do that here.'

---

* *On Writing: A Memoir of the Craft*, Stephen King (Hodder & Stoughton, 2000), p. 178.

Craft seems to have fallen out of fashion in recent years – lumped in with up-cycling, hobby jobs and DIY – relegated to a chintz Luddite faux-past. Craft as nostalgia. Craft smeared sentimental and twee, relegated to a verb league below Build, Engineer, Construct, and Fashion . . . while, to my mind, craft has always been kin to graft. To me, crafting something evokes the idea of deep knowledge and skill, but the word seems so divisive now – twinned with Pritt Stick and knit your own crackle-glaze cupcakes; interchangeable with *knocked together* . . . imagine a weakened, bed-bound William Morris being bludgeoned by the crazed kith of Barry Bucknell, well it's *exactly* like that. The last time I was in Norwich a former art school tutor grinned when I used the word. 'Ah,' she said, 'the C word.'*

---

* Since the introduction to this book was written the art school have axed a great deal of their part-time contracts and cut their technical staff numbers by about a third – nearly all the craftsmen and practitioners purged and phased out – more often the older ones with the hands-on nous and experience of making their skills pay the bills in the real world. Those that remain, having reapplied for their jobs and climbed over their fellows, are left 'explaining the blindingly obvious to the grossly inept', as one described it to me recently.
You know, one course technician to 210 students, that sort of thing . . .

The goalposts have shifted – but the Vice-Chancellor has merely brought the institution into line with current government policy – vocationally focused – at a time when some councils in England have cut their arts budgets by 100 per cent and the Education Secretary advocates a school curriculum and set of 'core' qualifications which dispense with the arts altogether but sees no problem in advocating teenagers get into five-figure debt to study it thereafter. Set against this, the art school seems positively benign, but the gleeful squeezing of staff numbers and fetishisation of campus facilities, as if unfettered interaction between students and the latest kit is the panacea, seems wrong-headed and short-sighted. I think they're prizing the wrong assets.
Knowledge abides in the hands and minds of those who've lived and experienced, worked, travelled and developed artistry. There is nothing more inspiring than interaction with such people – be they sculptors, writers, performance artists or graphic designers.

A tool without the facility to deploy it is dead – a lifeless machine.

So I love the fact that Stephen King subtitled his book on writing 'A Memoir of the Craft' – *the* Craft. It is a great statement from a writer who's honed and crafted some of the most memorable and horrific stories in the last forty years; meticulously engineered blood-soaked narratives, hewn and potent. King's craft gives them Hell.

VAUGHAN OLIVER (1957–) is a British graphic designer, best known for creating artwork for record label 4AD with his design studios 23 Envelope and v23. His unique, distinctive design is noted for its expressive use of type, emotive photography and creative collaboration.

VAUGHAN OLIVER

Epsom
November 2010–July 2012

Home is the fulcrum of this chapter. I've previously explored ideas of landscape, habitat and workspace in the book, but here those ideas coalesce and I find out what happens when that place is lost . . . as well as exploring other pressing questions such as:

> What is the purpose of a record sleeve?
> What is typography for?
> And why deny the beauty of a squashed frog?

Vaughan Oliver's graphic design celebrates, challenges and progresses the idea of packaging at both a physical and cerebral level, playing with ideas of collectability, belonging, significance, and insinuation. You can fall into his oeuvre and immerse yourself completely – swaddled in a visual world itself wrapped round the aural.

Employed and given space within the record label 4AD to create an aesthetic, almost all the music which emerged under that moniker – one of the first things he designed –

was branded with his imprint; artwork both individual to that group and congruous with the parent body – fleshly, visceral, tactile visuals . . . made in 15 Alma Road, Wandsworth, London.

My relationship with Vaughan Oliver began with the bull terrier and haloed monkey pictured on the covers of seven-inch singles by the band Pixies;* a great band with a great aesthetic – devised and helmed by Vaughan:

'I stand in the glory of their shadow.'

A *Surfer Rosa*** poster followed me through university – every time I moved house it was pinned to a new wall. After I graduated it returned home with me. I still have it.

Today I'm stumbling about in the cellar of Vaughan's house. Stepping over crates in the dark, skinning my knuckles on brickwork while lifting boxes out of the way, searching for a cache of original PMT proofs.***
Once back up in Vaughan's study with our boxes he begins to lay them out:

---

* Pixies are an American band who formed in Boston, Massachusetts in 1986. The group broke up in 1993 but reunited in 2004.
Tectonic bass lines, screaming, ripsaw solos, Quiet – Loud – Quiet – LOUD, Pentecostal gonzo . . . I last saw them play at The Troxy in Limehouse – a converted Art Deco cinema.
They opened with 'Cecilia Ann' while I was in a queue for the bar . . . the drinks line froze and then sped up.

** *Surfer Rosa* was Pixies' first full-length album, released in 1988.

*** PMT: Photomechanical Transfer – a process that photographically translates a drawing or collage into a black and white image on glossy paper. Can be used to produce a film positive or to make a photo stencil.

'That's probably one of the best record sleeves you'll ever see in your life,' he states, deadpan, daring me to disagree, 'although I don't want to build it up too much . . . It's one of my favourites, let's say. That's a proof of it. I think it was a bit of a breakthrough for me; this process, this camera, this PMT camera, it's how we used to do all our own type before scanners. You'd get the type in from a type-setter, you'd chop it round in a different order – or what I used to do, I used to go to old encyclopaedias for old typefaces, thirties and forties sort of stuff, and copy them out. You can see each letter I've spaced out is individually hand-spaced; so you create a bit of artwork, you shoot it on a camera, black and white . . . I was always fascinated by the underexposed bits around the edges.

So this, as a part of the process, you then subvert and play with the parameters that were there. I was so excited that day I thought, "Well, why don't I just shoot the whole thing?" It's underexposed to put in some extra texture and the revelation for me was taking a track listing and making it into a picture rather than merely information and illustration – in that, my approach to typography is similar to that of an illustrator, perhaps – because I hated type at college. Didn't study it. It was words I had to put on my pictures. I wanted to be an illustrator. So then, when I was obliged to use it in my first studio job working in a packaging design studio and specifically working on drinks labels I suddenly saw, "Oh! If I take a fat face and a skinny face and a script face and a big face . . ." because that's what it was to me. It was like texture.'

I guess, because you didn't come at it with preconceived ideas of typography you were perhaps less bound and more open.

'Some folk, like teachers, like to say, "You can't break the rules until you've learnt them," but I wasn't aware of the rules. What rules? I'm still just doing what I feel. I'm aware of a hierarchy of type, making things read and words that work in a certain order.'

This would seem to go back to the core point of type.

'It has to communicate information.'

It's not text and art, though.

'No, it's homogenous and I think that is what I aim for in a lot of my work – especially the early work. When we were shooting something, I had in mind the kind of type I wanted and where it was going to go, so it became part of the picture. That's really what I was aiming for all the time – although my aesthetic changed over the years.'

You can see here how the type bleeds into the main image.

'So these prints, they would come out of the PMT machine. You see you couldn't get this organic sensitive edge to things now . . . these are just fabulous, aren't they? You know, look at that, you can see the artwork on the table – taped down and the bits of card on there, are you with me? That's the quality. All this, I love and got great satisfaction from. It's like knitting. You're knitting this stuff together and it was fantastic, really rewarding for me in terms of design.
The PMT machine allowed me to go back in on the images, change the images and add new stuff to it. These are obviously a work in progress but, isn't that lovely, just black and white?'

You can't do this with scanners?

'No. It's not got the same softness, the organic quality with a scan because it has to go through another process after that – it has to be scanned then printed but the original, this . . .'*

This was a one shot thing.

'Yes. It's a stand-alone process.'

And this is not possible any more because they've stopped making the chemicals?

'Some of the students the other day said, "Well, it's a photographic process, so why don't you use photographic paper and, you know . . ." But it's not. I can't. It's that positive/negative going through that certain chemical that gives this quality.
Was that worth a trip downstairs and a shaved knuckle?'

Yes. It was.
This is absolutely what it's all about.

•   •   •   •   •

I first heard Vaughan speak about his work in October 2009 at a lecture he gave at University College London. The talk

---

* Despite his reticence, Vaughan has done some notable work with scanners – the cover of *This Rimy River: Vaughan Oliver & V23 Graphic Works 1988–94*, is a particularly sanguine example. He laughs when I mention it:

'Ha! Yes, shows how I've mellowed. The first thing I did when I got a scanner was slap a lovely great ox's tongue down on it . . . that was fun. Bugger to clean up, though.'

was steeped in anarchic humour; darkly beautiful artwork was projected behind him while he spoke, framing Vaughan as he laid out his methods, approach and scope:

> 'I've brought along a selection of my best work from the last three decades. This evening will be an informal affair but what I'd like to do is explain the role of collaboration in my work and also pick out and explore the idea of graphic authorship – that is, I've always employed and commissioned other artists and photographers to work with me as an art director and to work with me as a graphic designer; those are my roles. The images are created by other people – photographers, artists and illustrators – but I think you'll manage to see a thread that runs throughout, something of me that runs through that work. Now, I might describe it as being a love of texture or particular use of typography or a certain sense of humour in the work, but when I was teaching a Design for Music short course recently, I showed the students designs I'd done for the Pixies, the Wolfgang Press, Colourbox and Throwing Muses and, though they all look very different and have different identities and brands, I said I saw a thread running through it and a Portuguese student said, "That's your soul."
> We tend not to talk in terms of soul in this country so I'll keep it quite simple but I like that idea.'

Later that month I meet up with Vaughan at his home.
We sit in his current workspace, a study lined with white built-in shelves. On the shelves sit thousands of books, records and discs – their coloured spines making odd patterns as your eyes pan across.
A large window looks out onto the street. In front of this is a plan chest. On top of the plan chest stands a massive ceramic

bull which casts strange shadows on the floorboards. In the centre of the room is a white desk with a white Mac. A considered space.

At this, our first meeting, we speak about his current environment and how it's changed since the early days at 4AD. He warns me that this Epsom semi* and study doesn't provide the best picture of his physical space as he'd like it.

> 'I had a very nice studio in the last house. This one's smaller. The parallel motion boards, the drawing boards, they were at 4AD – that was a good studio.'

---

* Formerly home to Aubrey Beardsley – noted aesthete and kindred exponent of the lush, grotesque and fleshy.

That space no longer exists?

'It houses a different art department now. We were obliged to leave there in the middle of the nineties when 4AD went a bit pear-shaped – they culled their staff from something like eighteen to three and we were some of the first to go – me and my two assistants at the time . . . but those assistants were needed and we had deadlines every day. That was at a point when we were thriving; halcyon days. It just imploded on itself really, got a bit too big for its boots, I think. Ivo* had already gone . . . it was on the wonk after that because Ivo was a bit special – if you had the money for a trip to Santa Fe you'd get a good interview out of him. He defines enigma, I learnt at the time – but he was just twenty-four hours a day, driven. Driven by his love and passion for music. A very special fella I had a great empathy for. It's worth saying that, when it began, 4AD was an independent label. It still is an independent label, technically, but independent in those days was more about a philosophy and attitude whereas today it's become a style, I think, but in those days it was about kicking against the pricks; it was about providing an alternative to the mainstream and it came out of punk – it was post-punk.
Where I was fortunate was that I bumped into Ivo when he was setting up 4AD. I'd bump into him in clubs, watching the same bands, and I'd an empathy for

* Ivo Watts-Russell (1954–) was joint founder of 4AD. As well as overseeing the record label for twenty years he produced and curated several records, notably the output of This Mortal Coil. He used the title 'Musical Director' to explain his role. Watts-Russell sold the label back to original distributors Beggars Banquet Records at the end of 1999, moved to California and now works in photographic and art publishing.

the kind of music he was putting out . . . and over the course of an evening I persuaded him that he needed a logo and some kind of consistency in terms of what he was doing. In time, I became his first employee. We both shared what I suppose are very old-fashioned values – we both cared about how the product was perceived and how the music was packaged and we both had an inherent sense of quality. Ivo was putting out music not because it would sell but because he loved it and he wanted other people to hear it.'

Where did you go after 4AD?

'We moved on and went independent. Chris Bigg, my assistant at 4AD, and I set up partnership and had a studio in Battersea for three years. The black years . . .'

Not good?

'No . . . but it took me three years to realise that I'd lost this very impressive retainer that I was earning at 4AD and I'd taken on thousands of pounds' worth of debt . . . small numbers but, for me who hadn't had that before, who'd had free use of a studio and not paid any bills – telephone bills, assistant bills . . . It took me a long time to realise that I'd lost this much (mimes) and I'd asked myself to get this much (mimes much larger amount) and I was never going to bridge it, not from where I was coming from. I'd been cocooned for so many years, never networked, never met people.'

They all came to you.

'Yeah, but suddenly I was in a position where I was in business and I couldn't do it. I couldn't work out how to do it. We tried to employ people to do that for us and they didn't work out – so it was three very hard years getting into debt.

So we knocked that on the head and then I pulled it all back into the house. Everybody said that's where I should have started anyway, and I had a much bigger space in a place in Wandsworth and that felt like my own, I had room to breathe. Coming here, it's almost like the studio is in storage, in limbo. So today you're seeing me in my house and it's a sort of home office; it doesn't have the atmosphere of where we used to work, it takes experience and being without to understand that; I lost my home, and there was a sense of bereavement as well, I guess . . . and on top of that was the technological revolution which was my *bête noire* for ten years at least; I couldn't get on board with it. I lost my balance. I was bringing in assistants to work machines because I didn't know how. Control moved away from me.'

Things came between you and your work.

'From being in total control, I was suddenly a baby. I didn't know where my work was. It used to be over there in cardboard job bags and then it was in folders on a desktop . . . this might all sound strange but with digital I was suddenly relying upon this person who had just come into my studio to find things for me on the computer and it was too intimate . . .'

You were all about ink on paper.

'I always used to describe the colours as "electric". I suppose if you were to go to an audiophile and talk about the warmth of vinyl it would be the same; it's just a quality that you can't read on a graph, you feel it. There's something there, this extra dimension and if you're talking about food you're talking about that Japanese thing they discovered – you've got the five taste senses and then you've got "Umami", this other element of taste that's always been there but only the Japanese have a word for.'

It makes sense, you're experiencing something – when I'm listening to records I will sit there with my record player, take the vinyl out of the sleeve, put the record on, place the needle on the grooves. It commands my attention.

'I'll go with that. That whole part – the ritual – you take the vinyl out; it's a different package – it's not a little booklet in a stupid bit of plastic. It has physical presence, you've objectified it. It's something to have and to hold, I think. Sexy black vinyl. Needle on the record; it's all experience . . . and I need to get my record deck set up in here really . . .

I did a project with my MA students at Kingston on "Home" – which is a great project for them because I've got twenty-five students and they're from all over the world . . . and it struck me whilst doing that project that that's where my home was, at 4AD. I didn't know it at the time but in retrospect it's easier to say, "This was the place where I was most comfortable; this is the place I had control; this is the place where I was allowed to be creative."

We were in the building. It was a very creative place, so when that came down it took me a long time to recover and I miss it. I just think that way of working – Chris, Paul and myself stood at parallel motion boards in the same space – just that physical thing of standing up, and having banter, working on your board . . . you're

311

cutting this artwork out and I've got a comma on the end of my scalpel and then you're placing that in the artwork. Most important, that physical connection, a satisfaction and reward at the end of the day.

I miss that old process, the simple process of crafting a sleeve with paper and glue and a scalpel.'

Do you have banter with your students?

'To a degree, yes, and one of the reasons I got into education was because I was missing that banter, I was getting a bit of cabin fever I think, left to my own devices. I don't have great self-discipline so it's nice to have a bit of structure in your life and know you're going to be in Kingston on a Thursday and Epsom on a Monday. Going into those environments as well, the tutors down at Epsom have been so much fun and there's a sense of care that I get from them. They're not just old farts that are just doing their job and ticking off the days, no, they're keen and they're interested.

I would love to be the person who can be left to their own devices for a week but I can't. I need deadlines and I need interaction, and I didn't realise how much I needed that until I was sat for week after week . . .'

How much was that impacting on the work you were doing?

'It was impacting only inasmuch as I wasn't motivated to do it as much as I am these days because my time is split – I'm getting a buzz from going into Epsom; I'm getting a buzz from going to Kingston, you know? It carries on; the dialogue carries on. Otherwise, when I'm left to it, I get stuck inside my head and I didn't realise until a few years ago how much I need that collaboration, relationship, getting out . . . that's what

was missing from my life. Perhaps people from the outside think, "Oh yeah, he's a typical person that works
on his own," you know, "in his own world." But I'm not
like that! I'm a collaborator and I need people coming
through the door.'

Maybe this is down to your work, though – at once tailored
and idiosyncratic – suggesting an uncompromising nature; a
resolute person; not somebody to stand fools, perhaps.

'Does it? I don't see it like that, I see the whole process
as collaborative; I like to get on with my clients and I
don't like to fight them. You know, once I saw myself as
in the business of educating the clients – so it was really
a gentle process to work without offending that band
by saying, "I know better" . . . It's an interesting point
you raise, though.'

Do you think people might be intimidated by your oeuvre?
I mean, I told people I was going to interview Vaughan Oliver
and the reaction was 'Really? How did you get that!?'

'What do you think, coming today? He's alright,
isn't he? Down to earth . . . I mean, it's not an image
I've sought to build up. That's one of the reasons I'm
on Facebook and it's lovely and weird. I meet people on
Facebook, you know, there's a farming game I play
on there, so Jane Bloggs from Seattle might post a message saying, "It's so surreal, I'm playing Farmville with
my design hero! I do what I do because of you." I've
had so many great reactions and responses from people
who've written to me or I've met at gigs or exhibitions,
they say, "I'm doing what I do because of you." That,
to me, is success; inspiring somebody to do that, to
go and make their way, and I would say a lot of that

inspiration comes from being linked with music and the work touching people in their formative years; they're a bit more vulnerable to inspiration then . . . but you used a very strong word there, Daniel: "Uncompromising". I think I compromise with every project. I'm listening to the client's needs – if the client is a musician, if it's Charles,★ I'll listen to what he wants, what the music is about; clients would never accept something that they didn't agree with.'

Vaughan leaves the room to take a telephone call.
While he's away I think about him on his Facebook farm, spending his evenings feeding cyber cows and growing his cyber crops.

★ Charles Michael Kittridge Thompson IV, also known as Black Francis and Frank Black – Pixies' frontman and solo artist.

I go online to take a quick tour of his plantation and see corn planted to spell out words, flower symbols in psychedelic patterns and shapes. The nature of the digital make-up of the site and the repetition of its design bring to mind an auto-stereogram.

Is there something behind the corn shaped into phalluses and hearts? Is this Vaughan's own set of Nazca Lines, geoglyphs laid out to speak to those of kindred tastes . . . didn't the Nazca set out dogs and monkeys too?

Iconic dogs and monkeys . . . or maybe Vaughan just does it for a bit of a laugh.

My Farmville reveries are interrupted as Vaughan returns with a wooden board:

> 'I used to work on that when I was fourteen. Lovely piece of board, isn't it? The patina of age . . . I'm at home. I've got *Doctor Who* on, right? Patrick Troughton and the fella before. Banana sandwiches. I'm going into *Dixon of Dock Green*. Saturday afternoon; the wrestling's just finished and I've got the African rift valley on me lap. The interface between the African rift valley and my fourteen-year-old thighs is this bit of wood.
>
> What I didn't talk about in the lecture was my mum's poetry book.
>
> After Mum passed away I was going through her things and I found her anthology of poetry, I wish I had it at hand. This was poetry she collected, the general theme was absence – Dad's away at war, up there in his Wellington bomber.
>
> Not a crossing-out in the book.
>
> Beautiful fountain pen, beautiful writing.
>
> I've got that of hers. I have this board which was my dad's but, with the advent of the Mac, collecting memories and things, what do you pass on?

A disk is not going to have the same objective connection as when my mum was writing that poetry with
that pen or when I was doing my artwork with parallel
motion boards and a scalpel, it goes into your tools.
There's a great poem by Seamus Heaney about him
looking out the window watching his father digging;
he talks about digging with his pen, and it is about that
digging, it's about the tool and the physical connection,
isn't it?'*

· · · · ·

Vaughan begins to take me though his plan chests of archive.
The colours are so vibrant and the textures so tactile – a treasure trove of lush print and graphics – shiny lacquers, deep
matte blacks, glossy card sets . . . Prints and proofs from 4AD,
commissioned posters by theatres and magazines, college
work, photographs, PMT type experiments, contact sheets
and layered-test prints overwritten with instructions to the
printers on tracing paper and flaking tape.

'This layered feel is typical of the way we used to work
 – all analogue. A lot of students can't get that and I
have to explain, "It was in my head and then it was on
separate sheets of black and white artwork that were
then specced to the printer."
I'd have some of Simon's photographs and be thinking, "Oh, what colour will that be? What colour will
that be?"'

Vaughan pauses and grins as he looks over the copious notes,
diagrams and arrow attached to the sheet.

---

* 'Digging', *Death of a Naturalist*, Seamus Heaney (Faber and Faber, 1966).

'As you can see I've given the printer no specification whatsoever on this one! Jesus.' (Laughter)

'Here's a negative sheet which I've stained with chemicals and, again, talking about what excited me and what I put to the foreground, it's all about the edges of the print. The edges and the unintended. The edges, the accidents, the incidentals.

This is a nice bit of artwork, one of the first, 1982? And that's what we spent years doing – building this identity for the label at the same time as working for the bands.'

Other designers, with the shock of the new, must have got rid of their physical archives – so many archives on floppy discs, SyQuests and Zip discs must have been damaged or lost. These proofs and copies and clippings are a great resource to have kept.

'I was encouraged right from the beginning to keep a record of it all.

You would drive round Hammersmith roundabout and get an insight into what was going on at the cutting edge of graphic design if there was a Peter Saville poster there, a Neville Brody poster there, a Vaughan Oliver poster. Stuff from really obscure bands but full size, 60 x 40s. Not just heads and shoulders and logos. It was fantastic. It gave a fabric to the city.

So, again, as a label we used to do these for the record shops and then we got to the stage where we'd do the bigger ones – the A2s – and we collected those and sold them as a set, as a unit. Doesn't happen today.'

So, apart from the really large-scale posters, your archive is all here in your house; you've kept it all to hand?

'All the artwork stuff is stored in a cupboard in Wandsworth.'

Do you have crates of artefacts – Perspex planets, hair hearts, stuffed monkeys and the like?

'Not really. The monkey was rented.' (Laughter)

You do appear to be a bit of a hoarder, though, Vaughan.

'Me? Well, graphic designers often are. I can't throw stuff away.* The archive in Wandsworth is costing me more money than makes sense but I like to think it's going to be worth something one day, you know? I might not be here to appreciate it but the boys will . . . or I find a nice investor who wants to buy the archive, if you like, which would be fabulous – put the boys through college . . .

Somebody suggested that I should get it valued and assessed the other day actually, get Christie's or Sotheby's in – their modern graphics department – and if it's only worth ten quid I'll stop paying the £200 a month rental on it, you know? But I would like to sell it. I don't want to give it to somebody unless I found a college to really look after it properly. You used the word "resource" earlier but I'd have to stipulate that I wouldn't lose the copyright and it's there as a teaching resource. That's something I'd like to do. I'd like to have it catalogued because at the moment the archive

---

* Exhibit A, M'lud: one drawer containing a desiccated umbilical cord.
Exhibit B: one framed piece of toast; carbonised.
Exhibit C: forty-six galvanised buckets bearing the V23 moniker arranged in the drive to spell out the word 'TITS' . . . (fade out to much coughing and rustling of papers).

is a mess. I'd love it to be archived, catalogued and digitised but it's a big project, that's why I'd like a pro-fessorship here that would allow me the time to do that . . . The Design Museum have been interested in the past but they want a proposal, writing stuff down, I never got round to that . . . because in the past some-body has always gone, "Los Angeles – come and show; Tokyo – come and show, Paris – come and show," so I've always just gone with them but this is now me having to go to them and say, "Is this good enough?" . . . and the other thing is I'm very aware that it does your head in, having an exhibition on that scale. You know, Jon Barnbrook? It nearly broke him, nervous break-down; Neville Brody when he had his, nervous break-down, almost went bankrupt – what's that about?'*

You're all very emotional, open people perhaps?

'I think I've developed an emotional quotient over the years and that's what I bring to a lot of work. I think I'm less prepared for upheavals than another man might be who knows how to steel himself for business.
I'm someone who has worked on allowing emotional response. I develop my emotional response in the work that I do. I haven't cut it off and got on with business; and that's a big thing to say and it might be a silly thing

---

* Jon Barnbrook (1966–) and Neville Brody (1957–) are eminent British graphic designers – friends and peers of Vaughan.
The former has a website which promises a 'Multi-disciplinary design consultancy based in London, specialising in graphic design, motion graphics, and custom fonts'; the latter is currently Head of Programme & Dean of School for the Royal College of Art's Visual Communication Programme.
Vaughan's website features an email address and a picture of him naked, wangling some eels about.

to say but I think I have allowed my emotional, poetic, artistic side to develop way beyond the business sense.'

What did your dad do?

'He was a simple fella, a very simple fella. Where I come from, County Durham, the land of the Prince Bishops, the earth is underscored by amazing lines and veins of coal and mining. The National Coal Board. That was his work. He was a mining surveyor.

His neighbour told a great story about how, on my dad's retirement, the neighbour made him go and play golf and he said, "Everywhere we fuckin' went in County Durham, all your dad would talk about as we were walking up to the next green was what's going on underneath."

Man, that is so beautiful. He described the surface as a skin and all his knowledge was underground.

I said to him, "I'm going to scatter your ashes on Sunderland's football ground," and we'd just moved to a new ground called The Stadium of Light – which all the Newcastle fans make great fun of, obviously, with their poetry – but I thought, "All of a sudden it makes sense, The Stadium of Light."'

Was it a particular place on the pitch?

'Yeah, you weren't allowed on the pitch because of the acidic quality of ashes – obviously it's a popular thing to do – so you had to put it round the edges, but what was fabulous was, off the touchline was the turf that they'd taken from the old ground, where my dad and I used to go. The old Roker Park.

So, Sunderland was the football team but we were south-west Durham. I grew up in a new town, a satellite town. After the Second World War they built a lot of new towns (rummaging among his shelves); these books are great, you should check them out, *Festival of Britain*. They did these guides to the whole of Britain and this was the journey up . . . (flicking through) so we get to:

"The Great North Road and the main line of British Railways penetrate together the heart of the Durham coalfield. Leaving Darlington, the traveller is woven through a monotonous landscape and the road cuts through the factory estate and new town which is growing like an inflammation around the old agricultural village of Aycliffe."★

★ The *About Britain* guides were published by Collins in 1951 for the Festival of Britain Office.

'The Festival shows how the British people, with their energy and natural resources, contribute to civilisation. So the guide books as well celebrate a European country alert, ready for the future,' wrote the general editor, Geoffrey Grigson.

'Not everyone has ten shillings or fifteen shillings to spend on a fat topographical volume. Here are 94 pages of lively matter including upwards of 50 illustrations for a very reasonable price.'

– Dust-jacket blurb

1 *West Country* by Geoffrey Grigson
2 *Wessex* by Geoffrey Grigson
3 *Home Counties* by R.S.R. Fitter
4 *East Anglia* by R.H. Mottram
5 *Chilterns to Black Country* by W.G. Hoskins
6 *South Wales and the Marches* by W.J. Gruffydd
7 *North Wales and the Marches* by W.J. Gruffydd
8 *East Midlands and the Peak* by W.G. Hoskins
9 *Lancashire and Yorkshire* by Leo Walmsley
10 *The Lakes and Tyneside* by Sid Chaplin
11 *The Lowlands of Scotland* by John R. Allan
12 *The Highlands and Islands of Scotland* by A. Dunnett
13 *Northern Ireland* by E. Estyn Evans

Each illustrated volume contained ninety-four pages.
Published price was three shillings and sixpence.

'That's where I grew up.
I grew up in a bruise . . . although an inflammation's
worse than a bruise, perhaps . . . a pus centre.
It wasn't a very colourful part of the world.
A very monochrome place.
Mum and Dad were just ordinary folk. Dad worked for
the Coal Board; Mum was a housewife. I don't know
where the artistic influence came from . . .'

Where do these visceral qualities come from then?
I'd imagined he might have been a butcher because of the
viscera of your work. The heart on the sleeve, the innards
exposed.
Last night while changing channel I caught a split second
of Hugh Fearnley-Whittingstall slamming down a great load
of kidneys onto a kitchen counter and I thought, 'I'm seeing
Vaughan tomorrow.'

'Mmm. I suppose most of my stuff's intuitive.'

From the gut? Guts would work well with this analogy I'm
making.

'The Chinese say the liver is the seat of creativity . . .
Where does it come from? Okay, I'm going to go right
back; it doesn't come from my parents, okay, where
does it come from? I can remember where it would
pick up and I can remember studying Jonathan Swift
and *Gulliver's Travels*. I love telling adults the story –
when you get to the fourth book you've got the Yahoos
shitting out of the trees! You've got the Houyhnhnms
– the horses endowed with reason . . . him taking his
gloves off and them seeing it as him peeling his skin
off . . . Wow! That's fabulous. I loved the third book
as well when they go to Laputa – which is peopled by

academics – and even then I was getting this idea from the book of academics being unable to communicate on a regular level; so these academics employed runners, and those runners each had a stick with an inflated pig's bladder on the end and they'd knock it against the chap who was meant to do the talking so as to remind him to talk and they knocked it against the chap who was meant to be doing the listening – "Use your ear." Fuck me! That's fabulous. I think I was the only one to enjoy the books, certainly to that extent, at fifteen or sixteen.'

Do you have many touchstones like that you return to?

'In terms of methodology while approaching a job, Junichiro Tanizaki's book *In Praise Of Shadows* and a book on Wabi-sabi – a Japanese aesthetic which asks us to look closely and appreciate the beauty of decay, the patina of age and natural shapes; a kind of comparison between the modern aesthetic, which might be epitomised by a white ceramic cube, and Wabi-sabi, an open wooden bowl.★

That was a book I came across maybe ten or fifteen years ago in Los Angeles. You know when you see or read something and go, "Thank fuck somebody's explained to me why I like that and what that's about!" So it's quite nice to return to that and, again, it's like that feeling, it's a comfort thing. I know where I'm at, there. I'm in the zone. I can do that with *In Praise of Shadows* and I can do that with this Wabi-sabi book.

★ *In Praise Of Shadows*, Junichiro Tanizaki (Vintage Classics, 2001). Published in Japan in 1933, the first English translation was by Leete's Island Books, 1977.

Visually, when I'm starting a project I'll pull books off the shelf that I think relate to the sound . . .'

Your house is very good in that respect with all these shelves.

'I like books. That was my main vice when I was earning money; I could buy them for dollars in Los Angeles, as opposed to pounds here, and 4AD would ship them back for me. So I was going over and doing commercial jobs, TV stuff, earning money and going into this one bookshop – this bookseller knew me, he'd previously had a record shop, so he knew the aesthetic . . .'

He'd have them lined up.

'He'd have them ready for me and I'd go through them, "Yes. Yes. Yes. No. Yes" – such a decadent way of buying books. Lovely things, books.'

At this point one of Vaughan's two sons pops his head into the study and enquires what's for tea. He's called Beckett, it transpires. Vaughan and Beckett discuss fish fingers. I never discover what the other son is called; Sillitoe, I imagine, or Osborne.
When the tea situation has been sorted, both boys return to haring about the house, thumping up and down the stairs. I ask Vaughan about Beckett and he grins.

'Yes, Beckett: *The Unnamable*.'*

---

* *The Unnamable* is a 1953 novel by Samuel Beckett – the final of his 'Trilogy' of novels, the first two of which are *Molloy* and *Malone Dies* – originally published in French as *L'Innommable*.

Moving through to the kitchen, Vaughan lays out one of his most recent projects, *Minotaur*; a block of a tome, a downy grey case embossed with PIXIES, as big as a briefcase, with the look and heft of a rectangular seal pup.

A monster of a box-set, *Minotaur* holds all of the studio albums by the band Pixies but is made up of completely new artwork – re-imagined by Vaughan and photographer Simon Larbalestier* – funded and distributed by Jeff Anderson of Artists in Residence (A+R).**

The collection is the definition of deluxe, the pelt clam-shell case is just the beginning – care and attention and love have been lavished to such an extent that, as more and more of the collection is unpacked and placed on the glass breakfast table, I begin to giggle. It's mad. People don't do this any more, if they ever did – a 54-page book with gold-plated CDs inside, all the Pixies' albums on heavy vinyl, a Blu-Ray disc and DVD, Giclée prints and a 72-page hard-cover book.

> 'You're dealing with that French word *oeuvre* here; it's not about the specific albums. Where I was proud of work in the past, here I was doing things individually for each piece of music. This is about a body of work.'

(Looking through the books and prints) If the singles were images for individual songs, this is a collection of images for a catalogue and career.

> 'Yes. That's what I had initially on the title page, "Catalogue", but then I tried to think of a better word, like

---

* Simon Larbalestier (1962–) is an English photographer who has collaborated with Vaughan for many years, notably on 4AD / Pixies projects.

** Artists in Residence is a production company based in California, responsible for the release of deluxe editions (limited, exclusive and otherwise) of record and film packages by bands such as Sigur Rós, Nine Inch Nails and Beck. Founded by Jeff Anderson, A+R usually work by licensing recordings from an artist's regular record company.

"Compendium" or something, but didn't. I settled on
"A Visual Tribute". Have a look.'

I begin to pick through the pages of 'electric' images and fur-
lined record sleeves.
Squashed frog!

'Anybody else would have stepped over it but Simon
Larbalestier's in there; he's not going in there because it's a squashed frog, though; he sees the textural
relationship with the tarmac. It's tremendous.'

I think this is an astonishing and beautiful thing.

'You have to remember, I'm somebody who works on
his own, not even in a studio; so any feedback . . . I'm
really glad you like it!
Did you see the posters inside?
This is one of my favourite parts of the whole thing;
it's the lay-down for the slipcase. When I was doing it
I thought it looked great. To me it looks like an Issey
Miyake garment or something . . . so I thought I'd run
them together.'

How did Jeff Anderson respond to the mooted re-imagining
of such iconic sleeves? Did he originally approach you with
the offer of a free rein?

'He called me, then came over and we had a very good
meeting where he seemed supportive of everything I
wanted to do. He guided what the package was going
to look like in terms of that box. I showed him a few
things and he went for this clamshell case for everything to fit inside – so he had a creative role there, he
inspired me.

He'd set two precedents with Nine Inch Nails and the
Sigur Rós packages, but when I suggested we do something new he went for it.
I mean, it would have been a lot easier for him just to
take the original sleeves and make a nice package out of
them; he could have done that with another designer,
he didn't have to come to me, so immediately I knew
that it was going to be a good collaboration.'

You worked with some of your students on *Minotaur*. Were
they familiar with Pixies?

'They'd mostly heard of them. Since the reunion there's
been a resurgence of interest. One of the lads, a first-
year lad, had an album but not the cover and he didn't
know what the original cover looked like (laughs);
so here was us about to do the antidote to all that; I
thought that was funny.
They didn't take a lot of introducing to it and I'd handpicked them, obviously, so I knew what certain students could do. I think a major part of my role was to
get them to relax and say to them, "Don't worry about
it, it'll be alright. It's a professional job and you're going
to get nervous but, you know . . . not to frighten you but
it's probably the best job I've ever worked on."
To get them to relax I suggested that they didn't work
towards a finished image or graphic; they were going
to provide the ingredients for the pot. I thought of it as
"found graphics" with which to make the package. You
can see that, it's just like snippets and snapshots. It's
not a polished final thing which wouldn't have fitted
with the music . . .'

Is it the lyrics or the music which usually fire you up?

'If you're designing a book cover, you need to read the book. If you design a record cover, you need to listen to the music; you need to talk to the band, to my mind, otherwise it's worthless.

I think, when a record sleeve really works, it's actually creating a third thing that is much bigger than the sum of its parts, that's what I always aim for, and I would say I use the lyrics as a jumping-off point although there's nothing in *Minotaur* that's specific to lyrics while on previous packaging there might be a line in a song . . .'

Monkey Gone To Heaven.

'Yes, specifically. It had the right atmosphere.

The photographer in all of these cases was Simon Larbalestier.

I'd seen Simon's photography two years previous to actually working on the Pixies' stuff, and when that work came up I immediately went to him. He's like the fifth Pixie for me because his own personal work had echoes of the same themes – whether it was sex . . . and lust . . . or lust . . . and sex, sex and lust, oh, and religion as well, yeah, he had a kind of Pentecostal thing going on . . . (Laughter)

Simon was already dealing in that subject matter, and it seemed very natural to put him on the end of that process but not to look over his shoulder, I don't do that, I'm not that kind of art director. I think, to get the best work out of a photographer, you have to have chosen them for the right reasons. My job's done when I think, "Yeah, Jim's going to work well with Lush, Simon's going to work well with Pixies."

. . . There's no need then to stand over the shoulder of the photographer and impose myself, my ego, my ideas on the situation. It's all there in the music, it's all there in the lyrics. We'd discuss that – let that photographer run with the project.'

I dug out some Pixies' singles recently – 'Dig for Fire', 'Allison', 'Velouria' . . .

'I think *Barbarella* was the inspiration for "Velouria".'

They're very foily and layered, those sleeves.

'With the *Minotaur* book there are no layers. The book is sparse and pared down . . . it's a book of real things. Analogue. All done in the lens.
I think that's the key to enjoying *Minotaur* in all its vitality and energy: everything is real. That was the idea of bringing the type in, wanting to do all the type in a spacial, expressive way and getting the team to make it. Getting all their input. The images are not layered or built up digitally – all the images are of actual things that exist in the world.'

Vaughan steps into the garden for a cigarette and we speak about our favourite Pixies' songs. It turns out we come from a slightly different perspective to each other, musically. If Vaughan were going to pull out Pixies' songs he'd go to the more existential, animal ones – 'Where Is My Mind?' and 'Hey'.

'Stuff that's so loaded with scream and emotion . . . "Vamos", that's a great one. "Tame".'

I think back to Vaughan's UCL lecture and how he described each piece of artwork as it flashed up behind him:

'All these images, unless I point it out, were shot in the lens – there's no Photoshop work involved; so

we built the Pixies' planet for *Bossanova*★ – we had a model-maker build it out of Perspex and shot it in its environment. The image on the back sleeve, the hairy heart – there was a period in my life where I wore a shaven head, any girl who came into my life finished up with a shaved head and sometimes I'd keep the hair in a little black bag. This was Anne's. I remember taking it out after six months and seeing it had formed itself into a hair heart and, being a romantic, I thought, "Yes, I'll use that one day.'"

I remember the nervous laughter in the audience.
Vaughan looked up to meet our gaze, impassive.

★ *Bossanova* was Pixies' third album, released in 1990.

This is a man, I thought, who heard the last Pixies' album, *Trompe le Monde*,* and went straight for the bull's eyes. A homage to *Un Chien Andalou*,** perhaps, or a wilful mishearing as 'trompe-l'œil' – a play on orbs; a visual gag.

When we're back in Vaughan's study I ask him and he replies instantly:

> 'School memories of cutting open eyeballs, Daniel. The bull's eyes were very hard to obtain actually, it was around the time of the mad cow disease and butchers weren't letting them out the back door.'

Reopening the plan chest beneath the window and the glowering ceramic, Vaughan begins to rifle afresh, drawing out several satiny sheets of brightly coloured proofs – icy blues and whites, splintering into lava reds.

> 'Now, I'll bring you, well, not right up to date but I'll show you a little bit of work, The Breeders and an album called *Mountain Battles*. The brief from the band was that they wanted something sleek, slick and shiny; a bit Futurist.
>
> Their ideas of sleek, slick and shiny are in there but when I looked at the Futurist paintings there was something much more fractured and brutal going on so I had this idea of recreating that effect with broken glass – which is all very well for me to say but how does a photographer do that?

---

* *Trompe le Monde* was Pixies' fourth album, released in 1991.

** *Un Chien Andalou* is a 1929 silent surrealist film by Spanish director Luis Buñuel Portolés and Salvador Dalí. The film has no discernible plot and is infamous for the scenes which cut between the moon and a middle-aged man slicing a woman's eye with a cut-throat razor.

So this is Mark Atkins, an English photographer living in the middle of France, and he did this in his studio which I find absolutely bloody extraordinary. I mean, the glass looks like it's on the point of breaking, but this is an inanimate thing! This is dead. This is broken glass sitting on his studio floor. How does he make it look like that?'

We both hunker down over the images, peering into the flaked and breaking glass. Some shots look like stratum glass, some like paintings by Lyubov Popova, Fillia or Mikhail Larionov. Another of Vaughan's curated worlds, 12 x 12-inch dioramas, stage sets for the music to play out.

* * * * *

Just before I leave, I check back through the notes I made on the train up – I want to ask something more about Vaughan's mum – but Vaughan is distracted, peering at my handwriting.

'Very interesting writing style, you see. What you do is, you spend a long time going down and a long time going up but, in the middle, *shooooo*. It's an interesting rhythm. Has that ever been commented on in the past?'

Loose knitting, mad spiders and doctor's scrawl, yes . . . I can read it but, I mean, I handwrite a lot of letters and sometimes wonder if the recipients are pleased or nonplussed. I don't send an enormous amount of emails.

'Good for you.'

I wanted to ask about something I read in *This Rimy River* –
'It's a great life if you don't weaken' – Doreen Oliver.★
Your mother?

> 'That's right. You must have had some catchphrases
> rattling round your house?
> We never discussed it but I remember it was something
> that she always said and I thought it was a pertinent
> quote rather than take something from the scriptures
> or whatever. I don't know where it came from but when
> it came to writing something in the back of the book it
> came to mind.
> I dwelt on it briefly and thought, "Yes, you do have to
> be strong. You have to be driven."'

It's a striking phrase.

> 'Yes, I think it's a brilliant phrase. It strikes a chord.'

•   •   •   •   •

On my way back to the station I feel my optics have been
retuned, heightened:

Rust bubbles on a Morris Minor.
Frayed rope in a gutter.
Splintered bark on a car-smashed tree.
The patterns of trampled chewing gum.
Paint sprayed on water.
Crimson whirling maple seeds.

★ *This Rimy River: Vaughan Oliver and V23 - Graphic Works 1988–94* (V23 Publishing,
1997).

Ink runs where rain seeped into bus shelter hoardings.
Peeling Teflon on a thrown-out pan.
Spilt coffee on Epsom platform in the shape of a bird.
The raindrops which slink down my train window, like chemical veins on a Polaroid.

JANE BOWN, CBE (1925–2014) is a British photographer known for her work on the *Observer*, where she has been producing portraits since 1949. Recognised for her pared-down, technical approach, Bown has famously captured many images of notable subjects, including Samuel Beckett, Evelyn Waugh, Björk and Queen Elizabeth II. Her portraiture and photojournalistic work have featured in countless solo exhibitions and publications.

JANE BOWN

Alton, Hampshire
24 January 2011

Jane Bown's hands lie in her lap as she talks, the negative
space between them framing an absent camera.
'I've never been good with words,' she warns me. 'I've always
been speechless.'

The walls around us are crowded with portraits taken over
Jane's remarkable career at the *Observer*. Onion sellers hang
beside bishops, actors and painters jostle politicians, dancers,
poets, musicians, writers, colliers, and barefoot children –
each looking bright into the lens, giving themselves away.
Beckett like a peregrine, Björk behind her hands, Bacon's
moon face gazing from beside a tower of rags – the mirror
behind him strafed and spattered, the whole shot steeped in a
silver patina. A creature in his habitat, sat within a den.*

---

* The recurrence of Samuel Beckett, Björk and Francis Bacon form bridges here to
Jane Bown from Jenny Saville, Judi Dench, Vaughan Oliver.
Björk, although I didn't know it yet, would lead me on to Steve Gullick in the next
chapter.

I tell Jane how her photographs of Francis Bacon in his studio helped inspire this project and, quite suddenly, given a frame of reference, she lights up:

'They were done in terrible circumstances. I mean there was no light, no nothing except all these mirrors. He was very sweet but I wasn't winning at all – I know when I'm winning and then I stop. Do you know? I thought, "Oh dear, this isn't going well." I just wasn't getting it – I was using his face against those round mirrors – then I said, "Well, I must go," and gave in because I never stay long; and he let me out of the door, which was a stable door, and he leant on it. Bingo. It was perfect.'

How was he? I've read he was difficult.

'He was okay. I was always nervous of people; apprehensive, not nervous perhaps but, you know, unsure; but he was fine.'

I tell Jane about Jenny Saville's Rorschach radiator, how it bore painty witness to her methods. I'm not a photographer, I explain, but I sometimes see photographs.

'See them, yes.'

Do you still see them?

'Not as I used to, not in the same way. I remember when I began I saw photographs everywhere.'

The earliest photographs of yours I've seen were taken on Dartmoor.

'That's when I got my first camera, a second-hand Rolleiflex. I learnt about taking photographs because I could look through that little box and see things . . . so that's what happened. I was at Guildford art school with a marvellous Welshman, Ifor Thomas, he was absolutely marvellous for taking one on.'

I was interested to read that you didn't like taking part in the discussions at Guildford.

'Dreadful. It was awful. I suppose there were twelve students and each week one would have to put their work up and the others would have to criticise it, and I couldn't. I just could not.'

You couldn't put your work up or you couldn't talk about theirs?

'I couldn't talk about theirs. Couldn't. You're lucky to have a way with words but I never have. I don't think I've ever talked about photography much.'

At Guildford or generally?

'Just generally! (Laughs)
I learnt to talk on the *Observer* when I used to go out with journalists but I was always a listener, never a talker. Some people are, aren't they, but I'm intuitive – I'm a Pisces so I'm intuitive – I could see the people at once and I would know what to do with them and very quickly, which was good because the sort of people I used to do, they want you in and out in a flash. They used to say, "Send Jane, she'll only take six minutes."'

Did you develop your own shots at the start?

'Yes. I loved it. Later it was done in the *Observer*'s darkroom but at the very beginning I used to make my own
– fill a bath with water and wash all the prints in the
bath. As basic as that. I always used to do it myself at
night; wipe the film down with my finger; hang it up
to dry; get up again in the middle of the night; chop it
up. I loved the processing. Can't say I was so keen on
printing. I knew a good print when I saw one but it was
very wasteful – I was always conscious of using a lot of
paper.'

I've never heard you talk about this side of it, the development, I mean. I imagine few people have asked?

'No! (Laughs) The early days were lovely. At the end
of the war I was in the Wrens* and we were sent up
to a school on top of one of the hills around Bath and
there was a road where we were billeted and you could
look down and see all the lights. I was sent there to be
de-mobbed so we used to kid our time yapping. I didn't
know what I was going to do but we were given a sheet
of paper one night of the different things you could do
and I didn't think I could do any of them but then I saw
photography and I thought, "Well, that sounds nice."
Never taken a picture in my life, but I decided, "Well,
I'll do photography." Easier said than done. I couldn't
find anywhere in the country where you could learn to
take photographs except Guildford, and that was run
by a man called Ifor Thomas – an alcoholic Welsh chap;
super he was – and he said well he was full up but as he

---

* Women's Royal Naval Service.

was ex-RNVR★ and I was a Wren he would take me.
So I fell into Guildford to learn how to take pictures.
He had a wife who was also marvellous; she was prob-
ably better at teaching but he just said, "Correct expo-
sure, correct development and you can't go wrong."
He taught me that and I was very good at always know-
ing exactly what exposures to give without a meter.
Correct exposure and correct development.'

Was it he who showed you how to use the back of your hand
to gauge light?

'No, that was me; but that's very obvious really. I'd go
to a window and look at my hand. I never used a meter.
I'd just look at my hand to see what the light was doing
on it and assume it was doing the same on my face.
That's all I did. Nothing very clever . . . and of course,
once you're doing people by windows, it all falls into
the same category after you've done half a dozen of
them, you know.
Light doesn't change that much. It's brighter one day
and darker another but I always handled that.'

Did you use the Rolleiflex for a long time?

'Yes. I'd never used 35mm and then somebody suggested I should buy a Pentax so I was using a Pentax,
getting used to it, when Eamonn McCabe★★ came along

★ Royal Naval Volunteer Reserve.

★★ Eamonn McCabe (1948–) joined the *Observer* in 1976. He has won Sports
Photographer of The Year a record four times, covering three Olympics. In 1985
Eamonn was named News Photographer of The Year for his work at The Heysel
Stadium disaster. In 1988 he joined the *Guardian* as Picture Editor. He has won
Picture Editor of the year a record six times.

and said, "You should use an Olympus," and I found the Olympus was lovely because you could see through the viewing screen, very clear. So I've used an Olympus ever since. Still on Olympus 1!'

You'd always have the two cameras with you when you went out and two rolls of film on the go at any time?

'Yes. One was for security in case something went wrong but I got used to taking two and I'd put a film in each and that would be that. You don't need to take lots.'

· · · · ·

While at Vaughan's I showed him some of Jane's work. He knew about the Beckett shots, of course, but her first early studies were something else; fragile treasure, like frost. Dartmoor, a cow's eye, a fair child peering at a murky white bottle, hair obscuring her face, tiny nails seamed with dirt; river oysters proffered on an iron fork – the sort of abstract glacial shots which I knew would excite him.

Afterwards, back at home but still buoyant after my tangible time in Epsom, I began to think about cameras and tools – the scalpel with the comma on the end, the lustre of contact prints and proof sheets.
I dug out my Lubitel camera – a Soviet copy of a Rolleiflex – a rectangular box with twin lenses out front. A hefty matt block of a coaly patterned plastic which puts me in mind of binoculars – useful rather than graceful. Knobs and levers pock the box; the metal parts stand out silver. The spring-loaded viewfinder snaps up to reveal the bright TARDIS below – a crisp orb of light; the scene; the shot; bigger on the inside. I find it fascinating, but this is camera described as

object rather than machine for taking pictures. It's not a description Jane would recognise or subscribe to because, like Richard Lawrence, she sees herself as a technician.

Lord Snowdon once called Jane a great artist, but she described herself to the Queen as 'a hack'. So there.

As a press is a tool for printing, so a camera's a tool for capturing light.

I tell Jane I'd be interested to see her cameras and she laughs.

Is that a daft request? You've made a face.

'You'll be appalled. If you ask Em, she'll find them for me.'

I go through to the kitchen and ask Jane's friend Emma where the cameras might be. She finds them in a carrier bag in the hall which I take back to Jane.

'Any luck? Aren't you appalled?'

No, not at all. (I take out a silver Olympus) This is your main one, is that right?

'That's right. 85 Olympus. Yes.'

I pass the camera to Jane, who takes it up in her hands.

'I loved my Rollei but, isn't it awful, I used to chuck them in my bag – never had a lens cap, never had a case. Never seemed to matter.

The thing about the OM-1 is that you can still buy them for an absolute song – a hundred and something, for £150 you can still get one. I think I might have once had an OM-2 but I'm not sure.'

You always used that lens?

'I used the 85; a good portrait lens. I have got a sort of wide angle . . . I'm not particularly concerned with equipment, you know.'

Did you have a preferred film?

'Always what I was given; Triax, which is Kodak. At the beginning I used the film that the *Observer* gave me. Great boxes of it.'

● ● ● ● ●

I tell Jane a little more about the book and mention John Parish⋆ who I recently met at his home in Bristol. He works a lot with a musician called PJ Harvey, I say.

'Oh, she's wonderful! I went to America to photograph her. I used to take a portrait a week for the *Observer* Magazine with Andrew Billen. He'd do the interview

---

⋆ John Parish is a musician and composer who I spoke to at his home in Bristol about songwriting, collaboration and composing music for films. In the end the conversation didn't make it into this book but I hope to revisit him at some point because he is a very interesting man.

Lucy Johnston and I visited him at Toybox Studios in Bristol to take his portrait while he was working on an album with *Giant Sand* frontman Howe Gelb.

Shortly after this he went on tour with PJ Harvey, with whom he's worked for many years, playing her album *Let England Shake*.

In 2015, the pair took up residence in Somerset House, London, for a project called *Recording In Process*:

'Recording In Process is a project conceived by PJ Harvey, in collaboration with Artangel and Somerset House, for the Inland Revenue's former staff gymnasium and rifle range in the recently opened New Wing of Somerset House.

and have one page and I'd take a black and white picture and have the other. We were always doing jobs together and he loved interviewing showbiz types. Polly Harvey . . . I remember her because she lived on a farm. That was all she wanted to do, live on a farm and breed chickens and things.'

Going out into the world but always returning home.

'That's right. We talked about my going down to see her there one day – I'm sure I was in America at the time. They were all moving on. I went to a concert which finished late and they all got onto this great charabanc and they were all going somewhere and I thought, "How lovely, I'd love to sit in there and travel with them all." Polly Harvey, yes.'

• • • • •

Andrew Billen confirms this when we speak later in the year:

'Jane's recall is excellent, it's absolutely true, she did say she wanted to run off with them; hop on the coach and go round America.

—————

'Harvey has chosen to record her ninth album inside an architectural installation designed by Somerset House-based Something & Son. The installation is a recording studio in the form of an enclosed box with one-way glazing, displaying PJ Harvey, her band, producers and engineers as a mutating, multi-dimensional sound sculpture.

'Each visitor experiences exactly what is happening at a particular moment in the studio, as Harvey and musicians, together with her longstanding producers Flood and John Parish, go through the creative process of recording an album of songs.'

– Recording In Progress pamphlet

There's something of the bohemian about Jane; and PJ's from Dorset as well, I think, so they had that connection . . . people were often surprised when I'd pitch up with this little old lady. It was really good of her to get on a plane and go through all of that.

Sometimes I'd go on my own and sometimes she'd come along; there was one hectic three days when we did the Coen brothers, Kate Millett and Michael Moore in New York. Kate Millett was living up on a lesbian collective farm in Poughkeepsie, the Coen brothers were just hopeless to interview, but if you know their movies you'll know they'd be amused by someone like Jane. She took a very nice photograph of them.

It was an extraordinary period because I was aware of Jane Bown – as everyone was at the *Observer*, whatever age they were – she was legendary. Her career was so long she could have busy decades and not so busy decades, but the thing we did in the paper every week made a big difference and rejuvenated her. We were in our thirties at the time, our group – about the same age as her youngest son. It was a happy time. She was in her late sixties by then and it was a great privilege to work with her.'

How was she to work with?

'She's got a very mischievous sense of humour and, as you will have discovered, is completely unpretentious about her art. She has that room of her own photographs but there are no photographs on her wall, I don't know if she thinks photography is an art, really . . . not many books of photographs in her house.

Eve Arnold – we went to see her together.'

Did they compare notes?

'They did, actually. As I recall the piece, I really got Jane to interview Eve Arnold* because I thought it was much more interesting to record them talking rather than ask Eve Arnold direct questions myself – contemporaries finally meeting; but she'd never leap in with her own questions, unlike some photographers. She'd keep quiet and keep looking . . . some of it was a mixture of charm and bullying but she just always got people to do whatever she wanted. I remember doing Paul Merton and, because Jane only uses natural light, she made him lie down on the floor of his Soho office in a shaft of sunshine; when she was finally done and off he got up and said, "Ooh, it's nice to sit down, isn't it!" (Laughs)

Back in Jane's room of pictures, I'm struggling to hear her over the crying of Mona the cat who wants our attention. She gets it. We stop talking, Jane tells her off and I pick her up and fuss her for the rest of our conversation – her tortoiseshell hair covering my jacket for months afterwards.

'So go on telling me who you've done and what you do.'

Well, I'm a slightly odd proposition, perhaps like you were.

'Not normal.' (Laughs)

---

* Eve Arnold, OBE, Hon. FRPS (née Cohen; 1912–2012) was an American photojournalist. She joined the Magnum Photo agency in 1951 – one of the twentieth century's foremost photographers and a pioneer of photojournalism.

'It is the photographer, not the camera, that is the instrument.'

– Eve Arnold

No, not particularly normal; because of that people don't mind talking to me whereas a journalist might give them more pause. I don't turn up with a list of questions.

'That would be like me turning up with a great barrage of lights and things. I just used to go with a camera and not look like a photographer – more like a district nurse, somebody once said.' (Laughs)

Well, here we are, two odd propositions. I'm here following a conversation with a man called Vaughan Oliver, where we spoke about the idea of workspace and home. You've taken so many candid shots of people at rest, at work and off guard over the years – not only the likes of Bacon but those Grimsby dockers cycling to work in the sixties, for example – these rare, unvarnished encounters. Maybe that was only possible because of your district nurse aspect?

'I never thought I'd be known. I was never ambitious. It just happened; a lot of it chance – the *Observer* deciding to take me, an interest in pictures . . . I was snowballed around because people do snowball you around when you're young. I got some pictures together and Ifor used to say to me, "If you get six pictures together you can go round the world, just showing," and I did show with somebody and she made me show them to somebody at *Picture Post* and she picked out a man with a long neck and did a juxtaposition with a giraffe, you know, and she saw my cow's eye picture and said, "Anybody who can do that can take a portrait," so before I knew where I was I was photographing Bertrand Russell – because she'd seen that picture of the cow's eye and decided from that that I could take portraits. Then I was asked to do another one and another one – though it took me years to really get any good at it.'

Was it very difficult when you started?

'Yes, I didn't know what I was doing half the time. I was an absolute novice. I came across some pictures the other day, taken with the Rolleiflex while travelling up to Scotland with Danny Kaye, of all people, and I really honestly didn't know what I was doing, but I was looking. I was looking. That's what I do best, because I think I see.
But I could never tell anybody what to do. I'd always watch; and the better I got, the quicker I could see if somebody did something, turn their head, crook their finger or something.'

It must have been hard starting out as a photographer on Fleet Street in the late forties.

'And a female one, yes. I mean, the *Observer* were one of the first papers to start taking pictures seriously . . . no, people were all right about it because I wasn't threatening and I was quite young. I think they were quietly amused. (Laughs)
I always had two enemies, time and light, and that had to be sorted the moment I got into the room. But of course, when you were given someone like, well, some of these American stars who'd come over and take a suite of rooms in the Dorchester for the journalists and each one is allowed one hour . . . if I went with a journalist, he would take fifty minutes and I'd get five or ten, so I had to be quick on the draw. The main thing was the light – making sure the light fell on their face – I had to act very quickly and that's what I did; made sure their eyes were bright . . . no, I wasn't exactly threatening and because I was a woman they had to be reasonably polite.'

• • • • •

While Jane roved to take her pictures in the fifties and sixties, the *Observer*'s offices at 22 Tudor Street were her base; buildings variously described as cramped, tatty and poky by those who worked there, a muddled warren* – the *Observer* was

---

* *Observer* film critic Philip French recalled his first visit in 2009:

'Forty-six years ago this month, I delivered my first film column to the *Observer's* offices in Tudor Street, the most staid of the seven London premises the paper has occupied since I became a contributor . . . Expecting to be taken to a bustling newsroom, I was shown instead to an austere

one of many papers crammed into a ward of lanes evoked in Michael Frayn's 'Fleet Street novel' *Towards the End of the Morning*, heir to Evelyn Waugh's *Scoop*.* A murky male world steeped in ink and drink – an affiliate pub for each paper with 'Auntie's' furnishing the *Observer*. Jane recalls a gentle collegiate atmosphere of long lunches and afternoon halves of mild and bitter nursed until the vibration of the presses began beneath their feet to signal the close of play; a world where you might bump into a sozzled Kim Philby or pass George Orwell on the stairs.**

Andrew Billen explained to me how the *Observer*'s then editor, David Astor, held the view that women would always be supported by their husbands so didn't need to be paid very much,

'and, indeed, that is what happened with Jane because her husband was a successful businessman. You have to remember that the post-war *Observer* was so small, I mean, all papers were smaller – it wasn't long after paper rationing – all these ex-public schoolboys would

---

conference chamber where, after a short wait, I was joined by Terry Kilmartin, a tall, handsome Irishman who had been literary editor and arts supremo since 1946 . . .'
– The *Observer*, Sunday 5 April 2009

* 'It even had its own characteristic smell. Just as Southwark, where my father worked, on the other side of the river, was immediately identifiable by the delicately sour smell of the Kentish hops that were warehoused and factored there, so the alleys and courts of Fleet Street were haunted by the grey, serious smell of newsprint. I catch the delicious ghost of it in my nostrils now, and at once I'm back at the beginning of my career, struggling to conceal my awe and excitement at having at last arrived in this longed-for land.'
– Michael Frayn, the *Guardian*, 24 June 2000

** Although not on the same day – Orwell having died in 1950, Philby having been 'hired' as a foreign correspondent in 1956.

take her out to the pub. In the nineties she thought we were all pretty boring if we didn't go out for lunch and get drunk all the time.'

David Watkinson, the *Observer*'s darkroom printer for thirty years, sketched me the atmosphere of 22 Tudor Street in the sixties:

'I met Jane in about 1961. I started in the post room and front office in 1960 and got to know Tony Prime, who was in the darkroom at the time – Photographic Technicians they called them, and he was the only one. I used to go down there in my lunchtimes and eventually the work got so much he asked for an assistant, and he suggested me and that's how I got into the darkroom. I started developing the films and doing the contact sheets and washing the slides, whereas Tony Prime used to do the printing – very good printer – lovely character. He used to be round the corner in the pub. A photographer would come in and I'd process the film, get it contacted, and up to the Picture Editor to get marked up; when it was marked up I used to whip round the pub and tell Tony, "They're ready to be printed!" and he'd come round, print them and go back again.'

The photographers would drop their films off to you there?

'That's right, and then some of them would hang around, you know, looking to see what the negs looked like.'

Was Jane like that?

'Well you always got a good quality neg with Jane, believe it or not! (Laughs) She was one of the few you didn't have to worry about. Some of them – we used to inspect the film at the developing stage; we had this dark green light so you could make out whether the image needed more developing or was there; we got that technique going.'

Which gave you an edge.

'Bryn Campbell won the News Photographer of the Year with one I pushed, Paris Riots.* I looked at his film when he got back and one half was there, ready to be fixed, and the other half, you know, it needed more developing; so I cut the film in half and put one bit back in the developer and that was where the picture was that won the award! So if it wasn't for me doing that he wouldn't have got that picture.'

The Paris riots were late sixties?

'Tony Prime left in '65 so we're talking . . . about '68? Late in the sixties . . . but sometimes they'd come in and say, "The light was dodgy, it might need a bit more; push it," as we used to say, push it – so you'd give them the normal development and then go in, have a look, and judge how much longer to give it. It was only by experience you'd get to know. You'd get a bit of grain but there you go.'

Where was the darkroom in Tudor Street?

'In the basement, and all around it was books and the system for the lighting and god knows what else – that

* News Picture of the Year, 1969 – bryncampbell.com – Paris Riots.

building was all little narrow corridors ... some photographers would hang around outside, you know? Waiting to see what the negs looked like and maybe take the contact sheets up themselves where they could have a good look. Jane sometimes did, sometimes didn't – like all of them. She was no different really to the others in that.'

Do you remember developing specific shots of Jane's? Something like the Beckett?

'Yeah, I would have printed that . . . course you lose track of what you printed because she wasn't the only one but, from what I remember of that, there was terrible lighting on one side. I had a hell of job to get the shadow a bit lighter. They weren't her best negatives.'

• • • • •

I wonder if there are any photographs of the time itself, a document of the space – a who's who of photographers lined up in the Tudor Street basement – Bown, Campbell, McCullin, Berry, Donovan, Hedgecoe, Cranham . . . some or all stood awaiting a look at their shots, what a thing! The sort of picture that was Jane's bread and butter, but perhaps a scene too mundane to record at the time.

Both Jane and David describe their time in rich detail but I can't help but see it in black and white in light of Jane's catalogue: Jane in The Beatles' dressing room, caught on the cusp of world fame and clearly knackered; Jane running around to the stage door of the Royal Court Theatre to get those famous five shots of a scowling Beckett, glowering, stern and raptor-like (not her best negs, mind); Jane's desk upstairs in Tudor Street, 'up on the fourth floor with the music critic and book

reviewers, next door to the sport; shelves of 15 x 12-inch box files full of prints and negs – alphabetically arranged, a hopeless filing system – Actors. Artists. Business. Dance.'
Her kit in a bag, to hand.

And while their telling may be quiet and understated, the stories and impressions are electric and vital in Jane. Far from being taciturn and muddled, she speaks in trim vignettes.
She describes a meeting with Don McCullin in London, the latter recently returned from documenting the war in Vietnam:

> 'He was amazing. I was having a coffee with him, I think I'd been sent to photograph him, and we were sitting in a Bar Italia in Soho and some obviously photogenic old chap went across the road so I went to photograph the scene and Don, at speed, snatched the camera out of my hands and went over and he clicked. The speed at which he operated was incredible. Just some man who looked vaguely interesting so I poked my camera up, but he'd grabbed it before I knew where I was, as I say, the speed at which he moved; he was amazing, had a death wish, Don. Lovely chap.'

• • • • •

In November 2011, I went to see Vaughan Oliver give a talk at the St Bride's Institute, a year since we'd first met. Vaughan was one of several interviewees I'd kept in touch with and seen socially post-book conversation – Stanley Donwood and Judi Dench were others. 'How's the book?' they'd ask. 'How's *our* book?' Judi once enquired.
After Vaughan's lecture was over we went for a walk. ('How's that book?' he probably asked.) We went along Fleet Street to the Inns of Court, below the vehement dragon on the Temple

Bar marker, left down Essex Street and its arched steps and left again onto the Victoria Embankment. The Thames was slack and low behind the far parapet as we sloped along beneath the plane trees, past the railed and gated gardens of Inner Temple and left up Temple Avenue to Tudor Street.
the *Observer's* offices at No. 22 have gone, the large windows of the shop-like front and all else replaced by a dirty brick box so dull it isn't worth describing. The sash windows above the shops next door are my only clue that this is the spot, since they're a peripheral detail in the only picture I have of the building (circa 1960). In it, three men sit talking on the steps below a double door, 22 painted in white above them and, above that, centred, 'THE OBSERVER'. A Hillman Minx and a Vespa stand in front of the wood facade and basement vents which dove down to David Watkinson's darkroom . . . all gone now. Just Vaughan and I stood at the junction of Tudor and Carmelite Street, punning on Gang of Four's 'Armalite Rifle'.*

· · · · ·

Mona is making a voluble fuss again. I tell Jane about my own cat, Morrissey.
You've taken a portrait of Morrissey the man, I say.

'Yes. I don't think it was very good.'

No?

'Perhaps it was alright. He wasn't easy; by that I mean, people aren't deliberately difficult but he was in a flat

---

* 'Armalite Rifle' – B-side of Gang of Four's debut single 'Damaged Goods' – Fast Product, 1978.

down towards Putney Bridge somewhere and the awful thing with me is not only do I not talk much but I don't really know what's going on in the world and I didn't know who Morrissey was – which apparently is an appalling thing to say.'

I'm sure he'd say so, yes.

(Laughs) 'He didn't give anything out . . . it's not a picture I'd have chosen. I didn't know what to do with him.'

He's quite a taciturn fellow, I've heard.

'Yes. Exactly that.'

Do you have doubts about many of your more celebrated pictures?

'I don't know. The one I'm always asked about is Beckett; but what I used to like doing – like with those onion sellers on the wall there – was move about; I'd cycle everywhere and I'd see pictures. I was really look-ing for pictures. Shots. I've got a very quick eye and I'm quite an opportunist. I see quickly – which held me in good stead after a bit because I could actually go in and get a picture very quickly. If nothing else was going for me I'd just look straight into their eyes, always works.'

Did you ever have any disasters where you returned empty-handed?

'No. Thankfully. One didn't always pull it off but I was good at getting something. I was good if I could be quick, usually the first picture or the last. The first one was often the best but I'd go through and then, when I got another one that was good, I'd say, "Right; finished," and shut the camera.

I don't know what it is about taking photographs; it's nothing to do with clicking the camera, is it? It's wonderful when you see in people's eyes.

You see, when I first used to be sent out, I'd take any old picture; (referring to a shot in the rack beside her) that was Cowes Week, that little car. I was sent to Cowes to do Cowes Week but I came back with the car – not boats – but we used to have something on the *Observer* called the Weekend Page where they would use "an original photograph", something odd, a strange shot.'

When did you stop?

'Not that long ago. Five years ago? I remember I photographed the Queen when I was eighty. We got in touch with Buckingham Palace, it was a joke really, we just did it for fun, my idea; I said, "Shall we ring up the Queen to see if, on her eightieth birthday, she'd like an eighty-year-old photographer to come and take her picture?" We thought that was very funny. Then I didn't laugh because the next day they rang back and said, "The Queen would be delighted."'

She called your bluff.

'She called my bluff, yes.'

STEVE GULLICK (1967–) is one of the pre-eminent rock photographers of the past twenty years. In the early 2000s he co-founded seminal music magazines *Careless Talk Costs Lives* and *Loose Lips Sink Ships*. His pictures have appeared in the *Times*, *Mojo*, *Rolling Stone*, *Wire*, *Q* and *NME*.

He has exhibited worldwide and published four books: *Pop Book Number One* (1995), *Showtime* (2001), *Nirvana* (2001) and *The Nirvana Diary* (2014).

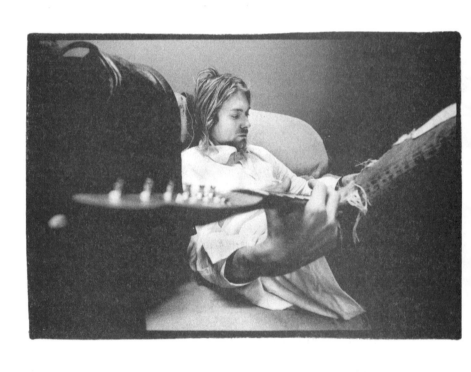

STEVE GULLICK

Manor Park, London / Cambridge
2010–2013

As I made to leave Jane Bown's house, packing away my kit, she spied my Dictaphone and brightened.

'I'll tell you a funny story. I was asked along by Björk when she wanted to interview David Attenborough. She'd never done it before but she just worshipped him and so she asked if she could interview him and I was to go along and take photographs. She didn't know what she was doing really, and they had a marvellous conversation and I got some nice pictures but at the end of it she found her machine had not worked, hadn't recorded; so he very kindly did it all again for her. I didn't go along the second time. It was so funny because she hadn't a clue really.'

I bumped into Björk last year, I tell her.

'Oh, she's lovely!'

She was walking down some stairs to leave and I wasn't sure what to say – I wanted to tell her about the book . . .

'She's zany. She's mad as a hatter.'

I should have asked her if I could speak to her for this book, but instead I said, 'I think the work you're doing to protect Iceland's natural resources from big business is really important,' and she said, 'Thank you.'
And then she left and I thought, 'Damn.'

> 'She's a great character. I got to know her well over two or three sessions; always dressed like a Christmas tree fairy.'

• • • • •

The Björk incident was unexpected and occurred in the middle of an odd night.
I'd gone to Shepherd's Bush Empire in London with my friend Roz to see Bonnie 'Prince' Billy and The Cairo Gang play. Roz knew The Trembling Bells, the support band, and so we ended up backstage after the gig, drinking beer in a bar with the band while the venue below was being cleared.
The photographer Steve Gullick was there, wearing a suit. He looked very dapper. I told him so.
Björk was also there, sitting in the corner. Small Björk.
I asked Steve if he'd reintroduced himself – having taken her picture in the nineties. He said no.
Later I spoke to her briefly on the foyer stairs.
I addressed her as 'Ms Björk' and rambled about how it was good she was fighting the multinationals threatening Iceland's environment – when I should clearly have been asking her to be in this book.
She was polite but clearly befuddled by me. It was late and I was tipsy but, you know, in for a penny . . . so I stumped back

up to find Will Oldham* and tell him how much I'd enjoyed his set and he seemed genuinely pleased by my enthusiasm but the important thing, the apex of the night, was when we spoke about Steve, how he's the only person Will likes to take his picture. 'He's my guy,' Will said, with genuine warmth. 'He's my guy.'**

• • • • •

Manor Park, London
July 2010

The week before, I'd spoken to Steve Gullick in his darkroom where he sat in the half-light, perched on a bench between two photographic enlargers which stood either side of him like concertina'd birds.

Steve is wolfish, intense and spare. Sharp. Knotty. Hungry-looking.

To see him amid his kit – deftly handling cameras, riffling prints, spooling film – I'm reminded of an early description of Jim Prideaux in *Tinker, Tailor, Soldier, Spy*:

---

* Bonnie 'Prince' Billy is Will Oldham's stage name.

** It was a long, strange night . . . I remember Roz held Will's hand and reminded him of their first meeting at Cambridge Corn Exchange when they'd spoken about Jeanette Winterson.

Then we were all turfed out – well, not all; Roz stayed behind with the band – but Steve and I marched off towards Greek Street – a very straight walk of four miles down Bayswater Road. A march, a bit of banter with strangers and then, a door; Steve knocked. A big chap answered. We waited while he sized us up then it was all warm handshakes and down the stairs to a warm cellar with beer and a record player . . . and Roz and the band – who'd passed us in a taxi some time ago, apparently.

Roz told Steve he'd clever and beautiful eyes before disappearing again.

We got turfed out of the cellar (all of us, this time). It was 3 a.m. or something.

I said goodbye to Steve at Centre Point.

The Astoria was gone or coming down behind blue hoardings.

'Taking the marble he slowly rolled it round in his hard, powdery palm and Roach knew at once that he was very skilful at all sorts of things; that he was the kind of man who lived on terms with tools and objects generally.'*

During several hours of conversation that day and after, he spoke about his fears about his future as a film photographer and how he's become adept at shooting people who don't like being photographed.
At one point he opened a fridge; full of film.

'I'm running out of film because the film I like they've stopped making; Kodak EPP.
You can't get it any more. This is all I've got left, that bottom row, and when that's gone . . . I don't know what I'm going to do.'

What do you like about it?

'I can control it.'

Running out must be a huge worry.

'Constant worry, yeah, has been for a few years. Digital's made it much harder for me because (nods to the work and machines around him) as well as doing all this, which is incredibly time consuming because I process the film myself and do all the prints myself, now I've got to do all that scanning shit.'

It must take a long time.

---

* *Tinker, Tailor, Soldier, Spy*, John Le Carré (Hodder & Stoughton, 1975).

'It does. I've got a really slow scanner. I bought a scanner to do *Careless Talk Costs Lives** because I printed everything 12 x 16 – "THUNK!" – that big (finds and throws down a pile of prints). I got a scanner that size because I wanted everything to be as good as it could be, you know? And that's what I'm still using but it's eight, nine years old.'

Do you scan the negatives?**

'No, I scan the prints. Brilliant quality but because the industry standard is now digital, if I gave someone a contact sheet or a print and said, "Here you are," they wouldn't know what to do with it. It's immensely frustrating because it's effectively doubled my workload; I mean, I'm getting paid less and working a lot harder which, you know, I haven't got a massive problem with because I did go through a few years of earning a lot of money, but fucking hell it's hard work. (Laughs) Really hard work . . .'

---

* *Careless Talk Costs Lives* was a magazine Steve set up with the writer Everett True. It ran for twelve issues between January 2002 and November 2003.

> '*Careless Talk* was a good magazine because it was designed to run for twelve issues and then stop. Everett did try to talk me into doing Issue 0 but I wouldn't. No . . . but Everett and I came at publishing from different perspectives. That's probably why *Careless Talk* was good; I didn't care about the words and he didn't care about the pictures – that's not strictly true but we used to fight a lot and that's why it was so great.
> The magazines were meant to be an antidote to magazines, if you like. They were designed and laid out around the pictures – full bleed – we put bands on the front that nobody was ever gonna hear of but who we liked. It's my best work. Undoubtedly my best work.'

** Several of these questions were asked by Lucy Johnston who was with me to photograph Steve at this first meeting. All the intelligent questions about photography in this chapter, unless otherwise labelled, are hers.

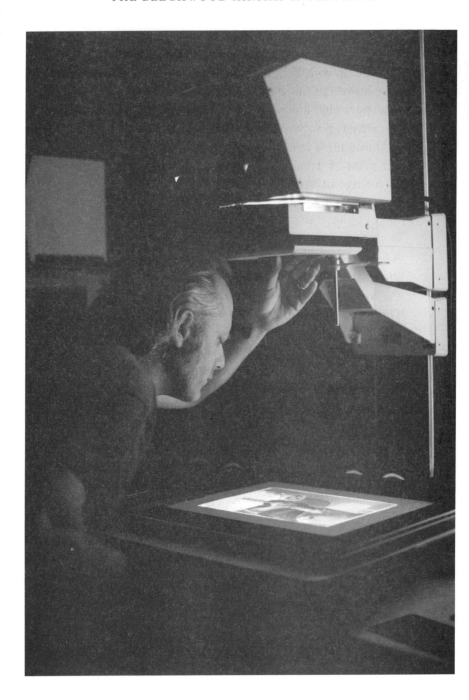

Steve's process may recall Jane Bown's memories of processing film in her bath, but I think his most obvious parallel in the book is with Vaughan Oliver and his PMT machine, because Steve's prints, particularly the landscapes and monochrome portraits, have the same focal layerings and subtle grain – rich as powdered rust.

Steve shows me a landscape he shot in North Wales, a silver gelatin print of a field of sentinel wheat crowding the lens below a ridge of serrate mountains. The sky a lowering fist of cloud, the whole shot roughed and blasted as if by pelting ash.

'That's cropped from a panoramic shot but this kinda blurry thing is made by printing through something else to get that texture.*

The thing about film and darkroom work is that it's a craft – something you need to learn and it takes a lot of work. It's a big deal. I've had a darkroom since I was fifteen. I had a darkroom in my bedroom; used to do it at night – black the windows out and print and that's all I used to do in my spare time . . . but I think, personally, for me, it's not just that I shoot with film it's the fact that I process the film – the times I've experimented and worked things out for myself; worked out what film works best for certain conditions, you know? Worked for years and years trying to perfect my own style.

Photography is as much science as it is art – probably more science than art – and I'm not scientifically or technically minded so I've had to work hard to learn

---

*The texture of these landscapes puts me in mind of Jim Jarmusch's film *Dead Man*, which Neil Young soundtracked. When I tell Steve this later it turns out he knows about it – '*Dead Man* is often in my ears, although I've strangely yet to see the film, the music has been with me for years.'

those elements, but I've persevered because without that I'd just be pissing around in the dark.* I've done a lot of experimenting to know what I know, but the basic laws of photography are science and you have to know about that to be able to do your own thing.'

All the way through, with all the people I've met, it boils down to – How do you do that?

'You do it for about twenty-five years and muck it up a lot but, after a long time, you can do it better than you could at the start, hopefully, and even then, you're winging it a bit . . . but by then no one wants it!' (Laughter)

You said earlier that photographing people who don't like having their photograph taken has turned into one of your main lines of work?

'Yes.'

Do you enjoy that?

'Yeah. (Grinning) It makes me feel special. (Laughter) Yeah, because they don't mind me being around. They're usually the people I like anyway.'

You've worked with Nick Cave quite a few times.

'Yeah. I work with Nick Cave 'cos I'm quick.'

---

* 'I did a photographic diploma and failed it. I wasn't paying attention. I wasn't interested in it because I felt I'd learnt what I needed to know and took it to do my own thing.'

He doesn't like it.

'No. I remember having a conversation with him about doing a photo session and him saying, "You can have six minutes," and I talked him up to ten and actually got twelve!
Yeah, Nick can't stand it. Will Oldham hates it. Will Oldham's probably the most difficult of the people I've photographed.'

Less than six minutes?

'The last time I saw Will he said he wouldn't be photographed ever again. Our band played with his band in Turkey, in Istanbul, and he said to me, "I ain't doing any more photos" . . . I said, "I was hoping to photograph you getting old." (Laughter)

Do you mind having your photograph taken?

'Um, well, because I'm in this band I have to be in photos. I hate it. It's tedious. It just bores me, it's a really tedious thing and that's a really good position to be in as a photographer because I can now see how shit-boring it is.
So it's been good in that respect . . . bores the fuck out of me, I hate it. I hate doing it myself. There's been a couple of occasions when someone else has taken pictures and that's actually been fine.'

You're able to switch off?

'Totally. I really don't care. If it looks good it looks good. And that's an interesting perspective – doing the band thing and being photographed has been really enlightening for me as a photographer because, from the band perspective, I don't care whether it's shot on digital or film so it's made me question why I'm so . . .'

You've realised you wouldn't hire yourself.

'I wouldn't hire me. There's no question. I don't like the kind of photographs I take! (Laughter) Well, I do – whenever I'm processing film and looking at the negs to see what's come out, then I'm in love with it again, you know? Because it really is exciting.

I'm doing these contact sheets at the moment and when you've got a set of good pictures and you're doing contact prints and you can see how good they are, it's fucking thrilling.'

It's the process again.

'Yeah; you see, because I'm confident processing film and pictures, I want to spend as little time in the dark-room as possible, but there are thousands of pictures over the years that I would really like to print but it's just . . . it's really draining doing this. You know? Being in the dark fucks with your head when you've been doing it for as long as I have.'

The chemicals too?

'The chemicals . . . well, ventilation in this darkroom is pretty good, but when I taught myself to colour print I did it all in a sink with trays and you had to be in total darkness for that. I was in the dark for days and days and days.'

No light or red light?

'No light at all. And then you're feeling about, trying to find the right chemical, putting your print through – colours can be quite difficult – and then, seeing it (mimes pained horror) after a ten-minute stint in the dark and it's awful and you don't still have no clue where to go with it . . . and you go through it again and again. Now I've got machines to do it; as soon as the exposure's done I can put it in the machine. I still have to wait but it's not in the dark . . . but there have been times when I haven't left either the darkroom or office at the top of the house for weeks because there's not been much work on and not working does my head in because I'm used to working. I'm from a family that always worked really hard.'

What did your family do?

'My dad worked in a factory and my mum looked after us. Then he took redundancy from the factory and became a cab driver.'

That work ethic of always having to have work.

'That's ingrained in me and, doing this . . . it's not a working-class job. Being freelance, I don't get paid regularly. I don't work regular hours. It doesn't fit with my background.'

•　•　•　•　•

Maybe it's Steve's hawser toughness which endears him to his tricky clientele. He talks in terms of tools and work and hours, he's self-effacing but knows the worth of what he does – there's steel there; when art is mentioned it's in the context of arts learnt and earned. Perhaps it's the fact he's clearly not

one to suffer fools and looks like a scrapper? It may be that you need to chance your arm for the best shots and trust your instinct; go with it:

'Some of my best pictures were taken under the influence of alcohol. In fact there's one great photograph which I don't even know if I took – a picture of the Yeah Yeah Yeahs live. Karen O's legs. It's an ace picture but I don't know if I shot it. I remember handing the camera out to the people in the crowd.'

My favourite Gullick shot turns out to be a sagacious case in point – a picture of Jason Pierce from the band Spiritualized

stood in front of an active Mount Etna, bronze mountain steaming. Pierce is wearing a silver space suit, helmet under one arm, black hair streaming. An unearthly panorama.

I ask Steve where he got the suit from.

> 'They're furnace suits, Jason's got two and he got his mate to go to Rugby to pick it up so he could take it to Sicily – because we were doing some photographs in London and he said, "Have you seen Mount Etna on the telly?" And I hadn't. He said, "Yeah, it's erupted ..." I said, "Shall we go there, then?" and he said "Yeah!" So a couple of days later we did.

He got his suit sent down and took it and, on the way, my bag of equipment was stolen – lighting equipment and six cameras – but in another bag I had a Canon F1 and a Widelux* and some film so we did the whole session with that. We got to a lava flow and he had his suit on sat next to me in the hire car and I had an out-of-date press pass from Brixton or somewhere and the police on the line waved us through – we could have gone and danced on the fire if we'd wanted. Incredible.

You asked earlier about my best shot, Lucy. That's it.'

What's your main camera?

'Hasselblad. I like to travel light so I've got a bag with a Hasselblad, Leica and Widelux in it – enough to guarantee a good shot.'

· · · · ·

Arts Picturehouse Cinema, Cambridge
January 2013

You're looking well.

'I am well. Never been weller. Haven't been ill since we moved over this way.'

Clean fens air?

---

* The Widelux is a panoramic camera with a motorised, pivoted lens that swings around to capture a sweeping 140° overview. Pictures are letterbox shaped – the widescreen film plane attuned to landscape vistas.

'Probably something to do with the amount of exercise I get; being out in all weathers. You know, we've got a dog. Gotta walk it.'

Steve hands me an LP then goes to the cinema bar to get coffee. On the front of the record sleeve is a Prussian blue seascape, swell waves sweeping towards the lens, white horses bolting up a cove, colours napped and molten:
End of the Road, Tenebrous Liar (035/100)

'I mean, the music may not be to your taste.' says Steve, sitting back down, 'but the picture on the front's good – it's hand-printed; biggest edition I've ever done and all different because they're printed through paper.'

For the patination?

'Yeah. Never lays the same on any picture twice. Every one is different, which I like a lot. I meant to re-photograph each one again, digitally, and turn it into an animation because there would be a visible change as it cycled through – but there's loads to occupy my time; I just wish I didn't have to earn money. If I didn't have to earn money I'd be the happiest person ever but, you know, even on that score I'm still getting away with it.'

Is it less expensive living out here?

'No! (Laughs) Even more expensive. It's all rich fuckers out here.'

You're near St Ives?

'Yeah, about two miles away. Huntingdon's about five but St Ives is closer. Fifteen miles from here. Middle of nowhere. In order to get to our house you'd have to, well, if you're me you'd get the bus to St Ives and walk, but I like walking. I don't mind.'

I wanted to ask about how you've got your darkroom set up now and the state of play with that.

'It's funny actually, I had to abandon all the water supply pipes last week because they froze. The dark-room's in my garage, we've only been there a year, and I've rigged up a temporary water supply and drainage with a view to digging up the concrete that separates it from the house and laying proper pipework, but before I got to that point it froze so I had to just chop it all out and rig up a hosepipe.
Drainpipe froze as well!
I did some printing yesterday and had to wash it all in the shower in the house – it was like the old days – anyway, really boring, that, but the darkroom's amazing, yeah. A while ago, you asked if I had any pictures of me working in there and I took one. I think I'll show it to you.* (Rummages in his bag and finds a shot of himself working in the darkness)
Can you see what's going on?
That huge thing above my head is the head of the en-larger. So that's projecting the light down onto the baseboard and that light's reflecting into my face.
That there's the safe light, and that's taken in the dark so it's the nearest you're going to get to me at work.'

---

* I had emailed Steve to ask if he had any shots of the darkroom. I think I asked if infrared film might work in pitch dark but he shot me down. No. No it wouldn't. The picture he took and now showed me was taken in very low, reddish light.

Very cool. It looks like you're working on the *Nostromo*.*

    (Laughs) 'It looks scientific. Ideal, I would think, for your requirements.'

Could I have a copy?

    'I'll send you one but I'd appreciate it if you didn't credit me. I don't want people thinking I take pictures of myself in the darkroom.' (Laughs)

How's the film situation?

    'I'm fine for film. I've got access to everything I want. I've got enough of a certain type of film to last me for my career.'

The slide film? I thought you said you were running out and that it was going to finish you off.

    'Nah. Photographic paper's the problem – as opposed to buying boxes, it's now only available on rolls. So now I have to chop it up in complete darkness. It's hard work . . . but that's the difference between me now and then, when I spoke to you first; three years ago I was pretty lazy. The idea of cutting paper in the dark: I ain't got time for that shit – but the work has slackened off to such a degree that I've probably got five days a week when I could be chopping up paper, you know?
So it's not a good situation to be in but I think, for my art, it is good because the less work I've got, the more attention I can give the jobs I do have.'

---

* The *Nostromo* was the spaceship in Ridley Scott's 1979 sci-fi horror film, *Alien*.

Are you still getting gluts of work, big jobs which tide you over for a while?

'Yeah, in the last couple of years I've managed to get a couple of massive corporate band jobs . . . and I mean, often they're nice chaps but it's not a job I'd . . . they're ones that pay to support the family.'

I remember we had a conversation about Beady Eye at our first meeting.

(Laughs) 'I just have to bite the bullet because it allows you to live but I actually got on really well with Beady Eye and I went on to photograph Liam Gallagher for Umbro for a lot of money. That got me through the year.'

And the Foo Fighters recently too, I saw.

'Yeah, but I go back years with them. I mean, obviously, I knew Dave in Nirvana – and I always really liked Dave – and when he formed the Foo Fighters, so soon after Kurt died, it wasn't a case of "Oh yeah, I wanna go and photograph the Foo Fighters," it was "Oh, I'll go and sit down with Dave," and that's how it was at the start of their career, I did them quite a bit. But then I didn't see them for nineteen years or something, but when they did the *Wasting Light* album they got Butch Vig to produce it; they obviously wanted to reintroduce that kinda family thing to the equation.'*

---

* 'In August 1991, mere weeks before the release of *Nevermind*, Cobain told me: "I think denying the corporate ogre is a waste of time. You should use

It wasn't about the photography, then.

'I don't think the photography comes into it, quite often. I don't think it was an issue with the Foo Fighters. They didn't want me to work with them because of the way I took pictures – in fact that may have stood against me – they just wanted that association, that link to Nirvana; and they could have gone for Michael Lavine or Charles Peterson, but they're not working any more! (Laughs) I dunno.
It was great. Such a nice thing to do and so great to catch up with that lot.
Tenebrous Liar even supported them at Dingwalls – I said, "Oh I play music as well," and Dave said, "You must support us in London!' I said, "You haven't heard us, we're probably shit!" He said, "All our friends' bands are shit!"
So, yeah, they gave us a gig – which was fantastic ... but what decided me ... I've basically spent the last seven years on this project, the band, and I've put all my creative eggs into it ... (picks up the LP he's just

---

them, rape them the way they rape you. I don't believe in closing off options to make your own world seem more important." He then paused for a long while, before smiling: "I think 'empathy' is a really nice word."
Cobain wrestled with the contradictions of being an instinctive anti-establishmentarian trying to maintain his soul amid a corporate machine for the rest of his life. In 1990 he aspired to sign a million dollar record deal yet proudly displayed the tattoo on his arm of the K Records' logo – K being the ultimate repository of punk rock artistic integrity ... *Nevermind* was the declamatory fist in the air of angry young men with nothing left to lose and nothing to offer but themselves and their music. Because of their grounding in the punk ethos, global success was something to be ridiculed, because of its sheer elusiveness. Once achieved, so dramatically and unexpectedly, Nirvana were profoundly, and permanently, confused.'
– Keith Cameron, *Mojo*, January 2003

given me and holds it) and I feel I've achieved every-thing I wanted on this record and I don't really have anything to say now . . . for the moment. I haven't told the band but I'm not planning on being too involved with it for a while because I want to concentrate on photography; I've kinda got the bug again – 'cos I think there's a certain amount of creativity which is floating around me and I have to put it all in one place.'

All or nothing.

'I think it is, yeah, because I think I've been doing photography on autopilot for a few years, to be honest, you know? Which ain't good but I got good at it so . . . it was a possible thing to do, but I want to start really working at it again.

I'm really excited about photography for the first time in years, but to my mind it takes a fairly grand gesture to actually move on in any way . . . and I don't want to give up the music but I do want to focus on photog-raphy so that's what I'm going to do.

I don't particularly enjoy taking photographs but I do enjoy trying to turn it into something great. I like taking these kinda pictures, landscapes, and I've been thinking a lot about my photography, and the kind of pictures I get to take of groups of people is kind of creatively stifling because the ideal ingredients for making a great picture are almost taken from you – I mean, in my experience the best pictures are usually of one or two individuals where you're engaging with them and that comes across in the picture – it's much more difficult to engage with a group of people; although, I think I do take good group photographs, which I think is a very difficult thing to do.'

You've developed strategies for that?

'I have, yeah.

I mean, I'm quite shy, so it's kinda conflicting with my nature in a way, when I'm in these situations but I think . . . you know, I try to be nice . . . and accommodating . . . and I'm sympathetic to what these people want and how they want to be portrayed and I try to help them with that . . . I think it's 'cos I love music and my sympathy is always with the artist.

I kinda want what they want. I try not to go into situations with a really strong visual idea. I'd much rather use whatever I'm presented with and work around it, you know? As opposed to having a concept. I much prefer a reportage approach to work.'

Did you see the recent Don McCullin film?

'Blew me away. He was the first photographer whose work – the first photographic book I ever saw was a book of Don McCullin's pictures and although, you know, his pictures are disturbing, there's always . . . I mean, it's mad but there's always beauty in his pictures and a sensitivity . . . so much creativity goes into his pictures; he's obviously a brilliantly natural composer but, you know, I think it's the darkroom thing – that's where you really nurture the mood of the picture.*

---

* I wrote to David Watkinson to ask for clarification regarding McCullin's print process during his time with the *Observer*. He wrote back:

'Dan,
    When Don McCullin worked for the *Observer*, he was treated the same as any photographer, sent on an assignment, film either brought back or sent and was processed and printed at the *Observer*, I will always remember when he went to Berlin just when the wall was built, great pics,

His sensitivity comes through in his pictures. They're so moving because he was obviously so moved when he was making his prints – imagine that reflected – because it's a very solitary environment, being in a darkroom . . .'*

After the reportage he also went back to landscapes.

'I think it's a default – I'll just walk round the manor taking pictures and printing – I mean, that's what I do, to be honest; I should be off exploring the world but, it's funny . . . when I started I did a really crap photography B-Tech in Wednesbury near Walsall and the first project was "Make Wednesbury beautiful".

Now, Wednesbury's a fuckin' shithole, but that's always stuck with me; not that I did a good job of it back then, but I do really believe that you can take a great picture wherever you are – it's about how you record it.

So, yeah, I'd like to travel the world taking beautiful landscape photographs, but I'm content just to walk around where I am doing it because I think there's always a picture to be got, it's more of a challenge in a way, to make somewhere slightly mundane look fantastic.'

---

also I was still learning the trade, Tony Prime was the printer then (my mentor), and in those days Don was not well known.

I hope this is useful.

Regards,

D Watkinson'

* A 2005 interview in the *Guardian* stated that Don McCullin still spends long days in his functional, bare darkroom – 'I like the consistency of the dark. It keeps me safe' – in a shed at the back of the house.

However, I found the writer's reference to McCullin 'getting into tizzies about the increasing scarcity of good photographic paper' callous and thoughtless – I'd fret too if my livelihood were threatened.

But then, you spend a lot of time in your own head, Steve.
I think a lot of photographers do, don't they? In their own
head in the dark.

'Yeah.'

Is that helpful?

'No.
Often not.
I've got a pretty unique view on things. I don't really
read very much. I don't know why. It's not something
I'd regard as pleasurable, reading; it takes much too
much of my time up, I'd rather be doing stuff.'

Working. Looking.

'Yeah.
I've read a lot of Charles Bukowski books . . . (laughs)
but that's probably not particularly helpful either.'

I don't think Steve hates people . . . but perhaps he feels better
when they're not around, to paraphrase Bukowski. I think it's
fair to say that he associates work with struggle and process

with art – perhaps it's his darkroom alchemy which marks him out; the mysterious thing that must be done alone in pitch black – that struggle and graft are what colour the fruits – the lustre is the labour.

When we first met, in Stratford, 2010, he was at an impasse. Kicking disconsolately against the pricks, pissed off and worried; seriously considering a career as a gardener –

'Maybe I'll enrol at horticulture college for a bit, learn up and see if I could get a job with it . . . but that's probably as much of a pipe dream as being a photographer.'*

Now, three years later, he's fired and inspirited again – although still as contradictory as before.

What's your plan for the year ahead? I ask him.

'I'm hoping to do three exhibitions this year because I've realised that people don't necessarily understand what they're looking at any more and I think the only way that anyone's going to appreciate what I do – what they've seen all over the internet and whatnot – is if I put it on a wall.
So in March I'm doing an exhibition in Whitechapel of pictures taken between 1990 and '93. I'm trying to

---

* 'I think, in an ideal world, I could keep myself entertained and occupied through the things I do. I like the effort involved in making music and doing photography; I think I'm a craftsman and I put a lot of time into everything I do and, at this point in my life, it's all concentrated on the music. But it could change. I might get into gardening. I might get into shed building.'
– Steve Gullick, Manor Park, 2010

think of a name for it at the moment, but it's basically pictures from what they called the Grunge era so I'm taking it from when I got involved in it up until Kurt Cobain died or, rather, the last time I photographed Nirvana – December '93 – 'cos it kinda ended there, certainly my involvement in it was pretty much forcibly halted, because the music press essentially turned their back on American punk rock music at that point – just cut it. For those three years I was probably in America every other week doing some really great American rock band . . . so it's all that stuff but I don't want to be elitist about it; I'm putting a lot of British bands in who were part of the scene. So that's going to be in March.'*

You've got quite a complicated relationship with a lot of those shots, haven't you?
I heard that after Kurt died you took your shots of him out of circulation and even considered burning your negs.

'I wanted to do that, yeah, because I never wanted to be in this position.
To be perfectly honest I never wanted to take a retrospective look at my career because I wanted it to go on until I died.'

Only have a retrospective after you were gone, you mean?

'Yeah, because then it's done.
It's ended. There it is. The job's done. Concluded.
But, unfortunately, I've found myself getting older.

---

* *Punk as Fuck: 90–93*, Steve Gullick, 1–13 March, 2013; INDO, 133 Whitechapel Road, London.

Which I never wanted.
I'm enjoying some aspects of being older – I don't regret not having burnt the negatives. The only reason I wanted to burn them was because I didn't want to be able to exploit them as I got older . . . I don't regret my decision not to do it but I also know, if I had done it, I wouldn't regret that either. Things like that you stick with – but I didn't do it so it's hypothetical.'

What's the next exhibition after that, then?

'The next one's in the spring, in Istanbul, and that's a more general overview of the work I've done, and there's a third one later this year of my Nirvana stuff which I've never shown on its own.'

Do you think people need to physically confront the work on a wall to have a dialogue with it?

'I just think I'm in a position where I can show people real photography, and I want to take that opportunity as much as I can now because I can't compete digitally.'

That situation's changed since I first met you, though.

'I've got two of the fucking things now!
Yeah . . . but the reason I bought a digital camera was as a consequence of the Foo Fighters job, because their management were having so much trouble viewing the scans of contact sheets – because what happens with digital is that you do the pictures and then make an on-line website and every picture comes up screen-sized looking sharp and perfect, whereas when you're doing them with film you've got to mess about zooming into a contact sheet and stuff; moving it about, it's not as

easy . . . and I could have chopped out each individual picture and done a website of it but, you know, because I hadn't worked digitally I didn't know that was desirable or a possibility . . . and it was so difficult because, you know, when you're talking about a band at that level it's very corporate and, you know, it looked like they'd paid me quite a lot of money to do a photo session that they couldn't look at . . . so it was incredibly frustrating . . . we made it work but I don't think they enjoyed the process.

They got the results but it wasn't easy for them. It was really stressful and I kinda gave in at that point and bought this digital fucking thing – but then, you know, using that thing; it's got some great uses. I was initially using it instead of Polaroids just to get the exposure right and check composition, but I actually kinda quite got into it.'

Earlier this year we met near Brick Lane and went for a walk and you spoke about it then . . .

'I just wish it had never been invented because it's fucked up my life! (Laughs) That's the truth because, you know, I had these relatively elite skills. Now there's probably a fucking button you can press to make your pictures look like mine.

So I'm competing with that culture – but you know all this, that's why you're doing your book – and it's a very difficult thing to compete with, on a surface level, so you've got to take it beyond the surface, but then who are you going to take beyond the surface? It's only going to be discerning folks and there ain't that many of them around these days . . .'

Have you backed down now?

'I have backed down. Yeah.

I still shoot film in every session I do but, what's been happening is, because I'm presenting these mandatory convenient online websites where everyone can look at every shot individually – you know, I'm a commercial photographer and I've got to do what the client wants, essentially – without exception, the digital shots are being selected.

I don't think people are even looking at the contacts, because they're not presented like the digital pictures . . . and I think it boils down to convenience and what somebody needs from me. What a band needs of a photograph of themselves . . . if it's for press, it's probably better if it's digital because it's easy. I can turn a digital shot round immediately whereas I've got to go in the darkroom and do a print, scan it . . . digital, for what people want, it does the job.

As I say, without exception, every job I've done where I've shot film and digital, it's been the digital ones that have been selected.

Then there's also the additional cost of doing a print . . . I think they think, well, that's fine. Let's just use that – but I do work really hard on the digital pictures. I mean, it's not photography but it looks good.' (Laughs)

'Throughout my career . . . I don't think I've ever made it easy for picture editors, it's just that they used to be a lot more professional and knew what they were looking at, whereas now everything's been made so simple for them, I think . . . and I'm not accusing anyone of anything here but I think picture editors go for the easy option over something they'd have to invest more brainpower in.

My photography isn't for everybody.

I don't know why some people commission me, because they don't want what I do.'

What's your redeeming feature then?

'It's my sparking personality, Dan. It's because I have an empathy with artists, I think. That's traditionally why I've worked . . . take Will Oldham: I've got a track record with supposedly moody bastards — but then, those people, they're only that way because they have to deal with idiots quite often.'

STEWART LEE (1968–) is a British stand-up comedian, writer and musician. He made his name in the 1990s after his work with fellow comedian Richard Herring. Author of *The Perfect Fool* (2001), *How I Escaped My Certain Fate* (2010) and *The 'If You Prefer a Milder Comedian Please Ask For One' EP* (2012). His BBC television series, *Stewart Lee's Comedy Vehicle*, has won a BAFTA.

STEWART LEE

Paddington Station, London
11 March 2011

There is a footnote on page 299 of Stewart Lee's book, *How I Escaped My Certain Fate*, which reads:

> 'The chiselling here, where I tapped the mic stand with the mic, went on at some length, sometimes un-interrupted for minutes at a time, with me varying the rhythm and intensity of the tapping. This doesn't work on the page, and ideally, my ambition is to get to the point where none of my stand-up works on the page. I don't think stand-up should really work on the page, so the very existence of this book is an indication of my ultimate failure as a comedian.'

The mic stand chiselling serves to colour the image of *Daily Mail* columnist Richard Littlejohn carving pedantic misogynistic addenda into the graves of murdered women. In the flesh, it's very funny, sad, uncomfortable and frus-trating – each arrhythmic salvo building towards another reveal, another line of Littlejohn's hateful pedantry. It's not comedy as it's normally understood; closer to challenging claustrophobic theatre perhaps. The audience are complicit in the performance, we trust that Lee's apparently esoteric flights will pay off and take us somewhere unexpected and rewarding.

It's a dance and a journey, a game. It's all about faith and manipulation and it hinges absolutely on Lee's ability to hold the audience and take them with him.

When we meet, I ask about the idea of stand-up as an entity which inevitably dies on the page, stripped of cadence, tone and swing – rendered flat, just 'funny writing'.

'Today, as a stand-up, the idea is that you're a content generator generating content, and that content can be chopped up into a seven-minute form for a roadshow, a twenty-minute form for a corporate gig; an hour for your DVD that you'll do and which'll then get on the television; or it could be thirty seconds for an App on a phone or it could be a one-liner to be quoted in *Zoo Magazine* underneath a funny photo . . . and I think, "No. Let's make the art form the thing it's meant to be. Let's not try and make a cross-platform thing."'

Alan Moore* hates the film adaptations of his books

---

* Alan Moore (1953–) was born, lives and works in Northampton, England.

The writer of many great comic books, he is currently working to finish a book about Northampton called *Jerusalem* which will be longer than the Bible when it's published – 'but hopefully better written'.

I heard him speak about the book at the Northampton Fish Market a few years ago, specifically about the discovery that James Joyce's disturbed daughter was incarcerated in the asylum next to his school.

In 2010 I met Moore briefly in the Old Vic Tunnels, below Waterloo Station, and had a light-hearted conversation about Stanley Donwood and swimming pools of blood. He was dressed in a blue cloak, I remember, a blue cloak and Dalmatian shoes . . . a magical, benevolent host. I asked him then if I could travel up to Northampton and

because he says they are comics and they were written to be comics and they're about comics and they're not supposed to be films. So that's the end of that, right? (Laughs) And I think I want to make stand-up that really is stand-up. Not things that can become something else. What's the actual essence of trying to be funny in a place without being a clown?

So, yes, ideally it shouldn't work off the page because it should be about intonation and performance and that scraping thing was a good example of that.'

Have you experimented further with that idea since?

'In the show after that, I had a giant coffee loyalty card that I'd made – a big, badly painted painting of a coffee card – and I said, "Yeah, look at that," and I found that, if I hit the mic at it at a certain speed and angle it would make a particular kind of scrape that would get a laugh out of the audience but if you tried it too hard or too soft it wasn't there. So I found that there was a funny sound that a microphone would make on a piece of card and there was a not-funny sound as well and I thought, "That's really great because somewhere in radio and television commissioning a man is reading a script and going through it putting ticks or

---

speak to him about the city but somehow our subsequent wires got crossed and I think he became concerned that I wanted to poke around his house and look under his kitchen lino, and so the conversation never happened but the fact remains that he is a unique exponent of the local being key to the global – as Ms Marple's life in St Mary Mead furnished her with insights into crime – because Northampton is a microcosm of everywhere else, as good a centre of the universe as anywhere – an idea explored in Moore's 1996 novel, *Voice of the Fire* – each chapter a story set in a different era, slicing through Northampton, from pre-history to the present day. He is missed in these pages: the one that got away.

crosses by lines that he imagines will work but if the sound of a scrape can be funny or not funny then a line must depend on who said it and what their face looked like when they said it. It doesn't exist in isolation; that's writing and we're not talking about writing. We're not talking about journalism or funny scripts, we're talking about stand-up and the timing, the space, the pitch of the person's voice, all those things – so in many ways the content of the actual words are the last thing about it.'''

•   •   •   •   •

Paddington Station is not where Stewart Lee works, as a rule. He generally works in theatres and comedy clubs because he's a comedian but, as we shall see, that doesn't matter much because he's cheerfully despairing about how he works – his grail of an office at home having failed him.

The great Victorian engineer Isambard Kingdom Brunel still has an office at Paddington, although he's not called in for a while; his reinforced hat rack now dusty and sad, his steam-powered pencil sharpener rusted and seized, its copper funnel pocked green grey.

Lee and Brunel are united in their love of nuts and bolts; one fascinated by the nuts and bolts of comedy, the other by actual nuts and bolts . . . trains, stations, big bridges, ships, cigars and hats – but he never wrote a book! No.*

Stewart Lee has written a book, though, a book about his comedic nuts and bolts, a book born out of his work on- and offstage – as this book began with an airship.**

---

* For all his steam-sharpened pencils, he never wrote a book, I don't think.

** Which had fourteen nuts and bolts in its nose.

I enjoyed your book, I tell him, when we meet.

'Thanks very much. I keep meeting people who've read it and it's weird. A theatre lecturer at Kingston University told me that all the people in the department had read it and they call it the "all practice, no theory" book.' (Laughs)

I explain a bit about the airship, and the comedian Stewart Lee listens, head cocked slightly to one side. He is small and wears a checked shirt. Both hands on the table cup and nurse his paper coffee. Habitually forlorn, his tousled quiff greying at the temples, today he resembles a cherubic crumpled Morrissey subbing as a lumberjack but, when he talks, he dances down long avenues of crackling thought and when he laughs, he cackles, rocking back in open glee.*

•　•　•　•　•

'So your book stems from frustration with the lack of process in art school? Good idea. The way books get

---

* 'Crumpled Morrissey' is Lee's own description and he extrapolates further on unflattering doppelgängers in his 2009/10 show *If You Prefer A Milder Comedian, Please Ask For One*:

'In April, March last year I did a telly thing for BBC2, and it was the first bit of telly I'd done for over a decade, and I was just worried that someone in the queue was going to recognise me and go, "Ooh look, there's that bloke off the telly. There's that bloke off the telly trying to steal two-ninths of a cup of coffee."
But as it happened, I needn't have worried 'cause the viewing figures were actually so low that I was less likely to be recognised as me than I was to hear someone go, "Oh, look, Terry Christian's let himself go." "Oh, look, Morrissey's let himself go!" "Oh, look, Edwyn Collins has let himself go!" "Oh, look, Ray Liotta's let himself go!" "Oh, look, Todd Carty's let himself go!" "Oh, look, Leonardo DiCaprio's let himself go!" "Oh, look, KD Lang's let himself go!" "Oh, look, Hattie Jacques has let himself go!" . . .'

made now is that they ask a load of E-list celebrities to come up with ideas. I noticed when my TV show got announced that people came out the woodwork from all these publishers saying, "Do you want to do a book?" and what they wanted was a book that would tie a name in with something like the television show title so they could get it into Tesco; but I'd already started working on the book that you've read and I wanted to write that . . . but most books by comedians are . . . I mean, I really like Dave Allen and I'd read a terrible, terrible biography on Dave Allen by a woman who used to work with him.'

The one which didn't touch on his process or where any of his ideas came from?

'Nothing about that, no. It was all about who he played golf with, or whatever. All the books about comedians now are about the funny things that happened to them at school. I thought, well, what about a book that had no personal information in it but was really about actual process? Because that's sort of what I'm interested in as a comic; I don't really care about whether people had a hard life or not, so I thought I'd write a book which I'd want to read. It's also the sort of book which very rarely gets written about musicians, they're normally personality driven; as if that explains everything.'

James Dean Bradfield told me he has certain spots where he sits to write, do you have a similar approach?

'I don't know what I do any more. Twenty years ago I carried a little notebook everywhere and I used to write things in it when I had ideas and then I'd go home and type them up on an Amstrad. Sometimes I'd have ideas in the middle of the night. I used to write for a radio show called *On The Hour* and I heard a repeat on the radio recently and it was about a thing in the country-side, like these barometer museums or the pencil museum – Worm World; An Exhibition of Worms:

'"You don't have to worm your way in, there's a gate. Tame worms are tossed towards your hands by trained volunteers."

'I remember I woke up with all these phrases in my head and wrote them down and a week later they'd been done by a voice-over artist, really weird, but now . . . because I always thought the place was the answer, right? I'd always said, "One day I'll have a space in a house and that space will have my desk and it'll have all my books on shelves and I'll be able to write there." But I've got that now and it doesn't seem to be the answer. I've still no control over where it will come from.

For stand-up, I used to write it all at home. I'd try to sit at the computer and work it out with my little note-book and crumpled bits of paper, but that ended after about 2007, which coincided with having our first kid – and therefore no time. What I tend to do now is write a skeleton and do enough little gigs around little clubs where I can sort of jam it onstage. I deliberately leave spaces where stuff's never fixed and that's a strategy in a way due to the fact that I'm now lucky to be popu-lar enough to do the same show 120 times . . . but as to where I work, I don't really know where that is. Nothing seems to happen where it should. That book, for example, I just couldn't do it. I did it all in hotel rooms on tour – and I've got the bloody room at home now! I've got the room that I thought was the answer and it hasn't been . . . so I'm still none the wiser and I read with interest these people who have their rituals – Peter Ackroyd writes lying on the floor while drinking whisky and he stops at midday. Other people say, "I put my pen here, I have to have it all just so . . ." but I've got no idea.'

Nicky Wire writes a lot in hotel rooms and collects hotel stationery for that reason, to put him back in that space. He said he can write well on aircraft because he feels close to death, and always in a hotel room because he feels that he's nowhere.

'Nowhere, yes, I like that. They are nowhere; none of your stuff to distract you, yet I always imagined that I'd be writing in my forties in my house that I'd own, thinking, "Oh yes, that's a bit like something Samuel Johnson said," and reach out and get the book down . . . but it's actually just not the case. The sterility of the hotel room, yes.

I've had to write an extra chapter for the B edition of that book – and we've just had a little girl, admittedly – but I was struggling, struggling, struggling with it at home – the deadline was two weeks ago – but then I got more done in six hours in a hotel room in Cardiff last weekend than I have done in the previous month and I know I can do the next book next year because I've got a four-month tour in the spring . . . but, also, I find I can't force an idea. My last show came together in the process of a walk from Central London to Camden which I was kind of obliged to do because I'd got my son with me in his pram and I couldn't go on the tube so . . . I had an idea on Oxford Street – he was asleep – and by the time I got to Camden I knew what the next live show would be. I could have probably sat in my room for ages and that not happen but, again, as

STEWART LEE

to where stuff happens, it's just . . . where stuff happens. How you do it, no idea. I wish I knew and I envy people when I read this sort of thing . . . although I don't believe them half the time.'*

---

* Now, I enjoyed the maudlin image of Stewart Lee pushing a pram from Central London to Camden beside a canal. In my imagination the pram was Victorian, the sort with spoked wheels – small at the front, large behind; suspended on a leaf-sprung undercarriage . . . beside the Regent's Canal he tramps, awning bassinet bouncing, muttering his way to Camden Lock – dressed as Morrissey, dressed as Brunel, dressed as the villain Quilp.

But when I got home and listened to the tape I discovered that the canal was my invention, Stewart Lee didn't mention a single canal in all the time we spoke. Maybe, in light of 'Crumpled Morrissey', I was dwelling on Kevin Cummins's photographs of actual Morrissey beside the Rochdale Canal and my mind sped ahead to plot a route a Camden-bound pram-pushing Lee might take from Oxford Street – Regent Street, Portland Place, Regent's Park, Regent's Canal, Camden Lock . . . in this scenario, a canal is a perfectly reasonable waterway to walk along.

But there were no canals on the tape. Never mind, never mind; at no point had Stewart Lee said canals were antithetical to the composition of stand-up. I decided I much preferred my version of events to the ones actually described: there was a canal and the canal was important.

Besides, it was very unlikely that Lee would publish a detailed psycho-geographic account of his journey home that day and thought processes en route.

Imagine, then, my black despair when I read pages 6–8 of the recently published book *Stewart Lee! – The 'If You Prefer A Milder Comedian, Please Ask For One' EP*:

'The purpose of the lunch with my live promoter was to decide a title for my forthcoming tour. I left the Caffé Nero in a huff, un-caffeinated, but as I traipsed north towards Camden [and we're off] I began to imagine how a TV observational comedian would deal with this mishap. He would speculate as to how and why the *barista* assumed he had faked the stamps, I thought, as I passed the now-closed Fitzrovian hang-out The Black House on Rathbone Place. [Disaster! He's started at the Tottenham Court Road end, not Oxford Circus . . .]

He would wonder what would be the point of only faking three of them instead of all nine, I decided, as I headed up Charlotte Street [He's going to take the Hampstead Road straight up past Mornington Crescent . . . There's no saving this . . .] and past various production companies, where Channel 4 filler is fermented in giant vats. As I crossed the street grid in a north-westerly direction to skim the edge of Regent's Park, via Albany Road [In the park! Get in the park!] where Edward Lear once lived, sketching parrots

405

Judi Dench learns tricky plays in a chilly bath, Bill Drummond restricts his palette, Jenny Saville works long hours alone – people have developed devices to get things done.

'Rich Herring, who I used to do a double act with, writes a blog and he says that he does it because it means that, every day, he's forced to get into work mode in some way. I don't think that's strictly true but, to be forced to do something would be quite good . . . as an "artist", you sort of think, "Wouldn't it be great to get to the point where I didn't have to do other stuff" – really devote yourself to whatever you want in the broadest terms – but actually the blank slate is pretty intimidating as well . . . so, talking about how your hand is forced, I don't know how you force yourself . . . I don't know.'

---

from the zoo, I worked through ever more exaggerated responses to the incident in my head. Against my instinct, I began, as I passed The Dublin Castle and the pet shop on Parkway, to find the whole idea genuinely funny. [Damn! He's cut over the Euston approach – below the canal . . . you know, I was thinking of Camden Lock when he's obviously headed for Camden Town . . . fair enough – I set my sights too far north. I should just let it go.] . . . As I wheeled the pram past The Good Mixer [towards the canal!] – where, throughout the Britpop years, the toilet cubicles were always occupied – I got out the Caffé Nero loyalty card and looked at the small print. Squirrelled away between the blue and white blocks of the company's distinctive corporate livery was the phrase: "If you prefer a milder coffee, please ask for one." 'By the time I met my promoter outside the Japanese restaurant, I had a poster design etched inside my eyelids, and a title which would seem to say something about the axiomatic modern dilemma facing the contemporary commercial comedian. Family-friendly funster or bile-spewing hate merchant? *If You Prefer A Milder Comedian, Please Ask For One.*'

I happen to know of a good Japanese restaurant in Camden Lock. By the canal. I flung aside Stewart Lee's book EP with a snarl.

I've read that Nick Cave chooses to write and compose during office hours – sitting down to work at nine and finishing at four.

'Well, Chris Morris* has an office and very specifically has it offline; he won't have a computer link in there

---

* Chris Morris is a writer, actor, director, musician and satirist in the good, sharp, weird sense of the word. He made a funny film about suicide bombers in 2010 and the spoof documentary series *Brass Eye*, among many other TV and radio programmes. These projects were very dark and caused much dull controversy in some quarters with the 'Yours, Outraged' brigade demanding that it stop and everyone involved apologise and then be banned – a sure sign of an interesting endeavour (see *Jerry Springer: The Opera* footnote, 192).
Chris Morris has been known to script-edit the television programme *Stewart Lee's Comedy Vehicle*.

. . . one of the things that's hard to explain now I have kids is that a lot of where ideas come from is apparently wasted time, right? Wasted time used to be where you'd lie on your bed and read in a grazing kind of way, then the internet came along and there's no parameters to that, no reason to ever stop hopping from one thing to another, and sometimes something does come out of it but it's quite difficult to explain that what looks like nothing, that's sort of where ideas come from; and as a parent you have much less dead time for stuff to bubble up, but that which you do have seems almost ultra-vivid.'

Do you ration out your time with your wife? 'Can I have three hours of dead time and you take the kids to the zoo?'

'Yeah, I mean that's quite brutal and it's quite hard to explain . . . funnily enough, since she's started to get stuff commissioned, she understands it a lot more but, yes, sometimes it's about having time to do nothing and I'm sure that would seem incredibly irksome to any civilians that read your book – "All these fucking people sitting around, trying to find the time to do anything!" But, I mean, God, pubs as well – to be in a pub on your own, it feels like you're king of the world – especially in the daytime – and it's convenient to say that it's a microcosm of society and all that sort of thing but it is also true that you do see things playing out . . .'

All this links in with the perception of wasteful decadence in education at the moment, perhaps.

'Well, this ties in a bit with what you were saying about the cutting back of facilities at art schools but also

about this current attack on the idea of education –
basically, you know, what do they do? They spend three
years wasting their time doing Norse studies and now
they should be charged £27,000 for that but, you know
what? Sometimes you don't know that it wasn't a waste
of time until it's over; you must have had this?
You often don't realise that you're working on something in your head until it's formed – you might have
had something that you thought you were doing for
fun or was just interesting you, but suddenly you realise
that it's all adding up into the shape of an idea.

'Before I did a double act with Richard Herring I lived
in a house with him and some other people, and he was
a very good person to say, "Have you noticed, you're
always talking about these things . . ." or "This thing
that you do to amuse yourself, you should do that on
stage" – things that had been staring you in the face;
and Bridget, my wife, is very good at pointing out
things that I'm unconsciously doing or seem to have
become interested in, but it maybe doesn't occur that
that's what you should actually be doing. Time's passing and you're doing something and then you realise
that actually that's the next project.

'Tom Morris,[*] who runs the Bristol Old Vic now but
ran the Battersea Arts Centre during their nineties
renaissance, he provided spaces for people – a bit like
what I imagine the sixties and seventies arts labs did –
just for people to try something:

'"I've got an idea about storage units."

---

[*] Tom Morris is the brother of Chris Morris, if that helps.

"Alright, you can have this space for two months. Is it an installation or a play or, what is it?"
"I don't really know yet."
"Okay."

'The problem with funding and jobs and the way things get commissioned for television or radio or theatre is that they normally want to know what it is at the beginning, but Tom was very good at talking about the process of finding out and I was lucky enough to work with some other people like that, Improbable Theatre. Eventually we ended up stealing their guys to do the set and design aspects for *Jerry Springer: The Opera*.* Improbable, again, there's four of them and no one knows who the director is:

'"Who's the director? Who's the designer? Who's the writer? We don't know.
We all sort of are."

'And it's obvious! It's obvious who's who – Velum's the director, Julian's the designer, it's obvious, right? But they won't accept that because they say that the things are all inter-related and obviously the design affects the

---

* *Jerry Springer: The Opera* is a musical written by Stewart Lee and Richard Thomas which was protested out of existence in the UK in late 2006 despite critical acclaim and four Laurence Olivier Awards – that very dull, insidious controversy again. This time protestors took severe umbrage with the Christian themes of the piece and – though they mostly hadn't seen the show, no – were disgusted and insisted, no, demanded it all stop and everyone involved apologise profusely.
Blasphemy charges were brought and dismissed, there were a lot of complaints and all attempts at adult discussion and dialogue were lost or rebuffed in the self-perpetuating cloud of pious outrage – OUTRAGE!!!
Which was a shame because it was a great, surreal, funny show of rare inclusivity and tolerance.

direction and whatever . . . they encouraged me with things I was working on; encouraged me to go down what appeared to be blind alleys. They said, "You have to get to the end of it before you know that it doesn't work, you can't abandon it at the theory/writing stage, you've actually got to knock into things; and maybe, if it's part of a theatre thing, get as far as getting people to sort of 'do it' before you don't do it."
The good thing about stand-up is that it's no trouble to do that; I can just have a go. You haven't got to get loads of things in place.'

Do you think it's tougher to find the time and space now that the arts are so squeezed? I mean, perhaps the idea of finding out who you are and what you want to do while in higher education seems like an offensive luxury – I've written in the introduction about the dawn of a 'post-impulsive airship epoch'.

'Well, you know, it's an offensive luxury when people around the country live in damp, rat-infested houses but it is also . . . if you're going to have universities, historically the idea of them was to improve the cultural and mental life of the country by association – so we had some people that were finished, you know?'
(Laughs)

But now, the debt and its influence on the courses taken; it's set up an antagonism – vocational focus versus wasted decadence. You mentioned Norse literature earlier.

'Yeah, it's like we've all got to be good little citizens. It's a shame.'

•   •   •   •   •

The big problems with art school, as I found them, were that each new intake of students was being squeezed harder for money while getting fewer cross-curricular opportunities and less interaction with professionally experienced, knowledgeable teachers and technicians. For all the money involved, they were being sold short on personal engagement with specialists who could open their eyes to the possibilities inherent and implicit in their courses . . . and if this book has revealed anything, I hope it's that expertise and experience help open one up and reveal the possibilities.

In the past few years, by means of labelling specialists as narrow, restricted practitioners and requiring staff to work longer hours, institutions have been able to justify replacing deeply knowledgeable part-time experts with generalists who could be spread more thinly – teaching more students on more courses and thereby cutting the wage bill.
As such, while students were being pushed towards the particular, the tutors best suited to teach them were undergoing a purge.

The real deceit, the dirty trick, occurred some time ago when student courses were reframed so as to be more vocational and tuition fees rose to a level which altered the student/teacher relationship to that of consumer/provider. In this new situation, the student is encouraged (feels compelled, perhaps) to seek 'value for money', often pressing for *exactly* the course as written in the syllabus, in the hope of guaranteeing a return on their investment – art schools and universities having inevitably become beshitten with the language of the City – but this reductive methodology only closes their subjects of study down further.
Today, art students are under huge pressure to attain a useful qualification towards employment above all else, where in the past they might have hoped to learn about art. At a very basic

level the current situation makes an arts degree less fun and experimental than it used to be. This change is money driven and damaging a generation.

My fear is that students seeking *exactly* the courses as written in the syllabus are likely to get them: identikit vocational courses lacking the depth and breadth of skill-set available under previous regimes which were student orientated.
Everyone is worse off. Everyone is hampered. The language is monetary when it should be aesthetic. Vice-Chancellors write letters which state that 'all aesthetic judgement is entirely subjective' when 'whatever, just give us the money' might be more apt. *

This book is, at least in part, a reaction against this dogma; a study in the inter-relation of disciplines. An investigation of cross-curricular possibilities. I'm throwing myself against the wall to see what sticks. The part of the wall is played by my interviewees, our conversations are the 'throwing' . . . I play myself.

David Nash discovered his way through the woods while building towers in Chelsea:

'Here's a technician, he is your friend.'
'Give this man all the help and materials he requires.'

It was only by going down the massive painty Kandinsky tower route that he discovered where he really wanted to go. He evolved and worked things out by exploring his materials.

---

* See footnotes on pages 23 and 494.

A similar process is detailed in *How I Escaped My Certain Fate*, similar but different. It certainly revolves around the personality and graft of the maker.

Back at Paddington, I ask Stewart about this aspect of the book.

> 'Well, Frank Carson said, "It's the way I tell 'em." He said that repeatedly. (Laughing) As if trying to convince us.'

Or himself.

> 'Or himself! Yes, but it is like that and that's why . . . you know, I don't really believe that ultimately you shouldn't be able to write stand-up down and it be funny, but it is a logical end point – in the same way that I don't think Derek Bailey, the free jazz guitarist, actually thought that all composed music was wrong, but it's a point of view, isn't it? It's worth saying.'

A lot of people never learn to read or write music for fear it'll deaden it.

> 'Somewhere between those points of view is something that's really true, yeah . . . but it's also about trying to make work that is of itself. That's partly why there were loads of footnotes in the book because I wanted to engage with the reader and you have to turn backwards and forwards and I wanted the book to be an object. I didn't want it to be "content" that could be read on a Kindle or whatever because there isn't the same engagement.'

I liked the duality of the narrative voice.

Yes; the stand-up is written in the character of me the stand-up and the footnotes are me the writer – me[*] – so I'm trying to make the book as a thing but all around you have people trying to un-make it. "Can we adapt it for Radio 4?" No, you can't. You can't because a) you won't broadcast some of the words in it and b) it's a book, right, and that's what it's supposed to be. I wouldn't have made that as a radio programme because it's a different thing.

I mean, funnily enough, talking about Alan Moore, I got rung up: "Will you come and be a writer on a radio idea for BBC7 and what it is, it's a Victorian world and all different characters from Victorian books interact – from Dickens to H.G. Wells . . ." and I thought, "Isn't that Alan Moore's idea anyway?"[**] but they said, "We've approached you, and Alan Moore might be doing it," and they mentioned a few people and I thought, "I bet Alan Moore's not doing it," and then they also said "the characters must be visioned" – not "envisioned" or "written", *visioned* – "the characters must be visioned" – which isn't a word – "the characters must be visioned so that they can also have an online life where members of the public can decide their futures . . ."

---

[*] Just as I, Dan, am doing here – footnotes are very much in vogue; everyone having read Stewart Lee's books and seen how well it works for him – making all these contextual notes, digressions and asides his fault – particularly the ones about canals and prams.

[**] *The League of Extraordinary Gentlemen* is an ongoing comic book series which follows the adventures of an elite 'Justice League of Victorian England', combining and pitting characters drawn from disparate but coeval fiction – horror, science fiction, crime, melodrama – a salmagundi of dramatis personae written and illustrated by Alan Moore and Kevin O'Neill.
Brilliantly detailed and knowing, *The League of Extraordinary Gentlemen* is as layered, clever and rich as a lottery winning onion in a Mensa-sponsored hovercraft.

Anyway, I rang up Alan Moore and said, "Are you doing this thing?" and he said, "No." And I said, "Oh, they told me you were doing it," and he said, "Oh, that's funny, they told me you were doing it" – which is what they do, to get you to do things.

I said, "So you're not doing it?" and he said, "No. Never do anything where they have to invent a verb to try and convince you," and he also said, "The point of being a writer is that I get to decide what happens to the characters. It's not negotiable for the public. Little Nell is supposed to die at the end of *The Old Curiosity Shop* and that's it," and I thought, "Bloody brilliant!" Because that's what he wants to be as a writer of stories. He doesn't want to invent computer games or create an interactive world, but you're seen as somehow lesser for not doing that.

You know, I think a good novel should be novelistic and a good novel ought to make a terrible film. A terrible novel, like a Michael Crichton novel or a Dan Brown novel, might make a good film because it's just a list of events – "and then this happened, and then this happened".'

All exposition.

'Yeah, there's no internal monologues, nothing unique about the language; it's just guidelines and bullet points for a director to make into a film, but a novel that really does what a novel ought should be unfilmable . . . because, if your thing can be cross-adapted then it doesn't know what it is.

Again, for me, being my age and having children late and whatever and *Jerry Springer: The Opera* not providing the pension that people assumed it would, you sort of think, "Well, what am I going to do?" And I look at people and know I never can be like them but I can, I could, really just try and do what stand-up is – not be a personality or somebody trying to get a sitcom.'

Not a stand-up who also . . .

'Exactly.'

Better to do one thing well. Yes, this chimes with a lot of the people I've met for this book.

'Well, there's something enjoyably puritanical about a lot of the people you're talking about. I mean, a lot of sculptors are essentially refining the same objects over and over again . . . I'm thinking about Derek Bailey because I've just been on the radio talking about him this morning; I can't really tell the difference between something he made in 1963 and 2003. On one of the last albums he'd lost the use of his right hand but I can't even really tell that, you know? It so is what it is, but it's also got that feeling of Carl Andre's bricks that are just sort of there: *

---

* *Equivalent VIII*, Carl Andre, 1966

Firebricks
127 x 686 x 2292 mm
Sculpture.

'The sensation of these pieces was that they come above your ankles, as if you were wading in bricks,' Andre has commented. 'It was like stepping from water of one depth to water of another depth.' This was the last in his series of Equivalent sculptures, each consisting of a rectangular configuration of 120 firebricks. Although the shape of each arrangement is different, they all have the same height, mass and volume, and are therefore "equivalent" to each other.'

– Tate display caption, August 2004

"'There it is.'
"'Oh, they're some bricks aren't they ... is it supposed to look like something?'
"'No. It's just those.'
"'Oh ... could it be a logo for a bank or something?'
"'No.'
"'Would it look nice in my house?'
"'No. It's not an ornament. It's a sculpture. It isn't for anything else.'"

'Again, is it a great sculpture or a bad sculpture? I don't know, but it is a sculpture. It's not a piece of statuary or an ornament or something that might have made a better painting!' (Laughs)

* * * * *

Sculpting as writing. In retrospect I see how I've repeatedly rewritten and redefined this book over the course of its creation, subtly recalibrating after each encounter recorded here. I'd assumed that I was approaching it like any other writer would, but now I think that I may have been wrong in that assumption and I'm more like one of Lee's sculptors, refining the same objects over and over again ... Stanley Donwood has a theory that J.G. Ballard essentially perfected the same book throughout his life, the same compositional tropes and character cyphers perfected book on book on book ... the unbearable lightness of being an overlooked empty swimming pool in a dystopian hinterland ...

* * * * *

Stewart Lee is showing signs of wanting to chip off – anxious, no doubt, to dredge the nearby canal for his next show – but before he goes I want to ask about words; his love and deployment of language in his work. The C word again . . .

'Well, a lot of the things that I get criticised for, I can't see what the problem is. People say "repetition", but that's a rhetorical device, isn't it? It's in Churchill and it's in Shakespeare and it's in poetry and songs so why not do that? I try to use words that people can understand and maybe once in a while I'll use a really long word in a funny way, but I don't do what Russell Brand does which is to use really, really long words all the time to let you know he's read some books. I'll do the opposite of that and use more self-consciously simple words onstage than I would even in conversation . . . and the last few years I've tried never to use swear words unless there's a real weight to it. There's one in the current show and it's "cunt" and it happens once, because I think they've become a bit pointless unless you're really, really good at it. It's a bit like the cross-platforming of art, now that everybody's allowed to swear it's a bit meaningless . . . and I'm also aware that the Stewart Lee onstage – what he says and how he speaks – is not necessarily how I am and speak, although there is obviously a big overlap . . .'

Is there a point where you, at the side of the stage, change into the character of 'Stewart Lee'?

'Well, I used to maintain that there wasn't, right, and that I used to just go on without doing any warm-up or preparation, and I still don't do that but in the last eighteen months, as recently as that, because I've been doing so much – because, as I've got more popular quite quickly, I'm doing much longer runs of shows which I never used to do and, since writing the book about stand-up – I do think about "him", this other person and what he would say and what he would think. "He" would be really, really annoyed with Mark Watson for doing a cider advert, whereas I think it's a shame because I've got quite fond memories of his stuff which is a little bit compromised now . . . but the onstage me, I do think of that as a different person. He's much more informed by me as a fifteen-year-old, so sometimes it's the first thought that you have that's a bit stupid, that the adult-you softens, that's the thought I give to him.'

Is your approach to writing for newspapers and magazines about music very different? Do you use different voices there too?

'It depends what I'm writing for. When I work for the *Sunday Times*, particularly if I'm writing about an anarcho-punk band from the eighties or a hardcore free-improvisation sort of thing, I tend to try and write it as if I were writing for an old lady. I try to imagine an elderly reader and then write about pretentious or antisocial things in an almost genteel way. Then, weirdly, when I write for the *Wire* magazine I'm sort of aware that, in the *Wire*, I could quote some Nietzschean or Cageian diktat but, with that, I feel compelled to go the other way and make comparisons to music hall artistes . . . they have different registers that are both in their own way inappropriate – I think of it like that. When I got asked to write things for the *NME*, then I would write as if I was very old and didn't understand what any of the things were – while indicating that I actually did. So, depending on what the paper is, I try and do the wrong thing . . . which I suppose is a bit like the stand-up thing of "I'm not going to give this to you on a plate, but if you listen you'll feel so pleased with your-self for the fact that you got it . . ." It's a game really; appearing to push them away but actually they quite like it.'

THE BUTCHER OF COMMON SENSE (2009–) is a collaborative experiment by Norwich-based band The Neutrinos and visual artist Sal Pittman. In 2009 they handpicked five other artists (a writer, a filmmaker, a sound recordist and two musicians) to join them in Berlin for an intensive ten-day residency in a defunct East German radio station, Funkhaus Nalepastrasse. The idea was to become immersed in the surroundings and create an album which would take its inspiration from this extraordinary space and from the atmosphere and history of Berlin. Several years in the making, the result is The Butcher of Common Sense:

An album. An artbook. A performance. An exhibition.

THE BUTCHER OF COMMON SENSE

2009–2013

A few years ago I bought a copy of 'Revolution' by The
Beatles at a car boot sale. The record had no sleeve and the
middle was punched out. It had spent its life in a pub juke-
box, I was told, and after forty years on heavy rotation it
looked pretty rough as you'd expect – worn but apparently
unscratched. I took it home.

Now, 'Revolution' is a fuzztone tune, a dirty three minutes of
insistent buzz saw whup which starts with wrangled double
stops and screaming and ends with deranged barrelhouse
piano – and that's the version on general release – mine's far
madder.

When I got home and played my 'Revolution' I was met with
a white noise deluge. Four decades of stylus erosion had
ground the original fuzz down to an overdriven soup, and
now The Beatles were thrashing like Neil Young circa *Rust
Never Sleeps* . . . or Part Chimp: 'Revolution' as played by a
blender full of spanners.

As such this record isn't 'Revolution' any more but a palimpsest, played to death and reborn a squalling ghost. The pub

probably got rid of it because didn't sound like The Beatles any more – I think they missed out. Taken on its own terms it's a unique artefact and very exciting. It's rock and roll.

This chapter is about the The Butcher of Common Sense.

In 2009, nine friends, all musicians and artists from Norwich and London, travelled to Berlin to find a new way of working, turning away from the conventional wisdom associated with composition, each becoming something like the blank film in a camera or that reborn 'Revolution' 45 – allowing themselves to be influenced, overwritten, possessed, processed and developed by the city and the building they'd elected as their hub; an attempt to 'bleed a space' – osmosis in derelict Berlin; percolation at a defunct East German radio station.

Nine Butchers stood in the echoing dark:

Jon Baker
Karen Reilly
Mark Howe
Sal Pittman
Roz Coleman
Leo Thornely
Pippin Cotterill
Jonny Cole
Dan Tombs

An exercise in the unknown: inversion and transcription – insides outside far from home.
The making of a book and an album:
The Butcher of Common Sense.

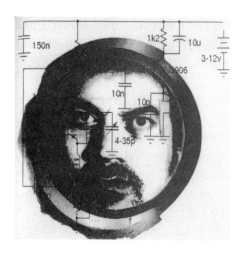

Jon Baker
Upper St Giles, Norwich
22 May 2009

Jon Baker and I sit opposite each other over his kitchen table. Jon is a choir leader, composer and musician. He has excellent hair. He's also a very skilled raconteur, evoking the Berlin the Butchers worked. The light, the sounds, the people, the cold and the architecture.

I've never been to Berlin. My Berlin is a collage of Christopher Isherwood, David Bowie, Fritz Lang and John Le Carré; *Cabaret, The Lives of Others, Downfall, Goodbye Lenin* . . . a muddled mishmash of Bauhaus, World Wars, ruins, checkpoints, the Cold War, faded decadence, art-squats, hipsters, the Neues Museum staircase . . . and I know the trouble is, unless you go, unless you explore and see for yourself, Berlin dissolves into cultural cliché and broad-brush cultural reference points; you have to delve deeper to find a Berlin a Berliner would recognise – the Berlin beneath the greatest hits and tourist surface grease.

My Berlin does not exist; it's other people's, once removed, whereas The Butchers went to work in the tangible midst:

'Part of the idea of the space where we worked in Berlin was that this old broadcasting studio, which was so important during the Cold War in terms of pumping out Beethoven and propaganda twenty-four hours a day – and quite a lot of Western pop music in the end, they realised they just couldn't resist it – would enable a sort of psycho-archaeology; so we weren't so much building things as uncovering them – feeding off the space and the city. We wanted to take that process, distil it and then make it into something we could record.'

It sounds like Brian Eno's card deck, the Oblique Strategies, in that respect.*

'Yes. That's essentially what we went and did. But we invented our own strategies which are based on a completely different set of ideas – some of which stem from a guy called John Stevens who had a band in the 1960s called The Spontaneous Music Ensemble. They used to do BBC sessions for Radio 3 and it was so socialist, the whole idea of it, that nobody wanted to be in the position of being a leader because that would have been too autocratic. So they decided that nobody would start and sometimes you used to have ten minutes of dead air . . . but of course that was part of the improvisation too because it was a choice people were making. They were

---

* 'These cards evolved from separate observations of the principles under-lying what we were doing. Sometimes they were recognised in retrospect (intellect catching up with intuition), sometimes they were identified as they were happening, sometimes they were formulated. They can be used as a pack, or by drawing a single card from the shuffled pack when a dilemma occurs in a working situation. In this case the card is trusted even if its appropriateness is quite unclear . . .'
— 'Introduction', Oblique Strategies: Over one hundred worthwhile dilemmas (Brian Eno & Peter Schmidt, 2001)

choosing to be silent. And somebody might eventually go "ping" but then "I'm afraid that's all we've got time for," you know. Or there might just be a huge clattery noise of someone pushing a drum kit over, or whatever the order of the day was. But John Stevens developed a whole set of principles and processes based around the idea of "search and reflect" and they're beautiful because they're all about space for music.

For example, we've got ten people sitting in the room, and what we're going to do is drop in some music; you're going to make the shortest piece of music you can. The only thing you're not allowed to do is coincide with anybody else. Now you don't know if you're going to coincide with anybody else or not, but if you do it's of musical interest. Or we're going to make a piece and the piece is dictated by the length of our breath. There's no judgement in that, it's just that people have different breath levels. You can choose any note you like and we're going to start now. It creates its own start point and end point and it has its own dynamic and contour; relationships are made depending on how people feel about the process.'▲

That idea of dialogue and the need for friction and tension – I told everyone I was building an airship long before I'd a clear idea of how that might be achieved. I set myself up for a fall and that's a way of working, I suppose, a conscious decision and tactic to get a result; manufactured pressure, a space to escape from – a similar approach to Situationists and actors, perhaps.

▲ *ROZ: I have to admit I had no idea we were doing any of this. Although I do remember writing a load of instructions on the back of a deck of cards in Berlin to try and give myself a creative constraint. I just had no idea it already existed as strategy, oblique or otherwise.*

'Yes, I'm very interested in that performance space, but I've done a lot of acting and I'm used to that and I'm perfectly happy there.

Barry Humphries* is going to be on *Desert Island Discs* this Sunday; I heard a trailer for it where he was asked, "What do you do to get rid of your nerves? I hear you get very nervous before you go onstage." And he said, "I go onstage."

I can understand that, it's a very nice place to be.'

How did you discover the Berlin space?

'We researched it, actually. We wanted to go to Berlin and, originally, what we thought we'd do was find a derelict space or an art-space of some sort. Another thing we thought was, "Let's go and book a studio in Berlin" . . . I mean, there's Hansa – Bowie's studio for *Low* and *Heroes* . . . eventually we came across a studio based in the Funkhaus complex and thought we'd book into that but it was just ridiculous in terms of money – we found a price that we thought was for a week but it turned out to be for a day, but Karen did her negotiating magic and transformed the daily price into a weekly price; then we were able to afford to rent a space within the Funkhaus but then we went and talked to the people around the place while we were over there and, in the end, they let us have the run of the building, the entire building! Hundreds and hundreds of rooms including the fantastic orchestral hall complex; and the more we delved into the place and worked there, the more we realised that these empty spaces were full of

---

* John Barry Humphries, AO, CBE (1934–) is an Australian comedian, author and artist.

shadows and ghosts and all kinds of things to set your imagination running – partly because of the time of year it was. It just felt so incredibly bleak.

As the light drained out of the building . . . you could almost feel it tugging at us.'

What did the Funkhaus look like?

'Quite a Brutalist building. Some of it's beautiful; it's in a derivation of the Bauhaus style so there's a slightly Art Deco feel to some of the spaces. There's a large office building which is a bit like the BBC's Broadcasting House – because that's what it was, the Broadcasting House of East Germany, set on the south bank of the Spree near Karlshorst . . . Brutalist and blocky and connected by a covered walkway across to the symphonic halls where privileged *Nomenklatura* in the Politburo would go to watch the radio symphony orchestras . . . I think they recorded an awful lot of Beethoven and Brahms and what have you in these spaces and they are acoustically superb, large, large halls – a big orchestral rehearsal space and a massive orchestral performance space – there was no expense spared. All the foyers are black marble and the spaces themselves are beautifully parquetted with amazing acoustic treatments which are integrated into the design of the building so they look fabulous and sound extraordinary – you can just imagine what a big string section or a big brass section would sound like – and then we met a man called Gerhard Steinke who was the main *Tonmeister*, the chief sound engineer there; he retired a few years ago but from about 1952 he was busy perfecting the sound in this place – quite obsessively, actually, in a good way. He was a great engineer, he's recorded some fantastic stuff but he'd also done some other weird things like build synthesisers – because they wouldn't have had access to Western kit – big, hot valve technologies and all the rest of it.'▲

What was your idea for the project at the very beginning?

'The idea was to go and make an album, but we wanted to make more of an artistic adventure about it. This was a discussion that I had with Jonny Cole, our co-producer and sound engineer. We wanted to steep our-selves in a way of doing things. The Butcher of Common Sense came about through a series of meetings where we invited people to this house for evenings which we

---

▲ *ROZ: The first time I walked into the building, Jon talked to me about sound as shadow, as imprint on the walls. We wondered about the sort of noises the building had heard, in its time as propaganda broadcaster, concert hall, radio station, recording studio, interrogation chamber . . .*

It became an experiment in hacking out your internal editor, disowning that part of you that has doubts. And alongside that there was always this background question, in every silent corridor or echoing atrium: what would it sound like, if all that collected aural memory suddenly played back at you, at once?

called "We made our own entertainment" and we did all sorts of musical experimentation – "We're going to do something in thirty seconds now, we're going to write a thirty-second lyric and then we're going to chop it all up into little pieces, then you're going to do this." We played with dice, we projected film and made instantaneous soundtracks, we made musical treatments to things, we did all sorts of Butcher-type stuff in rehearsal for putting a team together that would then go to the Funkhaus in Berlin.'

You had the Funkhaus sorted out by then?

'Yes. It was all extremely exciting. We packed the van up absolutely full of gear in the most appalling rainstorm and then set off – drove to Germany.
Karen and Sal, meanwhile, had gone over there as an advance art party to start gathering material – just trying to get the atmosphere and spirit of the place . . . and we were already presupposing that, because of the "We made our own entertainment" nights, we would go there and be able to develop those ideas and, to our total joy and delight, we found ourselves in this corner of slightly-forgotten-about, industrialised Berlin – nothing near it, you know? No bars or restaurants . . . there was a petrol station, I think . . . but we would sit around in Studio Four – P4 on the second floor – for the first couple of days, in an isolated control room we managed to make for ourselves – a treated broadcast studio so, sound-wise, it was pretty good – lots of pegboard, absorbent surfaces and diffusion surfaces. We had a couple of good rooms; a live-ish and a dead-ish room – this was before we started using the corridors. The Funkhaus had these extremely long corridors on every floor, hundreds of

yards long, disappearing almost into the infinite distance and slightly under-lit so there was a sodium light
effect going on which made them very yellow and
Eastern European as you'd imagine it . . . the building
was slightly crumbling and the lino floor was a kind of
yellow brown buff and it would squeak when you trod
on it . . . and there were other people occupying the
spaces in the complex so, behind these closed doors –
all sorts of things were going on. There was a kind of a
guy in his fifties, a German who'd probably seen it all
if you could mine him for information – a really nice
guy, we hired an amazing old Marshall bass amp from
him which looked like it had been through a war, it
was in a terrible state; and we noticed that on his walls,
he'd retained pre-Glasnost listening equipment – all
the kind of telephone exchange – because, obviously,
it's a broadcast station; there was a whole load of stuff
going on; everything was monitored by the Stasi . . . so
you got a real atmosphere from this guy and he looked
like he'd been there throughout, fossilised in this studio.
We dragged instruments around, experimented with

putting microphones along the corridors and all that kind of stuff – we'd run and walk around, improvise singing; we found an extraordinary depot and workshop outside; we spooked ourselves.'▲

And you were documenting this the whole time with recordings, writing and photography?

'Yes. And film. We documented absolutely everything. Everything was recorded.
We did lots and lots of improvising then, when eventually we got use of the huge orchestral spaces, we did things in there; put this tiny drum kit in the middle of this huge space.▲▲

'You never get the chance to do that sort of thing usually so we miked it from sixty feet away and it was extraordinary – this barrage of sound. We were miking up outside spaces as well, spent a lot of time in the black marble foyers and we'd do this re-amping stuff which is great fun; where you'd record something and then stick it through your speakers and then rerecord it within a space, at a distance, so therefore the artefact

---

▲ *ROZ: The Tom Waits 'What's He Building in There' Workshop, with the pit in the floor and the bent mirror outside and a sign that said 'Verboten'.*
Sal has a series of floating head photographs from there – we took it in turns to visit the mechanic's vault: a below ground cave of engine guts and grease.

▲▲ *ROZ: Hit snare, Pippin.*
THUNK
Hit snare, lad!
CRACK
Hit it again!
KABOOM
Thank you!

of the recording increases – you're starting to use the objects of extra-acoustic space – recording in a big space, playing it back through a small space, recording that and then playing it back through another big space – by the end of it you've got something unrecognisable.'

Like listening to exhausted vinyl or blowing up a photograph.

'Very much so.
Then we came back with all these bits and had to assemble them . . . and we were still applying all our so called Butcher techniques – nothing particularly new in it but it's the whole John Cage thing, that really interesting side of how you can make all sorts of things work, how you treat silence, how you treat the idea of decay . . . and we were drawing some, possibly slightly banal, connections between the idea of music and the idea of how the sound travels through the space and how the sound then becomes absorbed by the walls – we got very entranced by the notion that the building had absorbed everything that it had ever "heard" . . . we got very involved with that idea when we were over there, the idea of "play back" . . . you know, Berlin: what's it seen?'

In essence, then, you were steeping and immersing yourself in Berlin to become different and make a different kind of music.

'Yes. We took on characters.
The person who really carried it through was Mark.
He put on a different set of clothes and he acquired a walk and a hat.
He became an elderly man with a stoop . . . started to develop a perspective and a temperament . . . which

was great actually because that was part of the premise; we were all going to do that and I think we did each take on a character to a greater or lesser extent.
So it almost began to feel a bit like a theatre game . . . these drama games where you take a character on and a lot of actors will say, "Well, it all comes from the shoes . . ." you know? "It all comes from the ground up." You develop your walk and then you think from there . . .'

Now you've curated the sounds and music that you brought back and made a record and a book. The book and the record are the artefacts which play back the experience you had . . . is that right?

'I don't know, I think we've filtered it; it's mediated. In other words, you bring it back and what you would have done at the place you then change because you've come home; or you've gone and recorded somewhere else and you've added to it.'

You've overdubbed.

'Yes, and we've recorded things in different spaces, tried to find our equivalent spaces . . . quite often Butcher stuff is done in order to save time but it hasn't and doesn't particularly. (Laughs) It's that old argument of "when is something finished?" You know? I don't know. I'm not very good at knowing that one. I'd like to know "when is something finished," one day.'

The Machine – a film:

A light behind a dark grille.
Flash, flash, flash – after each flash, a spooled sheet.
Skimmed out at your face.
Paper mounts until it obscures the machine.
Self-same A4 sediment:
Arrows and squares.
Flash.
Arrows and squares.*
▲

· · · · ·

———————

* butcherofcommonsense.wordpress.com.

▲ *ROZ: I ended up falling in love with this Butcher character. I ended up writing to him. I'd invented such a vivid character that I was writing him letters at four in the morning . . . my need for correspondence, or a comrade, materialised (or so I thought) in the postman I kept seeing in the gloom before dawn. I'd be staying up in the apartment just off Friedrichstraße, trying to write or looking up half-remembered Walter Benjamin quotes or whatever – and I'd sit by the window (because I could smoke out the window) and at about four I'd look down to see this postman fellow who'd rock up the street with this big red wheelie deal and take armfuls of post to deliver to each floor of the massive apartment buildings opposite.*

Pitch dark, middle of November, properly freezing and he had so much to do! He'd take an armful, go up to the right floor, deliver to each door on that level, and then come back down to the trolley and get another armful – he'd spend probably twenty minutes doing each building, methodically making progress up the street.

Jon Baker
Upper St Giles, Norwich
30 June 2011

The Butcher led you into areas which your normal practice
wouldn't.

'It's about self-actualisation, a way of proceeding, a way
of looking at the world which leads to a set of ideas and
assumptions which then allow you to move beyond this
prosaic, "getting stuckness" which is the block which
affects us all.
It's about growing up in some ways.
How long does it take you to grow up?
How long does it take a human being to move into
itself?
It's a long time and I'm fascinated by that process and
the process of the artist as self-saboteur.
The second question of a questionnaire we gave out to
people at a "We made our own entertainment" night
was, "How do you poison your own water?" – a most
valid question.
I'm too cluttered.
The Butcher is a way of minimising the crap that gets

---

*I liked the idea of this 4 a.m. comrade – to the extent that I became increasingly annoyed as
the week went on that I kept seeing him and he never noticed me. At first I was amused to
be a spy but then I'd find myself smoking really loudly, or doing a big cough in this weird
bid to let him know that I was there too. Maybe I could send him a paper aeroplane – leave
him a note when he was on one of his trips then run back upstairs – except of course I
don't know the key code to get back in. It was already doomed, and I probably don't need
to take his ignorance that I was there too – that I was also up and working at four in the
morning – as a deliberate slight.
By the end I hated him a little bit.
And it's the same with the Butcher.
You hate him but, in the end, you want him to notice you.'*

me down. I'm not a neat person, I'm too lazy, but I like the idea of neatness.'

This is the currency of Ikea, isn't it?
They're tapping right into what you're saying by selling 'neat'.

'I can buy it off the shelf in a huge hypermarket of neatness and bring it back and assemble it and it becomes part of my psychic furniture, one's own mind and how you want to organise your life.'

But if you want to be neat, you need either less stuff or more room.

'Or self-storage, the biggest growth industry. It's created its own demand.'

Something about that makes me think of cities like New York where they send their rubbish away downriver . . . as if *downriver* is a solid destination.
Out of sight, out of mind.
Where does it go?
Downriver.

'Yes, it doesn't matter. I've been told there's an island in Tokyo harbour which is mostly made of white goods and growing – none of it more than five years old – because the Japanese always buy new. Their economy has been plummeting and part of the reason why is because there's no mending culture, they buy new; so this island is over-stacked and mounting.*

---

* 'Right from early on I was touched not just in an imaginative way – but as though some section of reality, of life, and movements in time, were influenced by the strange paradoxes of, say, a field of what seem to be

Big Yellow Company, that massive storage market, the question to ask is when are you ever going to get it back? You don't need it.

The Butcher is a filter, a clearing house, a lab – a licence to explore, change, mend and experiment.

I mean, in Berlin we believed, because we decided to believe it, that in the corner of that room there's a unique coincidence of time and space; there is a song to be harvested.

There's a song to be gained from that corner, so you'll

---

reasonable workable cars, washing machines or whatever, which have just been junked there. The rules which govern the birth and life and decay of living systems don't apply in the realm of technology. A washing machine does not grow old gracefully. It retains its youth, as it were, its bright chrome trim, when it's been junked. You see these technological artefacts lying around like old corpses – in fact their chrome is still bright. All these inventions touch a response to the movements of time and our place in the universe. There's no doubt about this. I think my childhood was spent in a place where there was an excess of these inversions of various kinds.'

– J.G. Ballard, *J.G. Ballard: The First 20 Years*,
Ed. James Goddard & David Pringle (Bran's Head Books, 1976)

go and make a huddle and you'll try and find it. It's ridiculous! It's just the way you feel at the time, we're basically deciding that that's the way it works but it's a way of working. It's a thing. Why not?

Why not try?

If I feel, on a sunny afternoon with the sun coming in at a particular angle, that that does something then I'll try and capture it; and the next day I'll have forgotten all about it and there'll be something else, you know? Or nothing. More often nothing . . .'

Folding Charts.

Now folding books.

Each book takes forty mins to fold all eleven sections.

Each page has a descriptive name, for example 'Double Doom Door'.

There are no printed page numbers.

Folding charts has made the task easier by 78 per cent.★

Sal Pittman
Wellworth Studios, Bermondsey
14 September 2012

Sal stands in her studio – a north-facing fourth-floor factory space – the grid of the window slanting squares across her face as she unpacks her head.

Sal's a Fluxus poster girl; bright words flying out to form a vortex in the room, spinning first about crumbs – 'One crumb! One crumb seeping through six pages of a book – Saturn rings of grease. One crumb!' – then Funkhaus paranoia – 'Those corridors, going about on your own . . . it was never

---

★ bookbuildingsite.wordpress.com.

that scary apart from this one floor shot through with bullet holes; strange indentations. None of us wanted to go there' – then off elsewhere, tangents intercut with associative snaps from the visual adventures she's had with Karen Reilly.

Pure dots of pointillist thought; the apparently scattershot coalescing to paint a picture of the Berlin Butcher project and the book built afterward, the beautiful grey cloth square book opened on the bench before us.

'The great thing about the book,' says Karen when I sit down with her later in the year, 'is that we've almost forgotten who took which photographs because we all did. The artwork began with all us contributing, a shared thing, then Sal took that material away and illustrated, painted, collaged, created abstract narratives from cut-up questionnaires — storylines which weave through the book . . . her hands have been on everything. Before it went in the book it went through her filter.'

'I want you to want the next page,' explains Sal, 'to feel tempo and sensation in the graphic. Some of the matter spills off the page. Here, the trompe-l'œil letter-pressing on the CD sleeve for where it slots into the book, the press box similar; see.'

The press boxes are tough brown cardboard, screen-printed and stapled boxes layered inside with plush smooth papers. Baader-Meinhof identikit pictures, lyrics, stories, maps, lists, plans . . . ideas of collage and layering proliferate the project, a subliminal sediment, symbiotic architecture; a palimpsest – a book and record built of spaces.

Apropos Sal, the next few pages will be impressionistic spatter:

Papers overspread the studio walls – crumpled, curling, pinned and wonky, Blu-Tacked brown paper, sun-faded cream paper wrinkled by moisture, masking-taped colour photocopies, black and white photographs, cutouts of the Funkhaus, sketches, coloured-in portraits of The Butcher team, contact sheets, legion black dogs, spattered lengths of corrugated cardboard, Post-its, printouts, newspaper cuttings, folded cardboard inner sleeves, tracing paper, ripped postcards, posters, A2 lists written in black marker, plans and diagrams.

This fourth floor overlooking.
Brick factory building.
H
A
R
T
L
E
Y
chimney.
Squared grey lino.

Radiators.
Trestle table desk.
Hands.
Plastic sacks.
Spray paint.
Oil paint.
Glass jars.
Stacked cardboard.
Packs of brown paper.
Scalpels, penknives, scissors, a pencil sharpener.
A Mac sat on a high chair – tall birch seat with heron legs.
A dressmaker's dummy where Sal hangs her brown coat.
Rust sprinklers jutting from the concrete ceiling.
Tins and cups of pencils and pens.
Box cameras.
Books – graded in height.
Ballet shoes.
A rocking horse.
A cutting mat, packets of stickers, box files, glue, headphones.
White gaffa/black gaffa/double-sided/insulation/parcel/cow-gummed strips.
The London Eye turning anti-clockwise in the distance.
Parliament's turrets glimpsed between two blocks.
The tall Shell building next to Waterloo.
Out there, finger pointing.
A page torn from a magazine – a man stands swathed in ticker tape and wires – a quadrophonic Cousin It.

• • • • •

'Early on, when I was working here, I'd have The Butcher demos playing or documentaries about Berlin or Hansa Studio recorded music. That was all I listened to, working here at all hours while this building percolated into the book.

445

You can't get away from the fact that the artwork was made here. It so, so suited this building – even the colour of the stairwells, the fact it's got a nasty old goods lift with a fantastic sound.'

Then Sal brews coffee by a corner sink and talks about the sounds around the book – the delicate jounce of the letterpress that printed up the record sleeves and press boxes; empty noise of clattering, a distant rhythm like a train, which grew and echoed at the Funkhaus – skittering down the corridors – music like a drunk trying to walk down stairs – the source of which nobody knew . . . thudding up the wooden stairs to the warm box of P4 'because you felt something was coming after you in the dark' . . . and then Sal's off and running about found footage and tapes of fairground tunes and a rabbit biting clout-nails out of its paws:

'In the late eighties Channel 4 had these fantastic 4mations – you'd get stuff on at midnight like Švankmajer. Around '87 – an hour or so of his work every night for a week. Amazing they had it then. I can't imagine going through a Sky box and finding a Švankmajer special now. It affected me, you know?'

You've mentioned Tacita Dean to me before.

'The catalogue for Tacita Dean's artwork *FILM* which she made for Tate Modern's Turbine Hall was a massive influence on how the multi-media exhibition work for live shows went together.* 'Ideas of splicing, editing and developing, the celebration of a dying medium, atmospheres, light and shade, all these things which we brought home from Berlin – bags of papers, photographs, song maps and lyrics. I built a narrative based around our separate characters and experiences, redrawn, spliced and re-edited, overdubbed – just as Jon, Karen and Mark did with the music; those narratives, literal and abstract, were woven like a soundtrack and a storyboard . . . but Tacita's work in general has been a huge influence since I first saw her work in Frith St Gallery in 1997. Her dedication to a medium because of its enduring ability to capture light.

Karen would come down for weekends where we'd work on projections, play with acetates and light-boxes. We spent about a year doing the artwork like that, back and forth, but we had all these lovely materials to work with; Roz's writing, all those narratives, questionnaires, song maps and lyrics . . . Karen was the link to the music; so a really nice cyclical process developed. I wanted to see if I could use the experience of the music to drive the imagery – keep feeding off the space and the energy of Berlin alive within that . . . I mean, I was taught film and colour theory at art school. Chemicals

---

* Tacita Dean is the latest artist to take up the challenge of filling Tate Modern's Turbine Hall.

Her response, entitled *FILM*, is a silent 35mm looped film projected onto a thirteen-metre tall monolith.

– tacitadean.tate.org.uk

and film reels, Polaroids and ink; every single page of the book has a hidden story; 340 of them. 340 artworks painstakingly made with attention to detail and love.'▲

Walking back to Borough from Sal's transmission tower, mind full of the Funkhaus, I thought of a kindred adventure I'd had in The Midland Grand Hotel, St Pancras, around 2003 – before its restoration, at a time when the rooms behind the brick facade stood empty and echoing; redundant except for occasional film work and the odd summer exhibition.

My father was exhibiting at an arts show in the building and after helping him unload and set up his work in a high-ceilinged room on the second floor whose lancet windows overlooked the Euston Road, I began to explore – first the corridors and stairwells I was allowed, then further, to the areas I was not, slipping away from the people and the light to the dark interiors.

When first built in the 1860s, Sir George Gilbert Scott's Midland Grand Hotel was the height of luxury, with hydraulic 'ascending rooms', Turkish coffee shops and a grand, uniquely cantilevered staircase. However, as time went on it became clear that what it lacked was decent plumbing and so

---

▲ *ROZ: I have an image of Karen on the footplate with Sal, stoking the photocopier in all weathers, driving the book onward; and it's a really obvious thing to say but it's the post-production that takes all the time – making the fucking book.*

It's so, so obvious but I didn't think about that at the beginning, I just remember worrying that I didn't know anything about Butcher-Of-Common-Sense-ry, all the time knowing that there was nothing I could do about that because it was like a reverse Death of the Author scenario, you know? Never mind the audience; you can't second guess the brief, whatever it is. This book, it's got to come out of you ... and it's coming out whether you like it or not; however much of a charlatan you feel.

I remember Jon telling me early on: 'I think we can afford to be pretty equivocal' – and having to look 'equivocal' up.

448

the establishment employed a vast staff to make up for this oversight with bedpans and the like – the cost of a full refit deemed unthinkable.

The hotel lumbered on but eventually closed to guests in 1935, thereafter becoming office space for the railway until they too quit in the eighties due to fire safety concerns.

In the years between 1935 and 2010 the Midland was left to moulder, many of the beautiful and intricate interiors forgotten or covered up – gold leaf and hand-printed wallpapers painted over with BR magnolia, ornate plasterwork concealed by polystyrene tiles, carpets and floorboards ripped up.

As I investigated I found Heath Robinson arrangements of strip lights suspended on flex from ceiling roses where chandeliers would have once hung. In the upper reaches heavy doors were screwed shut, random holes hacked in walls and floors and scaffolding poles rigged in lieu of long disappeared banisters. There were baths marooned mid-corridor, sinks ripped off the wall – pipework trailing; veined marble pillars half whitewashed, peppery dust pooling at the peripheries. I saw fuse boxes and switch gear bolted through delicate lath and plaster walls with iron strapping and wires streaming from moribund conduits – the place frozen mid-plunder, as if the wreckers might return any moment from tea break to continue their scupper, the *Mary Celeste* of arbitrary decor demolition.

A gated goods lift with a shaft dropping into pitch darkness.

Grilles and rusted skylights, the faint smell of soot and stale digestive biscuits. Floors which creaked and echoed. Gigantic corridors running to vanishing points fore and aft. A fawn wall smashed and dented; punched as if by cannon fire – screaming down the landing.

I must have wandered for a couple of hours, the distant sounds of London far below the grimy garret windows and attic cinquefoils.

In the book *Spirit of the Age* published in 1975 to accompany the television series of the same name, the architectural historian Mark Girouard describes St Pancras as Scott's great moment of glory, 'a vindication – the most ebullient, the most original and the most enjoyable of his buildings'.★

Girouard was a fellow trespasser, who investigated the innards of The Midland after slipping in out-of-hours through an unsecured back door, climbing the staircase 'like an explorer stumbling on a deserted temple in the jungle' – making it all the way up to the roof by way of ladders and a trap-door. I didn't get to the roof, although I did peer inside the bayonet clock tower, the interior soaring to a vaulted space of iron struts and timber beams, high workings, chains and weight boxes – the vault above receding to vacuity – while a smaller spire elsewhere gave a glimpse through crumbling brickwork of the vast train shed below.★★

Thinking back, the interior felt dormant rather than spooky or decrepit – although the spectre of The Overlook Hotel inevitably loomed, a bloody tumult mounting behind those locked lift doors.

It was a great thing to experience The Midland before it was restored to use to greet the arrival of Eurostar and once more hum to the sound of padding feet and voices, lifts, staff chat, bags, music, coffee 'jujj' and bells. I caught it in a hushed lull and stood listening to the building in repose. Before the cleaning; before they started the clock back up, reset the time, and shooed the ghosts away.

★ *St Pancras Station*, Simon Bradley (Profile Books, 2007).

★★ St Pancras Station will be familiar to millions because of its blackened appearance in the title sequence of Ronnie Barker's seventies sitcom *Porridge*. More recently, The Midland's grand staircase was deployed in a climactic bat-vortex descent in Christopher Nolan's *Batman Begins*.

The additions and aberrations of that eighty-year hinterland had produced a unique steampunk aesthetic: antique grandeur with brusquely pragmatic punctuation; an overgrowth of nodules, overwritten, worn away, accumulated foreign bodies and brutal interventions, but the building bore these scars stoically, bearing witness – like shrapnel found in the wood of old trees, barbed wire ingested from forgotten fences. Time was layered and porous in the corridors I'd walked, each branching door an invitation to unearth a facet of its past – which brings me back to that battered wall.

The story goes that, upon arrival at The Midland Grand, the 1930 Australian cricket team, determined to win back the Ashes they'd lost the previous winter, set up nets and practised in the endless corridors, insodoing rather trashing the place. They won the series and left their mark on St Pancras. From the shell holes I remember, their bowling attack must have been fucking terrifying.

•   •   •   •   •

Karen Reilly & Sal Pittman
The Horse Hospital, Bloomsbury, London
Friday 12 October 2012

The Horse Hospital cuts a slight figure in a quiet mews behind the sheer bulk of Hotel Russell. The only unspoilt example of a two-storey London stable – or so I'm told – a cobbled ramp slopes down from the front door; disappearing round right to a gallery performance space.
Now an arts venue, it's here The Butcher of Common Sense will be unveiled and tried out – the first night of a two-night tour; London today, Norwich tomorrow.
When I arrive, early evening, two hours before showtime, I see a stage area is lit by several slide projectors, while around it the walls are plastered with pages and photographs from the book, all washed with looping films which play across the whole space – a shifting document of the Funkhaus and subsequent visual and sound experiments.
Later, as the audience file in around me, I watch as they're drawn towards the pinned and pasted papers and the opera glass-like stereoscopes which suck the viewer into the endless parquet reaches of the haunting broadcast complex, before The Neutrino Butcher band take to the stage and the show begins in all its multi-layered intricacy – music, readings, soundscapes, film shows, light shards, megaphone monologues, teleportation, layers.

The next day, I ask Karen and Sal to explain a little about the ideas behind The Horse Hospital events.

Karen Reilly

'The idea was to make an experience as if you were walking into the book. So you walked down to a room which had pages and projections of some of the Funkhaus on the walls – projections which looked like they were going beyond those walls – especially the stereoscopes which really threw you back into the building – and then the added thing of playing the music in that space and having an audience there and us making music with them, around them, near them . . . the whole thing brought to life.'

Sal Pittman

'All new artwork was made over a three-week period – I totally zoned into how that space was going to look. I always knew and trusted that it was going to sound amazing. I knew they would nail that completely.
The walls were supposed to make you feel enveloped in the artwork and therefore the project – the Funk-haus, The Butcher world, so that when the music began the immersion would be complete and tenfold. The artwork was made to show you literal imagery, then the metaphorical and then the creative process and all its challenges – our thoughts, confusions, boredoms, desires – that's what I intended from the exhibition: an exploded book – like exploded cinema!
But I've stalked The Horse Hospital for years wanting to shape that space, planning how I would use it given the chance . . .' (Laughs)

Have you thought of the book and vinyl box as stored power to be loosed – like a battery?

Karen Reilly

'Yes. It's this huge thing which is bigger than all of us. I suppose I find it easy to say, "Look at this! This is great!" because it's not me saying, "Look! Aren't I

brilliant!?" I'm just a part of an extraordinary thing –
an immersive world which allows you to think outside
your box.'

The Undercroft, Norwich
Saturday 13 October 2012

The Undercroft in Norwich is even slighter than The Horse
Hospital, so slight as to be almost invisible: a door beneath
a war memorial beneath the City Hall. An antique portal
so subtle and familiar that, though a thousand people pass
it every day, it's implacable 'shut-ness' normally precludes
further thought or investigation, but it does open and it is
opening shortly and behind it, for one night only, prowls The
Butcher.
A crowd begins to form at the top of the steps that lead down
to the mysterious portal and then fifty are beckoned forward
into The Undercroft and the heavy door is shut firmly behind
them.
Thereafter, strange earthquakes resound.

. . . . .

Sunday 14 October 2012

How did it go?

Karen Reilly

'Really exciting! I was very conscious that we had to reserve some of our energy in order to come back to Norwich the morning after The Horse Hospital to do quite a complex show – something we'd never done before – and everyone had to be there, alert and on time because the shows were early as well; very different to London.'▲

Three shows in a new space.

'Yes, scary stuff! But taking people into a new space is always great because they're naturally nosy and also, with The Undercroft, we managed to hide three-quarters of the space from the people coming in and say, "Welcome into this little black cube, have a look around at these things on the wall, have some hot rum" – because that's great for making people feel nice – and then use the acoustic to sing un-amplified, very close up and they could hear all the definition . . . making sound-waves very near people is moving, literally, it's affecting. So we made curious people feel comfortable,

---

▲ *ROZ: Shows like this bear out the reality of time travel. Seemingly, ten thousand things are falling into place as you race through the eye of an itinerant hurricane and it's unbelievable but, somehow, five minutes before show-up everything is pre-set. We do a final idiot check and it's time to open the door. Roll it out. This is my favourite space to exist inside. The sound of deadlines whooshing by – the last half hour of power when you're knackered but everything's somehow ready, and you change gear from fast forward to real time, and then everything is Technicolor until you're turning it round again.*

we did some weird stuff – me in the ceiling, Mark through the megaphone – and then took them round for the surprise of "follow the drummer and mad guitarist on the trolley in the long low darkness up to some big noise and scary lighting!"'

Can you tell me a bit more about The Butcher's preoccupation with lighting?

'It's really an ongoing rant about how music gigs are lit. With music, you want it to break through conventions and be exciting and surprise you and move you, and yet the format of a gig has become extremely conservative: you walk through the door and there's a band onstage – a support band – and then there'll be a gap and then there might be another band but then there'll be the headline band and the lights will be brightly coloured, flashy flashy, on and off, you might have a bit of visuals behind, there'll be an encore, the band will go off but come back on, you know . . . it's just daft. But it doesn't have to be like that. There's room to finish a gig in a different way . . . so, with The Butcher gigs, we've done a whole series of performances that we've taken offstage to get away from the flashy flashy lights . . . How much more exciting is "I'm just going to light your eyes"!?'

Sal Pittman

'You know, the slide projectors aren't unusual, any more than a guitar is in a band. They're tools, from our histories, for our process and the common outcome – it's the work that matters. The technique of turning projectors and slides into analogue 3D abstract sets which we used last night draws directly back to

456

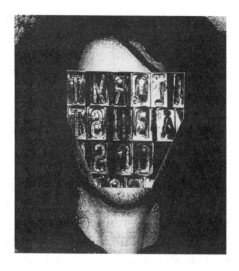

Expressionist style prints from my early collage work . . . and the work in the book, the whole Dada German Expressionism method, is a long-time fascination and inspiration.

For The Horse Hospital and Undercroft shows I made specific slides and shifted one transparency over another to create distinct atmospheres and focal points – using very small shafts of light to pick out details in people's faces, sliding graphic lines across the band.'

Karen Reilly

'Which was just perfect, brilliant.'

And you played The Undercroft three times last night.

'Three times on the same night, yes. That came about because it was a question of "Okay, we're only allowed fifty people in the space; that's not that many." "Okay, let's do it three times." "Okay, we'll do half-hour shows." But I didn't really think about the turnaround time so I put them back to back and that went into the programme. Then it was a case of "Right. That's what we've got to do!"' ▲

Were they each very different?

'When you do something three times that quickly, each one is different. You live in it in a different way.
The second one was the best.
You do the first one and think, "Ow! If only I'd . . . I just wanna . . ." and then you do it again and think, "HA! Yes!" And then we did it a third time – when we didn't have to push people out afterwards – and the energy went a bit.
The second one was the best.'

Sal Pittman

'I loved it! I loved all of it. Reloading and going again. Reloading and going again . . . Bloody marvellous!'

I'm struck how all these Butcher installations and happenings are primed and designed to tap into the Funkhaus's energy.

▲ *ROZ: This reminds me of the album in an hour. Completely regimented structure. Total immersion after all the planning eventually to surface somewhere later with stacks of findings, reams of results.*
When we were in Berlin, making an album in an hour seemed like the pinnacle of what was possible within an available time constraint but I think it started as a joke. 'What are we trying to do here, make an album in a week.' 'Yeah, right – an album in an hour, I heard.' And then that was it. That was the next thing to do. Keeping up with the improbable.
And you might not use any of it, you know? You might just keep it as an exercise – a place where ideas start – but, for energy levels and exhilaration, turning three shows around in one night was totally similar to the album in an hour exercise for me. The nerves beforehand, the giddy fatigue after. You wonder why you don't spend all of your time doing things like this. You'd get so much done.

In fact, The Butcher box feels a little like the compacted brick of ashes Bill had made with the remnants of the million quid the KLF burnt up: a document of rare ominousness, a charged object, a battery for the imagination – a kind of Berlin wormhole.

'When I think back to Berlin, the overwhelming memory I have is of barely controlled panic. You know, we set up these conditions to make something but we had no idea what it was going to be and that was really frightening but – a bit like you with the zeppelin – we found the building, took the people, set up the situation, made sure there was food . . . and it became a thing but there was no way you could have predicted it. The real excitement lay in the unknown.

I remember once when we were doing some gigs in New York and I went to some art galleries, and the art that I saw wasn't by any artists I knew of, and I was so excited to have no idea how their imaginations had come up with the things that I was looking at. You get very used to cultural reference points in this country, hearing about things before you've seen them – and I suppose The Undercroft show was a slight mirror of a show we held last year in an old McDonald's restaurant; we brought people inside in the dark, moved them along, scared them, played to them, blasted them, took them down the stairs, made them feel okay and pushed them out into the sunlight – all research and development, as it turned out.'

The Undercroft reminded me of Sigur Rós's film *Heima*.*

'I was looking toward the band Efterklang** when I hit upon holding it there. They went to an abandoned Russian mine and went around all the mental buildings and the big tubes and went "Oooo" and recorded things and they had a polar bear person to ward off polar bears.'

---

* *Heima* – Icelandic for 'at home' – is a documentary film about the Icelandic band Sigur Rós's 2006 tour around Iceland during which they played in such places as abandoned fish factories, water tanks and mooted dam sites.

ROZ: It's funny you mention this, Dan. In Berlin I spoke to Sal about Gregor Schneider and black bin bags, and I kept quoting The Waste Land all over the place – Unreal City this and that. And the word for uncanny in German – which I actually got from Mark Z Danielewski's House of Leaves – is Unheimlich (unhomely) or Nichtzuhauszein (literally, 'Being not at home'). I wanted to invoke those notions because of everyone working out of their comfort zones but also because I couldn't think of a more uncanny place – than Berlin, I mean. And when I got there and I saw where we would be working – in fact, the whole week, I mean, peering through the windows of a deserted Tempelhof only to discover when I got back I'd missed the closing party by two days – or stomping to the Bauhaus museum in the rain on the deserted day Obama got in, or just being in Tacheles. I got more than I could ever have imagined.
[The Uncanny is Berlin's stock in trade.]

** Efterklang is a band from Copenhagen, Denmark. Their name comes from the Danish word for remembrance or reverberation.

▲ Butcher Endnote –

In July and August 2014, Karen Reilly, Jon Baker, Mark Howe & Sal Pittman took The Butcher to the Edinburgh Festival Fringe in the form of an immersive, crowdfunded show named *KlangHaus*.

The team took over a former animal hospital inside the Summerhall venue, guiding their audience through twelve rooms of 360-degree visceral live experiences, immersive soundscapes, architectural projections and full band bombardment.

KlangHaus was performed over forty times at the Edinburgh Fringe and gained a cult following, enthusiastic media coverage, rave reviews, huge acclaim and several awards in the process.

▲   *Tonight, I suddenly realised the misery that Dan must have forborne this past however-how-long, sifting through our conversational jetsam.*
My last job was to scribble these notes, 17 book-style at the margins – a vague homage to the stalking silhouette that echoes through this compilation, consciously or otherwise.

Roz Coleman – Norwich, 2013

ROBERT MACFARLANE (1976–) is a Nottinghamshire-born author recognised for his contribution to the tradition of nature and landscape writing. A Fellow of Emmanuel College, Cambridge, his works *Mountains of the Mind* (2003), *The Wild Places* (2007) and *The Old Ways* (2012) were all published to award success.
He chaired the Man Booker Prize in 2013.

ROBERT MACFARLANE

Cambridge & Dorset
2009–2012

'Like creases in the hand, or the wear on the stone sill
of a doorstep or stair, they are the result of repeated
human actions. Their age chastens without crushing.
They relate to other old paths & tracks in the landscape – ways that still connect place to place & person
to person.'*

Robert Macfarlane – Holloway

• • • • •

I first met Robert Macfarlane in Cambridge, December 2009.
Snow spun about us and crunched underfoot as we crossed
the Emmanuel College quad. A sparrowhawk flew over with
its dark dove silhouette. The lido was frozen over – thick
enough to support a morose duck – and the famous oriental
plane tree stood out black bronze in the stalling light.

---

* *Holloway*, Robert Macfarlane, Stanley Donwood and Dan Richards (Quive-Smith
Press, 2012).

465

When we got to Robert's rooms I found my tape recorder had broken so the notes I have of the day were written on the journey home.*

They record that we spoke about Robert's books and writing, and that we looked at a book of fires, pyres and stoves by David Nash – a gift from Roger Deakin.** Robert knew about my great-uncle, I.A. Richards, and his wife and fellow mountaineer Dorothy Pilley, and we found a shared interest in the artificers and trench diggers from The Great War, polar sastrugi, the painter Paul Nash and the band Pixies.

As I was leaving, having agreed to meet again, I paused – recalling another, earlier, conversation in Bath – and said, 'You know the sunken road in Dorset which you explored with Roger? I spoke to Stanley Donwood a while back and he's haunted by it. I think he'd like to seek it out. I think he'd like to make a book.' And then I ran into the snow for my inevitably cancelled train.

•　•　•　•　•

Dorset
September 2011

The late September light is flat and warm. We are in Dorset – Robert, Stanley & I – sitting on a grass slope which runs down to a hedgerow beyond which a small farm can be seen

---

*　'The most inept interview I've ever been involved with'.

– Robert Macfarlane

** Robert became Roger Deakin's literary executor after the latter's death in 2006. A trusted friend and collaborator, he oversees Roger's literary estate and archive – housed at The University of East Anglia (UEA), Norwich, Norfolk.

stars★ ... specifically in this place, this deep, forgotten sunken road, because of the pivotal role it played in the novel *Rogue Male*, published by Geoffrey Household in 1939.★★

I say, 'this place' but 'general area' or 'sense of place' might be nearer the mark since the locations described in Household's book appear to have been composite spaces, sewn together from the author's intimate knowledge and experience of the landscape and deployed to best serve his narrative:

'The outer or northern slopes look down upon the Marshwood Vale. Here I passed out of chalk and into sandstone; the lanes worn down by the packhorses of a hundred generations plodding up from the sea on to the dry, hard going of the ridges, were fifteen feet below the level of the fields. These trade-worn cantons of red and green upon the flanks of the hills are very dear to me.'★★★

Roger and Robert searched the labyrinth of holloways around the Chideock valley for a point where Household's patchwork clues converged – orienteering by the book – trying to align the sandstone of an embankment, the view down the valley, a steep hillside behind a lost road diving

---

★   'The various subtle shifts of position to get comfortable whilst sleeping out on wild land / long grass.
     To change my head from elbow to forearm or to twist my feet from resting on the ankles to resting on the insteps.'

– A note by Roger Deakin – written at the time of his visit to the holloway in one of his many notebooks archived at UEA

★★ *Rogue Male*, Geoffrey Household (Penguin Books, 1977).

★★★ Geoffrey Household, writing in *Rogue Male* – it's hard to read these words and not imagine the book's author and unnamed hero to be one and the same.

down into a darkness, sentinel barbs, a tree-formed tunnel
... but nowhere quite tallied with the spot where Household's
hero hid; the crease lines of the valley were too numerous and
knotty to be understood in a long weekend, a week, a month
... and the secret remained.

And now Robert is back, with Stanley and me in tow – that
comment in Cambridge having bloomed into a collaboration, a journey and an exploration of the dormant fosse
paths within these crescent hills with a view to documenting
this vortex space in a book of words and cross-hatched illustration:

'A slender volume with marbled endpapers, embossed details . . . loose leaves of additional notes, impressions engendered by the place – fragments of ideas.'*

Cambridgeshire
September 2011

I have caught the Cambridge train again but today it rolls out into heat haze and sunshine rather than dark snow. We pass over the green dikes which hem Ely and below its twin cathedral towers – 'Ship of the Fens' – tip of this island city's jut of Kimmeridge Clay.
This is the first part of my journey today, a trajectory which will see me dart south-west from Norwich, meet up with Robert in Cambridge and then drive down the Icknield Way – or as close as modern roads allow.
As the crows fly we're headed over the Ivinghoe Beacon, down the Ridgeway, through the Chilterns and on to Dorset with its chalk and plough-turned flint, barren burrow slopes and coast chock-full of dinosaurs.
Were we flying or walking we could head dead straight but, since we're in a car, we jive about all over the place en route, through a gathering landscape of slowly building hills – a sine wave waggling out from the fens.

Passing beside the Icknield Way, Robert tells me about the route and a walk he made along much of its length for his most recent project, a book called *The Old Ways*:

'*The Wild Places* was an investigation into why we need wildness – a book rooted in Wallace Stegner's

---

* A note from Stanley, written around the time of our visit.

"geography of hope" – a brilliant and resonant phrase whereby certain landscapes, certain places, might do us good in ways that are unmistakable to experience★ but very difficult to articulate and I thought I was leaving those ideas but they kept coming back to me so, five years on from beginning *The Wild Places*, I found myself beginning *The Old Ways* . . . because they're fugitive questions, these questions of how we are shaped by our landscapes; how we think not just on them, not just about them but in some sense "with them" and, in my experience, they're best got at by means of action and anecdote rather than straightforward analysis; so I decided to set off and walk my way into this book and explore the relationship between walking and writing and paths and the stories they keep and tell. One of the first walks I took, in fact really the very first, was on the Icknield Way which runs from somewhere in the Norfolk heathlands down south-east of Cambridge and then, somewhere, frays into The Ridgeway – although where that actually occurs is a matter of speculation, as indeed is the proper age, the extent and the origins of the Icknield Way. For a long time it was badged as "the oldest way in England" and for that reason it has drawn dreamers and antiquarians to it for hundreds of years.'

As we drive, I imagine the Icknield rising from its Norfolk headstream, gathering as it goes, flowing past the car window now with a mounting potency, its furrowed course growing

---

★ 'We simply need that wild country available to us, even if we never do more than drive to its edge and look in. For it can be a means of reassuring ourselves of our sanity as creatures, a part of the geography of hope.'
       – Wallace Stegner's Wilderness Letter, 1964, *Selected Letters of Wallace Stegner*, Ed. Paige Stegner (Counterpoint, 2009)

strength and span. Robert tells me the route was a mile wide at the height of its use because it was a pre-enclosure right of way whereby there was nothing to stop you, if your rut was very wet, from stepping left onto the dry bit, and so when carts and people did that sufficiently often the path widened and became, as Edward Thomas put it, 'like the bars of the rayed Arabic mantle', and so now, in places, the Icknield Way is quite hard to trace – so vast that it hides in plain sight.

> '*The Old Ways* isn't studded with images in the course of its chapters – partly because the ghost of W.G. Sebald governs that method – instead I decided just to have one image, uncaptioned, at the beginning of each chapter but I'd have loved to use one of Major George Allen's aerial photographs of the Icknield Way, the railway and the A10, side by side, a car going one way, a train steaming the other trailing a plume of smoke and an unseen legion of Neolithic walkers on the path between.'*

Does the path run very close to your home?

'It runs so close that I was able to set out on a bright

---

* 'Major George Allen (1891–1940) was one of the first people in Oxfordshire to own an aeroplane – a de Havilland Puss Moth, named *Maid of the Mist*. He flew extensively across Southern England, and other areas, taking aerial photographs from 1933 until 1939.

Many of these photographs were of archaeological sites but he also took photographs of towns and cities, racing circuits, gravel pits and cloud formations.

The Ashmolean Museum has a collection of around 2,000 photographs taken by Allen, bequeathed to them after his death.'

– ashmolean.org

May morning while my family were still asleep, feeling very boyish and Famous Five-ish with my knapsack (technically a rucksack) filled with ginger beer (water). (Laughs)

I followed a beautiful field path away from my home which intercepts a Roman road, which I picked up and followed, and the Roman road in turn meets the Icknield Way at a perpendicular, and there I set out on several beautiful, endless days of walking . . . which isn't to say I had it all my own way – my initial dreams of elegiac time travel didn't always tally with the reality – as when the Icknield Way, arguably 5,000 years old, crossed the M11 on a metal footbridge – but that's because the old ways interlock, are overrun and wreathe with the very new ways and that was just one of those juxtapositions. So that was a clean cut but your eye, when you follow paths over a long period of time, starts to see in lines and you realise that paths are expressed in many different ways – some of them are debossed, others exist as phenomena of light and other unusual forms. Richard Long's *A Line Made By Walking* is a mighty example of the simplicity and immediacy of a path – that line was his own inscription in a flower meadow but one of the most strange, lustrous expressions of the path that I came across was when I was walking on chalk – that great lateral V of chalk in southern England on which some of the oldest paths appear to have been walked that we know – a beautiful lightning strike of inscription and incision that chalk paths produce, beckoning and leading the eye . . . and, of course, another phenomenon of walking chalk is that you become chalky. On dry hot days you beat up the dust from the ground . . . Flann O'Brien writes in *The Third Policeman* about how, when you walk, the continual cracking of your feet draws a part of the road up into you* – which is a wonderful line – but something not dissimilar happens when you walk chalk; you end up spectral at the end of the day, ghostly, faintly white as well as blistered and hip-sore . . . which was apt for me because I walked often with ghosts en route; Edward Thomas among them, conversing with the dead along the way.'

---

* 'The continual cracking of your feet on the road makes a certain quantity of road come up into you. When a man dies they say he returns to clay but too much walking fills you up with clay far sooner (or buries bits of you along the road) and brings your death half-way to meet you. It is not easy to know what is the best way to move yourself from one place to another.'
          – *The Third Policeman*, Flann O'Brien (Harper Perennial, 2007)

The holloway is a space steeped in absence. It reminds me of the overgrown canal network that can still be traced in the countryside around Bath. Built to carry coal away from the mines about Radstock, the Bath waterways were superseded by the railways – often laid on top of their drained courses – before they too were purged and faded from the map.

Cows now graze turf covering aqueducts; banked-up tunnels pass unseen under roads; forgotten abutments edge meadows, witness to an in-filled past, their stones scarred by the ropes from the horses which pulled the laden barges. Up-ended sleepers have become gateposts and barn stockades, deep oolite basins yawn ivy beside towpath cycle ways.

Such industrial archaeology tracks back to our Dorset bostle where feet and hooves and carts eroded a relation of the rock corridors near Camerton, the ruined flights of locks around Combe Hay and the echoing viaducts of Midford where two railway lines once crossed on limestone arches.*

This latent narrative and energy within landscape seems to be the driving force within Robert's work; the tension between elemental geology and the ambitions of man; the way we inhabit, plot and change the terrain – concerned with our place in the broader scheme and the traces left behind. In books about mountains, wild places and old pathways, he travels to the heart of worlds obscured, forgotten or apparently superseded to report and respond, and more often than not

---

* The opening shots of the 1953 Ealing Comedy *The Titfield Thunderbolt* were filmed at Midford and show the tracks passing one above the other – the Somerset & Dorset Joint Railway over the Limpley Stoke to Camerton branch, redundant even then.

Apparently the drivers on the S&D had great fun trying to disrupt filming with gratuitous whistling whenever they passed overhead.

Scenes of a manic Sid James driving a traction engine assured the film cult status.

he brings news of sites which have lapsed rather than died, altered but enduring unseen.

This is Land Writing, kindred of Land Art and similarly rooted in the ground; a response to the earth and its territorial imperatives.★

'The ways paths run through people as well as they run through places . . . these are things I've been writing about for three books now, for twelve years and about 300,000 words in published work and about a million in unpublished – because I throw away, for the good of everyone, a lot more than I keep – and I guess I've walked two or three thousand miles in the writing of these books, moving down from mountain summit to beaten path – but paths connect places to places and they connect people to people and they relate in the sense of joining and they relate in the sense of telling.'

Robert talks about Frost's poem 'The Road Not Taken', a work inspired by walks the poet took with Edward Thomas in the countryside around Dymock in the years leading up to the First World War:

Two roads diverged in a yellow wood,
And sorry I could not travel both
And be one traveler, long I stood
And looked down one as far as I could
To where it bent in the undergrowth;

★ 'The contemporary flâneur is by nature and inclination a democratising force who seeks equality of access, freedom of movement and the dissolution of corporate and state control.'
— An extract from Will Self's inaugural lecture as 'Professor of Contemporary Thought' at Brunel University, London, 2012

Then took the other, as just as fair,
And having perhaps the better claim
Because it was grassy and wanted wear
Though as for that the passing there
Had worn them really about the same,
And both that morning equally lay
In leaves no step had trodden black.
Oh, I marked the first for another day!
Yet knowing how way leads on to way
I doubted if I should ever come back.

I shall be telling this with a sigh
Somewhere ages and ages hence:
Two roads diverged in a wood, and I,
I took the one less traveled by,
And that has made all the difference.★

'That line caught my ear – *knowing how way leads on to way*.
Thomas always wanted to take both paths, as it were, but there's some sense that Frost knew about the connective power of paths and I now know that too – we all know it to some degree: the paths that I've followed took me in all sorts of directions and inaugurated all sorts of meetings.'

I ask about Robert's first meeting with Roger Deakin – his great friend and mentor.

'I think it's ten years ago now; I'd read *Waterlog*, somebody had sent him a copy of *Mountains of the Mind* – or maybe we'd met already, just before then. He wrote this

---

★ 'The Road Not Taken', *The Collected Poems*, Robert Frost (Vintage Classics, 2013).

incredible, generous letter about *Mountains of the Mind* and gave a fantastic quote about it.'

For the jacket?

'He'd read a proof copy, yes – this would have been 2002 . . . but maybe we'd met before then – a bit like you, I felt I'd crossed his path long before I actually met him – and I remember being told later that when *Waterlog* was published he'd come to Cambridge to do a reading but he'd gone for a swim beforehand down at the mill and then he'd sloshed up to Waterstones and left a trail of watery footprints which someone remembers following . . . so I definitely knew who he was though I don't think there was any particular reason that he should have heard of me. So we met, maybe, and then he read my book and then we really met onstage for a talking event somewhere at Cheltenham – and I was so nervous I had to lie in a darkened room beforehand. I didn't know how to talk, you see, and I was nervous about seeing Roger properly . . . but he was just so . . . great. And gentle. And kind. Generous and all the things that he was and then we talked before and we talked afterwards and we talked in public onstage and then he said "come over" or I said "come over" . . . it was location that made friendship possible because we lived an hour apart, although in completely different worlds – you cross the border into deep Suffolk from high Cambridge and you're into a mirror world, another land, and it was the same for him crossing back although he'd been here as a student, of course. So each of our worlds held different things for the other and there was lots of backing and forthing and talking and stopping and travelling.'

And, from the off, walking was an important part of your friendship, your thinking?

'(Thinks) Yes. We'd go walking – and there was a lot of good kitchen table thinking, I remember, as well ... and I say this at the beginning of *The Old Ways*, "this book could not have been made by sitting still," but actually, to tell the truth about that book and, indeed, pretty much all my thinking, I had to both sit still and walk to write. A lot of the book is born of sitting still and thinking and talking and reading with my bum fixed firmly on a seat; and the other part of it, the indivisibly "other" part of it, is born of walking and tramping, talking and exploring and seeing; so it's not quite true to say that all this thinking just gets done while walking or on foot because, as we know, pubs and kitchen tables and studios and houses are all involved . . . and that plane tree out there isn't going anywhere; that tree is a kind of office space for me, a thinking space – but we did walk. We walked from his house, around the fields, all those acres of meadow. There was a standard walk he liked to do which took in the wood at the end by the railway track and so on, and when we held a memorial evening for Roger, as just a few friends wanting to get together – on a fierce winter night – we walked Cowpasture Lane.'*

·   ·   ·   ·   ·

* Roger Deakin's relationship with Cowpasture Lane is detailed in his collected diary and notebook writings, *Notes from Walnut Tree Farm* (Penguin, 2009).

Autumn 2010

A photograph.

A winter field with a house beyond.
Bare trees frame the shot to the right, their fallen leaves
littering the straw grass below.
The house is Persian orange with an earthenware roof with a
twisted tower of chimneys.
White window frames. A black door. A hedge. A picket-
fenced bridge over a stream.

I crossed that bridge, unlatched a gate and knocked to no reply.
It wasn't Walnut Tree Farm, looked nothing like it.

Later, when I looked online, peering down from space to
hover above the field and house just described, I saw we'd
been walking on the wrong half of the common; the wrong
side of the railway line – pottering amiss on the off chance.
The dog enjoyed the day, though, and it was a lovely day –
ambling over Mellis's common ground with my friend Zoe
and Bramble the dog; drawn to the sound of a chainsaw –
crack and warp phantoms – peering into the closed pub,
looking down at the ducks and up into trees and recalling the
smell of childhood bonfires – the best to be had.

Roger Deakin was gone when we went hunting mapless for
his house.
There was no fire or tea awaiting us. We were not late for an
appointment with the great man – one of three East Anglians
whose work inspired this odyssey and whose paths I'm crossing, albeit latterly; seeking out the places which remain
behind where tea was drunk, thoughts thought and written
down, programmes made and records played.

The three: Roger Deakin, John Peel and W.G. Sebald.

Sebald was unknown to me when I arrived to study in Norfolk. By the time I discovered the dunescape of his prose he'd
gone; perhaps we passed each other in the grey corridors
of UEA – near missing, our paths overlapping but never
converging in the weeks before he died.

His great work, *The Rings of Saturn*, is best a found thing – a
book of lost images or spidery notes in a wiry hand, a thing
to be pored over and decoded – a map without a key or cross.
I found my first copy in a blanket box while looking for something else.

Nothing else I have read captures the depth and loss of the
broads; crawling into the landscape on a wheezing COPD
train; walking out – the dot of the man getting smaller and
smaller until he is swallowed by the landscape and only the
voice remains.
Rothko and Ballard near Benacre Broad.

I read it in one sitting in a Norwich student kitchen, the book
playing out until, suddenly, the end.
I blinked and peered about me to see where I was.

It was dark outside.

> 'For days and weeks on end one racks one's brains to
> no avail, and, if asked, one could not say whether one
> goes on writing purely out of habit, or a craving for
> admiration, or because one knows not how to do any-
> thing other, or out of sheer wonderment, despair or
> outrage, any more than one could say whether writing
> renders one more perceptive or more insane. Perhaps
> we all lose our sense of reality to the precise degree

to which we are engrossed in our own work, and perhaps that is why we see in the increasing complexity of
our mental constructs a means for greater understanding, even while intuitively we know that we shall never
be able to fathom the imponderables that govern our
course through life?'*

–W.G. Sebald

•   •   •   •   •

Was the *The Wild Places* the first book where you travelled
with a view to exploring ideas and landscape?

'Yes. Unlike the subsequent two books, I didn't travel
for *Mountains of the Mind,* that was made from what
I'd done in the first twenty-three years of my life, but
I set out for *The Wild Places*. Rog features a lot in that
book, as you know . . . and that book became explicitly
about thinking and place and ideas and landscape –
their inseparability in my mind and in the notion that,
when we lose certain kinds of landscape, we lose certain possibilities of thinking and that we can imagine
the world as a giant and complex cortex and that when
parts of that cortex are damaged or vanish irreparably
then parts of thinking go as well.'

And this all tied in with your childhood, which was spent in
a specific sort of landscape in Scotland and the Cairngorm
Mountains and the presence of your grandfather, to whom
you were very close . . .

'. . . Yes.'

---

* *The Rings of Saturn,* W.G. Sebald (Vintage Classics, 2002).

So you were exploring that?

'He has persisted and, well, we've talked before about climbing and the hold that high places have; the "beckoning silence of great height" – the inverted gravity of mountain-going – but I was brought up in rural Nottinghamshire which is very far from the Cairngorms and very far from the wild and is slightly tedious pastoral . . . I mean, I had a wonderful childhood and my parents are full of adventure and enquiry – Roger embodied many of the qualities they possess. My father loved making dens and shelters, enclosed spaces – relations of the holloway.'

Inner Space?

'Inner Space and concealment and encryption in the ways we've been discussing, yes. Rog and I talked a lot about dens and den-making – Richard Jefferies' Bevis, *Swallows & Amazons* . . .
Gaston Bachelard, in *The Poetics of Space*, talks about the purchase of the nest and the den and the hollow and I realise I began writing much more about mountains as places you enter – the wonderful writer, Nan Shepherd, who I write about in *The Old Ways* and was fascinated by how we walk "into" mountains and now it seems curiously logical, following *Holloway*, Nan and dens, that I'm writing a book about underground and the most enclosed spaces of them all – the womb tomb and the subterranean . . . so I guess, oddly, it goes back to Roger and *Rogue Male*; we're into an intellectual version of path-crossing and trail-meeting except, because they're invisible as you lay them, you don't know the trails are being made or that they're being crossed until you look back at where you come from.'

Have your rooms at Emmanuel College become your den to write now?

'Yes. You've been in my cave. You've seen it's a lined burrow – the nest has been feathered with all the stuff that my work's made of, which is words and bits of land – stones and boulders and feathers and pictures. That's where I write because I have children and a job and so I just try and guard one or two hours a day when I might write . . . having children is not the death of art, you just need to organise art more carefully and – I mean, what I do isn't art anyway but you know what I mean; I don't mean to over-dramatise the kind of things I do – and then it's just obsessive revision.

Listening to you talk about Steve Gullick and, indeed, almost everyone you've met, maybe, although there's a kind of spontaneity with some of them . . . but, for me, art is another word for craft, really, and your dad and you – you're craftsmen and you're artists when you're being craftsmen and vice versa.

I have a very crafty view of writing and it involves obsession and revision.'

Heideggerian in the sense of polishing ideas with repetition and returning?

'Working and reworking?*Yes, that's true, working and reworking and not the Keatsian idea of words forming "as naturally as leaves to the tree" which, as we know when we look at his drafts, is not true anyway** – which I think we talked about all those years ago while standing under the plane tree . . . but, ha! Look, there's the tree and I couldn't write without having been to specific spaces and those places then come back and distort themselves – that sense of going out somewhere and not knowing quite what you're looking for exactly but finding something else instead . . . at the beginning of *The Wild Places* there is a very specific description of a tree that I climb, but if you try and follow those instructions there is no tree to be found . . . and lots of people get annoyed about that and I've had to find

---

* Which I mishear later on the tape as 'walking and re-walking'.

** 'If Poetry comes not as naturally as leaves to a tree it had better not come at all.'

             – John Keats in a letter to John Taylor, 27 February 1818

a way, non-pompously, to say "find your own tree!"'
(Laughs)

Like *Holloway*: a map of its finding is not contained within those pages.

'It sounds like lostness is a key trope in the book. Losing and finding.'

Losing, finding, flailing . . .

'Do you know about Hobart's Funnies? They were the tanks to which they fixed great rotating chain flails out front to whip the Normandy beaches in 1944, flailing the ground in front of them to set off mines sufficiently far distant that they could be driven on and over – developed and tested in the Suffolk coastal woods, actually – anyway, whenever I think of flailing I think of Hobart's Funnies in the woods near Orford and strange things like that . . .'

Well, my Hobart approach to this book has led to a lot of funny, unexpected things . . . I drew the map as I encountered the landscape and met its inhabitants – the landscape of the book – and the book is as much a map of how not to write a book – a 'how not' guide!

• ◦ • • •

The book *Holloway* took some years to come together. Stanley first told me about holloways in March 2009. We met and spoke about it several times that Spring and I met Robert (in the snow) in December and was brazen enough to suggest that we three collaborate on something at that first meeting – which was an especially bold move considering that I'd turned up over an hour late (due to the snow) and without a functioning means of recording our conversation . . .* and it's possibly worth noting that, while I improved as an interviewer as the book went on, my method remained fairly unmethodical, but I think my saving graces were research and enthusiasm; throughout the project I kept books of notes and clippings, took pictures of my adventures and made sufficient connections, I think, to intrigue those to whom I wrote letters and at least prick their interest enough to respond.

Nothing happens unless you make a start and ask.

And so, in parting, I mooted the thing that would become the book *Holloway* and Robert did not say 'No.'**

•   •   •   •   •

And so we bedded down that first night in Dorset, Robert in the sleeping bag which has warmed him atop mountains and in the midst of wilderness, Stanley in a bijou one-man tent and I in Roger Deakin's hooped bivvy bag.

Robert read to us from a book of Edward Thomas's poems that he'd brought and then I burrowed my way to sleep, thinking of this confluence of work and people; how strange the Beechwood Airship should spin me down into this bush of ghosts.

•   •   •   •   •

'Waking in the holloway the thing that struck me, lying half out of my green cocoon and staring up – staring through the awning mesh of twigs and stems – was the way their patterns shone white when I blinked or

---

* See footnote on page 466.

** *Holloway* was self-published in an edition of 277 in June 2012.

turned away. A fretted photo-negative weaving with the vessels in my eye.

Burnt in. Of a piece.

'Once up, we sat round in the bank, ears pricked. We slept well but for the rain at four, faintly aware of the bird song swell with the sun – the hedges here are stuffed with birds; abundant, loud and brazen-bright as we are out of place. We hide ourselves as émigrés, as artificers in a trench, sat with our sub rosa gin below the parapet.

'Some 250 miles east, in an archive box, I found a card:

'"As an only child, the sheer solitude of the hero's escape and odyssey appealed to me. He was a swimmer too, dragged his tortured body into the Rhine like an otter – throwing off the guard-dogs that pursued him."'*

But let's be clear, our time in the hedge was more *Three Men in a Boat* than *The 39 Steps* – for all the doom intimated by our initial walk atop Pilsdon Pen with its glum cows and misted ramparts. No, for all the *Rogue Male* grounding, the endeavour felt much more akin to a daft farce – bicycles collapsing left, right and centre, we three hiding in our hole for fear of being discovered by irate dog walkers, drinking gin and eating cake like naughty schoolboys, falling over roots in the middle of the night; *Boy's Own* stuff but far from Household barbarism.

•   •   •   •   •

---

* An extract from *Holloway*. The last paragraph is a scribbled Deakin note I unearthed at the UEA.

Back in Robert's Emmanuel rooms, my last interview, almost four years to the day from the first, the sash windows again overlooking a tundric Parker's Piece, the snow drawing the eye and the room's little warmth outside.

The 277* copies of *Holloway* that we made have been sold and there's talk of a general edition to come in the Spring – we seem to have formed an accidental publishers: Quive-Smith Press – Macfarlane, Donwood, Lawrence & Richards. Time for a celebratory coffee to warm and cheer at the end of a circuitous climb.

Robert looks out the white common square, reflecting on the odd journey we've made.

> 'Getting lost is a very fine experience, you know. I like whiteouts and mist for that reason, but Edward Thomas was brilliant at looking at an Ordinance Survey map and following the old route where it was broken into fragments but still existed as place names, footpaths – he could almost see it in its shattered form – but I don't possess that capacity . . . but I'm fascinated by people who know places very, very well, as are you, I know.'

Yes, they are the source of so much else . . .

> 'Exactly. Even though *The Old Ways* is primarily about motion it's also to some degree about acquaintance so, particularly in the chapters which take place abroad, I was always in company and I really tried to reduce my presence to a pair of eyes almost on the shoulder, as it were, rather than any kind of interference of judgement – my ignorance was a constant companion

---

*The number 277 relates to the height of Pilsdon Pen – a book for each metre above sea level.

in Tibet, Palestine and Spain – so they tend to be the most observational, neutral chapters which allow detailed stories to tell themselves – whereas often in Scotland and England, those were chapters where I'd walk alone but in the company of ghosts – in one case my grandfather, walking to his funeral across the Cairngorms, and in the other, Edward Thomas.'

And then we finished our coffee, shook hands and went our separate ways; Robert home to his new son, Will, and the massing tomes of the Man Booker, and me to the station in the snow for my inevitably cancelled train.

Printing Endnote –

The original printing of *Holloway* was undertaken in Oxford in the Spring of 2012 by Richard Lawrence and Stanley Donwood.

At some point the decision was taken to use a Monotype caster to cast fresh type from molten lead for Richard's presses and employ the font Plantin – first cut in 1913 for the Monotype Corporation, based on a face cut in the sixteenth century by Robert Granjon.

The type was made by using a large keyboard to punch holes in a paper tape about five inches high – tape akin to that of a player-piano. This task, named 'keyboarding', was undertaken by Richard Lawrence and David Bolton of the Alembic Press.
The text was input 'blind'; that is, the person doing it has only their memory to tell where they were in the text and whether or not they'd made any mistakes. All they had to show for hours of punching keys was a roll of white paper, pocked with small rectangular holes.

The roll of paper in no way resembled a book, nor text, nor a typeface, nor, in fact, anything much at all. But it's where the book began, as it contained all the information needed to cast the type, which was done on the adjacent Monotype caster – which spat, ricocheted and hammered away madly in contrast to the reassuring 'Pish ti'coo; Pish ti'coo' of Richard's Heidelbergs, on which the finished type and Stanley's layered, hypnotic drawings – now photo-etched to zinc plates – were printed. A return to this book's beginning, although Richard's moved to Oxford now and the integrity of the roof above his printshop is noticeably less reliant on moss.

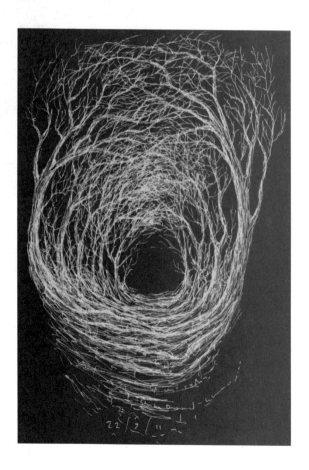

EPILOGUE

It is early evening. Light drizzle is falling. Dusk, as it has throughout this book, is settling on the land. I am standing in the middle of a field hefting half an airship into place above my head – seeking to slot the curving keel into a scaffold frame.

For several hours in the rain I rebuilt the zeppelin, fixing sections together with screws and wire, wielding an orange cordless drill in the lee of a pair of ancient oaks – sprung green and budding; calloused trunks screwed rough, deep veined and gristy.

After a couple of hours I'd patched and wired one half – a bisected envelope which I then hung well away from the shelter of the trees and hedge which had hidden my doings from the road. The spectral form, now visible to passers-by, stood out white in the grey scape – an odd swell of papered hoops and stringers set against a heavy sky.

A year ago, I returned to Norwich, lowered the airship down from the SU eaves and cut it up. It was a sad day. To compound matters I had to buy the saw myself, which I felt was a bit much.

I'd heard rumblings, tremors from on high, for months that the airship had 'been there too long'. Art school is a young man's game, after all, and pointed white elephants are not to be countenanced.

Shortly after graduating I'd begun a correspondence with the Vice-Chancellor – initially to ask why my certificate had a photocopied signature; although I had more questions as it turned out.

He employed a hilarious slash and burn policy to my queries, perhaps sensing that he was talking to a lunatic. He noted that I'd clearly had some little success since graduating and that my description of the school's new logo as a 'wonky N' was actually his idea of a dynamic logo. He went on to state that 'all aesthetic judgement is subjective'* – which I thought

---

* See footnotes on page 23 and 413.

494

was rather postmodern of him but might cause the institution trouble down the line in terms of marking work.

Returning to the SU I saw that the bar had moved on, changed hands and was now painted grey, wonky Ns encroaching at the margins like weeping angels.

So the ship was pulled from its bottle, displaced from the Jägermeister womb: a site-specific artwork shorn of an apt space, marooned like the last polar bear.

I helped the school out and got shot of the art. I bought the saw, borrowed some keys, lowered the ship and cut up two years' work – the line of thought it embodied having come to pass.

• • • • •

I am told that Bill Drummond plans to torch his Land Rover once he judges his work with The17 to be over. Immolating the crucible of the massed choir sound – an end to the space which bore it. Fiery coda; acrid flare full stop.*

Jerry can of petrol at my feet. I walk back and frame the field – horizon, airship, petrol.
I listen to the birds in the oaks and hedgerow – singing the daylight down.
Then I walk out and start to douse the zeppelin. At some level I knew this day would come; I chose to build a six-metre Hindenburg.

---

* Also, this may prove a good way of taking the Land Rover off the road because it was sounding a bit rough the last time I heard it – arson a cheaper option than bringing it up to spec for an onerous MOT.

• • • • •

This book was never designed to be vicarious – it wasn't really designed – it was experienced and relayed, a continuation of the tangible work in the Beechwood Airship. The people I sought out acted as catalysts to impel the journey on but I had no map of the territory ahead when I started.
As it turned out, I ended up in a holloway, that defiladed road, flailing for fear of getting lamped, having gone off to participate and immerse myself rather than simply interview and observe.

We had a bottle of damson gin in the holloway that my mother had made the previous year, the damsons picked from a tree at the bottom of the garden, deep rubine, the fruit macerated down to a sweet pulp, steeped and changed.

Robert Macfarlane has written of John Stewart Collis, a writer and worker of the land from the last century, a man of great empiric curiosity, that 'His only fixed belief, as far as I can tell, was that work – labour; contact; touch – was a prerequisite of durable knowledge.'*

I set out to submerge myself in this project rather than dipping a toe. Nothing beats the excitement of being inside something, moving and being moved, of driving a project and being changed.
That is what I missed at art school, I think, the shadow of escalating fees aside; I'd enrolled with hopes of being taught palpable skills – infused and enthused – but instead had to go it alone. But I was changed by the school: it fired me to seek

-----

* Robert Macfarlane, writing in the introduction to the 2009 Vintage edition of John Stewart Collis's 1947 book *The Worm Forgives the Plough*.

what I felt was lacking, to get on the road and into the mix like Stanley Booth and John Stewart Collis, like the damsons – implicated, from the Latin implicatus: 'folded in'.*

One of the first things Colin Henwood said to me in his boat yard, back at the start of this adventure, was that he respected people who got on with things. 'The people I admire are doing it,' he said, brilliantly blunt. For Colin and Richard Way it was all about the verbs, and it's notable that doings dominate this project – in fact a path through the book can be sketched in verbs:

Challenge. Research. Visit. Listen. MAKE SOUP. Build. Hoist. Meet. Interview. Narrate. Chronicle. Print. Translate. Chisel. Etch. Paint. Sketch. Sculpt. Compose. Play. Speak. Act. Doubt. Collect. Combine. Lose. Teach. React. Archive. Curate. Edit. Photograph. Develop. Perceive. Perform. Transcribe. Transmit. Write. Collaborate. Walk. Flail. Burn.

---

* Early on in Stanley Booth's *The True Adventures of The Rolling Stones*, he describes sitting down with Mick Jagger in an effort to secure the band's agreement and co-operation with the project and Mick asks what the book will be about, you know, what'll be in it?

> 'Maybe I can give you a comparison,' I said, and I told Mick that I had written a story about a blues singer who had swept the streets in Memphis for more than forty years, but he's more than just a street sweeper, because he's never stopped playing, if you see what I mean. I didn't look at Mick to find out whether he saw. You write, I told him, about things that move your heart, and in the story about the old blues singer I wrote about where he lives and the songs he sings and just lists of the things he swept up in the streets, and I can't explain to him, Furry Lewis, what it is about him that moves my heart, and I can't tell you what I would write about the Rolling Stones, and so, well, I guess I can't answer your question. No, he said, you answered it, and for the first time since I thought, long months ago, of writing this book, I felt almost good about it.'
> – The True Adventures of The Rolling Stones, Stanley Booth
> (Canongate, 2012)

Above all: Think and Work.

Each practitioner I've met interacts with the world in a different way and exhibits a unique methodology. Yet, at root, I think they're all speaking a common language and working at the same coalface: up against a risky frontier of chaos, accident and manifest skill – the childlike endeavour Judi Dench describes which entails both play and hard slog – odysseys into the unknown; long shadows of destruction; long hours alone; expedience as art; sudden revelations; decades of development – a life choice and head-space Stewart Lee struggles to explain to civilians.

This book chronicles an impulsive circuitous journey. I've visited high Welsh country and derelict London, sunken lanes, sitting rooms, workshops and imagined towpaths – you've just left me wrestling with a zombie airship in a field – but now, sitting here in my kitchen, fitting this epilogue together, I'm conscious of the fact that, if the conversations I've collected make any kind of sense or have a cogent shape, it's due to dialectic – the collision of ideas between the people I've encountered; time spent batting theories and polemics about, picking metaphysical ticks, because if there's one thing that links all the people I've spoken to together then it's the sense of the work emanating as much from 'about them' as within.

I first learnt this when I visited the boat builders in Henley-on-Thames to ask about beechwood and have discovered since that a huge amount of information, encouragement and knowledge is available if you have the gumption to ask – and that doesn't just apply to knocking on Bill Drummond or Judi Dench's door; more generally I've found how deep knowledge abides in the people who use it daily.

Norwich art school recently began rehiring specialists, a tutor told me last year. They need them back. The experiment hasn't worked out. He told me that with a smile and a shrug but I think my face betrayed me. It was the face of someone imagining they'd studied a degree during that time, aghast and unbelieving. Let down.

The cuts to funding, teaching hours and staff began years ago and continue. The social and pastoral sides of university have been trammelled, along with the cross-curricular opportunities they represented – the broader experiences limited along with the course remits and outcomes, the students' licence to explore tangential avenues and make creative mistakes lessened.

With all this in mind, I met up with my friend James Bulley, a composer currently studying for a PhD at Goldsmiths. I may have left art school and gone off gallivanting, but he's still working at the sharp end of arts Higher Education. Over coffee in Shoreditch we discussed the current state of play.*
I begin by asking him about his situation — working on a music PhD while making a living as a composer. From the perspective of a practising musician, what's his experience of the present system?

'Well, classical music is an interesting case, as it's always co-existed with academia – it's been a curriculum sub-ject in the academy since the medieval era – yet never had to justify its purpose. Fundamentally no one really cares about what that kind of music *means* so, if you're studying as a classical composer, you're at liberty to do pretty much what you like. It's retained its ability to be "for the sake of it" and I don't know what that brings to the argument, but I can't see why sculpture, writing, theatre etc. can't be treated in the same way rather than *quantifiable, knowledge-producing forms.*'

While writing this Epilogue I've been reading a lot about a European agreement called *The Bologna Process* and that's something you're dealing with in your PhD, I know.

'Yes, The Bologna Process is at the heart of everything we're discussing. It was launched in Bologna in 1999 as a joint declaration from ministers for higher education in the UK, France, Germany and Italy and created the

---

* Just as all workshops and studios seem to be badly heated, it's some sort of unwritten law that these sorts of conversations inevitably take place in Shoreditch. The conversation in question occurred in Autumn 2014.

three-tier structure of BA – MA – PhD we currently
have in an attempt to make the EU the world's biggest
knowledge economy.'

To make everyone's qualifications compatible across Europe.

'Yes, across the European Higher Education area.
Post-Bologna Process, for arts institutions to survive –
receive accreditation & assessment – they had to *become
academic*.'

* * * * *

It's notable that post-Bologna Process, terms like *Practice
as Research* came to prominence – a clunky term affixed to
those making work within the arts – and autonomous art
schools and polytechnics began to become subsumed into
universities; Goldsmiths became part of the University of
London, for example.
The need to quantify the arts in empirical and scientific
terms and bring everything into line with pre-existing judgement systems became paramount.

'The emphasis moved towards documentation,' agrees
James. 'What's the term? *"Articulated evidence of research enquiry"* . . . it's all the stuff you struggled with
in Norwich.
Practice as Research began relating practice-based
approaches with book-based approaches, and *Research
Audits* emerged as an intractable web of questions
about process and protocol, all caused by the enforced
integration of art schools into academic institutions.'

And that enforcement has trickled down, I see that. From
the policy makers at the top to the students at the bottom,

the pressure to conform and be absorbed by the system has never been greater, which is obviously concerning.

'The thing I have always found the hardest to accept is the physical boundaries set by courses – my situation over and over again is a mirror of your making of the airship – technicians and academics in other departments were baffled and gave me short shrift when I ventured into their domain for some reason or another. A huge amount of the craft element has gone. I was expecting and excited to learn about carpentry, electronics – how to make speakers, how to screen print – but getting access to those facilities at Goldsmiths is virtually impossible now. The loss of the textiles and ceramics courses are great examples of short-sighted, conceptual, theory-based judgements of which courses work and fulfil the new remit of a research-based judgement system. Crafts don't fit but that's only because the system is at fault.'

It often feels that arts degrees mainly focus on learning how to critique *work* and *making* before you've made anything, which is so obviously daft and wrong-headed, to me. Engagement with people and manual work have opened up so much for me.

'But in spite of it all, art degrees and art schools can still act as a wall to bang your head against, although they are less of the messy petri dish they used to be.'

Yes, even now – riven with quantified data and practice-based research – students can still, just about, mess around, antagonise and do things that have *technically* nothing to do with what they're supposed to be doing. They *can* go without an agenda but at massive cost!

'But it's important to remember that The Bologna Process was a strongly left-backed project and perspective at the time. In retrospect, I'm not sure that the people involved quite understood the onerous overarching repercussions of EU mandates on educational structure.

Essentially, some fundamentally dull, grey decisions of the 1990s that no one cared to properly interrogate or protest against have had a huge and lasting impact on the way art schools can function today.'

．　．　．　．　．

During the writing of this book I've been inspired by the emergence of Sweden's *Hyper Island* as a new model of higher arts education. Teaching both intensive short courses and degrees in digital culture, media and technology, *Hyper Island*'s ethos centres around masterclasses from industry professionals, while placing great emphasis on boosting students' leadership and communication skills. A *Hyper Island* year might consist of six months at school, followed by a four-month industry internship. One of the organisation's slogans is 'Real World Ready' and the focus on workshopping and autonomous learning aims to furnish and prepare graduates for the realities of working in fast-moving, rapidly changing environments.

I ask James if he sees the *Hyper Island* model taking off as an alternative to the UK's current Bologna-backed three-tier HE.

'It's a difficult one, as no one has actually had the gumption to do something in the UK as far as I'm aware. The obvious thing would be to run a three-month summer school where you learn a similar amount to a degree but pay markedly less, with incredible practitioners teaching you real skills, with great lectures and discussions.

For me, the *Hyper Island* model works and the *Black Mountain* idea works* – it should be about incubating and surrounding those learning with a variety of people and ideas from their field with the emphasis on *making*; making something of it and letting people do with it what they will. Degrees just don't, by themselves, contribute the necessary skills for somone to make work. You need real world drive and inspiration for that.'

But the reality is that *Hyper Island* teaches digital industry skills with financial backing from the digital industry. It's vocational training done right, in many ways, and that's how they can offer subsidised courses, but the lack of arts philanthropy in the UK means that any holistic Black

---

* 'Founded in 1933, Black Mountain College was one of the leading experimental art schools in America until its closure in 1957. When Philip Johnson, MoMA's first curator of architecture, learned that Black Mountain College was searching for a professor of art, he suggested Josef Albers, an artist whom he had recently met at the Bauhaus in Germany. Only a few months prior, the Bauhaus had closed its doors due to mounting antagonism from the Nazi Party, and Josef and his wife, the preeminent textile artist Anni Albers, readily accepted the offer to join the Black Mountain College faculty. During their 16-year tenure in North Carolina, the Alberses helped model the college's interdisciplinary curriculum on that of the Bauhaus, attracting such notable students and teachers as R. Buckminster Fuller, Elaine and Willem de Kooning, John Cage, and Robert Rauschenberg.'
– Francesca Wilmott, Curatorial Assistant,
Department of Drawings and Prints, www.moma.org

'Obrist told me that his own unrealised project is to found a new version of Black Mountain College, the defunct North Carolina retreat where, sixty years ago, top practitioners in the arts, culture, and the sciences taught and exchanged ideas.'
– 'Hans Ulrich Obrist: The curator who talked his way to the top',
D.T. Max, *The New Yorker*, 8 December 2014

Mountain-style start-up would probably have to be funded by a bank or an oil company. And here we are, sat here, putting the world to rights, waving our hands about, but I would have thought it was obvious that if today's arts institutions are in danger of becoming sausage factories then a more localised organic 'head, heart and hand' approach of Black Mountain seems to be in order, something akin to Germany's *Fachhochschulen*; a return to placements and apprenticeships with practitioners, perhaps; the provision of meaningful creative engagement with the wider working world both within and without the classroom as a matter of course. I'd love to see the emergence of practical, heuristic alternatives to the current UK model in the next few years, alternatives which don't patronise or deceive the young who are currently funnelled in a demonstratively unfair system devised and overseen by a generation who paid substantially less for their degrees . . .

'You big old Socialist.'

I know, right!?

•   •   •   •   •

I don't pretend to have the cures to the current system's ills, but this book records the thoughts of some great creative minds about the innumerable possible ways of working within and without the art school system. Repertory, boot camp, isolation, denial, single-minded pursuit, teaching, provocation, abstraction, happy accident, failure. There is no one right way. If anything, this book is an incitement to disagree, a spur for the reader to go away and question the contents, to go off and build their own airship – whatever that be – the beginning of a dialogue about change. My initial thoughts of what and whom art schools were for – the idea of

the airship, all of that – went out into the world and morphed into all sorts of other questions and interactions.

Time and again, the artists and craftspeople in this book tried out ideas aloud and ventured theories, as if for the first time; their process having crept up on them. Sometimes an interview turned into a proving ground where theories and standpoints were sifted and scrutinised but, more often, questions about practice seemed to trigger a sudden candid appraisal; the artist dragging ideas into the light whereas normally they'd be busy 'getting on with it'. As such, this new dialogue, forming and formative often came to light in a confused and contradictory form – *'It's about this . . . no it isn't; it's about that. And it's about this other thing too'* – the actual metamorphosis, the 'happening' occurring in the ineffable moment of creation, the doing; that split second or decades-long career.
They all started somewhere; they all built themselves and made it up as they went along. They'll be forever working to hone themselves and their work, it never really stops.

And as well as building themselves, creative types assemble a domain about them – a calibrated crucible in which to work. Francis Bacon famously said that he believed in 'deeply ordered chaos', and Jane Bown's portrait of him, sat owly in his shattered splattered studio, shows his deep devotion to the idea of creative maelstrom.

Jenny Saville's studio, though relatively ordered when I visited, adhered to the same notions of amassed collage and visual mulch. Manic Street Preachers have Faster in Bute; Robert Macfarlane, his Emmanuel rooms – stuffed with books; David Nash lives in his Blaenau Ffestiniog chapel, part house, part galleried arena of work, while his wood store and chainsaws live in a utilitarian knot of units down the road. Workspace is central to the process, a concrete collaborator whose physical presence affects the artists within. Each space I visited or spoke about had a creative character – often surprising and not always straightforward, sometimes seeming to exist and operate beyond their maker's control. The multitude of theatres which repertory afforded shaped the young Judi Dench. Stewart Lee's study doesn't work as it should. Cally has fashioned a manifest head-space at Marlinspike Hall. Steve Gullick stands in his darkroom, wapsed by fumes, at once despairing and elated by his lot. Richard Lawrence has built a succession of solid, no-nonsense sheds. Bill Drummond plans to set his Land Rover on fire . . . but the spaces used by artists are constantly under threat of getting swallowed up and redeveloped. Sal Pittman's studio has been sold and is shortly to become luxury flats. The Horse Hospital is possibly to be sold too, the Astoria's gone – and these are London examples but it's a national problem. There seems very little protection for the makers and creators from the powers that be – big business, educational institutions, local authorities, central government – happy to enjoy the fruits of the process while juicing the practitioners, as if they're unconnected.

It is a sad irony that, time and again, the atmosphere and attendant cool of creative hubs appeal and attract those who lack the empathy and insight to understand what makes them tick. The vampiric gentrification and rent rises which so often follow price out the community of artists who energised the place to begin with, leaving them bereft — the fate of *The Milk Bar* in Bristol is an excellent case in point.*

---

* 'Since 2009 a group of theatre makers, performers, and live artists have been based at 11 St Nicholas Street. Known as Residence, the 17 artists took over the space, paying a peppercorn rent, under a council scheme to bring empty buildings back into use.

In return the group have managed and maintained the building, known as *The Milk Bar*, and developed a national reputation for themselves as innovative artists and performers.

Now they have been told they could lose the premises after Bristol City Council put the property on the open rental market.

Although the group say they can afford the £8,000-per-year for the lease, it is understood that offers above-market rates have been made and the council has said it is obliged to make the decision based on financial value.

Residence member and artist Ella Good said: "Residence want to take on the lease at the rate that the council has advertised the property for – we're not asking for a freebie or a hand out.

"We believe the council should take into account Residence's six year history of managing and maintaining 11 St Nicholas Street. We've created an artistic hub which has made a huge contribution to the cultural reputation of Bristol.

"Losing the building means the livelihoods of the seventeen artists who work from there will all be put at risk".'

An open letter to Bristol has been published on Residence's website, with signatures including director of the Tobacco Factory Theatre Ali Robertson, Theatre Bristol's Katie Keeler, artistic director of the Bristol Old Vic Tom Morris and Guardian theatre critic Lyn Gardner who said that "the current explosion of work in Bristol has a lot to do with the mutually supportive environment of Residence".

Assistant mayor Simon Cook told the BBC that the council is "very supportive" of the group and recognises the "enormous contribution it makes to Bristol's thriving art scene".'

The petrol ripples down the frame and soaks the paper skin. I slosh until the can is empty, then stand back and light a Swan Vesta – 'The smoker's match' – 'The Original' – which spits into life and then the dusk blooms pink as flames spread down the airship's length, tail to nose, streaming fire, tissue bruising and veined with soot then writhing burnt and gone. Embers fleck the dark sky. The hot air blurs the picture but the beech frame stands out vital – a branded silhouette. Zeppelin, shorn of space, taken out and turned into another bright idea – the expedition down to Holloway and on.

However, he added that "the property is in a prime city centre location and we must realise the potential to achieve best value, now more so than ever".

He said the council was "fully committed to finding a solution, which accommodates the needs of both the collective and the council".

Tweeting back to Cllr Cook, Residence said: "If Bristol wants to be a 'creative city' then where else would we locate our artists but in those 'prime' locations?" and 'BCC say "prime city centre location" is why we're not 1st choice. Guess it depends what you want in your prime locations?"

– bristol247.com, 27 January 2015

Fire. Roger Deakin wrote,

> 'It begins with a slender, splinter stick of poplar, a
> matchstick. How many matchsticks are there in a single
> poplar?
> When wind blows through poplars, they sound like a
> match alighting when you strike it. To light a fire, you
> start from small beginnings. Good firelighters under-
> stand small beginnings.'*

Smoke from the pyre pools back in the trees which shiver in
the firelight, oneiric and doomy.
Half an hour later, the airship's turned to ash – a glowing
heart.

Combusted.
Gone.
Returned a book.
You hold it in your hands.

•   •   •   •   •

Dan Richards – 2015

---

* Page 289; *Notes from Walnut Tree Farm*, Roger Deakin (Penguin, 2009).

In memory of Jane Bown (1925–2014)

THANKS

Tim, Annie, Joe, Bob & Moz.

All the artists and craftspeople involved in this book, who gave so generously and freely of their time and work.

Carrie Plitt and all at Conville & Walsh.

Scott Pack, Rachel Faulkner and all at The Friday Project.

Tom Killingbeck and all at 4th Estate.

Lucy Johnston, for all her work, advice, belief and ace photography.

Kevin Parker, Katie & Sophie Utting for their encouragement and brilliant photographs.

Stanley Donwood and Natalie Dosser for creating this book's wonderful artwork.

James Bulley, Roz Coleman, Walter Donohue, and Rory Hill for their wise counsel and help to shape and hone the manuscript.

David Potter, for all his support and patience.

Special Thanks to Stanley Donwood, Richard Lawrence, Robert Macfarlane and all those involved with the printing, binding and publication of both the original letter-pressed Holloway book and its subsequent Faber & Faber incarnation.

All at Caught By The River, The Quietus, Rough Trade East, and The Faber Social.

Those at the workshop of Timothy Richards, Alembic Press, The Bicycle Shop, The Book Hive, Henwood & Dean Boatbuilders,

Lennie's Café, Mr. B's Emporium of Reading Delights, The NNF Spiegeltent, Norwich Art School Student Union, Outpost, The Playhouse Bar, The Scooter Cafe, STEW, and Stevens & Co. Ltd.

Malú Ansaldo, Laven Arumugam, Jon Baker, Oliver Barker, Jeff Barrett, Jay Barsby, Sarah & Lennie Beare, Amice Beaumont, Emily Benton & family, Andrew Billen, Björk, Rodney Blanch, Sarah Blunt, David Bolton, Jane Bown, Lee Brackstone, Megan Bradbury, Amanda Brisbane, Lucy Brownlow, Buckley, James & Havva Bulley, Will Burns, Cally Callomon, Kaavous Clayton, David Cochrane, Clare Coleman, Roz Coleman, Cristina Colomar, Will Connor, Adrian Cooper, Pip Cotterill, Sally Craythorne, Alec Cumming, Freya Cumming, Dame Judi Dench, Mark Dishman & family, Luke Dodd, Walter Donohue, Stanley Donwood, Bill Drummond, Rachel Faulkner, Sheryl Garratt, Liz Gould, Anna Green, Peter Green, Steve Gullick, Terri Hall, Nathan Hamilton, Dhugal Harrisson, Emma Hazell, Heavenly Records, Colin & Lucie Henwood, Nina Hervé, Liz Hilder, Becci Hill, Rory Hill, John Hirst, Milly Hirst, Nina Hobbes, Andrea Holland, Rob Howe, Jacob Huntley, Julie Hutchinson, Izzy & Ruth Iwamoto, Jasper, Sue Jennings, Ben Johnson, Lucy Johnston, Tom Killingbeck, Richard Lawrence, Henry Layte, Stewart Lee, David & Sandra Lees, Alex Lingford, Richard Long, Loomit & Juno, Robert Macfarlane, Manic Street Preachers, Lucy-Ann Martin & family, Stuart & Emily Masters, Dr. Giles Mercer, Virginie Mermet, David Mathews, Alan Moore, Joe Mounser, David Nash & Claire Langdown, Phoebe O'Donnell & family, Will Oldham, Vaughan Oliver & family, Scott Pack, Dan Papps, John Parish, Kevin Parker, Erin & Sam Patel, Lucy Peters, Sal Pittman, Carrie Plitt, David Potter, Adam Pugh, Push, Sheila Ravenscroft, Karen Reilly, Luke & Sally Roberts, Paul Robson, Gavin Rothery, Sonja Ruddick, Jenny Saville, Sabine Schlenker, Lorna Shipley, Charlotte & Simon Smith, Lucy & Tim Snelson, Ashley Stokes, George Szirtes, Ursula Terrell, Leo & Alice Thornely, Sarah Thornton, Dan Tombs, Tim Tracey, Trembling Bells, Robin Turner, Katie Utting, Sophie Utting, Jane Vance & family, Rohan Wadham, Jane Wallace, Andrew Walsh, Zoe-Rose Ward & family, David Watkinson, Dick Way, Amy Webb, Mark Wernham, Emma Wheeler, Christopher Whitfield, Marcus Williams, Jessica Woollard, Caroline Wright, Jo Wright.

This book is dedicated to all the artists currently working in bars.

BIBLIOGRAPHY

Ackroyd, Peter, *Hawksmoor* (Penguin Books, 1993)

Ackroyd, Peter, *The House of Doctor Dee* (Viking, 1993)

Ackroyd, Peter, *London Under* (Vintage, 2012)

Adams, Douglas & Mark Carwardine, *Last Chance to See* (Pan Books Ltd, 1990)

Amis, Kingsley, *Dear Illusion* (Penguin Books, 1983)

Amis, Martin, *Experience* (Vintage, 2001)

Ardizonne, Edward & Maurice Gorham, *The Local* (Little Toller Books, 2010)

Bachelard, Gaston, *The Poetics of Space* (Beacon Press, 1992)

Baker, J.A., *The Peregrine: The Hill of Summer & Diaries: The Complete Works of J.A. Baker* (Ed. John Fanshawe) (HarperCollins, 2010)

Ballard, J.G., *Extreme Metaphors: Interviews with J.G. Ballard 1967–2008* (4th Estate, 2012)

Ballard, J.G., *The Complete Short Stories I* (4th Estate, 2014)

Ballard, J.G., *The Complete Short Stories II* (4th Estate, 2014)

Ballard, J.G., *Empire of the Sun* (4th Estate, 2014)

Ballard, J.G., *Miracles of Life: Shanghai to Shepperton: an Autobiography* (4th Estate, 2014)

Barbellion, W.N.P., *The Journal of a Disappointed Man* (Little Toller Books, 2010)

Barford, J.E.Q., *Climbing In Britain* (Pelican Books, 1947)

Bayley, John, *Iris: A Memoir of Iris Murdoch* (Abacus, 1999)

Beckett, Samuel, *The Unnamable* (Faber & Faber, 2010)

Benjamin, Walter, *The Work Of Art In The Age Of Mechanical Reproduction (Or Reproducibility)* (Trans. J.A. Underwood) (Penguin Books, 2008)

Billington, Michael, *State of the Nation: British Theatre since 1945* (Faber & Faber, 2007)

Bonington, Chris, *I Chose To Climb* (Phoenix, 2012)

Booth, Stanley, *The True Adventures of The Rolling Stones* (Canongate, 2012)

Bown, Jane, *Faces: The Creative Process Behind Great Portraits* (Collins & Brown, 2001)

Bown, Jane, *Exposures* (Guardian Books, 2009)

Bradley, Simon, *St Pancras Station* (Profile Books, 2007)

Brautigan, Richard, *Sombrero Fallout: A Japanese Novel* (Canongate, 2012)

Brook, Chris, *The K Foundation Burn A Million Quid* (Ellipsis Books, 1997)

Buchan, John, *The Thirty-Nine Steps* (Penguin Books, 1999)

Burns, Will, *No Ordinary Poet* (Self-Published, 2012)

Chesterton, G.K., *The Defendant* (R. Brimley Johnson, 1902)

Clifton-Taylor, Alec, *Spirit of the Age: Eight Centuries of British Architecture* (BBC Classics, 1992)

Collis, John Stewart, *The Worm Forgives The Plough* (Vintage Books, 2009)

Conan Doyle, Sir Arthur, *The Memoirs of Sherlock Holmes* (Penguin, 1965)

Curtis, Penelope, *Modern British Sculpture: From the Collection* (Tate Gallery Publications, 1988)

De Quincey, Thomas, *Confessions of an English Opium Eater* (Penguin Classics, 2003)

Deakin, Roger, *Waterlog: A Swimmer's Journey Through Britain* (Vintage, 2000)

Deakin, Roger, *Wildwood: A Journey Through Trees* (Hamish Hamilton, 2007)

Deakin, Roger, *Notes from Walnut Tree Farm* (Penguin, 2009)

Donwood, Stanley, *Dead Children Playing: A Picture Book by Stanley Donwood & Dr. Tchock* (Verso, 2007)

Donwood, Stanley, *Household Worms* (Tangent Books, 2011)

Donwood, Stanley, *Red Maze* (Schunck Glaspaleis, 2011)

Donwood, Stanley, *HUMOR* (Faber & Faber, 2014)

Dorling, Danny, *Inequality & The 1%* (Verso, 2014)

Dostoyevsky, Fyodor, *Notes From Underground* (Trans. Natasha Randall) (Canongate, 2012)

Douglas Fawcett, Edward, *Hartmann the Anarchist, or The Doom of the Great City* (Bone, 2009)

Drummond, Bill, *45* (Little, Brown & Company, 2000)

Drummond, Bill, *How To Be An Artist* (Penkiln Burn (Book No. 6), 2002)

Drummond, Bill, *17* (Beautiful Books, 2008)

Drummond, Bill & Jimmy Cauty, *The Manual: How to Have a Number One the Easy Way* (KLF Publications, 1988)

Drummond, Bill & Mark Manning, *Bad Wisdom: The Lighthouse at the Top of the World* (Creation Books, 2003)

Dyer, Geoff, *Out Of Sheer Rage* (Canongate, 2012)

Dylan, Bob, *Chronicles: Volume One* (Simon & Schuster, 2004)

Eliot, T.S., *The Waste Land and other poems* (Faber & Faber, 1999)

Eno, Brian, *A Year with Swollen Appendices* (Canongate Books, 2007)

Foster Wallace, David, *The Pale King* (Little, Brown & Company, 2011)

Frayn, Michael, *Copenhagen* (Methuen, 1998)

Frayn, Michael, *Towards the End of the Morning* (Faber & Faber, 2005)

Frayn, Michael, *Stage Directions: Writing on Theatre 1970–2008* (Faber & Faber, 2009)

Frost, Robert, *The Road Not Taken; Mountain Interval 1916* (Henry Holt & Company, 1920)

Frost, Robert, *Collected Poems* (Amereon Ltd, 1996)

Gale, John, *Clean Young Englishman* (The Hogarth Press Ltd, 1988)

Gayford, Martin, *A Bigger Message: Conversations with David Hockney* (Thames & Hudson, 2011)

Gray, Alasdair, *Unlikely Stories, Mostly* (Penguin Books Ltd, 1984)

Gray, John, *Straw Dogs: Thoughts on Humans & Other Animals* (Granta Books, 2002)

Gullick, Steve, *Showtime* (Vision On Publishing Ltd, 2001)

Hartcup, Guy, *The Achievement of the Airship: A History of the Development of Rigid, Semi-Rigid and Non-Rigid Airships* (David & Charles, 1974)

Heaney, Seamus, *Death of a Naturalist* (Faber & Faber, 1966)
Heaney, Seamus, *Seeing Things* (Faber & Faber, 1991)
van Hensbergen, Gijs, *Gaudi: A Biography* (Harper Perennial, 2003)
Hess, Barbara, *Abstract Expressionism* (Taschen, 2006)
Household, Geoffrey, *Rogue Male* (Penguin Books, 1977)
Hyde, Lewis, *The Gift: How the Creative Spirit Transforms the World* (Canongate Books Ltd, 2007)

Ikeda, Mitch, *Forever Delayed: Photographs of the Manic Street Preachers* (Vision On Publishing Ltd, 2003)
Irvin, Jim, *The MOJO Collection: The Albums That Define Popular Music* (Mojo Books, 2000)
Isherwood, Christopher, *Goodbye to Berlin* (Vintage, 1998)

Judt, Tony, *The Memory Chalet* (Vintage Books, 2011)
Jerome, Jerome K., *Three Men in a Boat* (Oxford University Press, 1998)
Jones, Lloyd, *The Book of Fame* (John Murray, 2008)

Kerouac, Jack, *On The Road* (Penguin Books, 1999)
King, Stephen, *On Writing: A Memoir of the Craft* (Hodder & Stoughton, 2000)
Koren, Leonard, *Wabi-sabi: For Artists, Designers, Poets & Philosophers* (Imperfect Publishing, 2008)
Kunstler, James Howard, *The Long Emergency: Surviving the End of Oil, Climate Change, and Other Converging Catastrophes of the Twenty-First Century* (Grove/Atlantic, 2005)

Ladd, Brian, *The Ghosts of Berlin: Confronting German History in the Landscape* (University of Chicago Press, 1998)
Larkin, Philip, *High Windows* (Faber & Faber, 1974)
Larkin, Philip, *The Whitsun Weddings* (Faber & Faber, 2001)
Lawrence, D.H., *Selected Poems* (Ed. Keith Sagar) (Penguin Books, 1972)
Le Carré, John, *Tinker, Tailor, Soldier, Spy* (Hodder & Stoughton, 1975)
Lee, Laurie, *As I Walked Out One Midsummer Morning* (Penguin Books, 1973)
Lee, Stewart, *How I Escaped My Certain Fate: The Life and Deaths of a Stand-Up Comedian* (Faber & Faber, 2010)

Lee!, Stewart, *The 'If You Prefer A Milder Comedian, Please Ask For One' EP* (Faber & Faber, 2012)

Long, Richard, *Heaven and Earth* (Ed. Clarrie Wallis) (Tate Publishing, 2009)

Lynskey, Dorian, *33 Revolutions per Minute: A History of Protest Songs* (Faber & Faber, 2011)

Macfarlane, Robert, *Mountains of the Mind* (Granta, 2003)

Macfarlane, Robert, *The Wild Places* (Granta Books, 2008)

Macfarlane, Robert, *The Old Ways* (Hamish Hamilton, 2012)

Macfarlane, Robert, Stanley Donwood & Dan Richards, *Holloway* (Quive-Smith Press, 2012)

MacGregor, Neil, *A History of the World in 100 Objects* (Penguin Books, 2012)

Maitland, Sara, *A Book of Silence* (Granta, 2008)

Maxwell, Grace, *Laughing & Falling: The Restoration of Edwyn Collins* (Ebury Press, 2010)

McCullin, Don, *Shaped By War* (Jonathan Cape, 2010)

McCullin, Don, *The Impossible Peace: From War Photographs to Landscapes, 1958–2011* (Skira Editore, 2012)

Mishima, Yukio, *The Sailor Who Fell From Grace With The Sea* (Vintage Classics, 1999)

Moorcock, Michael, *King Of The City* (Scribner, 2000)

Moore, Alan & David Lloyd, *V for Vendetta* (DC Comics, 2005)

Moore, Alan, *Voice of the Fire* (Top Shelf Productions, 2003)

Moore, Alan & Kevin O'Neill, *The League of Extraordinary Gentlemen* (Titan Books Ltd, 2002)

Morris, Jan, *Fisher's Face* (Faber & Faber, 2007)

Mowthorpe, Ces, *Battlebags: British Airships of the First World War* (Wrens Park Publishing, 1998)

Murdoch, Iris, *Bruno's Dream* (Vintage, 2001)

Nash, David, *Stoves and Hearths* (David Grob Editions, 1982)

Nash, David, *David Nash: Pyramids Rise, Spheres Turn and Cubes Stand Still* (Annely Juda Fine Art, 2005)

Nash, David, *Wooden Boulder 1978–2003: The Whole Story* (Benteli, 2008)

Niven, John, *Kill Your Friends* (Vintage, 2009)

O'Brien, Flann, *The Third Policeman* (Harper Perennial, 2007)

Obrist, Hans Ulrich, *Ai Weiwei Speaks with Hans Ulrich Obrist* (Penguin Books, 2011)
Oliver, Vaughan & V23, *This Rimy River: Vaughan Oliver & V23 Graphic Works 1988–94* (V23 Publishing, 1997)
Orozco, Gabriel & Ann Tremkin, *Gabriel Orozco: Photogravity* (Philadelphia Museum of Art, 2000)
Orwell, George, *Cigarettes vs. Books* (Penguin, 2004)
Oswald, Alice, *Dart* (Faber & Faber, 2002)

Peel, John, *The Olivetti Chronicles: Three Decades of Life and Music* (Bantam Press, 2008)
Peel, John & Sheila Ravenscroft, *Margrave of the Marshes* (Bantam Press, 2005)
Peppiatt, Michael, *Francis Bacon: Anatomy of an Enigma* (Constable & Robinson, 2009)
Peppiatt, Michael, *Interviews with Artists: 1966–2012* (Yale University Press, 2012)
Pessoa, Fernando, *The Book of Disquiet* (Ed. María José de Lancastre/Trans. Margaret Jull Costa) (Serpent's Tail, 2010)
Pilley, Dorothy, *Climbing Days* (G Bell and Sons Ltd, 1935)
Plath, Sylvia, *The Unabridged Journals of Sylvia Plath* (Ed. Karen V. Kukil) (Anchor Books, 2000)
Poynor, Rick, *Vaughan Oliver: Visceral Pleasures* (Booth-Clibborn Editions, 2000)

Robinson, Douglas H., *Giants in the Sky: A History of the Rigid Airship* (G.T. Foulis & Co Ltd, 1973)
Ross, Alex, *The Rest Is Noise: Listening to the Twentieth Century* (4th Estate, 2008)
Ross, Alex, *Listen To This* (4th Estate, 2010)
Ruskin, John, *On Art And Life* (Penguin, 2004)

Sacks, Oliver, *The Mind's Eye* (Picador, 2010)
Saville, Jenny & Danilo Eccher, *Jenny Saville: The Rome Retrospective Exhibition* (Mondadori, 2005)
Schama, Simon, *Jenny Saville* (Rizzoli, 2005)
Sebald, W.G., *The Emigrants* (Trans. Michael Hulse) (Vintage Classics, 2002)
Sebald, W.G., *The Rings of Saturn* (Trans. Michael Hulse) (Vintage Classics, 2002)

Sebald, W.G., *Campo Santo* (Ed. Sven Meyer/Trans. Anthea Bell) (Vintage Classics, 2003)

Sebald, W.G., *On the Natural History of Destruction* (Trans. Anthea Bell) (Penguin Books, 2004)

Self, Will, *The Quantum Theory of Insanity* (Bloomsbury, 1991)

Self, Will & Ralph Steadman, *Psycho Too* (Bloomsbury, 2009)

Sennett, Richard, *The Craftsman* (Allen Lane, 2008)

Shepherd, Nan, *The Living Mountain* (Canongate, 2011)

Shute Norway, Nevil, *On The Beach* (Vintage Classics, 2009)

Sinclair, Iain, *Lights Out for the Territory: 9 Excursions in the Secret History of London* (Granta Books, 1997)

Sinclair, Iain, *London Orbital* (Penguin Books, 2003)

Smith, Andrew, *Moondust* (Bloomsbury, 2005)

Stegner, Wallace, *Wilderness Letter; The Sound of Mountain Water: The Changing American West* (Penguin Books, 1997)

Sturt, George, *The Wheelwright's Shop* (Cambridge University Press, 1963)

Swift, Jonathan, *Gulliver's Travels* (Penguin Classics, 2003)

Taleb, Nassim Nicholas, *The Black Swan: The Impact of the Highly Improbable* (Penguin Books, 2007)

Tanizaki, Junichiro, *In Praise of Shadows* (Vintage Classics, 2001)

Terkel, Studs, *And They All Sang: Great Musicians Talk About Their Music* (Granta Books, 2006)

Terkel, Studs, *P.S.: Further Thoughts from a Lifetime of Listening* (The New Press, 2008)

Thomas, Edward, *The Path: The Annotated Collected Poems* (Ed. Edna Longley) (Bloodaxe, 2008)

Thomas, Edward, *The South Country* (Little Toller Books, 2009)

Thornton, Sarah, *Seven Days In The Art World* (Granta, 2009)

Tusa, John, *On Creativity: Interviews Exploring the Process* (Methuen, 2003)

Trynka, Paul, *Starman: David Bowie – The Definitive Biography* (Sphere, 2011)

Vincent, Jim & George E. Lodge, *A Season of Birds: A Norfolk Diary* (A&W Publishers Inc., 1980)

Vonnegut, Kurt, *Slaughterhouse 5* (Vintage Books, 2000)

Waugh, Evelyn, *Scoop* (Penguin Classics, 2000)

Williamson, Henry, *Salar the Salmon* (Little Toller Books, 2010)
Wodehouse, P.G., *Summer Lightning* (Penguin Books, 2002)
Wyndham, John, *The Day Of The Triffids* (Penguin Classics, 2000)
Wyndham, John & Lucas Parkes, *The Outward Urge* (Penguin Books Ltd, 1970)

Yates, Chris, *Nightwalk: A Journey to the Heart of Nature* (William Collins, 2012)

Collections
British Prints from the Machine Age: Rhythms of Modern Life 1914–1939 (Ed. Clifford S. Ackley) (Thames & Hudson, 2009)
Caught by the River: A Collection of Words on Water (Ed. Jeff Barratt, Robin Turner & Andrew Walsh) (Cassell Illustrated, 2009)
The International Book of Wood (Ed. Martyn Bramwell) (Mitchell Beazley Publishers Ltd, 1979)
J.G. Ballard: The First 20 Years (Ed. James Goddard & David Pringle) (Bran's Head Books, 1976)
London: City of Disappearances, (Ed. Iain Sinclair) (Hamish Hamilton, 2006)
Spacecraft: Fleeting Architecture and Hideouts (Ed. Robert Klanten & Lukas Lombardo) (Die Gestalten Verlag, 2007)

DISCOGRAPHY

All the music listed below was listened to whilst writing this book. Some of it was on heavy rotation while building the Beechwood Airship, some of it is cited in chapter footnotes, and some of it was mentioned or recommended by interviewees. I recommend it all to your ears.

I Am a Bird Now, Antony and the Johnsons (Secretly Canadian, 2005)
Funeral, Arcade Fire (Rough Trade, 2004)
AMOK, Atoms for Peace (XL Recordings, 2012)

Improvisations for Cello and Guitar, David Holland & Derek Bailey (ECM, 1971)
Standards, Derek Bailey (Tzadik, 2007)
In the Flat Field, Bauhaus (4AD, 1980)
Mask, Bauhaus (Beggars Banquet, 1981)
'Strawberry Fields Forever'/'Penny Lane', The Beatles (Parlophone, 1967)
'Hey Jude'/'Revolution', The Beatles (Parlophone, 1968)
Travel Notes, by Patrick Bell (SIX INCH RECORDS, 2009)
I See A Darkness, Bonnie 'Prince' Billy (Domino, 1999)
Master and Everyone, Bonnie 'Prince' Billy (Domino, 2003)
The Letting Go, Bonnie 'Prince' Billy (Domino, 2006)
The Wonder Show of the World, Bonnie 'Prince' Billy & The Cairo Gang (Domino, 2010)
Noble Beast, Andrew Bird (Fat Possum/Bella Union, 2009)
Hands Of Glory, Andrew Bird (Mom+Pop Records, 2012)

Volta, Björk (One Little Indian Records, 2007)
Biophilia, Björk (One Little Indian Records, 2011)
Prolonged Exposure, BK & Dad (Gravy Records, 2010)
Borth, BK & Dad (Gravy Records, 2011)
Thickfreakness, The Black Keys (Fat Possum, 2003)
Gorilla, The Bonzo Dog Doo Dah Band (Liberty Records, 1967)
Tadpoles, The Bonzo Dog Doo Dah Band (Liberty Records, 1969)
Station to Station, David Bowie (RCA, 1976)
Low, David Bowie (RCA, 1977)
Heroes, David Bowie (RCA, 1978)
Modern Love, David Bowie (EMI, 1983)
Mystery White Boy, Jeff Buckley (Columbia, 2000)
The Butcher Of Common Sense, The Neutrinos/Various Artists
  (Self-released, 2013)

Tago Mago, Can (United Artists, 1971)
Ege Bamyası, Can (United Artists, 1972)
The Lost Tapes, Can (Mute, 2012)
Abattoir Blues/The Lyre of Orpheus, Nick Cave & The Bad Seeds
  (Mute, 2004)
Dig, Lazarus, Dig!!!, Nick Cave & The Bad Seeds (Mute, 2008)
Push the Sky Away, Nick Cave & The Bad Seeds (Bad Seed Ltd.,
  2013)
The Clash, The Clash (CBS, 1977)
Give 'Em Enough Rope, The Clash (CBS, 1978)
London Calling, The Clash (CBS, 1979)
Sandinista!, The Clash (CBS, 1980)
The Story of the Clash, Volume 1, The Clash (Epic, 1988)
Lullabies to Violaine, Cocteau Twins (4AD, 2005)

The Best of Nick Cave & The Bad Seeds, Nick Cave & The Bad Seeds
  (Mute, 1998)
Five Leaves Left, Nick Drake (Island, 1969)
Bryter Layter, Nick Drake (Island, 1970)
Pink Moon, Nick Drake (Island, 1972)

Porcupine, Echo & The Bunnymen (Korova, 1983)
Ocean Rain, Echo & The Bunnymen (Korova, 1984)
Crystal Days (1979–1999), Echo & The Bunnymen (Rhino, 2001)
Piramida, Efterklang (4AD, 2012)

Ivor The Engine: Original Television Music, The Vernon Elliott
    Ensemble (Trunk, 2007)
Here Come The Warm Jets, Brian Eno (Island, 1974)
Taking Tiger Mountain (By Strategy), Brian Eno (Island, 1974)
Another Green World, Brian Eno (Island, 1975)
Apollo: Atmospheres and Soundtracks, Brian Eno (EG Records, 1983)
Someday World, Brian Eno & Karl Hyde (Warp, 2014)

50,000 Fall Fans Can't Be Wrong: 39 Golden Greats, The Fall
    (Sanctuary, 2004)
Rounds, Four Tet (Domino Records, 2003)
Everything Ecstatic, Four Tet (Domino Records, 2005)
There Is Love In You, Four Tet (Domino Records, 2010)
Late Night Tales: Four Tet, Various, compiled by Four Tet (Late Night
    Tales/Azuli, 2004)
NonStopErotik, Black Francis (Cooking Vinyl, 2010)

The Fame, Lady Gaga (Interscope, 2008)
Damaged Goods, Gang of Four (Fast Product, 1978)
Entertainment, Gang of Four (EMI, 1979)
Felt Mountain, Goldfrapp (Mute, 2000)
Seventh Tree, Goldfrapp (Mute, 2008)
Pale Green Ghosts, John Grant (Bella Union, 2013)
The Sophtware Slump, Grandaddy (V2, 2000)
Sumday, Grandaddy (V2, 2003)
Appetite For Destruction, Guns N' Roses (Geffen, 1987)

White Chalk, PJ Harvey (Island, 2007)
Let England Shake, PJ Harvey (Island, 2011)
A Woman a Man Walked By, PJ Harvey & John Parish (Island, 2009)

'Anna Lee'/'Stranger Blues', Elmore James (FIRE FB 302, 1961)
Unknown Pleasures, Joy Division (Factory, 1979)
Closer, Joy Division (Factory, 1980)
The Beyond Within, The Joy of Living (SIX INCH RECORDS, 2009)
There Are Eight Million Stories . . . , The June Brides (The Pink
    Label, 1985)

Justified & Ancient, The KLF (Trancentral, 1991)
The White Room, The KLF (KLF Communications, 1991)
Floodplain, Kronos Quartet (Nonesuch Records, 2009)

Mug Museum, Cate Le Bon (Wichita, 2013)
Led Zeppelin IV, Led Zeppelin (Atlantic, 1971)
Physical Graffiti, Led Zeppelin (Swan Song, 1975)

Real Life, Magazine (Virgin, 1978)
The Correct Use of Soap, Magazine (Virgin, 1980)
Wig Out at Jagbags, Stephen Malkmus & The Jicks (Matador
    Records, 2014)
Generation Terrorists, Manic Street Preachers (Columbia, 1992)
The Holy Bible, Manic Street Preachers (Columbia, 1994)
Everything Must Go, Manic Street Preachers (Columbia, 1996)
Lifeblood, Manic Street Preachers (Columbia, 2004)
Send Away The Tigers, Manic Street Preachers (Columbia, 2007)
Journal For Plague Lovers, Manic Street Preachers (Columbia, 2009)
Classist, Max de Mara (SIX INCH RECORDS, 2009)
I Am a Wallet, McCarthy (September Records, 1987)
You Are There, Mono (Temporary Residence Limited, 2006)
Hymn To The Immortal Wind, Mono (Temporary Residence Limited,
    2009)

Stainless Style, Neon Neon (Lex Records, 2008)
Technique, New Order (Factory, 1989)
Retro, New Order (London, 2002)
Nevermind, Nirvana (DGC Records, 1991)
In Utero, Nirvana (DGC Records, 1993)
Klaus Nomi, (Klaus Nomi, RCA, 1981)

Who Is William Onyeabor?, William Onyeabor (Luaka Bop, 2013)

How Animals Move, John Parish (Thrill Jockey, 2002)
Once Upon a Little Time, John Parish (Thrill Jockey, 2009)
Chart Pimp, Part Chimp (Rock Action Records, 2003)
Brighten the Corners, Pavement (Domino, 1997)
Terror Twilight, Pavement (Domino, 1999)
Surfer Rosa, Pixies (4AD, 1988)
Doolittle, Pixies (4AD, 1989)
Bossanova, Pixies (4AD, 1990)
Trompe le Monde, Pixies (4AD, 1991)
'Bam Thwok', Pixies (iTunes, 2001)
It Takes a Nation of Millions to Hold Us Back, Public Enemy (Def
    Jam, 1988)

Fight The Power, Public Enemy (Motown, 1989)
Public Image: First Issue, Public Image (Virgin, 1978)
Different Class, Pulp (Island, 1995)
We Love Life, Pulp (Island, 2001)

Pablo Honey, Radiohead (Parlophone, 1993)
My Iron Lung EP, Radiohead (Parlophone, 1994)
The Bends, Radiohead (Parlophone, 1995)
OK Computer, Radiohead (Parlophone, 1997)
Kid A, Radiohead (Parlophone, 2000)
Amnesiac, Radiohead (Parlophone, 2001)
Hail To The Thief, Radiohead (Parlophone, 2003)
In Rainbows, Radiohead (Self-released, 2007)
The King of Limbs, Radiohead (Self-released, 2011)
Transformer, Lou Reed (RCA, 1972)
Berlin, Lou Reed (RCA, 1973)
Candylion, Gruff Rhys (Rough Trade Records, 2007)
Hotel Shampoo, Gruff Rhys (Onvi Records/Turnstile, 2011)
OX4 The Best of Ride, Ride (Ignition Records, 2001)
Their Satanic Majesties Request, The Rolling Stones (Decca, 1967)
Beggars Banquet, The Rolling Stones (Decca, 1968)
Let it Bleed, The Rolling Stones (Decca, 1969)
Sticky Fingers, The Rolling Stones (Rolling Stones Records, 1971)
Exile on Main St., The Rolling Stones (Rolling Stones Records, 1972)
For Your Pleasure, Roxy Music (Island, 1973)
Country Life, Roxy Music (Island, 1974)

Never Mind the Bollocks, Here's the Sex Pistols, Sex Pistols (Virgin, 1977)
Hvarf/Heim, Sigur Rós (XL Recordings, 2006)
Empires and Dance, Simple Minds (Arista, 1980)
Sons & Fascination/Sister Feelings Call, Simple Minds (Virgin, 1981)
Kaleidoscope, Siouxsie and the Banshees (Polydor, 1980)
Juju, Siouxsie and the Banshees (Polydor, 1981)
Figure 8, Elliott Smith (Dreamworks, 2000)
Hatful of Hollow, The Smiths (Rough Trade, 1984)
Meat is Murder, The Smiths (Rough Trade, 1985)
The Queen is Dead, The Smith (Rough Trade, 1986)
Karyobin, The Spontaneous Music Ensemble (Island, 1968)
Countdown to Ecstasy, Steely Dan (ABC Records, 1973)

Pretzel Logic, Steely Dan (ABC Records, 1974)
Katie Lied, Steely Dan (ABC Records, 1975)
Guerrilla, Super Furry Animals (Creation Records, 1999)
Songbook: The Singles, Vol. 1, Super Furry Animals (Epic, 2004)

End of the Road, Tenebrous Liar (TV Records, 2012)
Soul Mining, The The (Epic, 1983)
It'll End in Tears, This Mortal Coil (4AD, 1984)
'Doctorin' The Tardis', The Timelords (KLF Communications, 1988)

Needle in a Haystack, The Velvelettes (Motown, 1964)
White Light/White Heat, The Velvet Underground (Verve, 1968)
Live at Max's Kansas City, The Velvet Underground (Cotillion, 1970)
Loaded, The Velvet Underground (Cotillion, 1970)

Attempted Mustache, Loudon Wainwright III (Columbia, 1973)
A Pagan Place, The Waterboys (Island, 1984)
This Is the Sea, The Waterboys (Island, 1985)
Pink Flag, Wire (EMI, 1977)
Chairs Missing, Wire (EMI, 1978)

The Eraser, Thom Yorke (XL Recordings, 2006)
On The Beach, Neil Young (Reprise, 1974)
Dead Man, Neil Young (Vapor, 1996)
Live at Massey Hall 1971, Neil Young (Reprise, 2007)
Rust Never Sleeps, Neil Young & Crazy Horse (Reprise, 1979)
Live at the Fillmore East 1970, Neil Young & Crazy Horse (Reprise, 2006)

Genius: The Best of Warren Zevon, Warren Zevon (Rhino, 2002)

Compilations
Enjoy Every Sandwich: The Songs of Warren Zevon, Various Artists (Artemis, 2004)
FabricLive.07, mixed by John Peel (Fabric, 2002)
John Peel and Sheila: The Pig's Big 78s: A Beginner's Guide, compiled by John Peel & Sheila Ravenscroft (Trikont, 2006)
Power Corruption & Lies Covered, Various Artists (*Mojo* Magazine, 2012)

LIST OF ILLUSTRATIONS

1 *Beechwood Airship*: Nina Hobbes, 2009
2 Dan Richards, Widcombe Old School, Bath: Tim Richards, 2007
3 Wooden Hoops, Widcombe Old School, Bath: Dan Richards, 2007
4 Tissue Paper Sunday, Norwich: Dan Richards, 2007
5 *Beechwood Airship*, Norwich: Photographer Unknown, 2008
6 Bill Drummond, Stoke Newington, London: Lucy Johnston, 2010
7 *Poster 59*: Bill Drummond, 2003
8 *Poster 128*: Bill Drummond, 2006
9 Bill Drummond & Lucy Johnston with *A Smell Of Sulphur In The Wind*, Stoke Newington, London: Dan Richards, 2010
10 Richard Lawrence, Widcombe Studios, Bath: Dan Richards, 2008
11 Printshop Detail, Widcombe Studios, Bath: Lucy Johnston, 2010
12 Blind Emboss Bears, Widcombe Studios, Bath: Lucy Johnston, 2010
13 Ink, Widcombe Studios, Bath: Lucy Johnston, 2010
14 Richard Lawrence, Widcombe Studios, Bath: Lucy Johnston, 2010
15 Stanley Donwood, Bath: Lucy Johnston, 2010
16 *Night Bears*: Stanley Donwood, 2008
17 *Fleet Street Apocalypse*: Stanley Donwood, 2008
18 *The Universal Sigh*: Stanley Donwood, 2011